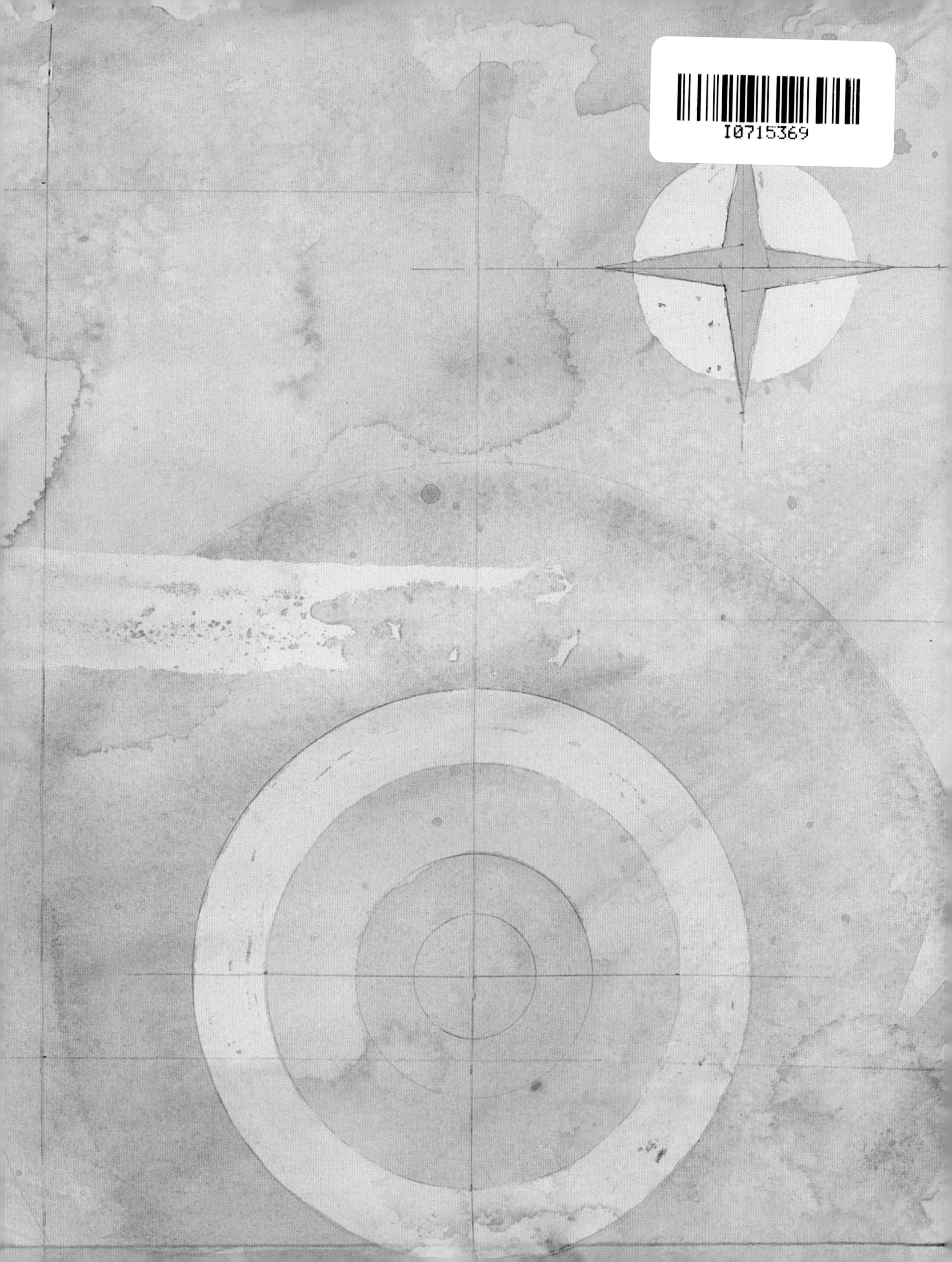
I0715369

The Path of Drawing

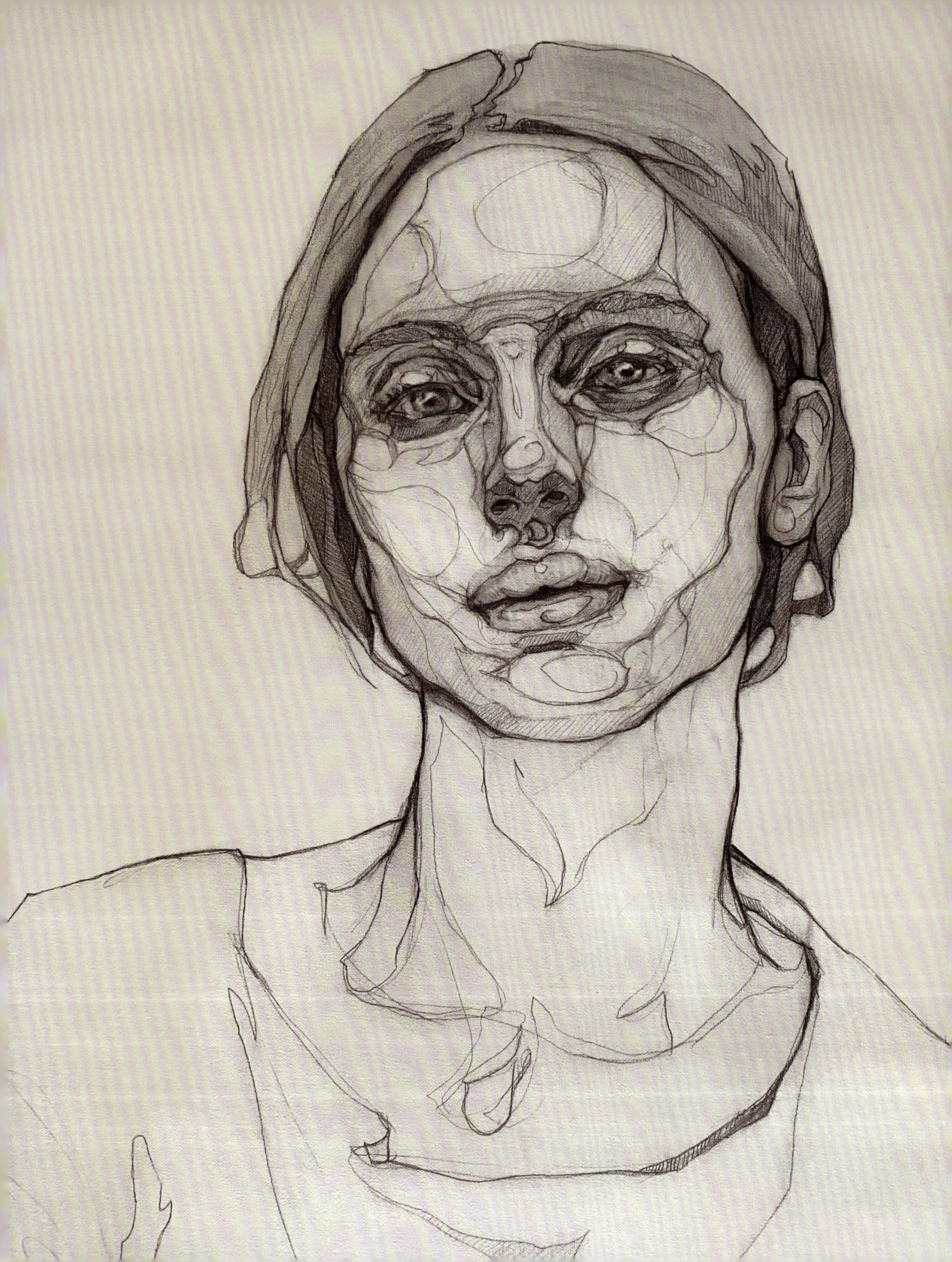

PATRICIA WATWOOD

The Path of Drawing

Lessons for Everyday Creativity and Mindfulness

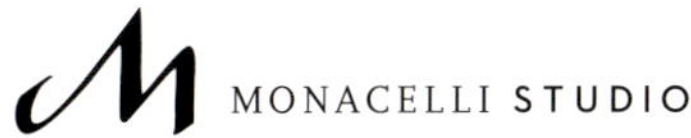

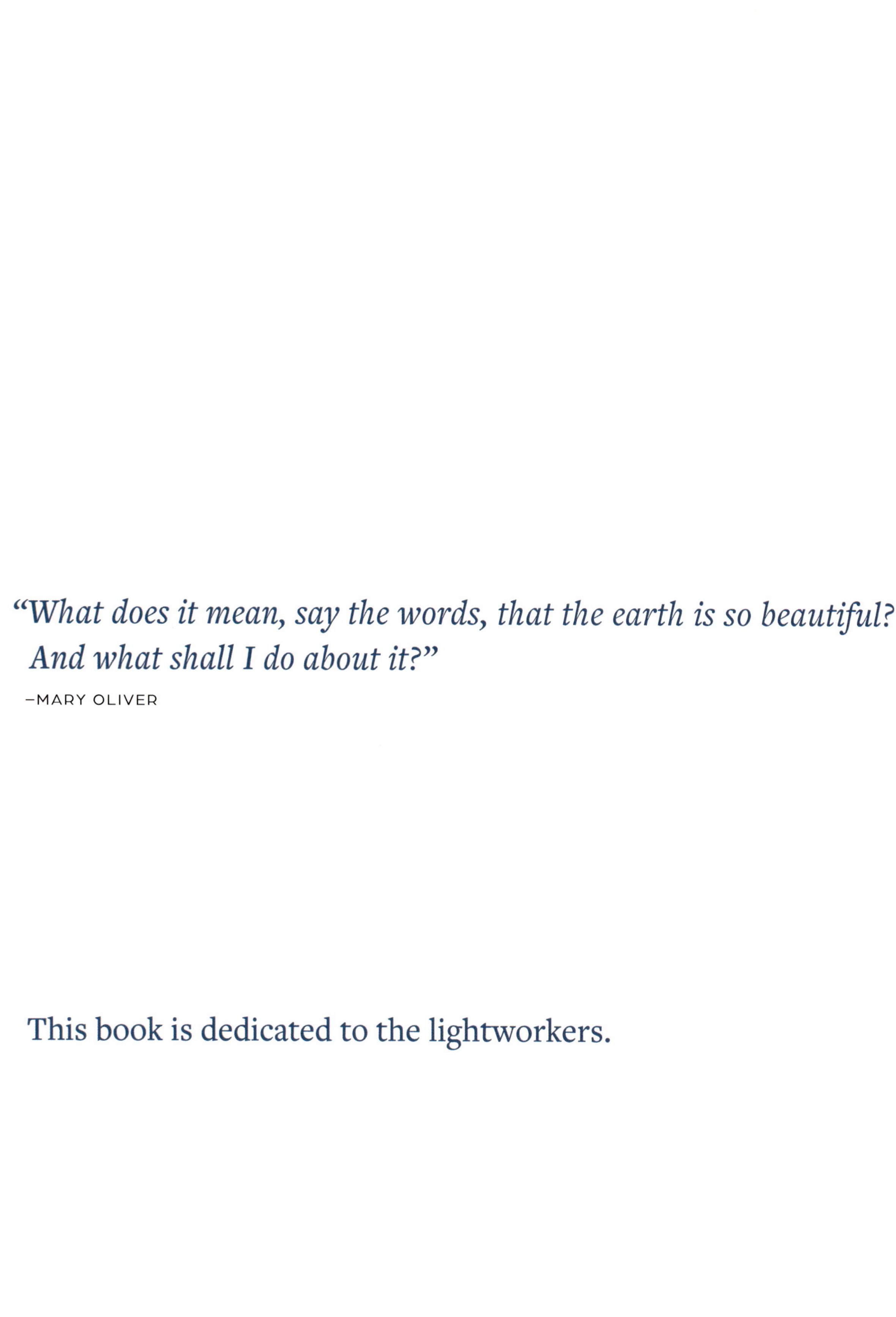

*"What does it mean, say the words, that the earth is so beautiful?
And what shall I do about it?"*

—MARY OLIVER

This book is dedicated to the lightworkers.

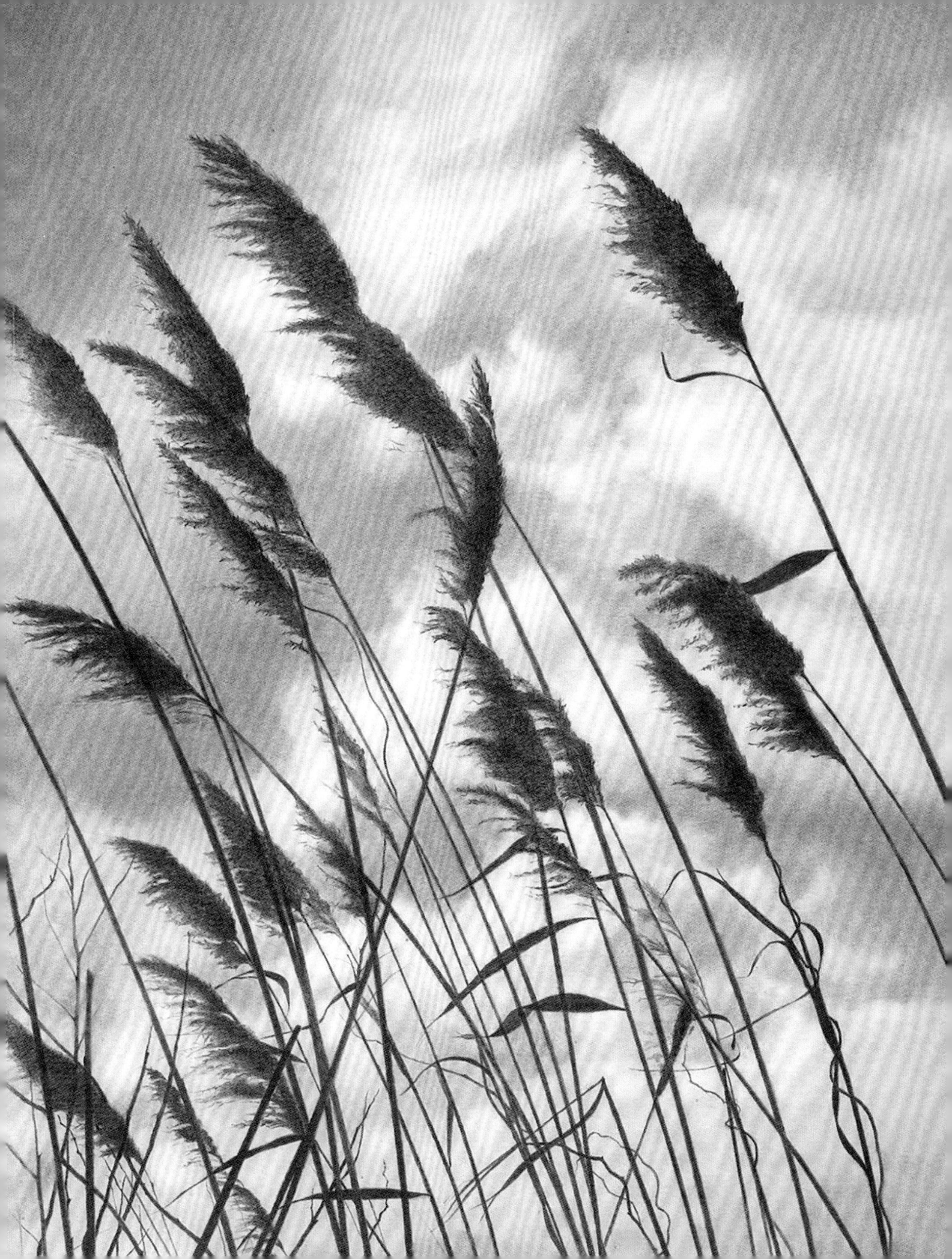

Contents

120   **CHAPTER 7**

The Shadow's Edge

The language of light and form

178   **CHAPTER 10**

Developing Creative Ideas

From the loosest of doodles to a completed work

140   **CHAPTER 8**

New Paths in Color

Exploring with watercolor and mixed media

204   **CHAPTER 11**

Lightworkers

Intentional practices for continued creativity

160   **CHAPTER 9**

Monsters and Mandalas

Taming the monsters that get in our way

Acknowledgments

A deep bow of thanks to the many people who helped me on the path of writing this book. First to Victoria Craven (1959–2021), the associate publisher of Monacelli Press and founder of the Monacelli Studio imprint. This book would never have come to being without Victoria's nurturing and patient encouragement. I'm so sad that you didn't get to see the finished book.

Deep gratitude to my dear aunt, curator, and writer Vicki Halper, for her insightful reading, editing, concise prose, and practical wisdom. I'm thankful for the support and help of two close friends: photographer Stefan Hagen, and artist and author Hyeseung Song. Special thanks to artist and author Juliette Aristides for her foreword and for helping me believe I could accomplish this task. Thank you to editor Carla Sakamoto, designer Shawn Hazen, April Hopkins for graphics, and to Sarah Paddock and Sarah Carlton Green for permissions support.

To the teachers who shaped and guided me: Steve Gilliam, Gary Faigin, Anthony Ryder, Jacob Collins, Ted Seth Jacobs, Martha Mayer Erlebacher, Steven Assael, Vincent Desiderio, Wade Schuman, and my friend and mentor Nelson Shanks. Thank you for keeping this tradition alive.

To all the artists whose illustrations were used in this book, and who generously gave their work and enthusiasm: Thank you for the gift of your creativity and for keeping faith in what you do.

To my beloved husband, Duncan, and my fantastic kids, Beaux and Jo. Thank you for your love, endless support, and for leaving me alone to work. To my amazing parents, Marjorie and Kenneth R. Smith, Jr., for unfailing love.

To God and my congregation at First Presbyterian Church of Brooklyn, who share the love that hopes all things.

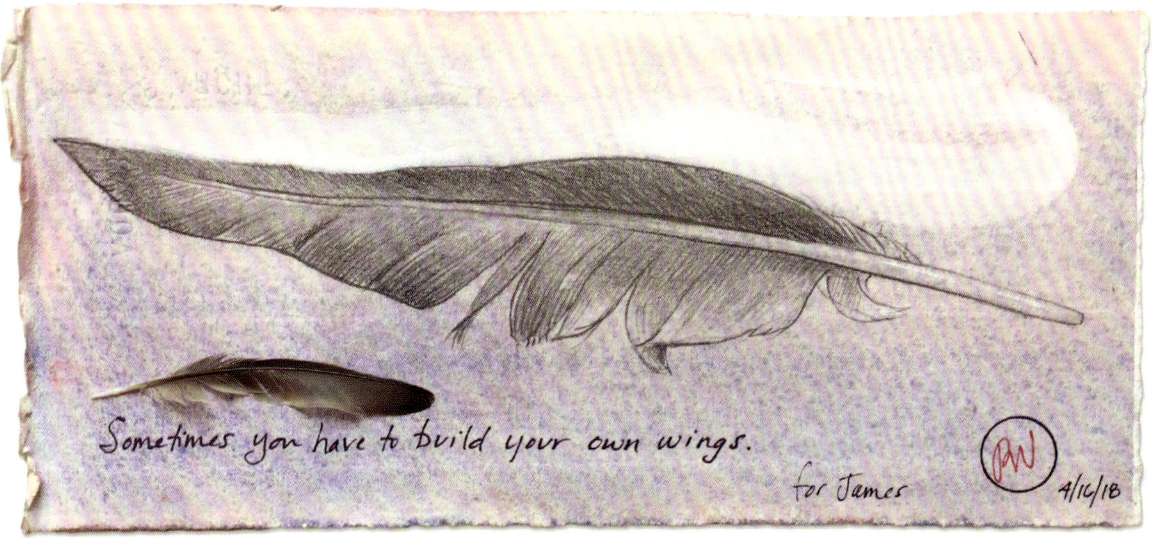

Foreword

BY JULIETTE ARISTIDES

I grew up in the woods of Pennsylvania, and, to this day, my idea of beauty in nature is rolling hills and lush forests. Years later, I moved out, yet the woods remained my picture of home. Life being of endless change, my mother moved to New Mexico and sent me a picture of her new house—a low structure on a barren field of rocks that extended as far as I could see. When I arrived, every suspicion I had was confirmed. It was as unwelcoming as I imagined: civilization an apparent afterthought, weightless and transient, built on a treeless and arid ground.

A week later, we drove into the desert to visit the Puebloan ruins of Chaco Canyon, where a thousand years ago there was a thriving community. In this protected land, without the strip malls and parking lots, the environment looked different, and the fragile golden walls of the village merged with the landscape. I descended into a kiva, a ceremonial room, and the light cut through the darkness, forming a moment of architectural sublimity. When my eyes acclimated to the light, I could differentiate subtle color and texture. Over the course of the day, my eyes followed the sun across the horizon uninterrupted. The arid ground was robed in a spare majesty. Returning to normal life, I glimpsed the ancient world alongside the modern one and saw its beauty—yet the only change was my perception. This story captures a secret long known by artists: that seeing is not a passive experience, but an active, malleable one.

Drawing retrains our sense of sight, and for this reason, learning to draw is often referred to as "learning to see." When we draw, we slow down and

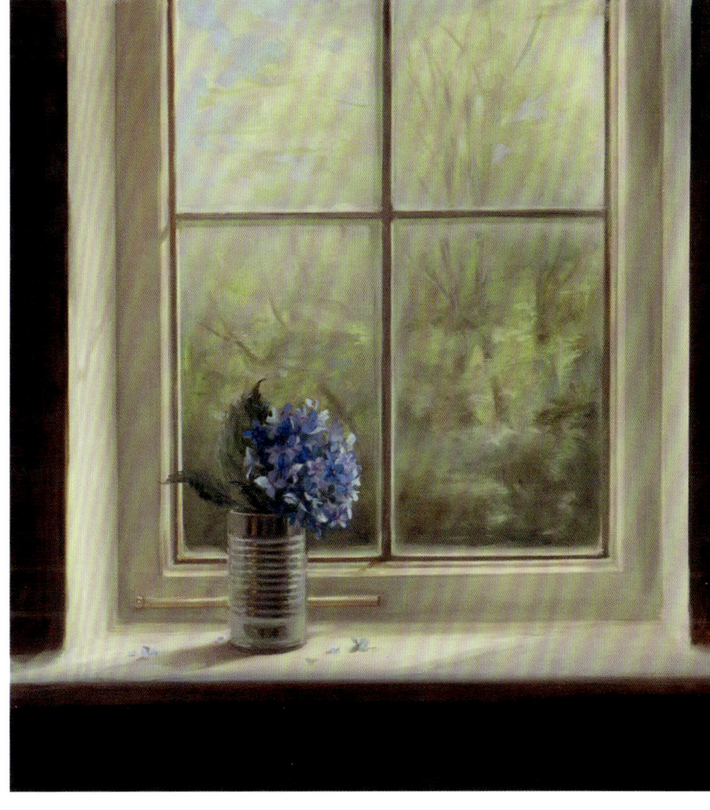

Juliette Aristides, *Hawthorn*, 2020, oil on panel, 24 x 22 inches (61 x 56 cm). Courtesy of the artist.

isolate our subject from the stream of life, pulling it into heightened attention by framing it. A pencil and paper help us pay careful attention, and we learn that anything, no matter how insignificant, can become an object of wonder and beauty. When we anticipate the beautiful and the interesting, we find it in unlikely places: A painting of morning light hitting crumpled bedsheets enables me to view my own bed as something worth noticing. A tin can sitting on a windowsill shows

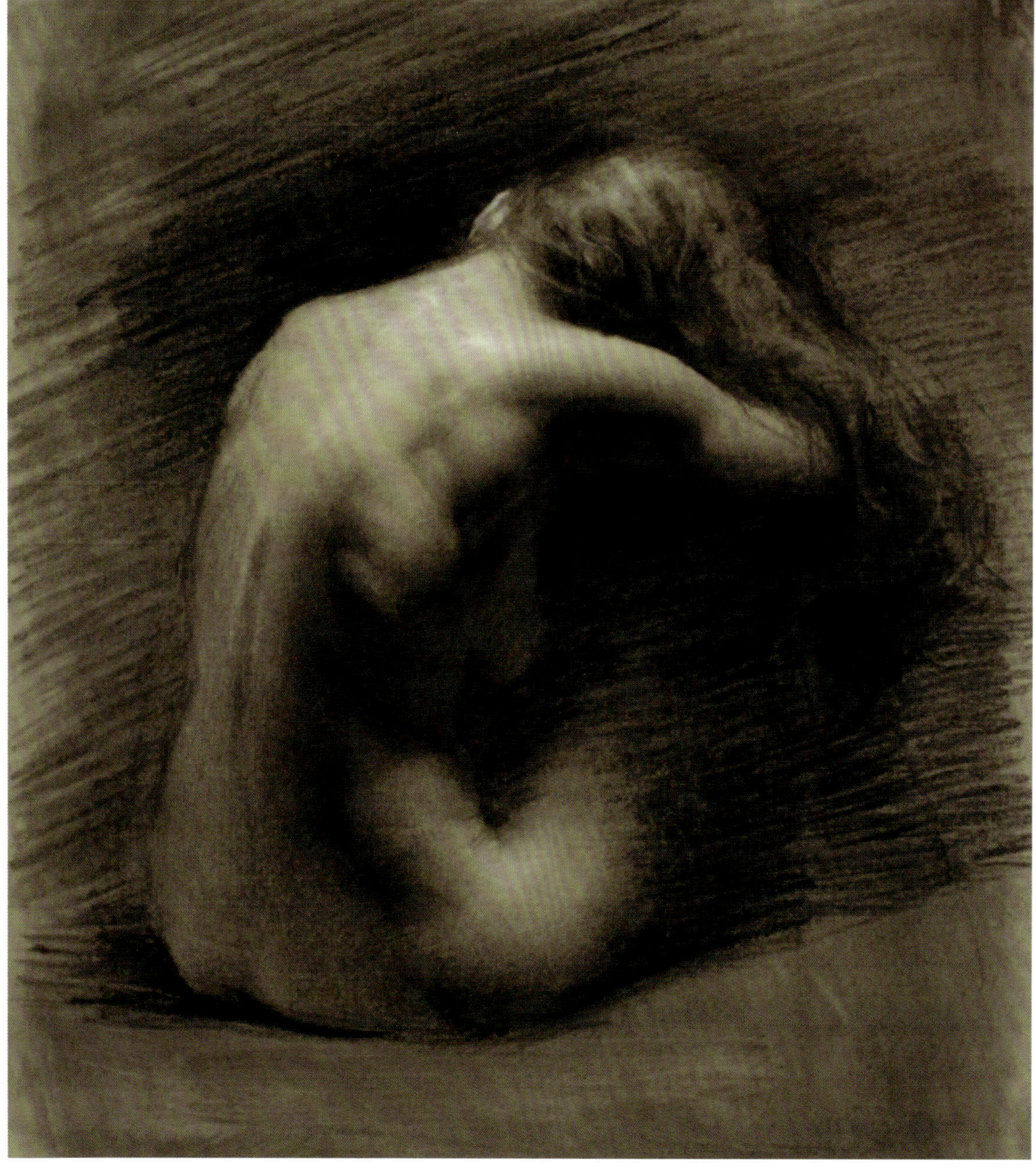

Juliette Aristides, *Repose*, 2017, charcoal on toned paper with white pastel, 22 x 18 inches (56 x 45 cm). Courtesy of the artist.

me that the visible world is a portal to something deeper and more vital if we only had eyes to see it. Finding beauty and interest is an act of cocreation.

In the pages that follow, Patricia Watwood introduces us to the practice of drawing and generously shares her technical training. She is uniquely skilled for the task. The first time I met her was as a student at Water Street Atelier. I was amazed at her confidence and talent. That admiration has only grown in the intervening years as she continues to push the boundaries of her art and has emerged as a leader in our field. Patricia knows that artists quietly transform the world as they transform themselves. Through careful looking and unmediated experience, they give voice to something essential. With nothing but a pencil and piece of paper, we can explore our own lives as a new country.

Preface

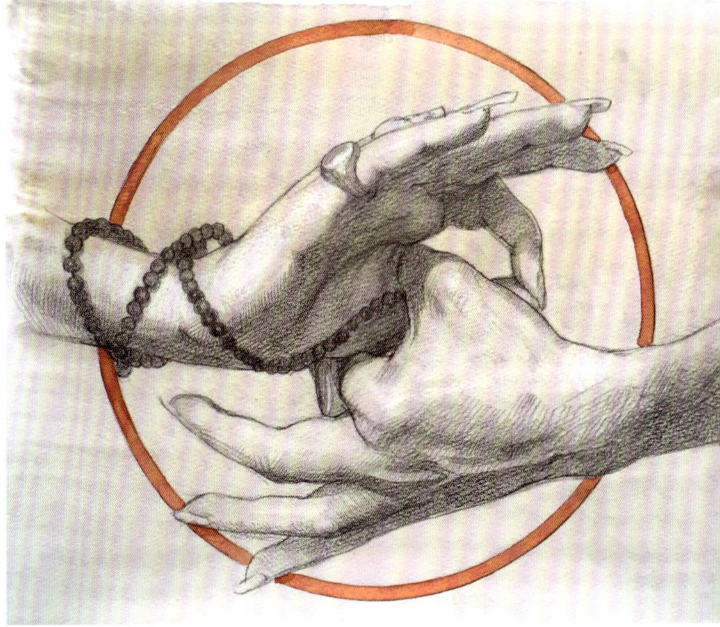

Patricia Watwood, *Spiral Mudra*, 2017, graphite, white Prismacolor, and watercolor on paper, 11 x 14 inches (28 x 36 cm). Courtesy of the artist.

When I was a child, my mother was fond of taking me to museums, cathedrals, and gardens, and I happily went along on these excursions to the land of beautiful things, intuiting early that these were important in the universe of pedestrian objects. She taught me to look for beauty and notice details around me, like a tiny blossom on an otherwise barren tree.

My first passion was theater, and in stage design I found a place that engaged my graphic skills and visual thinking. This seemed like my path, until the head of Yale's MFA theater-design program recommended that I hone my figure-drawing skills in a life class. Ming Cho Lee suggested the Art Students League of New York. (The fact that I lived in Seattle at the time seemed an inconsequential detail.) That little piece of advice was the beginning of the end of my time in theater.

Through investigation and kismet, I found my way to Gage Academy of Art in Seattle, whose founding director, Gary Faigin, had formerly taught at the Art Students League (aha!). Pencils sharpened and drawing pad in hand, I attended my first lecture from Gary. I remember to this day his explanation of drawing a life model using proportion, light, and shadow. I was hooked.

In Faigin's class I discovered an entire universe. Despite all those trips to museums with Mom, I was totally unaware of this cul-de-sac of the contemporary art world where living artists drew realistically and studied traditional methods. Not too long on this road, I took my first workshop with an artist named Anthony Ryder, who went on to write the foundational book in my field, *The Artist's*

Complete Guide to Figure Drawing. A couple of days into studying with Tony, I realized: "I want to know what he knows." Tony is a compassionate and generous teacher, and he encouraged me to take my artistic aspirations seriously. "To build a beautiful house, you must start with a strong foundation and invest properly in the architecture and design," he advised. Like Ming Cho Lee, that short conversation had lasting consequences. Not too long after that, my new husband and I moved to New York City, where I began studying with Jacob Collins. Collins had just begun the Water Street Atelier (it grew into Grand Central Atelier). I also enrolled in the MFA program at New York Academy of Art, a school founded in the early 1980s with the mission of bringing rigorous technical training to a new generation of artists.

Parallel to my artistic development, I have always been on another path. My other lifelong interest has been spirituality. I have a contemplative nature with a mystic bent. I'm constantly trying

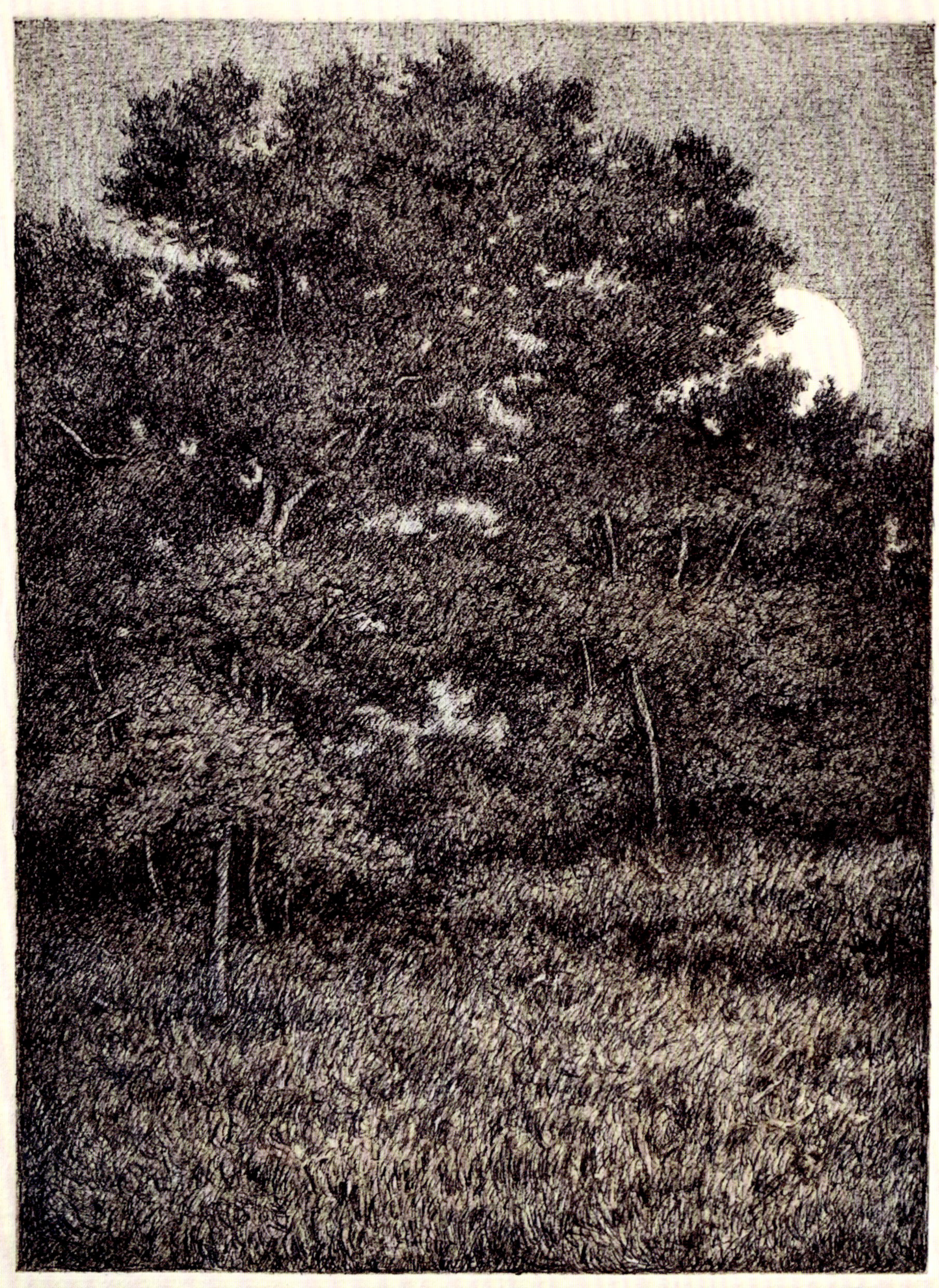

to chase down some kind of transcendental state, and this has impelled me to join a church, try Zen meditation boot camps in winter monasteries, spend a week in solitary silence in remote Nevada, walk around Walden Pond, read Rainer Maria Rilke and Kahlil Gibran, sing in a gospel choir, tend an altar in my studio, and buy a zafu, a zabuton, and a bunch of incense. I'm a spiritual junkie looking for a mystical fix, chasing after God. I had a clarifying moment when I learned about the Tree of Contemplative Practices,[1] which helped me see that all the different things I liked could be understood as varied expressions of one thing. Drawing, painting, walking, singing, or sitting—all of these were various paths to the essential quest for meaning and the goal to make a spiritual life centered peacefully in myself and my community.

It all started with drawing. I didn't know when I bought my pencil box for Faigin's class that I would carry that box on a long trip that would take me across the country and even abroad. Drawing has been the fundamental beginning point of my entire journey in art. To be honest, "becoming an artist" was never front of mind, and it would have scared me to think of—I just wanted to learn to draw.

I'm still trying to get better at drawing. I'm still dogged by a sense that with just a *little more practice* maybe I'll really get there. Perhaps this is like trying to understand the Himalayas. They are simply too big, too complex, too vast to master and own. Instead, I should enjoy the hike and throw a few snowballs. The profundity of the practice of drawing will always be wider, deeper, and larger than my own understanding. The wonderful part about that vastness is that there is always more room for anyone who wants to play about and make a snow angel in the land of art.

Instead of a skill to master, I have come to understand drawing as a pathway to a creative life. To learn the skills of drawing is to develop a practice and process that you repeat doggedly with the hope

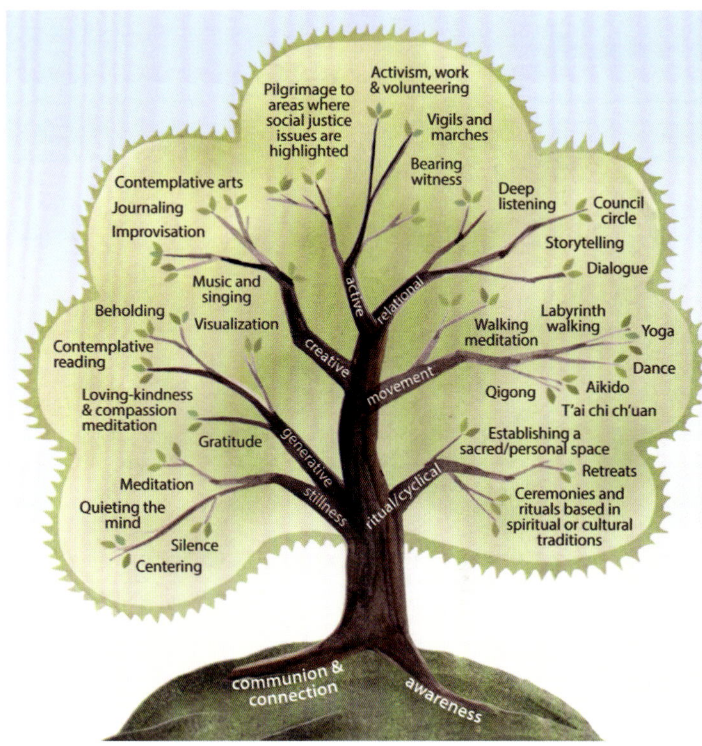

Above: *The Tree of Contemplative Practices,* © The Center for Contemplative Mind in Society. Concept and design by Maia Duerr; illustration by Carrie Bergman.

Opposite: Luis Colan, *Moonrise IV,* 2020, pen and ink over monotype ghost print on Rives heavyweight paper, 8 x 6 inches (20 x 15 cm). Courtesy of the artist.

that "Maybe, this time, I'll make something really beautiful." Even this misses the mark a bit. I've come to think of drawing as an artifact, a visible trail left by a journey of investigation. The end result might be lovely, might be worthy of a frame and public sharing—but that is a lucky by-product. A drawing is a vehicle for artistic travel. A means to go from one point to another—to observe more acutely, explore a visual puzzle, or unearth an image jutting up reluctantly through the sands of your mind. It's also a vital source—for when we are lost, drawing is one of the great lodestones for creatives to employ in helping us discover and connect with our inner creative voice.

Where do you want to go?

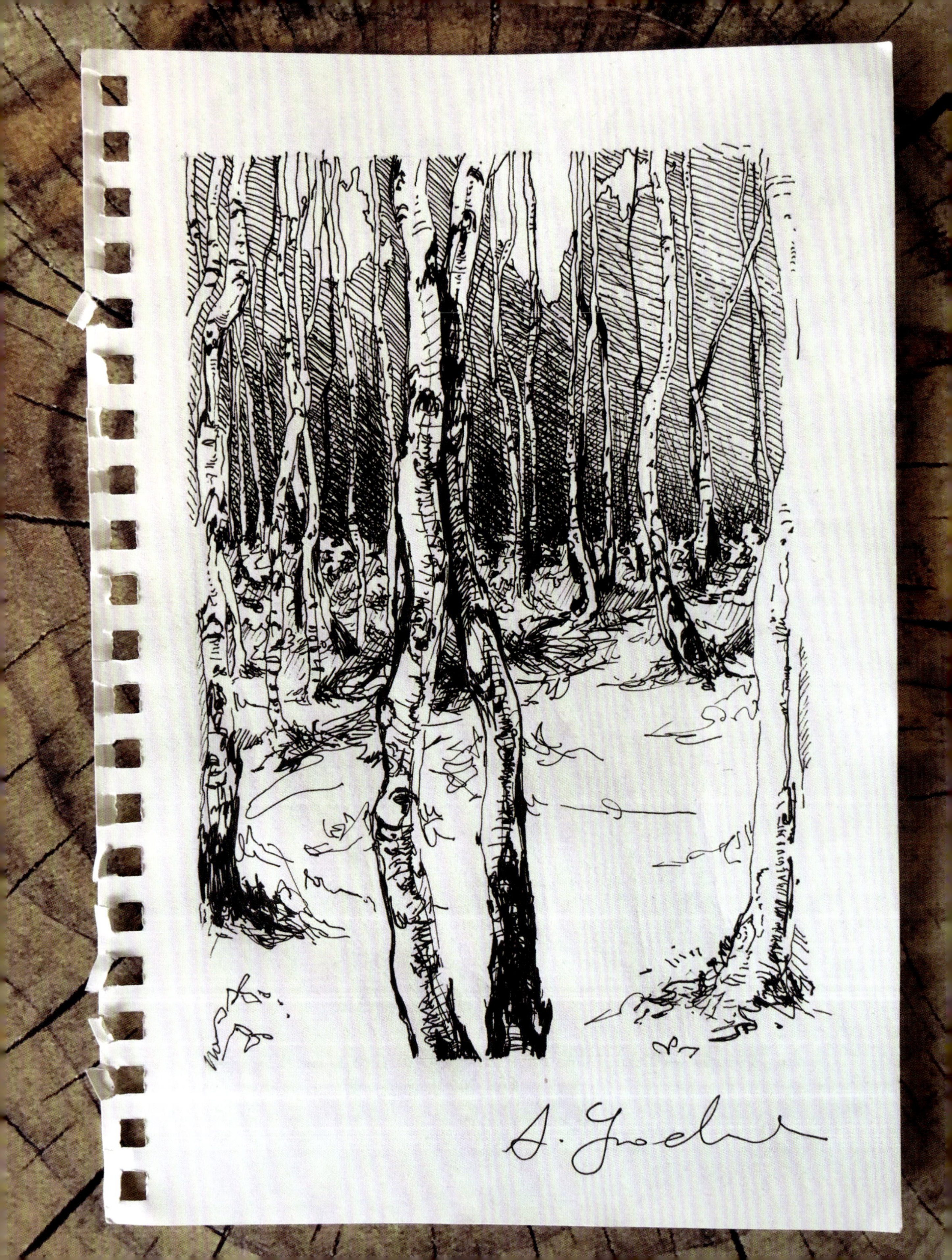

S. Groebel

Introduction

Today, many of us are learning that mindfulness can improve our lives by alleviating stress, anxiety, and depression and building resilience for experiencing joy in the present moment. Mindfulness is cultivating awareness of our thoughts and feelings as they unfold, so that we can understand our responses without being governed by them. The goal is a state of calmness and clarity toward the tumult of the mind. Our technological society constantly clamors for our attention, commodifies our anxiety, and invites our comparisons with others' lives. While contemplative practices like meditation and journaling work well for some, others find the idea of sitting totally still for twenty minutes more like torture than relaxation.

You might prefer to work through your hands in a visual, nonverbal way. This book is intended to teach you how to use drawing as a practice of mindfulness and inspire you to keep it as a habit. With consistent engagement, you can build healthy mental space for new ideas or get lost in a creative world. Drawing can clear your head, calm your nerves, give you joy, and help you reconnect with your inner voice. The demonstrations and exercises presented here will also serve as stepping-stones to your becoming a better observer while you learn the concepts of drawing in a realist style.

Where do creative ideas in art come from? How do we cultivate our imaginations? Even experienced artists can struggle when asked to engage their imaginations in visual work. This book describes some ways that I use drawing to refine and develop a creative idea from inkling to fruition. I'll share strategies I've developed to cultivate imagination and nurture inspiration. After many ups and downs, I've learned that the biggest challenges to a life in the arts are not technical, but emotional. I'll share what I've learned about overcoming obstacles to creating your best and most personal work. I hope this book will continue to reorient you should you find yourself a bit lost in your creative field.

"Wanderer, there is no road, the road is made by walking."
—ANTONIO MACHADO

Opposite: Agnes Grochulska, *Birch Forest Study #3*, 2018, ink on paper, 9 x 6 inches (23 x 15 cm). Courtesy of the artist.

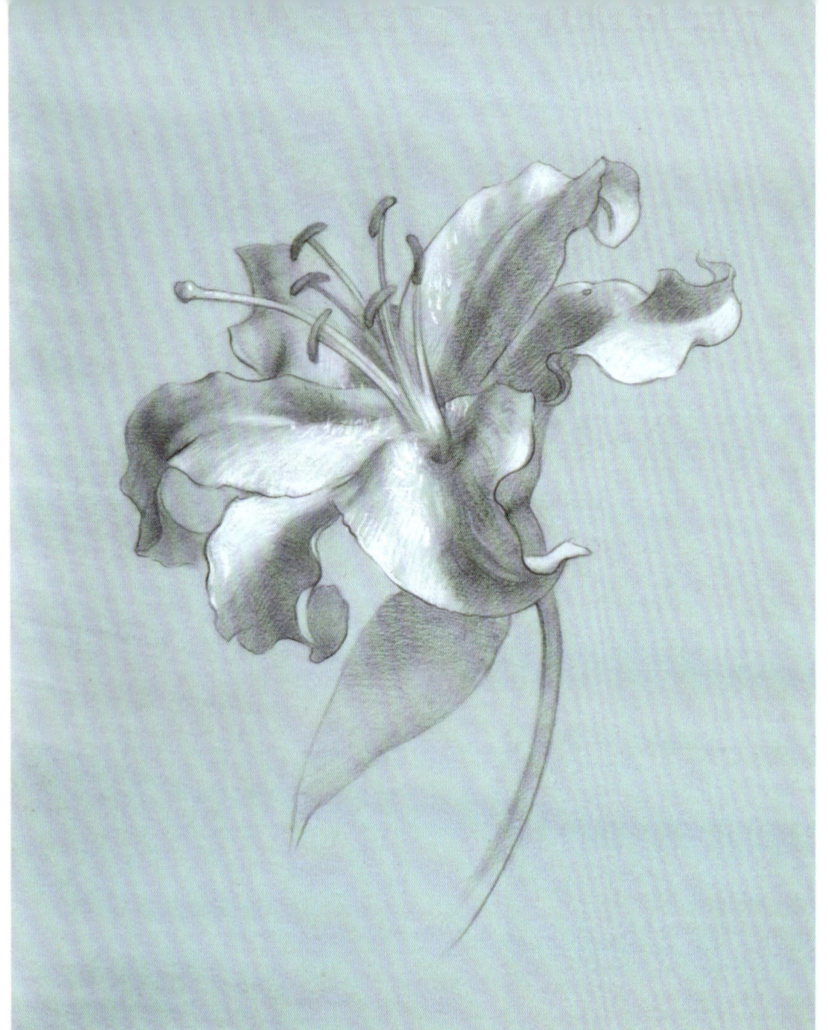

Patricia Watwood, *Annunciation Lily*, 2021, graphite and white pastel on watercolor paper, 12 x 9 inches (23 x 30 cm). Courtesy of the artist.

I have been writing this book in the middle of the coronavirus pandemic. The past couple of years have created overwhelming challenges, losses, struggles, and uncertainty. I hear artists asking, "Can you focus?" and "Are you getting work done?" Even in a normal period, we must at times range through rugged emotional terrain. I've dealt with depression and periods of professional frustration. I've come to think of depression as the opposite of creativity. We like to imagine an ideal state of creative flow: Inspiration! Clarity! Passion and energy! I've experienced that graceful and exuberant space once in a blue moon. I think that if artists required that emotional state for successful creative work, there would be very little art to look at in galleries and museums.

So how do artists persist without ebullient enthusiasm and creative bolts of lightning? How do we heal our troubled hearts to coax out focus and concentration? Instead of expecting a constant flow of inspiration, I have learned to navigate common emotional challenges such as wavering self-confidence and fear of imperfection. I follow a creative pathway and trudge along in fine weather and foul.

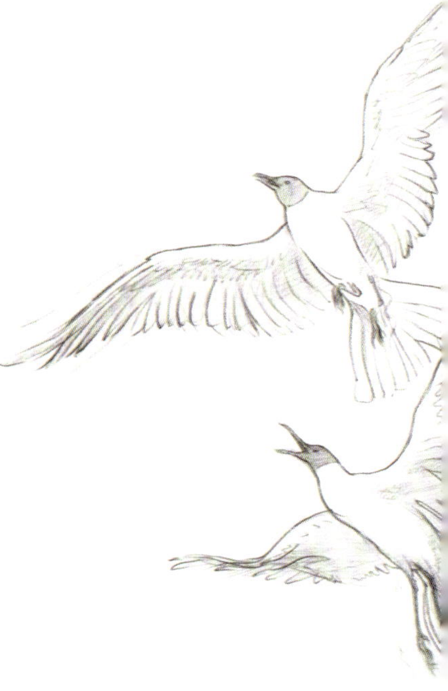

Even after years of making art, if I am not drawing, I am not getting better. The drawings might be doodles in a sketchbook, multimedia works on paper, observational sketches, or life-drawing sessions. I focus on processes, not goals. Artists draw to maintain our chops and explore new territory.

Can you devote thirty minutes a day to your creative growth? Or two hours a week? The projects in this book are designed to be manageable in a short period of time. They should fit into your day and bring creative thinking to every aspect of your life, grounding you in a practice that helps you feel calmer, more patient, and open to observing the joys of the world around you.

What do you do *each day* that creates happiness in your life? Too often, even though we enjoy making art, we allow life to get in the way. I'm inviting you to reframe your art hobby as a practice of wellness. Making art helps us bring our best selves forward and to those around us. I hope to encourage you to claim that time and prioritize creative joy in your days and weeks.

This book is for the young person who harbors a burning ember in her heart to be a creative maker. It is for the lawyer who sits at his desk at 6:00 a.m. with a book of poetry and a sketchbook to tend his soul before work. It is for the parent who wants to stay connected with the joy of art while the baby sleeps. It is for the teacher who loved art in high school but never had time until his retirement. This book is for anyone with an interest in visual art and a desire for more hands-on creativity. While the techniques in this book are grounded in traditional realism, the strategies for cultivating creativity and developing an individual voice are intended for a broad audience working in any style.

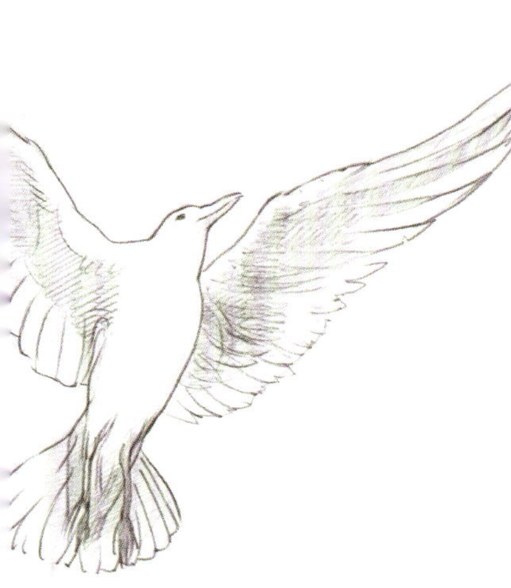

> *"'Hope' is the thing with feathers*
> *That perches in the soul,*
> *And sings the tune without the words,*
> *And never stops at all …"*
>
> —EMILY DICKINSON

ART AND RESILIENCE

The young climate revolutionary Greta Thunberg states, "Hope is something that you create, with your actions."[2] She declares that hope is not a passive position, a thing you simply "have" or "don't have." Feeling hopeful is not a by-product of a sunny disposition. Instead, it is earned through tenacity and work. Think of hope as a renewable resource rather than a finite asset. Did Emily Dickinson worry that her tune wasn't good enough or she couldn't find the right word? If so, I'm glad she kept singing anyway, perennially encouraging us to do the same.

After the years of pandemic, many of us are well acquainted with a miasma of fear and anxiety that makes it hard to move. Fear makes hope very difficult and drains our energy. Cynicism kicks in, and hope looks naïve and saccharine. When fear threatens to overwhelm, deregulate, paralyze, how shall we become wholehearted?

Shame researcher Brené Brown identifies key characteristics of wholehearted people: vulnerability, patience, open-mindedness, intuition, visualization, and imagination. My eye leaped at her last quality: creativity. She urges us to dive into creativity and reject comparison of the self to others. Brown's list overlaps remarkably with the qualities needed for artists. Her blunt conclusion is that "without vulnerability, there can be no creativity."[3] To be wholehearted, we must accept vulnerability and uncertainty, instead of barring them at the door.

Can we use the creative process to develop the very resilience we need to thrive? How shall we gather up our vulnerability and fear and step forward into greater wellness? If you want to awaken every day and be a positive force, you must adopt a system to retain your equilibrium and faith.

A PRACTICE OF WELLNESS

Art is a mechanism of hope. Engaging with and experiencing art is a lively well of renewal. Drawing takes so many different parts of your mind: eye-and-hand coordination, visual-spatial thought, and refining of complexity into simplicity. Mindful drawing creates a focused quiet that blocks out stray thoughts and distractions, restores calm, brings you happiness, and centers the mind. The very characteristics we wish to gain—patience, open-mindedness, and imagination—are developed while we learn to draw.

Creativity is not a panacea, but for an investment of four dollars on pencils and an eraser and ten dollars for a sketchbook, I believe that drawing is a pathway to wholeness, self-knowledge, and the resilience that comes from creative daring. Drawing can be a meaningful practice in developing your best self. This path begins by picking up a pencil.

Alexey Steele, *Mrs. O'Neal,* from the My Neighbor series, 2016, sepia on Fabriano soft press paper, 30 x 22 inches (76 x 56 cm). Courtesy of the artist.

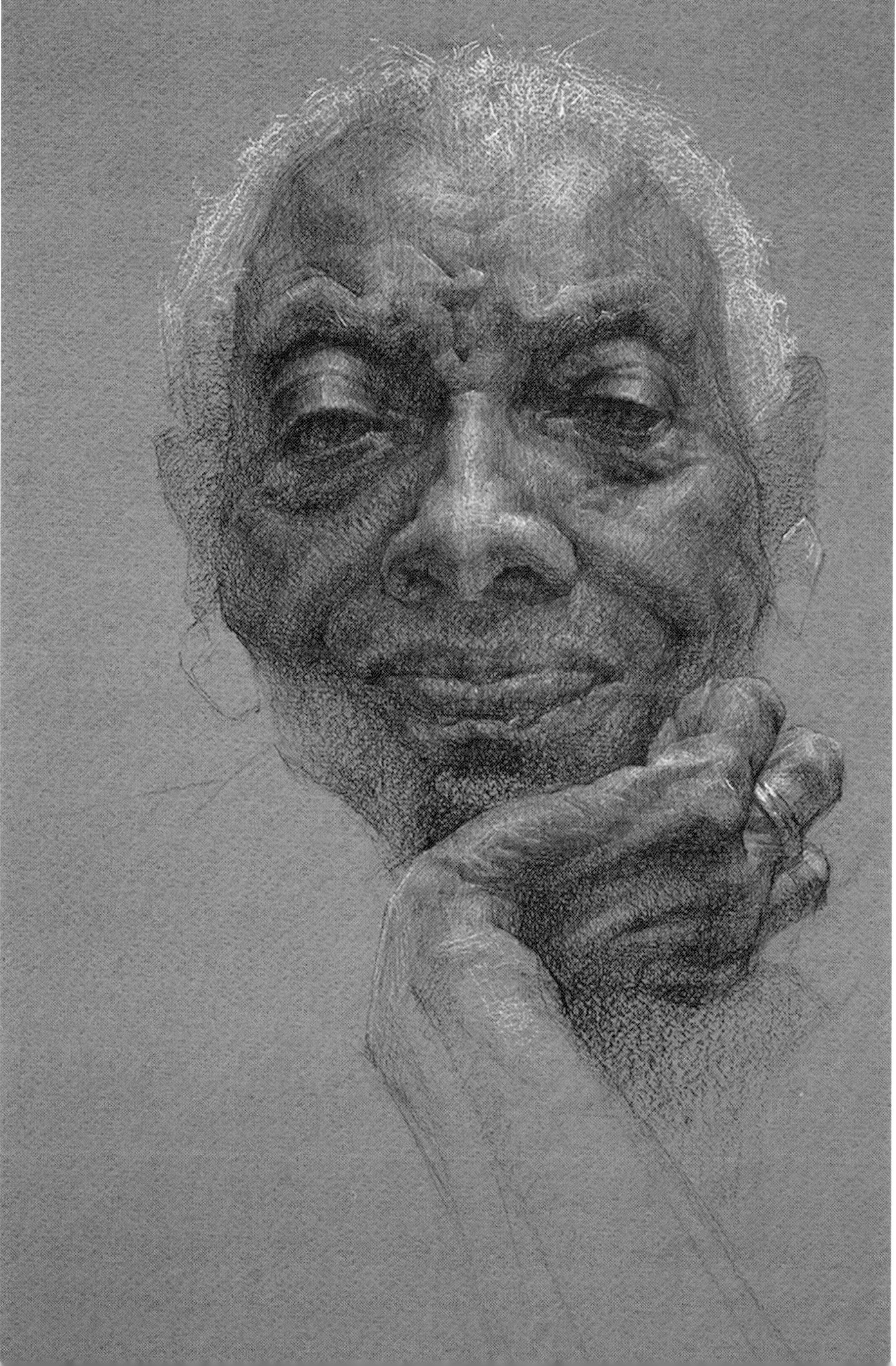

Materials List

Here's a list of all the materials I used in the projects in this book. Consider the drawing basics as essential to getting started, and all other items as possible enrichments for your creative work.

For the exercises in graphite, any simple sketchbook with smooth drawing paper, or loose sheets of unlined paper, will work.

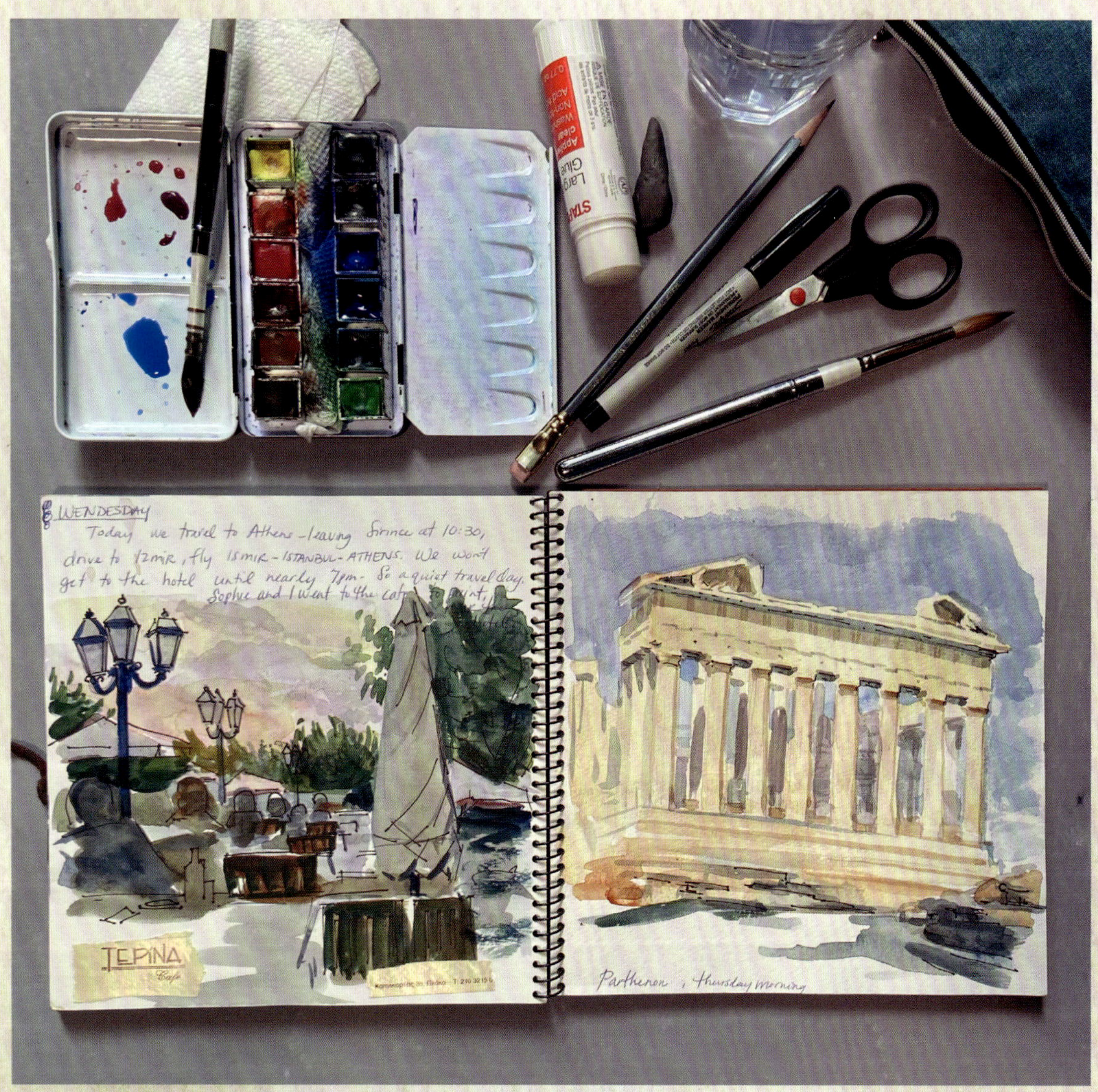

DRAWING BASICS

Mixed-media (or multimedia) sketchbook: 8 × 8 inches to 9 × 12 inches with a thick, smooth white paper (look for 90 to 140 lb. hot press), spiral-bound preferred

Graphite pencils in HB (or a yellow #2 pencil), 2B, and 3B

White vinyl eraser

Kneaded eraser, gray

Medium blending stump

Pencil sharpener

OTHER HANDY TOOLS

12-inch ruler

Glue stick

Scissors

Drawing board (13 × 17 inches)

Two large bulldog clips or binder clips

White vinyl eraser stick such as Paper Mate Tuff Stuff Eraser Stick or Pentel Clic Retractable Eraser

Slender 13- to 14-inch knitting needle or long barbecue skewer

Workable matte fixative spray

Presentation book with clear plastic sleeves (9 × 11½ inches)

Various round plastic container lids, diameters from 3 to 7 inches

Graphite Blackwing Natural pencils and Blackwing 602 pencils (my favorite)

OTHER PAPERS

Strathmore Drawing pad, 400 Series, 14 × 17 inches

Canson Mi-Teintes colored paper in loose sheets

Watercolor paper, white 140 lb. hot press, such as Fabriano Artistico

MIXED-MEDIA SUGGESTIONS

Ink markers, such as Paper Mate Flair medium in black

Sharpie Ultra Fine markers (or other waterproof type)

Colored pencils

FOR WATERCOLOR

Three or four short-handled watercolor brushes, including:

- One small, pointy sable round brush
- One medium sable round brush
- One wash/mop brush ½ inch across or more

Hake wash brush about 2 inches wide

For Travel:
Rosemary & Co watercolor travel brushes:

- R10 Pocket Golden Synthetic Pointed Size 8
- R3 Pocket Pure Kolinsky Sable Pointed Size 10

Small tubes (.17 oz./5 ml) of watercolors:

- Winsor Yellow or
  Sennelier Yellow Light (PY154)
- Alizarin Crimson (PR83)
- Phthalo Blue (red shade) PB15:1 or
  Ultramarine Blue (PB29)
- Burnt Sienna (PBr7)

Or try the Sennelier travel watercolor palette, Metal Pocket Box Set "A" of 12

Large white ceramic or plastic plate

Paper towels and water

1

Inviting Creativity In

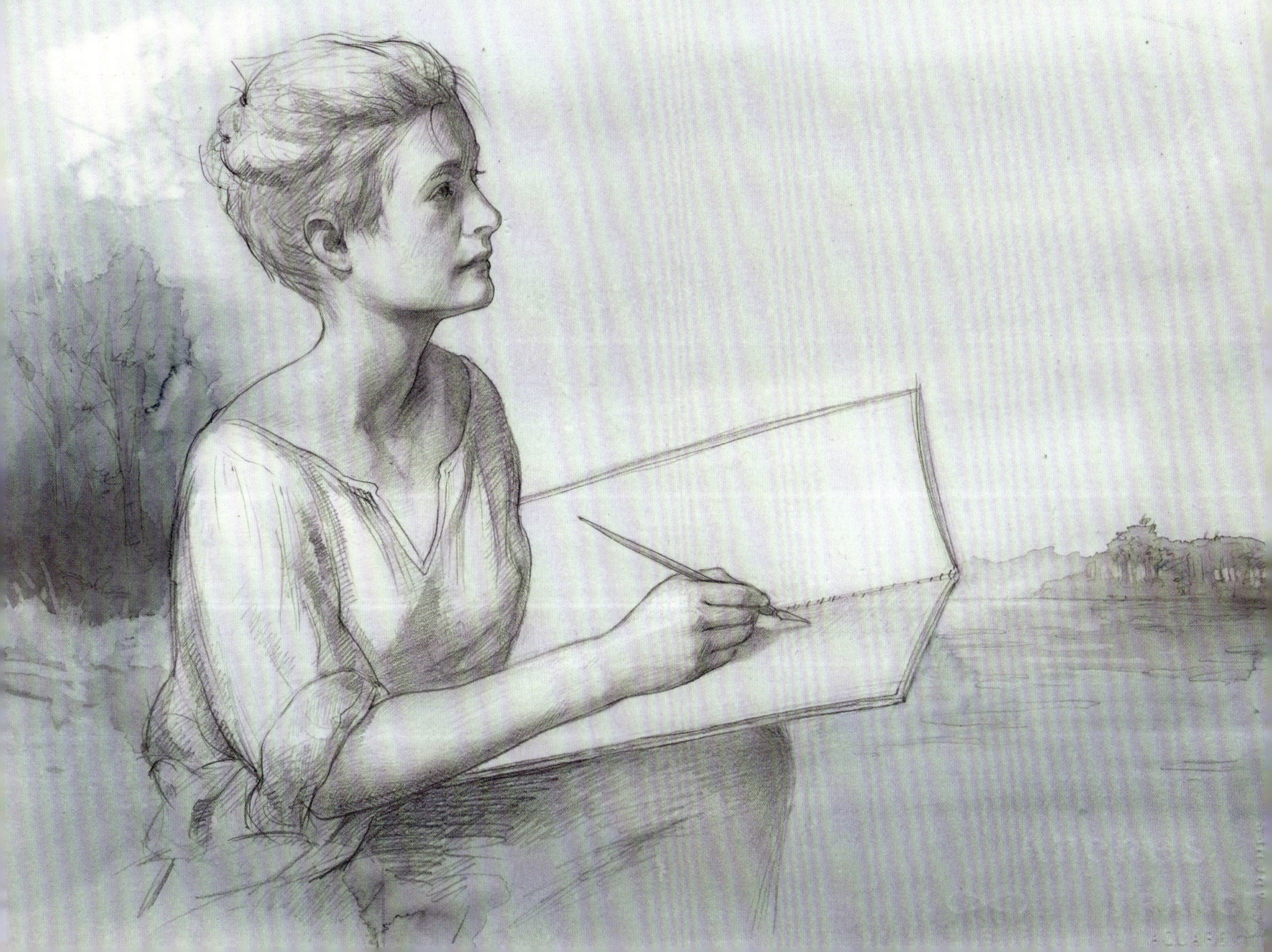

"A journey of a thousand miles begins with a single step."

BUILDING A CREATIVE HABIT

Do you want to make creative practice a regular part of your life? One hard lesson I've learned is that there's a big difference between thinking about doing something and actually doing it. Then there's another step between doing something once or twice and truly making it a consistent part of your life. With these common challenges, how do we make creating art a lasting habit? This chapter will give you some structure to invite creativity into your life.

Some of the most important steps begin before an artist puts pencil to paper. There are days when I don't feel like drawing any more than the next person. To build a habit, I've learned to set up my work space so that starting is as easy and natural as possible. Twyla Tharp recommends "rituals of preparation," simple repeated acts and conditions that help impel you forward, like setting out your running shoes before bedtime. "By making the start of the sequence automatic," Tharp advises, "[you] replace doubt and fear with comfort and routine."[4]

Starting this new habit requires three main components: materials, time, and intentions.

Be specific.

1. Plan for getting the materials you need.
2. Plan a space to work and store your materials.
3. Plan a regular time to do your project.

WHAT

All of the projects in this book are intended to be cognizant of your time and the accessibility of the tools you will need. The essential kit for this book consists of a mixed-media sketchbook, pencils, and erasers. Common household items such as scissors, glue, and a ruler will be handy. Later, you may wish to add watercolor, markers, or colored pencils. Look at the materials list section (p. 21) for full details, and spend a couple of minutes planning what you need.

Opposite: Patricia Watwood, *The Muse and the Source,* 2016, graphite and watercolor on paper, 11 x 15 inches (28 x 38 cm). Courtesy of the artist.

This book uses simple materials that are readily available: a mixed-media sketchbook, pencils, erasers, and, in later projects, watercolor and brushes.

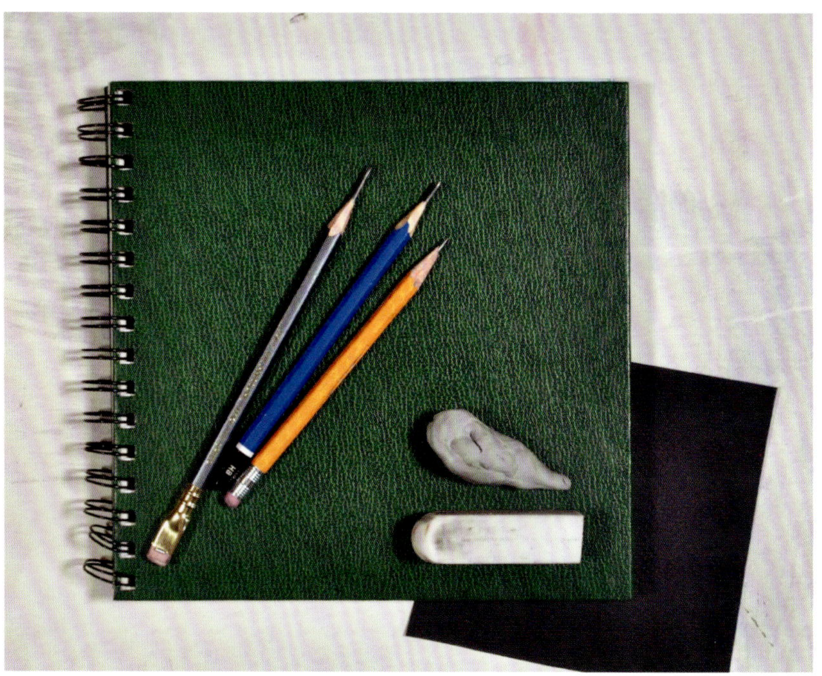

WHERE

You need to carve out a little space for your creativity. You may not have an entire room of your own, but can you dedicate a spot with a chair and table? It doesn't take much of a barrier to stall forward momentum, so consider where you will keep your sketchbook and materials. If the first thing you have to do is search for them, you might accidentally find some laundry to fold. I keep my sketchbook smack dab in the middle of my desk, with a pencil box and a few brushes standing by. As much as being handy, their visibility serves to remind me: *Done any drawing today?*

It can be hard to claim space for your creative work when you share your home with others. Do you feel shy about it? This little art hobby? Oh, it's nothing. Creative work can take up space and be messy. Maybe you are a little scared to draw attention to your art making because you feel compelled to justify your time as seeming productive. Maybe you feel vulnerable if other people see your creative attempts. If you have had these nagging hesitancies, know that it is common for creatives to feel shy about claiming space. Maybe these ideas can help: Creative practice as a component of mental health keeps you healthy, positive, and more joyful in your interactions with your friends and family. Cultivating imagination will make you more open to new ideas and innovative solutions to help you meet challenges at work and

"There are seven days in a week, and 'someday' is not one of them."

—BENNY LEWIS

in the world. A chunk of time away from the news, your work, the internet, and the din of social interaction will clear your head for renewed engagement. If you find it hard to claim space for yourself, remember that you help those around you by taking good care of yourself. You are entitled to claim that space for no good reason other than your own happiness.

A space to work can be a clear spot at your kitchen table. Is there a shelf in the kitchen where you can keep your stuff? Even better, set up a table and chair in a quiet area of your home, away from the TV and general hubbub. Arrange a storage space to keep your things, maybe a shallow plastic bin big enough for the sketchbook, some papers, and a pencil box.

WHEN

Can you devote thirty minutes a day to your creative growth? Or two hours a week? Take a minute and think about what amount of time, and how often, you might want to spend drawing. Some people find it's easier to build a habit with a short period every day, even ten to fifteen minutes. I get engrossed in my work, and I love to have at least one or two hours carved out to get lost in a project. It can be difficult to make real progress in anything with too little and too sporadic an amount of time. It's a bit like learning a foreign language—if you draw only once or twice a month, you'll forget what you gained between sessions. But small amounts of time, if consistent, will keep you connected with the thread of your creativity and allow you to make slow and steady progress.

Make an appointment with yourself, and write it down. Put it somewhere you will see it, or set an alert on your phone. Life happens, so you might need to reschedule, but too many people's favorite time to draw is "later." When is it possible to create a regular window? After breakfast? After dinner? Over your lunch break, or right after work? If you are trying to jump-start a new habit, I recommend that you make a commitment to spend time drawing every day for twenty minutes, for a week or even a month. When I am busy, I still keep to my practice three to four times a week. If you do this consistently, I promise that you will quickly see improvement in your skills and experience a shift in your daily routine toward a more positive and calmer outlook.

Luis Colan makes notan thumbnails (small sketches indicating flat areas of dark and light values only; see Chapter 10) in his sketchbook from imagination and then selects his favorite compositions to create a monotype print.

Luis Colan, sketchbook pages with notes and thumbnails, 2018, pen and ink on paper, each page 8 ¼ x 5 inches (21 x 13 cm). Courtesy of the artist.

Luis Colan, *El Arroyo,* 2020, pen and ink over monotype ghost print on Rives heavyweight paper, 6 x 8 inches (15 x 20 cm). Courtesy of the artist.

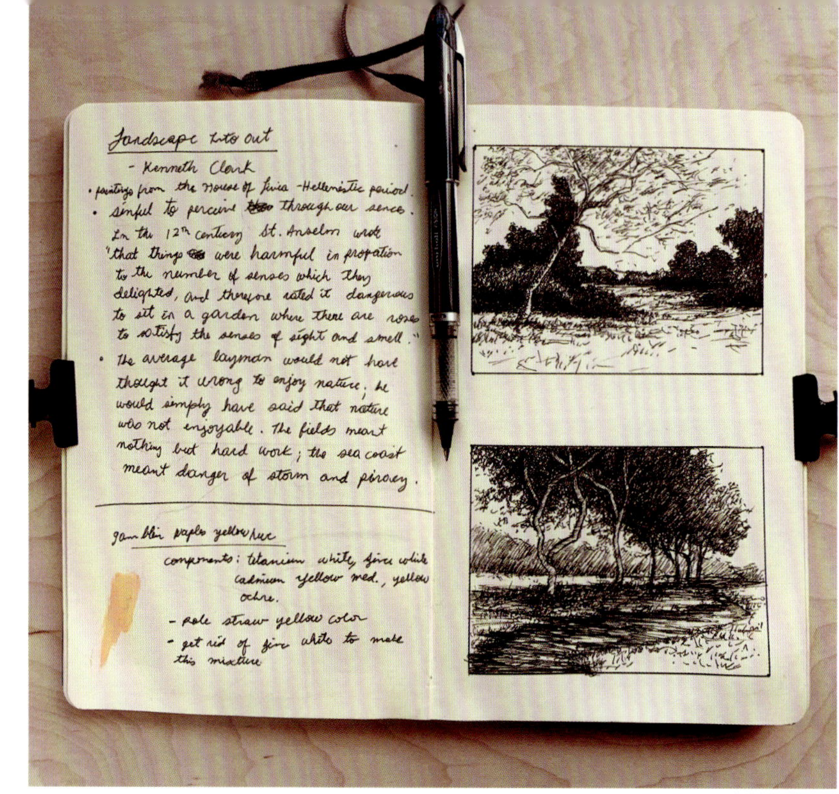

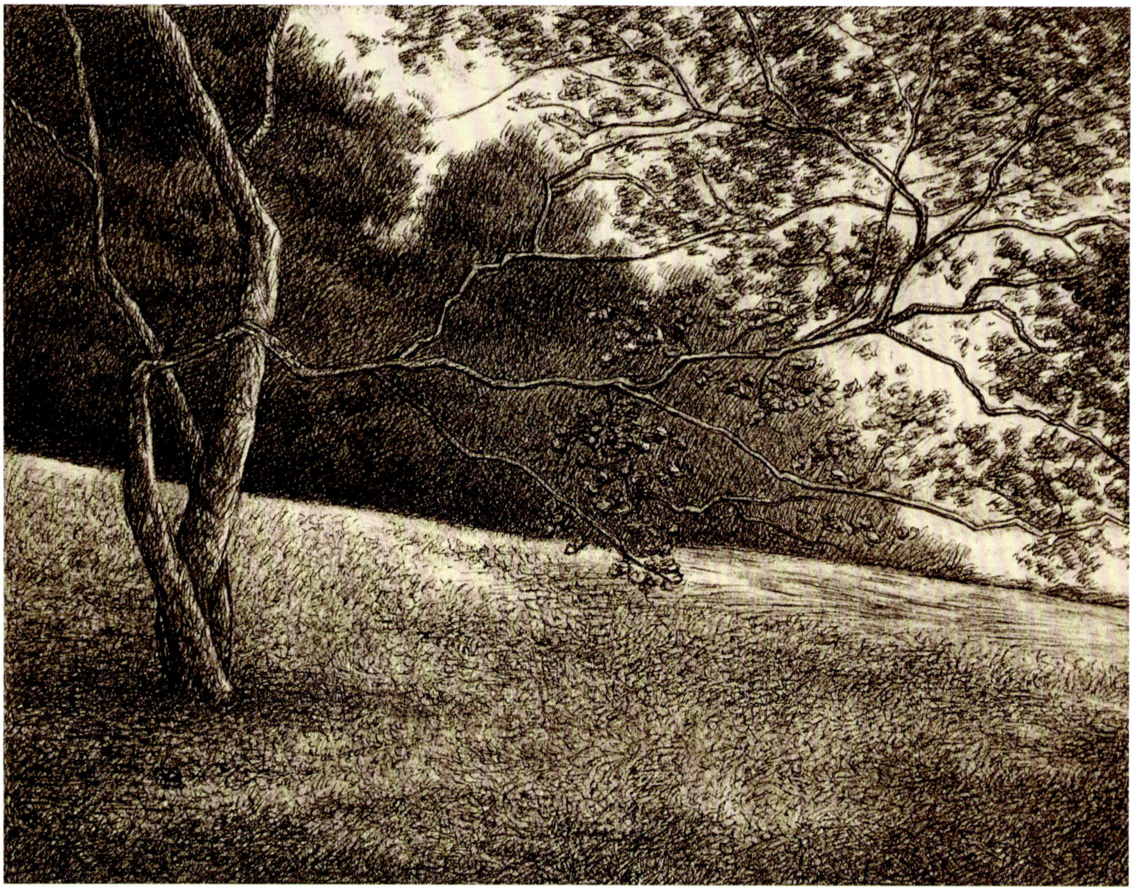

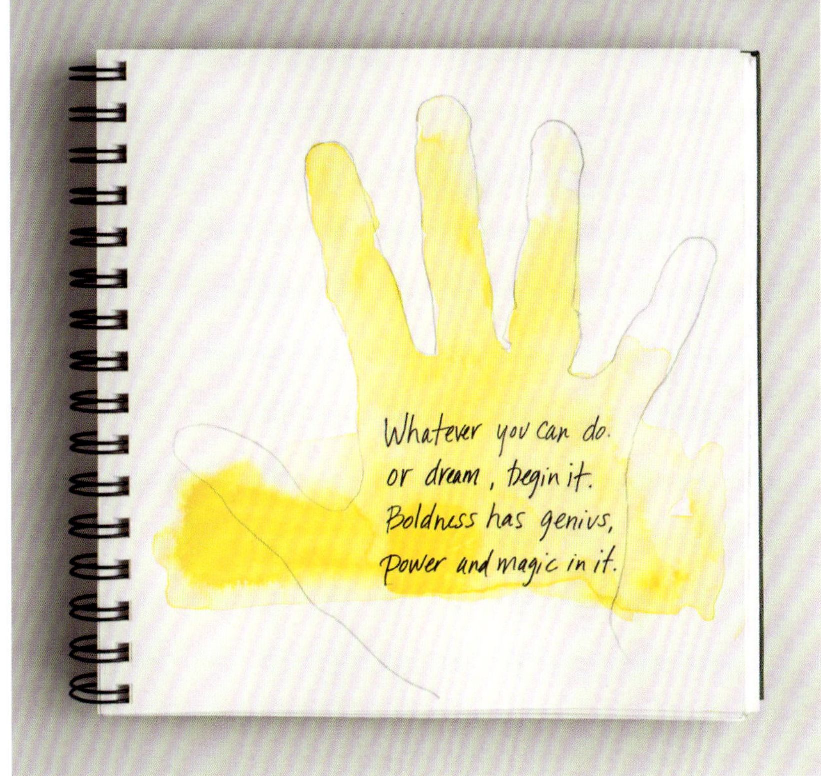

Artwork with part of a quote by William Hutchison Murray. The full quote is "Until one is committed, there is hesitancy, the chance to draw back, always ineffectiveness. Concerning all acts of initiative (and creation), there is one elementary truth, the ignorance of which kills countless ideas and splendid plans: that the moment one definitely commits oneself, then Providence moves too … Whatever you can do, or dream you can, begin it. Boldness has genius, power, and magic in it. Begin it now."

SET AN INTENTION

You've planned out what and where and when. Now the most important question left is WHY. To build a consistent habit, you need to stay connected with the motivation that propelled you to begin. Write out an *intention*: Use your sketchbook as a source of ideas that will help you stay connected with that goal. Add plans for how often and how long you wish to pick up that sketchbook over the weeks and months ahead. It may seem unnecessary to write these out—but too often our creative goals fall victim to life's interruptions and general procrastination. Writing it down will strengthen your resolve. My intention is to help you cultivate an ongoing relationship with your creative self.

TIPS FOR SUCCESSFUL STARTS

SET OUT YOUR THINGS

Prime your engine by setting up your materials the night before. In this book, many projects include a bit of preparation—still life objects, inspirational photos, maybe a light. To begin is to be half done. Five minutes at the end of the day getting out your paper and tools make starting the next day flow naturally.

SET A TIMER

I regularly use a timer when I need a little boost for my concentration. I set a timer for twenty minutes and begin. Until the timer runs out, I will not allow myself to be distracted. No checking my messages, no phone calls, no emails, no getting up from my chair. (If, oops, I find myself distracted, then I gently turn my mind back to drawing.) Twenty minutes may seem long at first, but once you become involved in your project, time will pass quickly. When the timer dings, I sometimes reset it. Usually, by then I'm happily involved and don't need extra structure.

TURN THINGS OFF

Our interconnected world is full of distractions. The economic interest in your attention is flourishing, and advertisers and corporations keep metrics on the value of your thoughts and time. Seeing my sister's new baby walk on social media is delightful, but these sites are designed to pull me down the rabbit hole to stay. Our attention (or lack thereof) has become so remarkably disrupted that folks are now studying the impacts of what is called the attention economy.

Every single action we take—calling our grandparents, cleaning up the kitchen, or, today, scrolling through our phones—is a transaction. When you pay attention to one thing, you ignore something else. Attention has always been currency, but as we've begun to live our lives increasingly online, it's now *the* currency.

If you have noticed a marked decrease in your ability to focus in the last year or three, just know that many people are similarly struggling. Between doom scrolling, disruption, and the onslaught of the Information Age, focus is fragile and elusive for everyone. Mindfulness begins with noticing the inputs and claims on our attention, then making a conscious choice of how and where to focus.

Silence, turn off, and disconnect your distracters. "Do Not Disturb," "Airplane Mode," and "Oops, my battery died" are great for drawing. Put a note on your door telling the kids to come back in an hour unless they are literally bleeding. Claim that hour for your own thoughts and creative growth.

Opposite: Marina Terauds, *Fern Urbanized*, 2014, etching and watercolor on paper, 32 x 26 inches (81 x 66 cm). Courtesy of the artist.

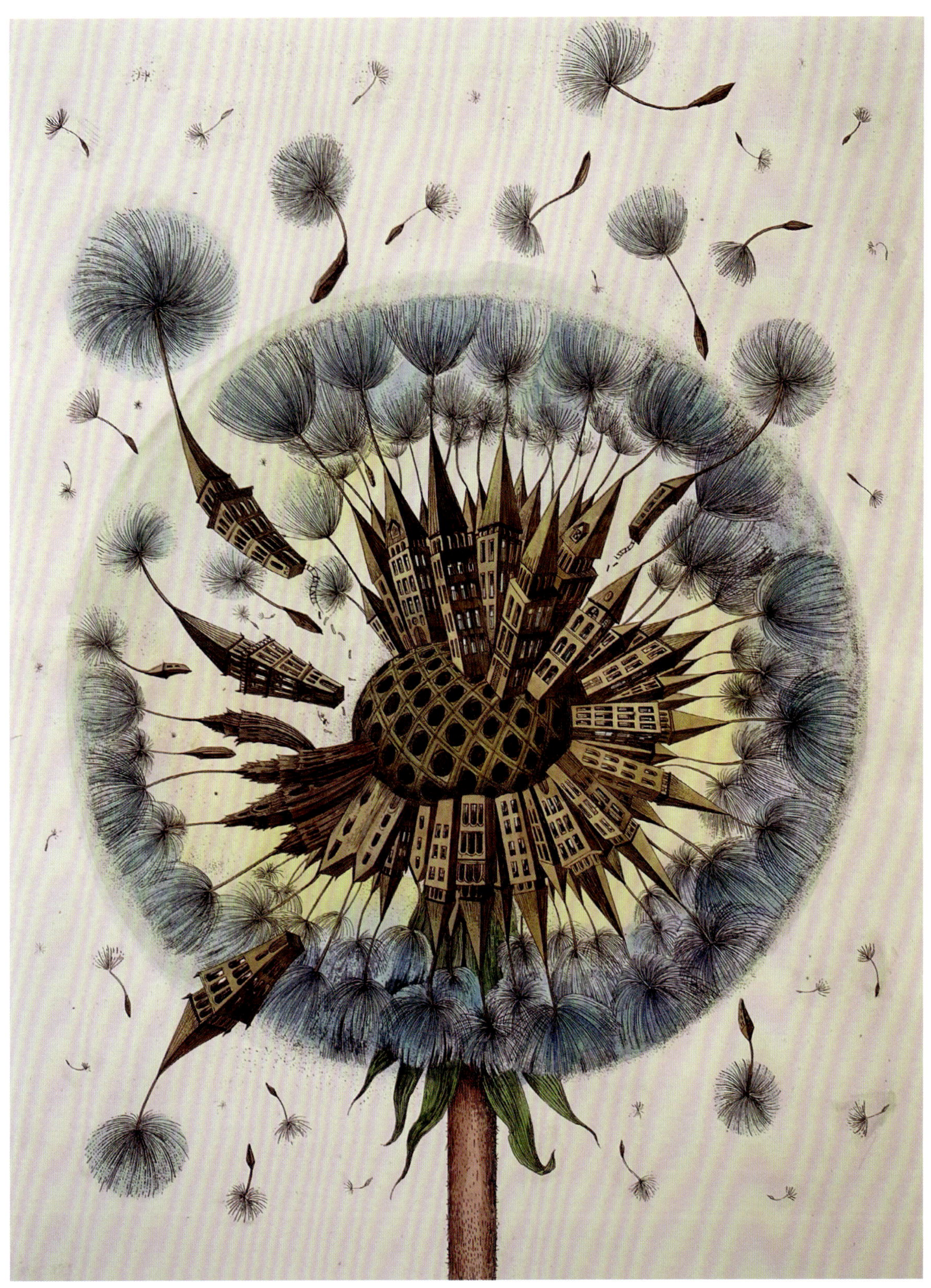

Pay attention to your aural environment. Email dings, radio chatter, honking horns, and the like pull us out of our thoughts and back into the world. I listen to frankly boring music to drown out other input. My favorite playlist these days is called *Binaural Beats*, a genre of music that is more like sound therapy. With headphones, the sounds coming in to each ear have slightly different wave frequencies. This is believed to encourage the same kind of brain-wave state found in meditation and helps create focus, increase relaxation, and reduce anxiety. It's not conventionally musical, so binaural songs don't draw my mind to melody or harmonies. Sometimes silence leaves me a bit too alone with my internal dialogues. With this non-music, I have an almost Pavlovian response—my blood pressure drops, I quickly relax, and I am ready to work. I would never have gotten this book written without it!

If this particular music isn't your jam, I recommend a playlist of non-verbal tunes that help you chill and go with the flow. A white-noise machine or playlist of nature sounds also can support your focus. Noise-canceling headphones or earplugs can help create a pillow of quiet for your head.

"The faculty of bringing back a wandering attention over and over again is the very root of judgment, character, and will."
—WILLIAM JAMES

One other idea I want to put out there—how does *silence* work for you? Having a period of silent concentration is healthy for the mind and nurtures your ability to tune in to your inner voice. If you are unaccustomed to silence, it can be disconcerting at first. Adjusting to periods of quiet allows space for imagination and thoughts to sift through your consciousness. If you wish to build up your tolerance for silent concentration, start with just ten minutes. If you are still bothered by the quiet, turn on white noise or nature sounds. Gradually build up to longer blocks of silence. I like to have about an hour a day of audio detox and listen to the sounds of life around me. Combining quiet focus with your daily drawing can be like meditation, calming and restorative.

GATHERING INSPIRATION

To end this chapter on preparation, I want to introduce a practice you can incorporate with your daily routine. *Creative composting* is the gathering of

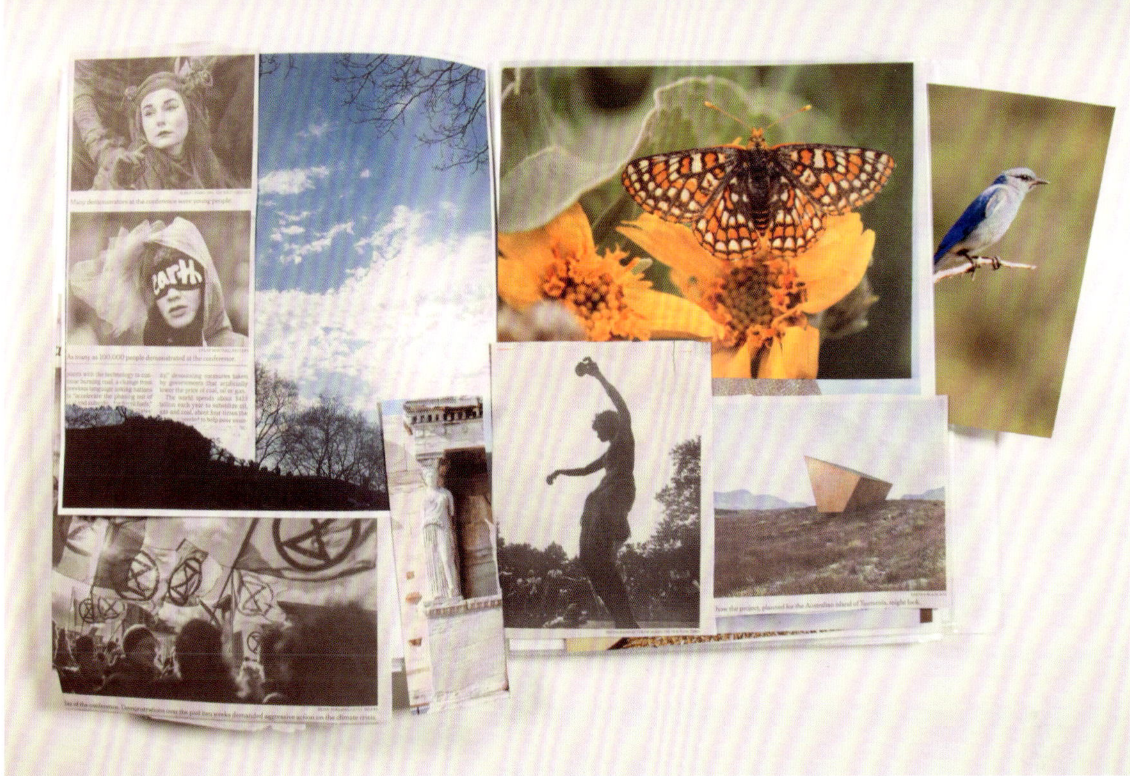

ideas and inspiration for later cultivation. Like collecting compost for gardening, you can amass scraps of visual materials and ideas that, through time, intermixing, and discernment, will create a fertile soil for new ideas.

I gather items such as postcards, magazine illustrations, and newspaper clippings for future use and reflection. I keep a small notebook in my bag at all times to jot down thoughts and quotes or capture a scene in a thumbnail drawing. Flickers of inspiration that pop into my day are a precious resource.

Later I'll share a creative compost project and tell you how I use it for nurturing ideas. For now, I invite you to keep an eye out for images you like, ideas, quotes, bits of poems, stray ideas. Tuck them into a folder or use your sketchbook like a scrapbook with scissors and glue. It doesn't have to be just full of stylish and tidy drawings. Instead, think of your sketchbook as a personal sourcebook of drawings, doodles, ideas, collage, and maybe a grocery list. Our lives are messy and complicated. Your drawing book can be a safe space for all the different parts of yourself.

VISUALIZING YOUR FUTURE SKETCHBOOK

If you just picked up a new sketchbook, flip it open. Do the pages seem full of endless possibilities, or empty and intimidating? Can you imagine what

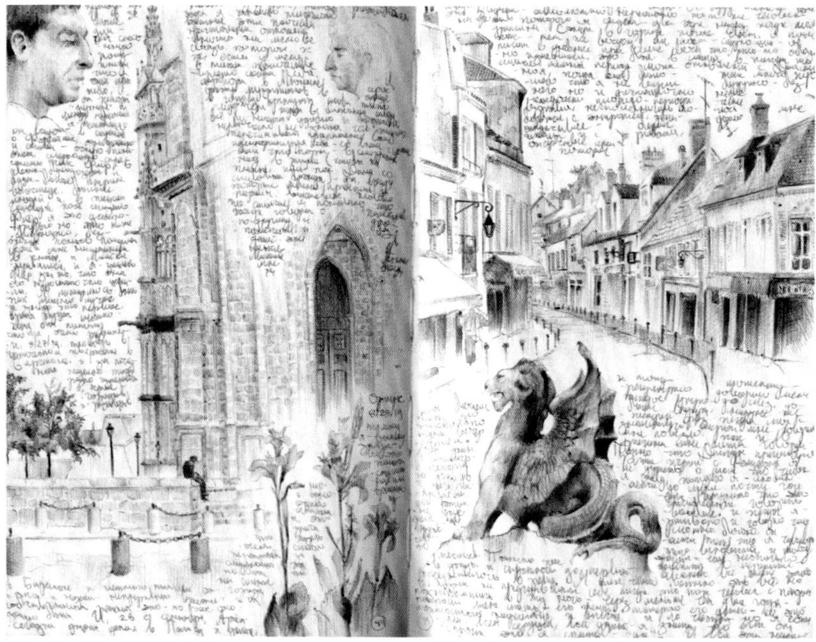

the book would look like with all the pages full? How would it feel to turn the pages, remembering the projects you learned and seeing the progress you have made? To imagine is an act of creative visualization. The more clearly we visualize our goal, the more committed we become to the process.

Connect with your intention—what impelled you to pick up this book and do some drawing? Perhaps it was kismet: a gift, a coincidence, an idle fancy. Perhaps it was a long-held dream to become an artist. Consider jotting down your thoughts to remind you of these intentions. In a creative practice, you must connect the instigating idea with the visualization of a goal and the implementation of a process. Every opening of your blank sketchbook is an opportunity to practice this sequence and make creativity a part of your life.

Discard expectations of perfection and loveliness in your sketchbook. I rarely show my own sketchbooks to friends or extract drawings to frame. To be honest, most of my sketchbook pages are clunky, disorganized, and full of drawings I consider subpar. I admire artists whose sketchbooks seem like polished presentations of finished work. (Perhaps those are just the pages they carefully selected for Instagram.) My goal is to fill a drawing book in whatever way makes me eager to start a new one. My approach could be slow, fast, tidy, sloppy, scribbles, or seraphim. Another idea to circumvent the daunting blank pages is to open to a random page a bit further in from page one. Sneak in the back door and make yourself at home.

2

Spiral Your Way In

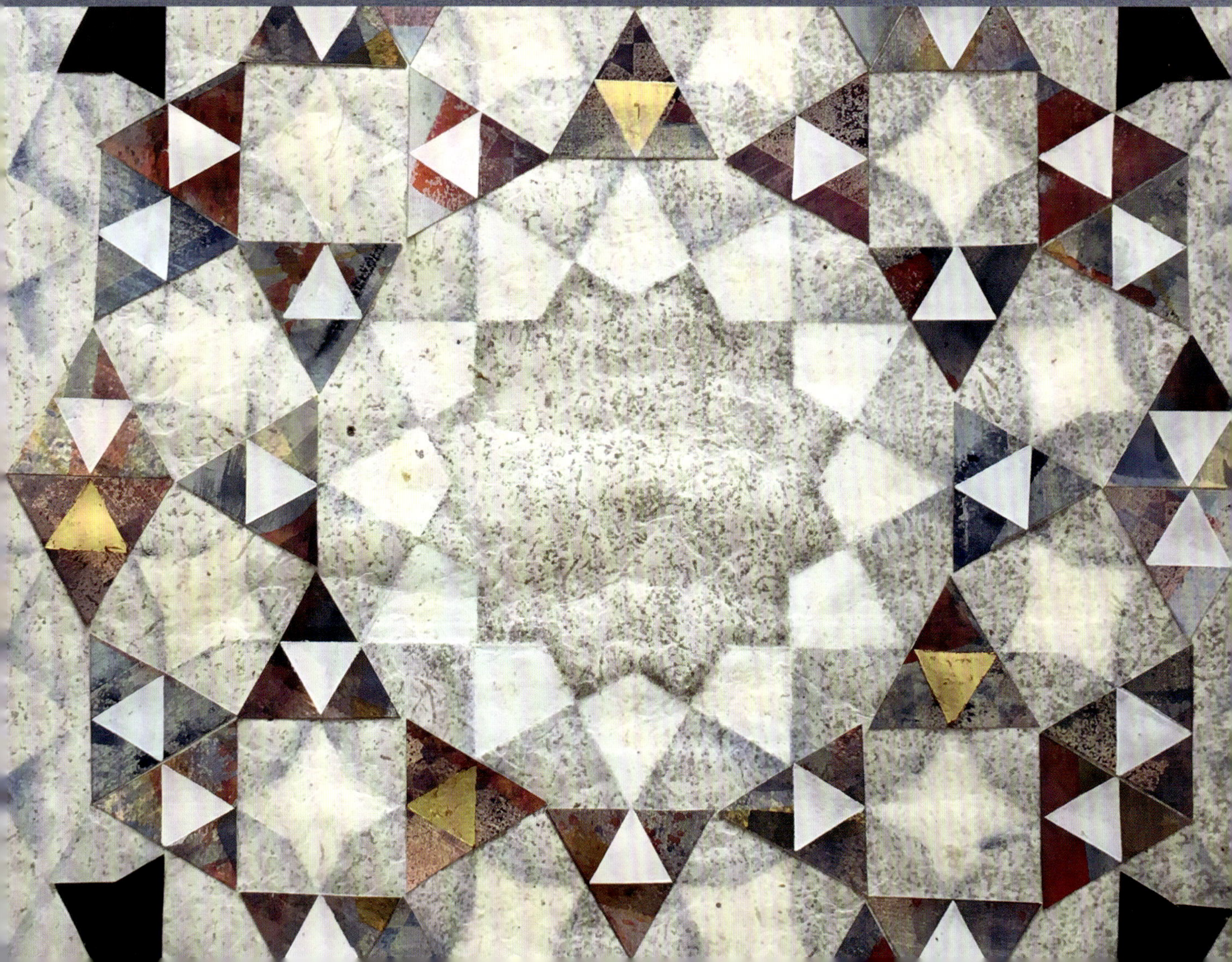

—RALPH WALDO EMERSON

As you travel this path of drawing, you will discover that often it's the stalling at the very start that impedes your progress. Every day, a new beginning. Every day, the same stumbling block. Every artist needs a ritual of focus.

Distractions and demands on your time are everywhere. I could really use (another) cup of coffee. Oh, look…there's a notification about an email; I better check that! This chair is really uncomfortable; where's a pillow? Oh, crap, I forgot to call my mom.

What's really going on here is that I'm desperately casting about for ways to avoid the blank page. Under the distractions is hesitancy and perhaps a little discomfort sitting quietly with myself. Mindfulness in this moment means that I notice the many things that pull my attention away, and then intentionally choose to ignore them. This ability to focus is incredibly important to our health and success in many things—work, personal projects, relationships, and health. This choice to spend time drawing will build your skills for focusing on anything that needs and deserves your attention. Remember that the world is literally spending money trying to distract you and get your attention (usually to buy something or to get mad about something). Build your focus muscles and choose what gets your time.

Incredibly simple acts can give you an on-ramp to the creative space. *Choosing* to focus might not quite get you to *actually* focus. This is where ritual helps us over that stumbling block. In this chapter, I'll share a few strategies that can serve as rituals for getting started. These easy skill builders will take you from distraction to moving forward. These starts are approachable for absolutely anyone and can build skills for a total beginner.

The cartoonist Lynda Barry begins with the prompt "Spiral your way in." Here's her strategy: "Before I begin writing, I set a timer for two minutes and I draw a slow, tight spiral and I let my mind's eye drift to scenes that come back to me… I just draw the spiral and drift."[5] This is a marvelously simple way to begin to connect your mind, hand, and materials.

Let's take Lynda's advice and start with a dumb, inconsequential spiral. This is a lifeline I love that pulls me into my practice.

Start with me as I pick up a smooth, dark pencil, like a 2B. I'm using a Palomino Blackwing, which sounds more like a bird or F-wing fighter than a

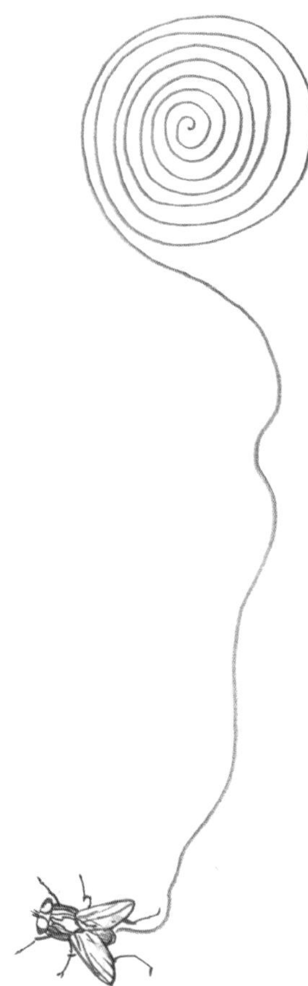

Opposite: Richard Henry's collage design is inspired by classical patterns from medieval Cairo and Damascus.

Richard Henry, *Harlequin* (detail), 2019, mixed-media collage with gold leaf on paper, 36 x 26 inches (91 x 65 cm). Courtesy of the artist.

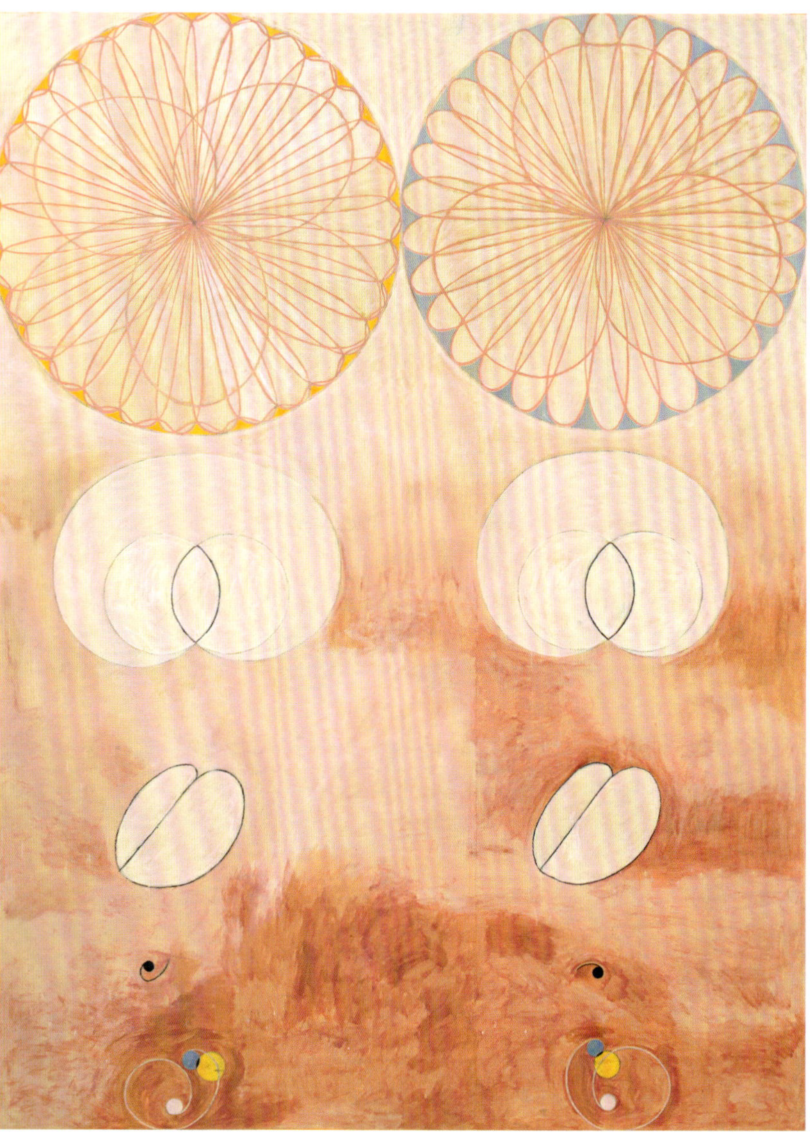

piece of wood and graphite. It feels like a good omen. I set the pencil down at a random place on my blank page. Inhaling, I pick a point and start to spiral out like a finger moving through water. Exhaling, I focus my mind on the pencil, the trail of lead, the white paper. My mind quiets, my shoulders drop, my heart rate settles.

I have broken the surface of the pond and submerged myself in the world of drawing. After about seven spirals, I notice that my speed and eye-hand coordination shift; I move left instead of right as my hand begins another spiral. There is no right or wrong, up or down, no purpose other than bringing my mind and pencil together on the page. The shapes and spirals please me. I have left evidence of a moment of my existence on the paper. I am no longer worrying about drawing; I am simply making marks and being present.

I invite you to come back to this simple practice whenever you need to anchor yourself to your seat and begin. I'm sorry to confess that after twenty years of drawing, starting is not particularly easier for me now than before. All the same clatter of nerves and distraction flutter in my mind. This is part of my emotional makeup, so I take a small step forward.

Sitting down to work, take a moment and notice your body: your tush on the chair, the space between your toes, the temperature of the skin on your cheek. If your nerves are particularly jangly, send your thoughts to feel the pressure of your feet on the ground and the earth pressing up underneath you. Take a deep breath and remind yourself of your intention—you are just going to engage with drawing for twenty minutes or so.

Our entire body participates in the experience of creativity. Every single time I begin to work, I use some variety of a centering ritual. If I'm not making spirals, I may start my practice at the easel with a yoga Mountain Pose: feet square, straightening up my spine, remembering to drop my shoulders, head lifted, body aligned. I notice distracting thoughts and then let them drop away. If I get worked up and frustrated in the middle of my creative work, I pause and recenter, remembering to take a few deep breaths. Imagine a gate in your mind and shut it to the clutter of distractions from all parts of your life. The emergencies of the world can usually wait. It is time to draw.

SIMPLE SKILL–BUILDING EXERCISES

The line between doodling and drawing is so thin that it is really imaginary. In fact, the only difference is the word you use to describe your activity. Spirals and squiggles begin an exercise that also builds skills in eye-hand coordination. When you watch a masterful artist knock off an elegant and terribly simple line, it looks like magic. Truly, it's the result of many hours of practice and muscle memory. If your simple lines don't look like Picasso's bouquet of flowers, it's not evidence that you lack talent. It only shows that your hand has not traced those flowers a hundred times. Most skills are completely available to you through repetition and attention.

"All art is quite useless."

—OSCAR WILDE

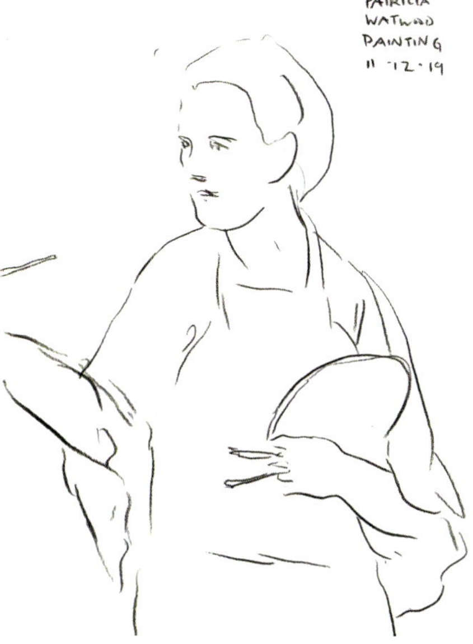

Daniel Maidman, *Patricia Watwood Painting*, 2019, black Prismacolor pencil on paper, 7 x 5 inches (18 x 13 cm). Courtesy of the artist.

Hit the Dot

Let's play a game called "Hit the Dot." If you have ever thought, "I can't even draw a straight line!" this is the game for you. Grab a pencil and paper.

On the left side of a blank piece of paper, make a vertical row of eight dots. About two inches to the right, make a matched row of dots. Don't use a ruler to line up the dots; just use your eye. (If you are left-handed, I recommend you reverse this and start the first row on the right side.) The origin of the word *draw* comes from "to pull." We "pull" a line more naturally as right-handers from left to right, and as left-handers from right to left.

Now, draw a series of straight horizontal lines between each set of paired dots (don't worry if they aren't perfectly lined up). Like hitting a ball, the trick here is not to look at the line—look at the dot where you are heading. The line is the trail left by the trajectory of your hand.

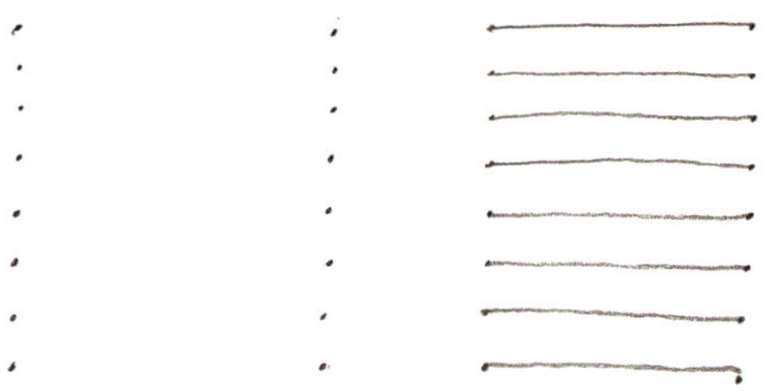

How did you do? Miss the dot a few times? Not really lined up? If your lines are crooked, even the process of noticing imperfections is part of learning to observe.

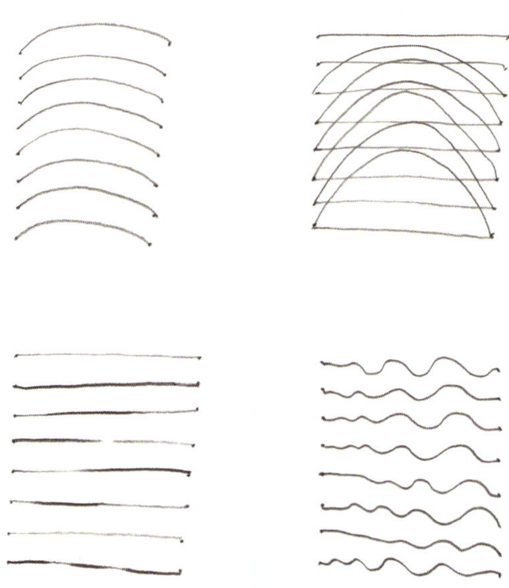

There are as many variations of this game as you can think up. For example, try to make a series of squiggly lines, improvising the first and then seeing if you can mimic the curves as you repeat. Or make a set of simple arcs, which are harder to control than a straight line. Next, practice varying the line weight, alternating between light and dark. Can you switch from light to dark within the same line?

When we draw, we build new neural pathways in our brains. Every time we draw, we strengthen the connections and muscle memory. The first time you ride a bike requires total concentration, but eventually you are flying down the road without touching the handlebars. The practice of drawing builds similar connections of nerve, sinew, eye, and mind. These simple exercises build skills and calm your energy.

Hatching Quilt

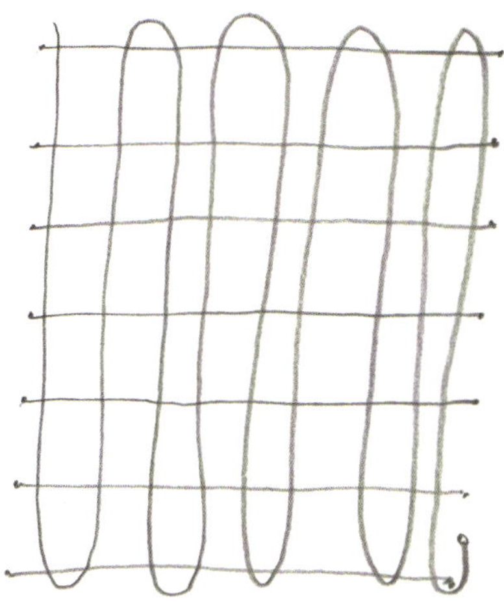

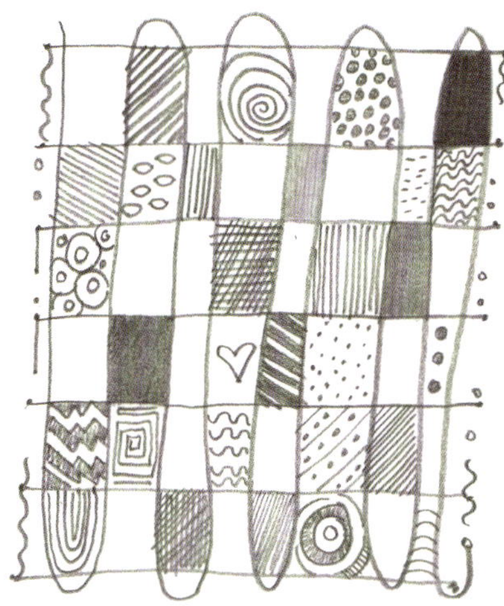

Let's extend this exercise into something I call a hatching quilt. Add an eraser and blending stump to your tools for this to start learning some shading techniques.

I made my grid of dots and lines a bit larger, about four inches across. I made a horizontal set of lines and then crossed them over with a free-flowing squiggle.

From here, improvise different ways of making marks and tones to fill in the boxes of your quilt. Try short parallel lines in one direction and then another. Try an even shaded tone, a light box, and one as dark as you can. Add some curves, spirals, squiggles, and zigzags. Every time you fill in a square, you build your dexterity; your consistency and line control will develop quickly.

As you have been working, you have picked up a few drawing techniques along the way. An area made of small dots is known as a *stippling*. Regular lines in one direction are *hatching*. Lines crossing in two directions are called *cross-hatching*. A controlled set of curves is sometimes called *cross-contour*. An even shade, usually laid down with a pencil and then blended with a stump, is called *tone* or *veiling*.

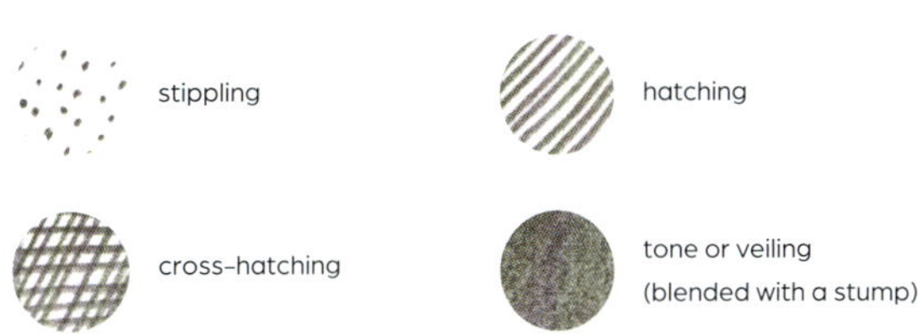

COLOR-HATCHING QUILT

If hatching quilts engage you, improvise your own variations. When creating these abstractions, I found my mind traveling to other lands. At what point did the lines and shapes become snakes and floating seaweed? Are those suns or drops of water on the surface of a pond?

The boundary between my marks and the vast imaginative space of my mind slips back and forth in the process of drawing. The line starts as a gray mineral trace on paper and then becomes a portal to another world. We humans are natural narrative builders. The simplest shape gives me a springboard. It's a sun, there's water and waves and a little snake and, oops…dinner is going to be late.

I want to emphasize that this is your personal creative time and space and should be free of output-oriented goals. Don't ask if your work is good or if it's art. The idea is growth and enjoyment, not product. Particularly if you are very new to drawing or haven't picked up a pencil since high school, set those questions of value aside. They are not actually useful, even for seasoned professional artists.

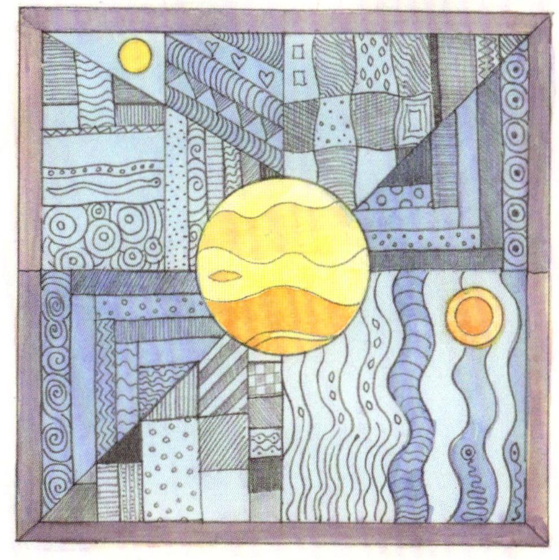

Color-hatching quilt: I made a few geometric shapes of circles and triangles, and then added watercolor for an abstract color design. When that was dry, I drew crazy-quilt blocks on top.

MAGIC GEOMETRIES

We started with drawings that seem rather like doodles, so take a step toward drawing that uses simple geometry as an inroad to an abstract graphic project.

Almost every culture has artistic traditions that are rooted in geometry, pattern, and abstract design—weaving, adornment, and bricklaying, for example. Humans find pleasure in shapes, lines, and repetition. We respond to the beauty found in geometry, which can have a spiritual dimension. I am fascinated by the connections found across cultures in art, mathematics, philosophy, spirituality, and geometry.

In Western civilization, we can trace back to ancient Greece the philosophy that the basic building blocks of geometry and mathematics reflect the cosmic unity of nature. I think of the circle, square, and triangle as the spatial equivalent of the primary colors red, yellow, and blue. Mathematical relationships are embodied in the Golden Section, and Platonic solids were incorporated into the art of Neoplatonists during the European Renaissance. They used geometry and mathematical intervals

Marie Milne uses Euclid's Postulates as a starting point for geometric abstract drawing.

Marie Milne, *Meditation on Equilateral Triangles*, 2021, ink on paper, 6 x 6 inches (15 x 15 cm). Courtesy of the artist.

with the belief that it embedded cosmic truths in their creative work. They believed that design grounded in mathematics transformed the representation of earthly forms into images of universal order.

For millennia, the study of geometry has been a discipline of scholars in exploring the nature of the divine and part of a contemplative practice. Geometer Robert Lawlor describes the connection between the work of a compass and ruler and the contemplation of form and philosophy this way: "A link is formed between the most concrete (forms and measures) and the most abstract realms of thought. By seeking the invariable relationships by which forms are governed and interconnected we bring ourselves into resonance with universal order."[6] Using creativity to seek order and calm in a universe of chaos has perennially been some artists' goal.

Islam has also placed tremendous religious and philosophic value on geometry. In 2008, artists Richard Henry and Adam Williamson created a school in London, Art of Islamic Pattern, to illuminate this art form. In describing his passion for Islamic design, Henry wrote, "There was a fundamental order underlying all of creation, and geometric patterns were a key to understanding it." Henry explains that the Sufis "describe

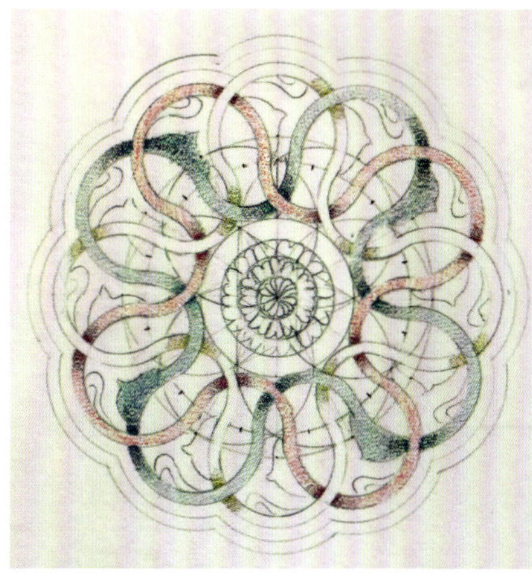

Mandy Theis, *Geometric Study of an Islamic Pattern,* 2020, graphite and colored pencil on paper, 10 x 10 inches (25 x 25 cm). Courtesy of the artist.

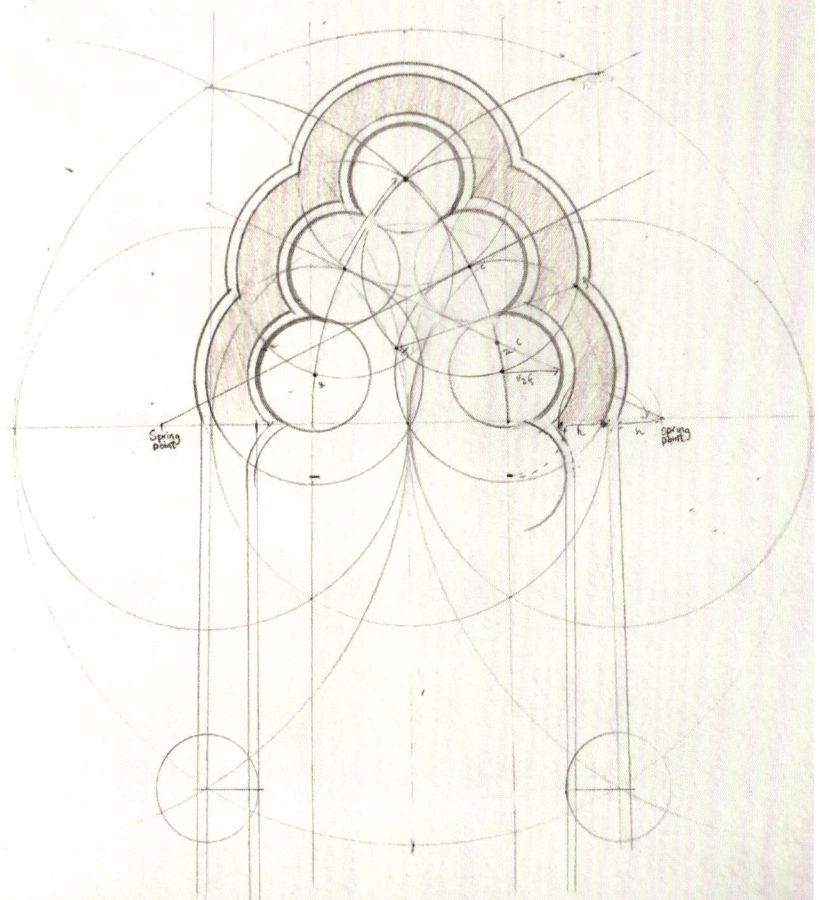

Mandy Theis, *Geometric Study of an Arch,* 2020, graphite and colored pencil on paper, 12 x 10 inches (30 x 25 cm). Courtesy of the artist.

"In designing, carving, and painting, the artist undergoes a journey of self-discovery and spiritual refinement, guided by the training that connects them to past masters in a chain of transmission going back millennia."

—ADAM WILLIAMSON

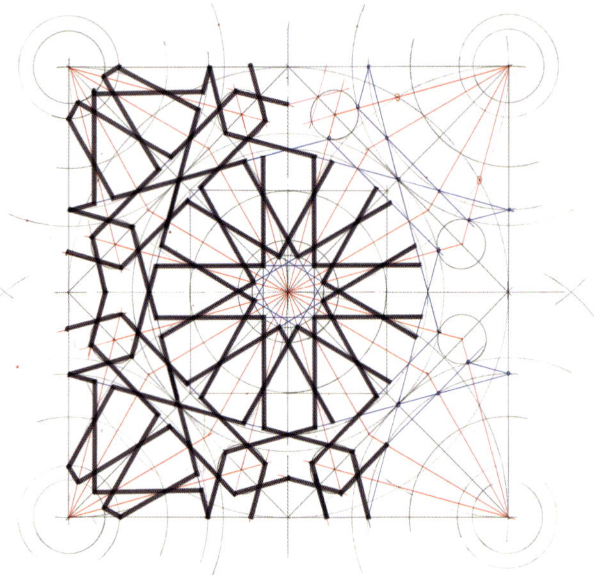

Above: Richard Henry, *Mumluk Study*, 2015, ink on paper, 32 x 24 inches (81 x 61 cm). Courtesy of the artist.

Below: Adam Williamson, *12 Fold Frontispiece, Sultan Uljaytu Quran, the Art of Islamic Pattern*, 2014, digital composite. Courtesy of the artist.

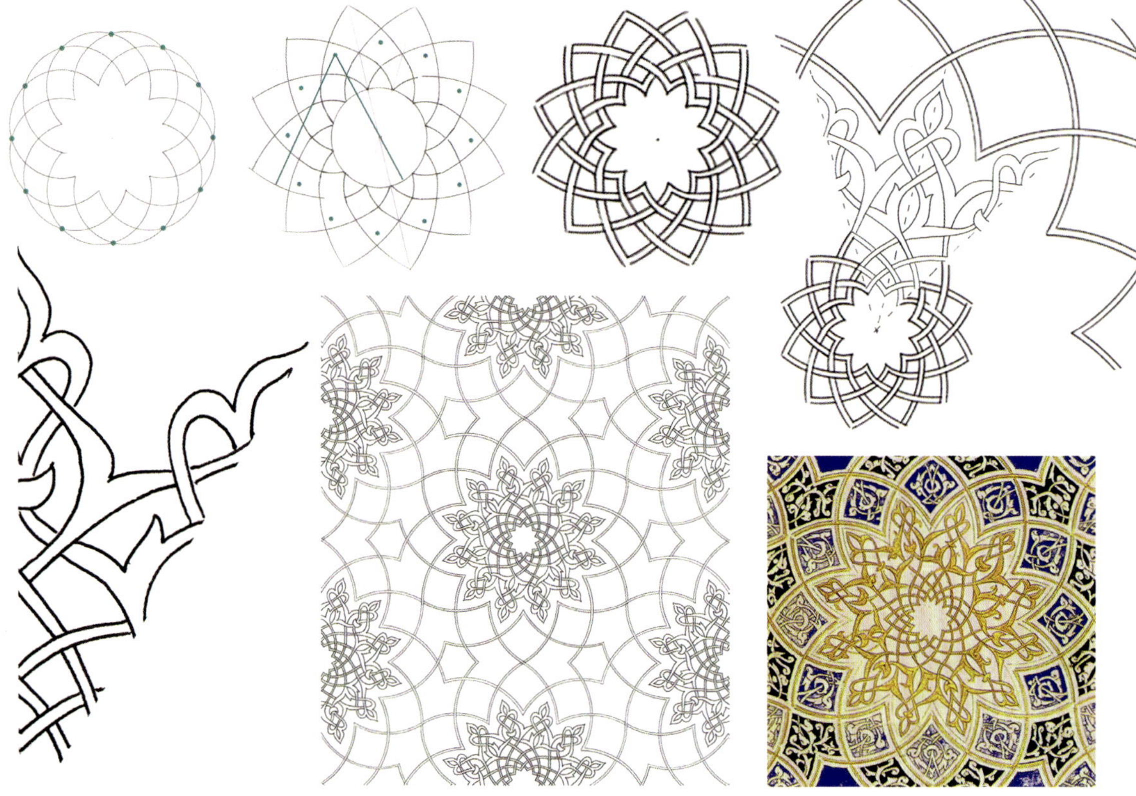

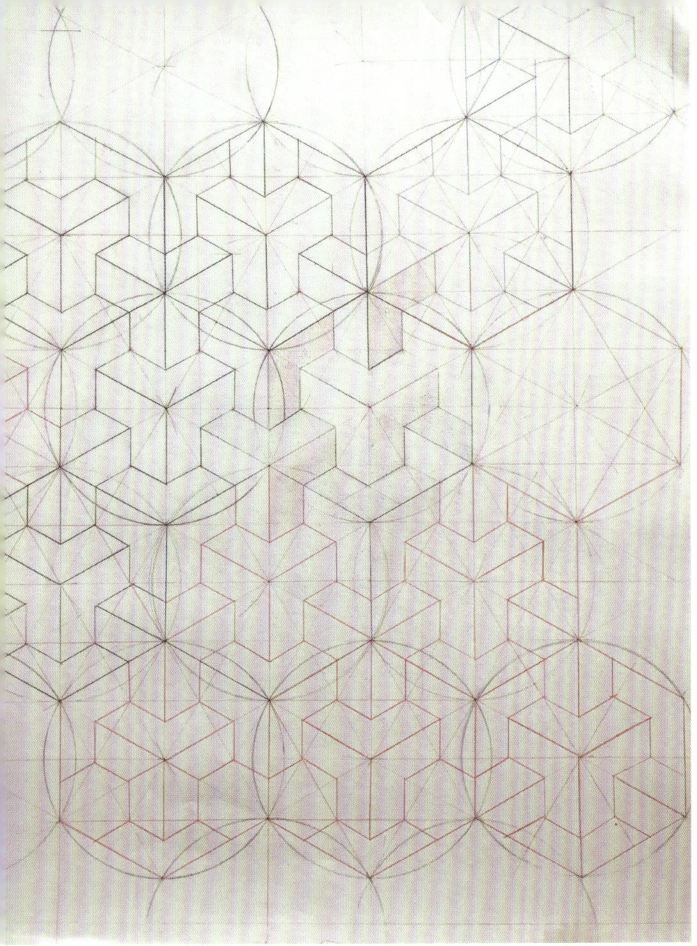

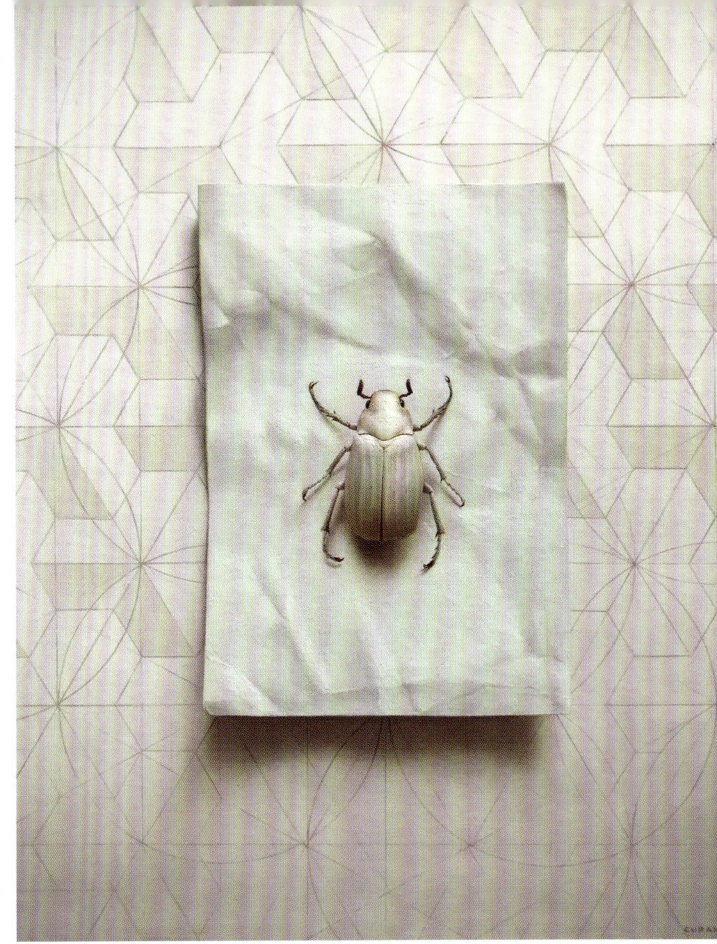

Tony Curanaj often creates elaborate geometric patterns on paper, and then uses the drawing as an element of design in a painting.

Above, left: Tony Curanaj, *Geometric Drawing,* 2020, graphite on paper, 16 x 13 inches (41 x 33 cm). Courtesy of the artist.

Above, right: Tony Curanaj, *Nimus 2,* 2021, oil on linen, 12 x 9 inches (30 x 23 cm). Courtesy of the artist.

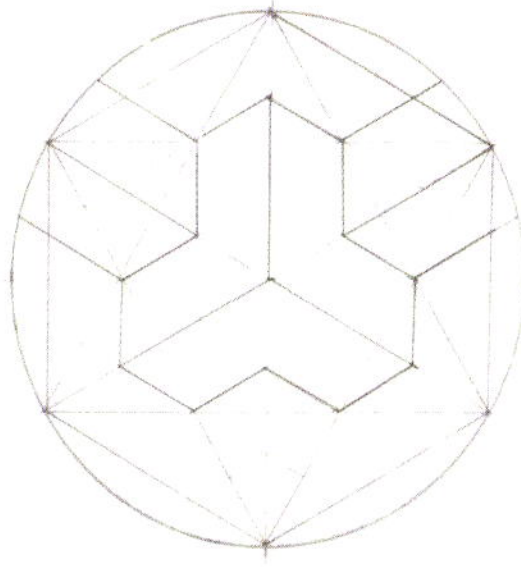

This drawing shows a single circle of Tony Curanaj's repeating pattern. Can you find the geometric forms of a circle, equilateral triangle, hexagon, six–pointed star, trapezoid, and the chevron shape? When we extract a simple geometric form, it trains our eye to see the larger, unifying structures within a complex image.

Islamic patterns as drawing us back to the source of creation," and adds, "I certainly regard the designs as having a powerful meditative and contemplative dimension."[7] As shapes and lines repeat, becoming an intricate design, so the patterns of our thoughts seem to fall naturally into a calm and beautiful order.

Making Islamic-style patterns gives us the opportunity to learn proportion, rhythm, harmony, balance, and elegance. Practice develops precision in forming lines and shapes, as distinct from accuracy in representation. Patterns and designs can also create a compositional foundation for a formal, representational image. The artist Tony Curanaj often creates an elaborate geometric pattern on paper, then layers it with a trompe l'oeil image to juxtapose elements of the artistic process.

Geometric Design Drawing

This exercise will build your ability to see simple and complex shapes simultaneously and develop your accuracy and precision in using line and contour. Create this geometric drawing using just a few tools: a pencil, erasers, a 12-inch ruler, and a CD as a template for the circle and arcs.

STEP ONE

Make a square, and divide it diagonally using light lines. Using a CD, trace a circle in the middle, then two more arcs on a diagonal that touch in the center of the circle.

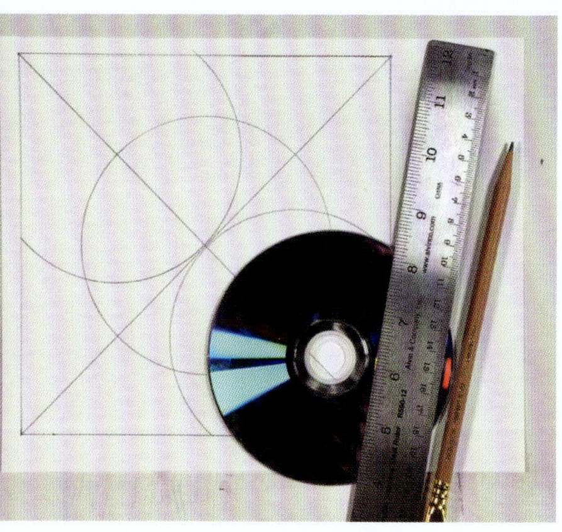

Tools: pencil, erasers,
12–inch ruler, and a CD

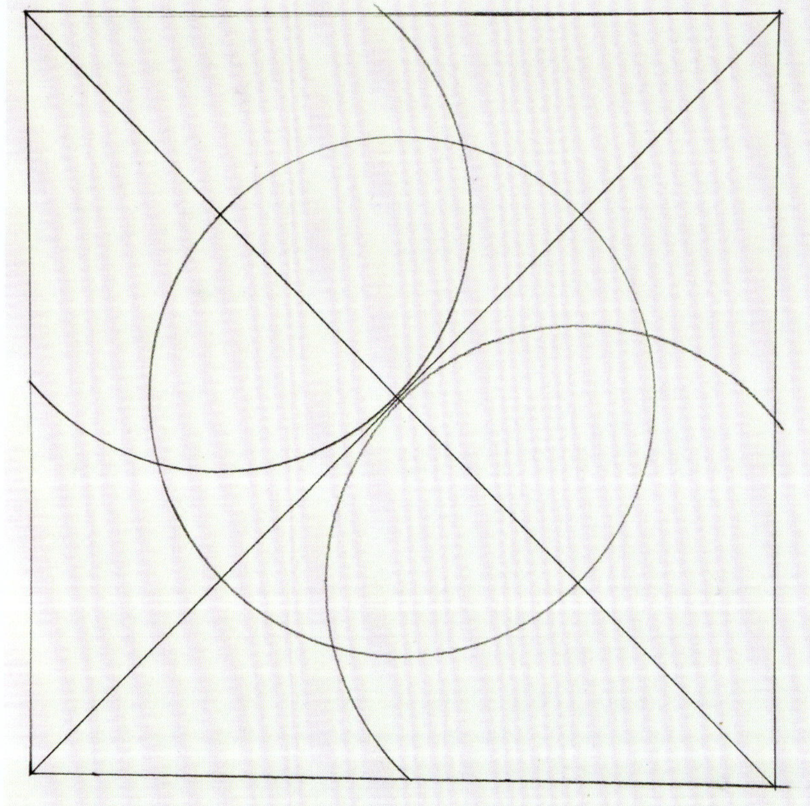

"Art cannot be modern. Art is primordially eternal."

— EGON SCHIELE

STEP TWO

Add four more arcs using the intersections of the central circle with the diagonals, and more arcs from the outer corners. Using the CD and ruler subdivide the larger shapes into repeating and symmetrical segments as you please.

STEP THREE

Following symmetries in the shapes you created, add flat tones and hatched lines to darken some parts of the design. Try a variety of graphic techniques, experimenting to build your skills. Use the CD and ruler to create regular lines if desired.

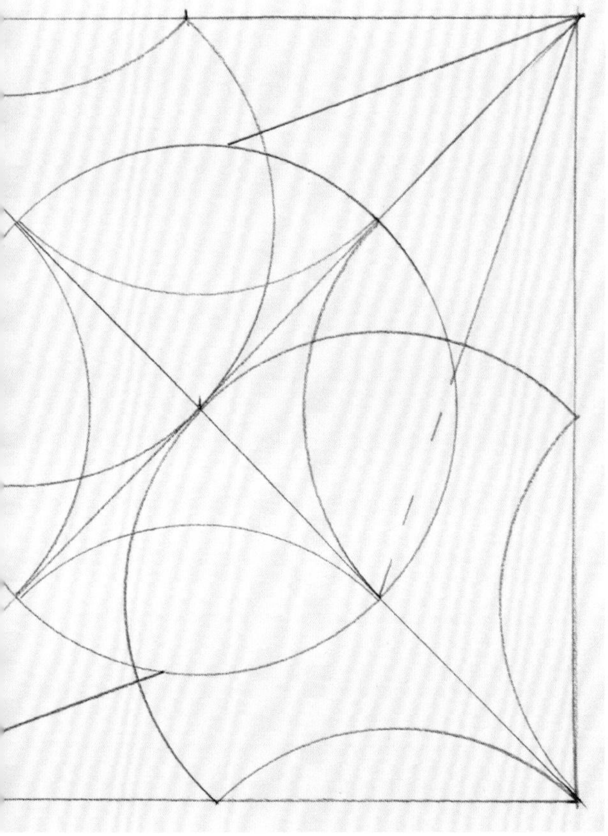

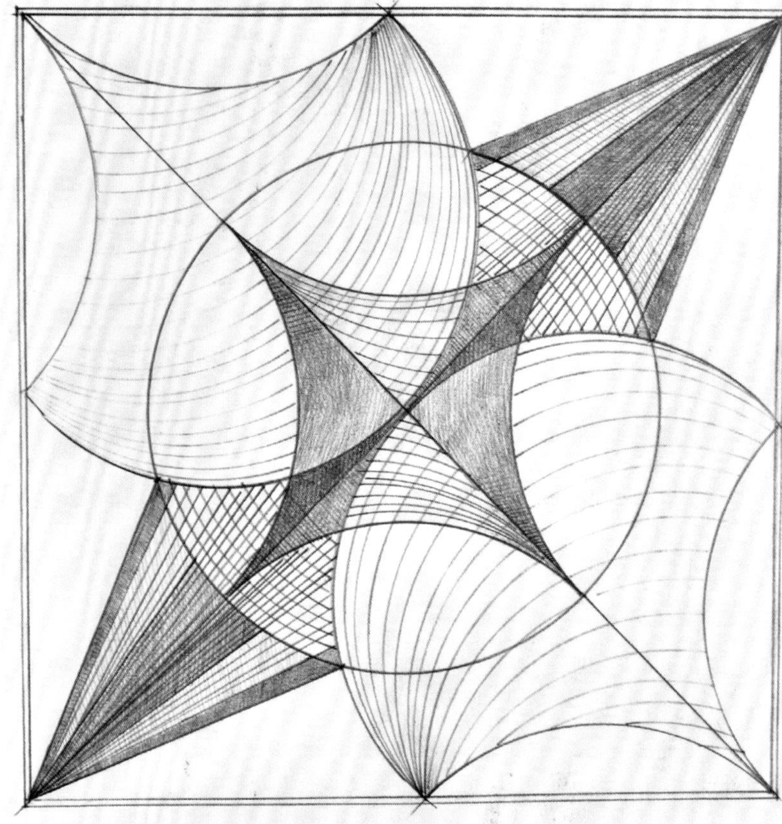

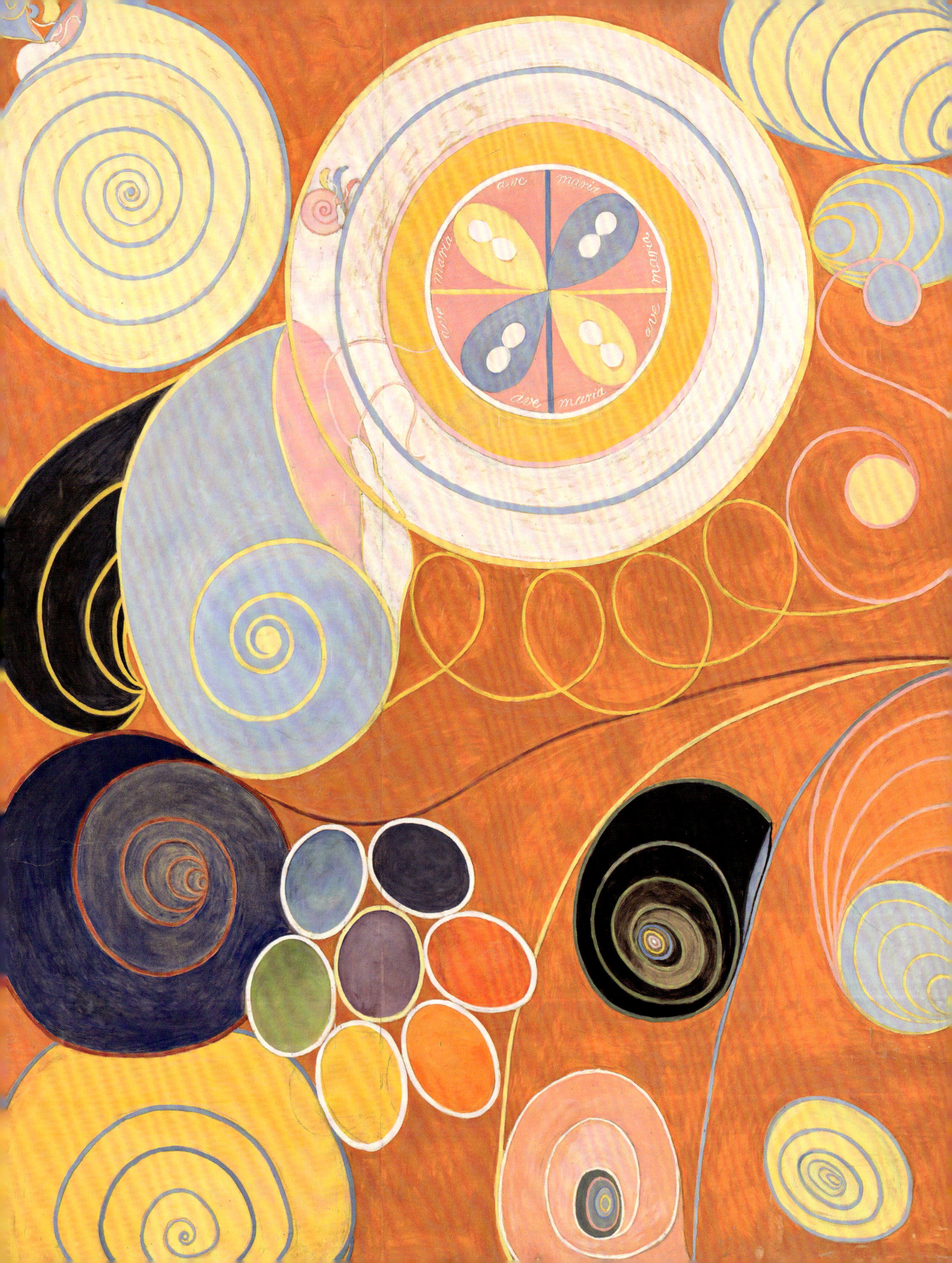

ave maria
ave maria
ave maria
ave maria

"It is six a.m., and I am working. I am absent-minded, reckless, heedless of social obligations, etc. It is as it must be. The tire goes flat, the tooth falls out, there will be a hundred meals without mustard. The poem gets written… There is no other way work of artistic worth can be done… The most regretful people on earth are those who felt the call to creative work… and gave to it neither power nor time."

—MARY OLIVER

Hilma af Klint, *Group IV, The Ten Largest, No. 3, Youth,* 1907, tempera on paper, mounted on canvas, 196 x 93 inches (320 x 238 cm). Courtesy of the Hilma af Klint Foundation.

Opening Up to the Visual World

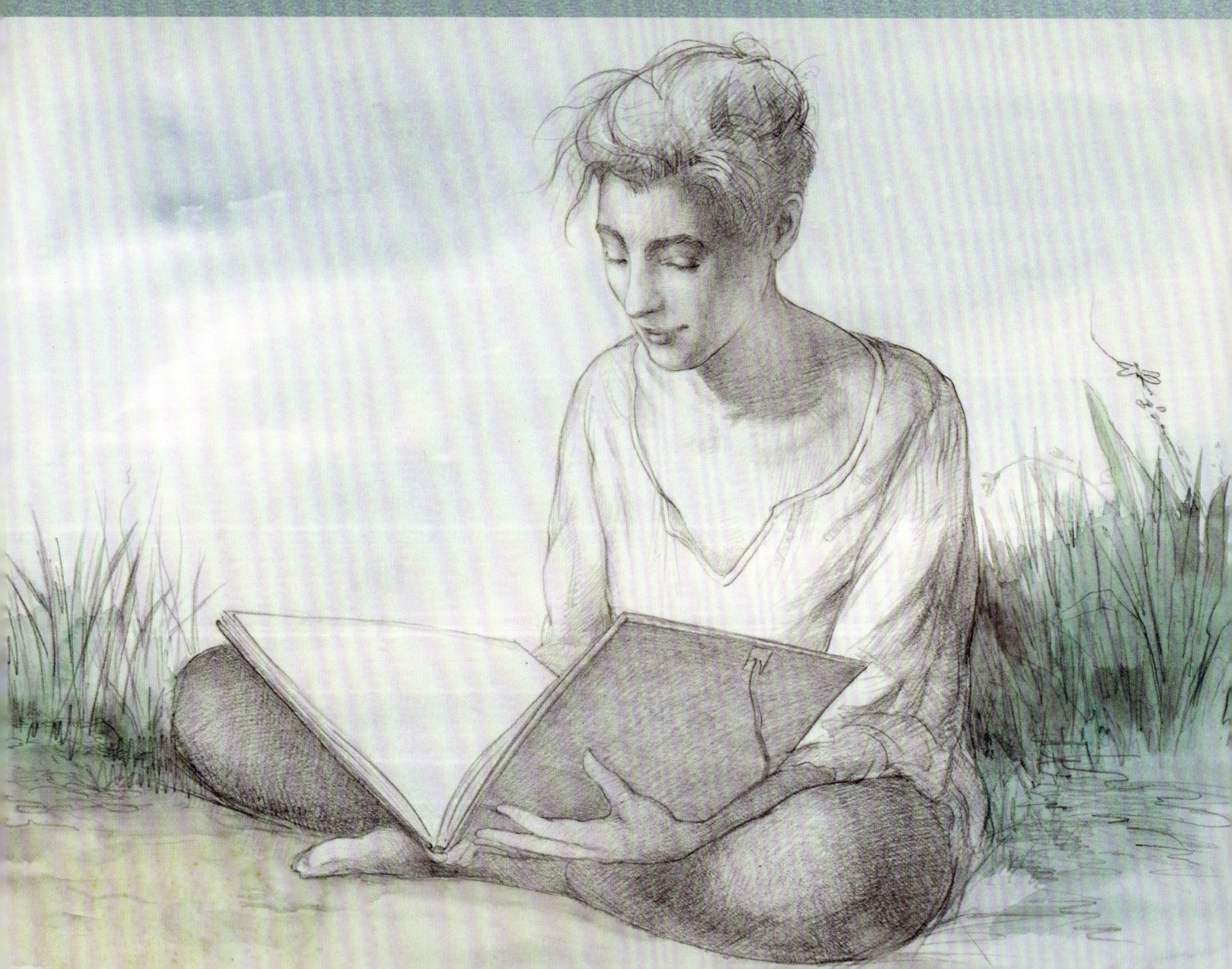

For the working artist, there are many parts of the creative process that happen before and after we put our pencil to paper. External to the technical and skill building, artists need to be receptive to inspiration and ready to work with it. I've come to think of the work of creativity as a cycle of input and outflow. I see myself akin to a vessel through which creative ideas travel. Ideas and observations come in, a process of making ensues, and the outcome is an expression of the experience—now transformed by the journey through my mind and hand. Sometimes I feel more like an empty bucket, and other times like an overflowing cup. Mindfulness has taught me to become attentive to the amount of flow, and when needed, take steps to fill up my bucket. Experience has taught me that empty buckets will fill again with time, and overflowing states are to be stored up and graciously savored.

In this chapter, I'll share a couple of practices I trust for priming the pump. One of the healthiest and most reliable tools I have for the empty-bucket problem is simply to *go outside*. There, I can coax my heart to gently open and carefully observe. I can gather inspiration for a drawing and find delight in the present moment. If I make a new drawing, afterward, I can reflect on the experience. While we cultivate technical skills, we want to encourage a mindset that supports a long-sustained practice. These mental skills are receptivity, open-mindedness, trust, and comfort in uncertainty. By opening up to the ample inspirations in the natural world around us, we learn to work with this process over and over again.

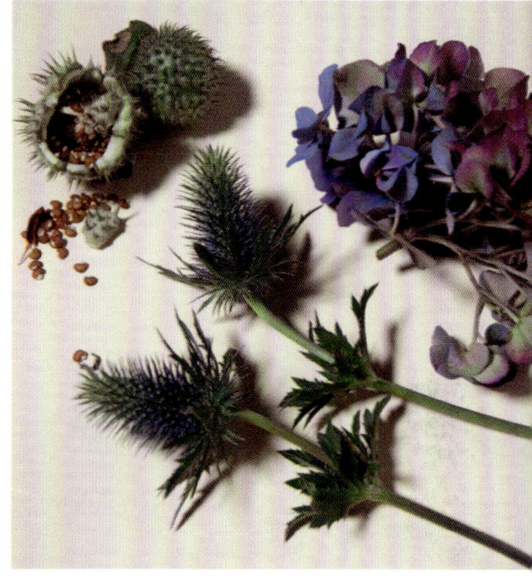

So many things found in nature make a marvelous subject to study.

WALKING AND OBSERVING

I tie my shoes, zip up my coat, let the door click behind me. I glance up at the great sky. What kinds of clouds are there? How fast are they moving? How

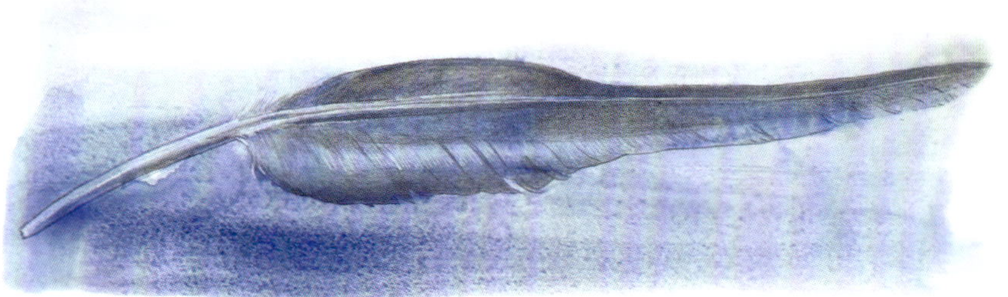

Opposite: Patricia Watwood, *The Seeker*, 2016, graphite and watercolor on paper, 11 x 15 inches (28 x 38 cm). Courtesy of the artist.

Left: Patricia Watwood, *Large Goose Feather*, 2021, graphite and watercolor on paper, 8 x 18 inches (20 x 46 cm). Courtesy of the artist.

cold is the wind on my cheek? I start with a fast pace in the direction of the nearby cemetery, eager to leave the clutter of house and mind. An even gait drums my heart into a steady rhythm. My thoughts are still racing—that thing I said, that thing he said, and those emails I forgot are zipping past like the cars. After five minutes of trudging, deep breathing returns and I can feel a little warmth in my perpetually chilly fingers. Finally, I start to *notice* the world around me. The ginkgo tree, the pigeon feather, the poofy dress in the storefront, the discarded mailer on the sidewalk, the face of the child in a pink mask waiting for the bus. That which is outside myself seeps in.

Soon I begin to *see new things*. I stoop to pick up the feather. It is all white except for the tawny brown where it tapers to a point. I notice the shape of the ginkgo leaf, ruffled as a dance fan for Barbie. The clouds streak out thinly from east to west in two rows of slanting, illegible scrawls. A low airplane that just lifted off from LaGuardia cuts diagonally toward New Jersey.

As a predominantly visual thinker, I am now as engaged as a child by the infinite variety of the world around me. I become anchored in the present.

NATURE, THE GREAT TEACHER

Our next drawing project is of gathered objects. Take a pair of scissors and a bag or basket and collect four to five natural or found objects. Leaves and plant cuttings are great for this exercise. Look for a variety of things of different sizes, colors, and structures. If you find yourself thinking, "There's nothing interesting here," slow yourself down and look at a few small things underfoot. That dandelion weed has a marvelous leaf. A crushed can has jagged geometries and folds to explore. Perhaps what you find is not pretty, but drawing has taught me that beauty unfolds even in the most unlikely and neglected places.

John Ruskin's classic treatise *The Elements of Drawing* (1857) was foundational to the styles of art like naturalism and realism, paying homage to the sublime beauty and infinite education offered by studying nature. These included the Pre-Raphaelite Brotherhood and the Arts and Crafts

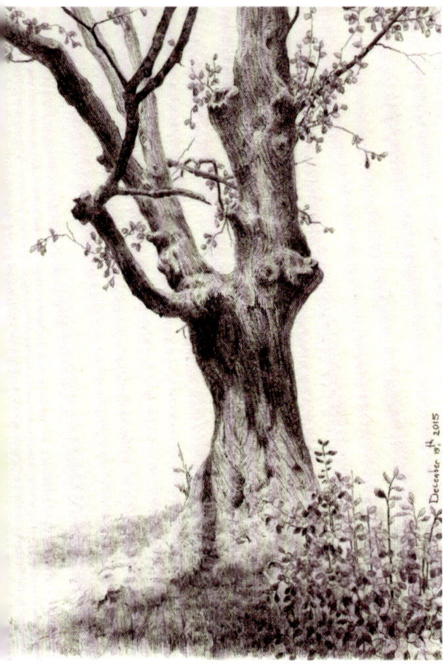

Above: Dina Brodsky, *Tree No. 42,* December 15, 2015, ballpoint pen on paper, 8 x 6 inches (20 x 15 cm). Courtesy of the artist and Bernarducci Meisel Gallery.

Opposite: Mary Reilly, *Wildflower, Central Park,* 2011, graphite on paper, 18 x 13 inches (46 x 33 cm). Courtesy of the artist.

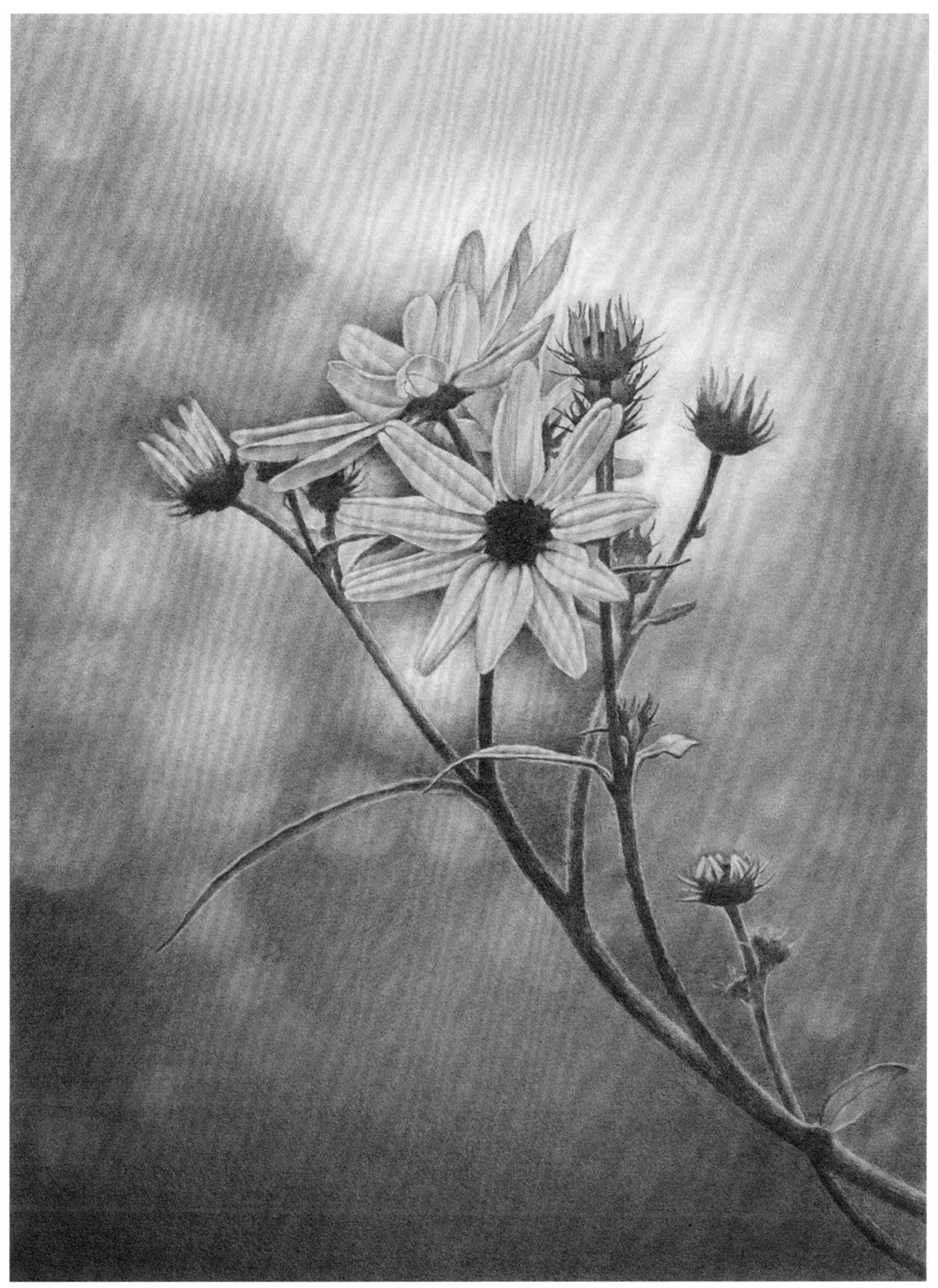

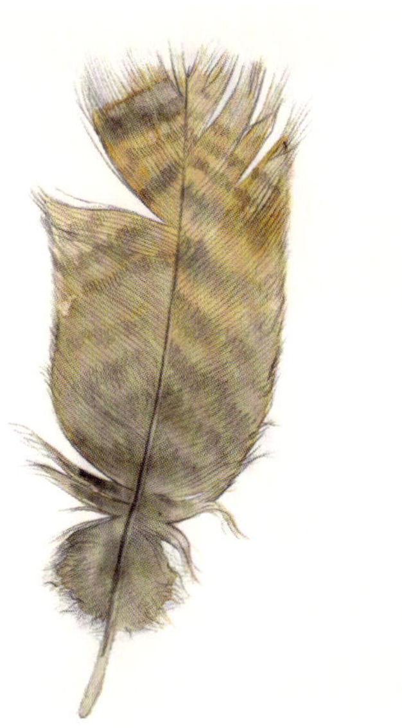

Patricia Watwood, *Turkey Feather,*
2016, pencil and watercolor on
paper, 7 x 5 inches (18 x 13 cm).
Courtesy of the artist.

movement advocated by artists such as William Morris, William Holman Hunt, and John Everett Millais. Ruskin thought that style had become based more on preconceived compositional and thematic rules than on intense observation. He believed that by studying the intricacies contained within a single leaf, an artist discovers that any portal into nature contains the mysteries of the whole.

Why go to the trouble to make an accurate and detailed drawing? What difference does it make if my leaf has six little points or seven? Who will know the difference? When speaking to our drawing class, my teacher Tony Ryder was asked, "Do you try to improve on nature?" (The world being full of imperfections and oddities, a certain frame of mind would suggest that the artist might "fix" things a bit by, say, making that nose smaller or those love handles disappear.) Ryder answered, with reverence, "No. Rather, I am hoping that nature will improve on me." My art is grounded in an understanding that the profundity that I seek to explore is always greater than my limited capacity to understand. In realist drawing, when we strive for fidelity to nature, we hone our ability to see details, proportions, and shapes accurately, cultivating the life skill of visual literacy.

Visual literacy not only makes us better artists, but also better able to apply visual skills to all areas of life. Wouldn't you appreciate greater visual literacy in your surgeon, your dentist, your car mechanic, and your handyman? Our mainstream education system prioritizes other types of learning such as textual analysis, critical thinking, and nimbleness in math. Visual literacy—developing our visual capacity to observe differences and spatial relationships—is just as important for cultivating our capacity for new and robust thought. When a scientist peers through a microscope or an engineer researches the construction of a coral reef, she is employing acute observation (visual literacy) to make discoveries and find innovative solutions to problems. Attentiveness to the complexity of nature through art can transform anyone's ability to see and process visual information.

> *"I do not want to die…until I have faithfully made the most of my talent and cultivated the seed that was placed in me until the last small twig has grown."*
>
> —KÄTHE KOLLWITZ

Gathering from Nature

This project will help you develop observational skills by considering the arrangement of the composition, looking for unifying geometric shapes, and carefully observing details like symmetry and asymmetry.

STEP ONE

Make a clear space on your table and place your collection on a sheet of paper the same size as your future drawing. Take a minute to look at each of your finds to get acquainted with their intricacies. You may want to pull away a few leaves to simplify the number of shapes.

Play with the arrangement of your treasures. Consider elements of design such as the directional axis of a branch or leaf. Notice the various sizes, and start with the biggest object, and place the rest in relationship to that centerpiece.

For a stronger composition, look at not only the leaves themselves, but the spacing between them and in relation to the edges of your paper.

STEP TWO

Look for the central axis lines and for geometric shapes. The central axis line may follow a central stem or middle vein. Next, create a simplified framework, or armature, for each object. Notice the number of leaves on a stem, and mark the stem first. Then lightly sketch the spacing for the elements of your composition.

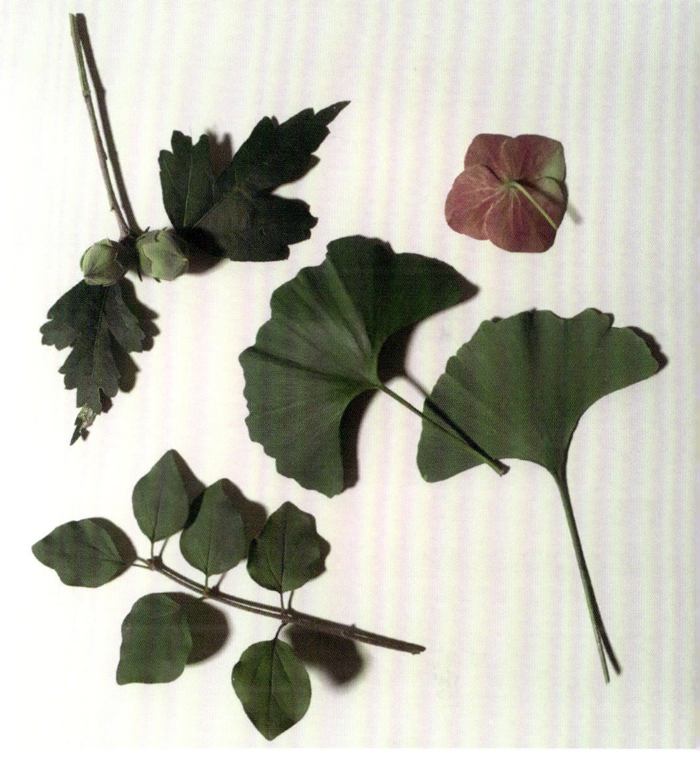

Look for geometric shapes, and sketch simple shapes for each element with light lines. The ginkgo leaf is basically a semicircle. The hydrangea flower has four petals, so it's nearly a square. Other leaf and flower forms can be simplified into diamonds. Look for tips and points of inflection to find visual landmarks.

Notice the variety of proportions, and try not to regularize the sizes and angles. Plan the spacing by observing the distances between things.

STEP THREE

Now change gears and turn your focus to discovering fine details. Working on one element at a time, navigate the contours attentively. Are the curves convex or concave? Even or uneven? What do the notches on the stem look like? Are they symmetrical or offset? How many points are there?

Patient discovery will add richness to the detail of your study. Erase the guiding armature lines to create a finished effect.

For fun and visual appeal, I love to add a few touches with watercolor. When I combine watercolor, colored pencil, or markers with my sketches, it feels more like play. I'll present some simple watercolor methods in Chapter 8.

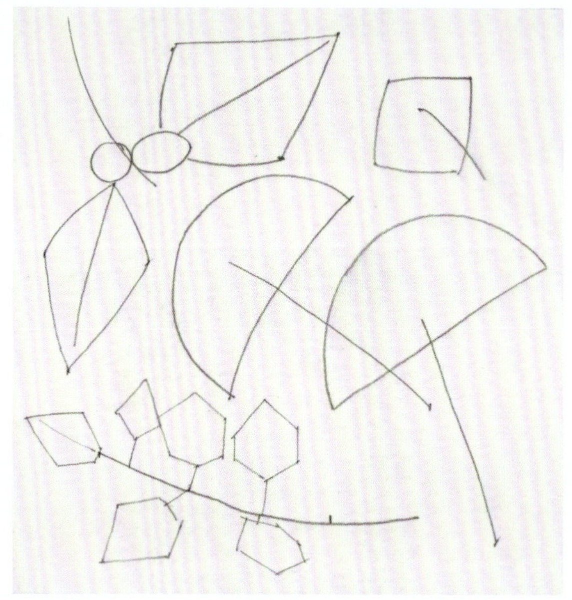

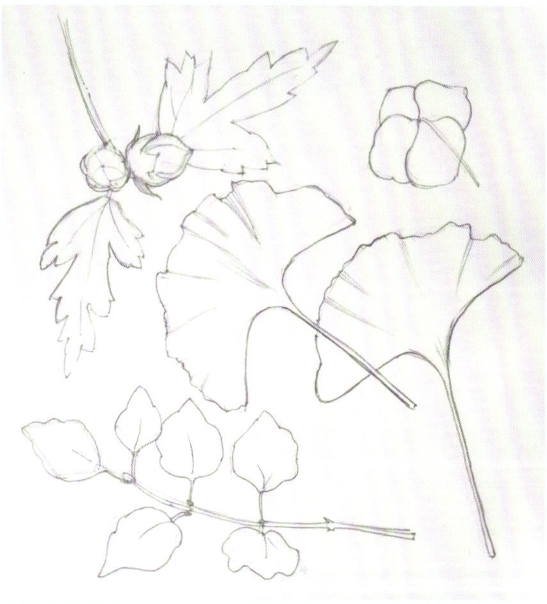

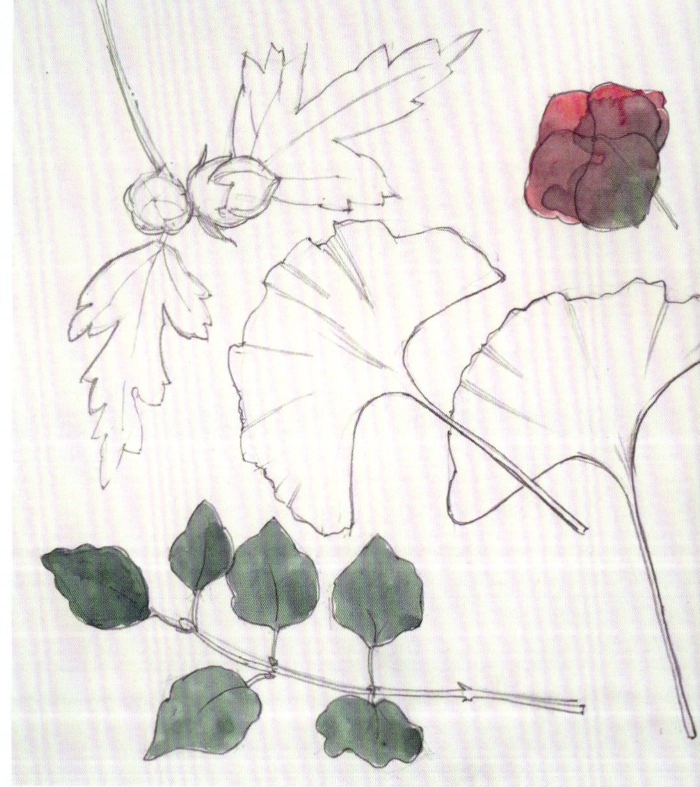

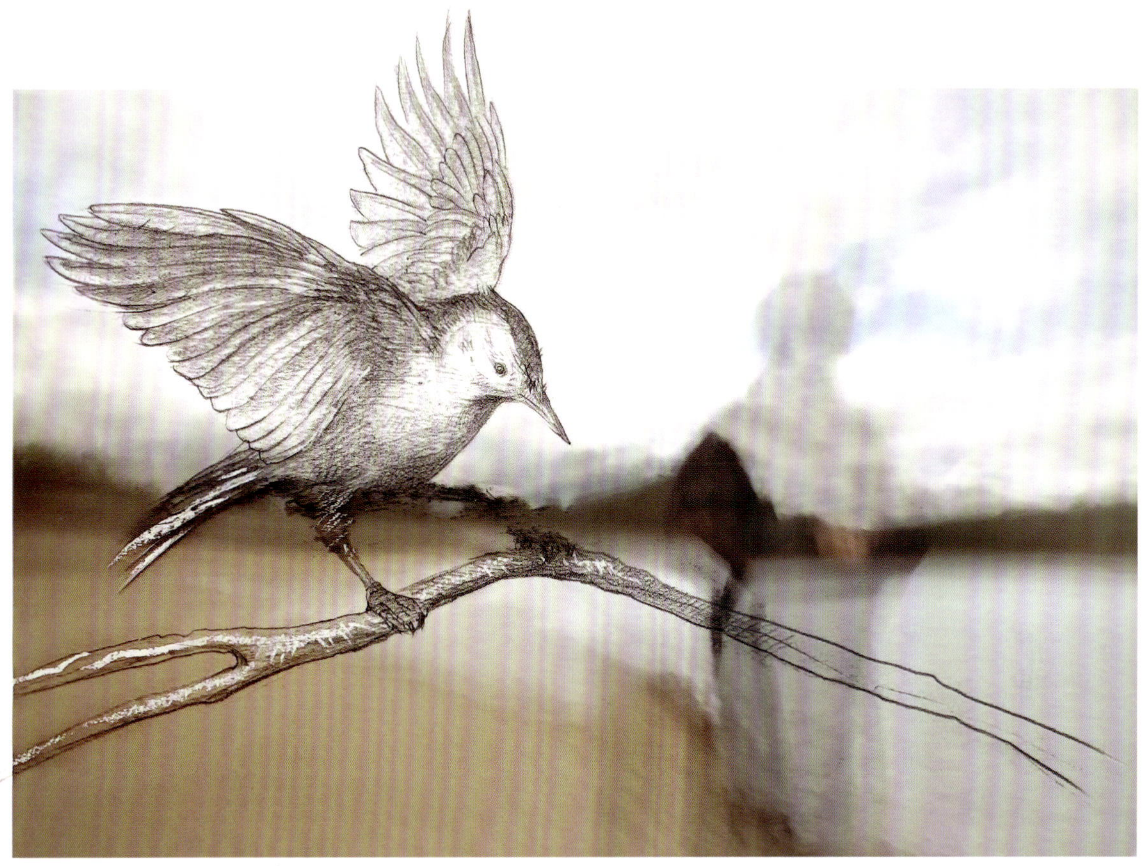

Stefan Hagen and Patricia Watwood, *Encounter at Walden Pond,* graphite and goauche on archival inkjet print, 13 x 19 inches (33 x 48 cm). Courtesy of the artists.

THE OPEN CREATIVE MIND

Bringing mindfulness to my thought process when I sit down to draw, I notice the gap between "I want to draw" and "I am drawing." That gap can be a small edge in the sidewalk that you trip on every time or a chasm too large to step over alone. The most important skill you have to learn to keep on the path is the skill of stepping over the gap. From my viewpoint twenty years down the creative path, it's not the drawing that is hard—it's the gap: Each day, you don't quit, and each day, you begin again.

I won't lie: The gap can be a legitimate challenge. It's filled with distractions, unpaid bills, and the terribly uncomfortable feeling that you don't know what you are doing. We like to feel competent, focused, and assured of a reliable outcome. But reliable outcomes are the purview of manufacturers, not artists. If the aim of your creative activity is a predictable and assured outcome, I'm afraid that you are already missing your mark. Creativity is built on a pliable and adaptable foundation of openness and a willingness to embrace uncertainty. By cultivating these traits, you can bridge the gap.

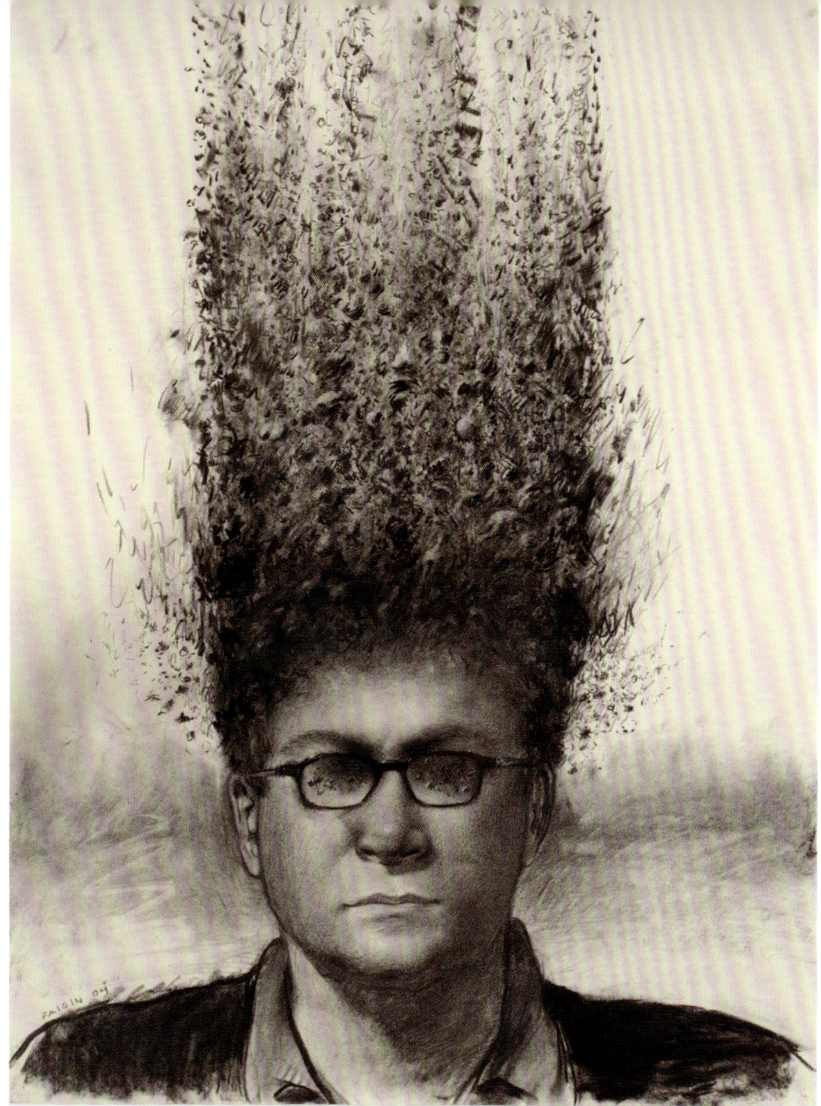

Gary Faigin, *Grey Matter*, 2004, charcoal on paper, 30 x 22 inches (76 x 56 cm). Courtesy of the artist.

> *"I'm good at being uncomfortable, so I can't stop changing all the time…I'll make the most of it, I'm an extraordinary machine."*
>
> —FIONA APPLE

Instead, we must become like Fiona Apple in her song "Extraordinary Machine": "good at being uncomfortable." In previous chapters, I discussed building a habit—I don't care if you feel like it, I don't care if you are inspired, just sit down and do it. Work on your work. To explore this skill of being uncomfortable, I want to convey the idea that *not* knowing—an attitude of openness and receptivity—fosters growth.

The phrase "closed-minded" identifies the state I wish to avoid. People who are closed-minded don't seem capable of changing their opinions, even in the face of good and relevant information to the contrary. They can become convinced of their own way of thinking, and this confirmation bias (with a dose of self-preserving denial) leads them to falsely fit new information into their old frames of reference. When you see someone else doing this, it is maddening. When we do it ourselves, we are usually oblivious.

I learned a great lesson from an elementary schoolteacher who asked my child's class, "How do you feel when you are wrong?" The kids said things like, "I feel embarrassed!" and "I feel sorry I said that!" But the teacher pointed out, "That is how you feel when you *realize* you are wrong. If you don't realize you're wrong, you feel exactly the same as when you are right!"

What does this have to do with drawing? In cultivating a creative mind-set and practice, we learn to reframe our ideas of "doing it right" and "making mistakes." As maddening as it can be to realize that you messed up the proportions or the contours, if you are *seeing* these mistakes, greet it

Edward Minoff creates drawings of waves from observation, finding endless variation in the eternally breaking surf.

Edward Minoff, *Split Break*, 2015, graphite and gouache on gray paper, 5½ x 7½ inches (14 x 19 cm). Courtesy of Cavalier Galleries.

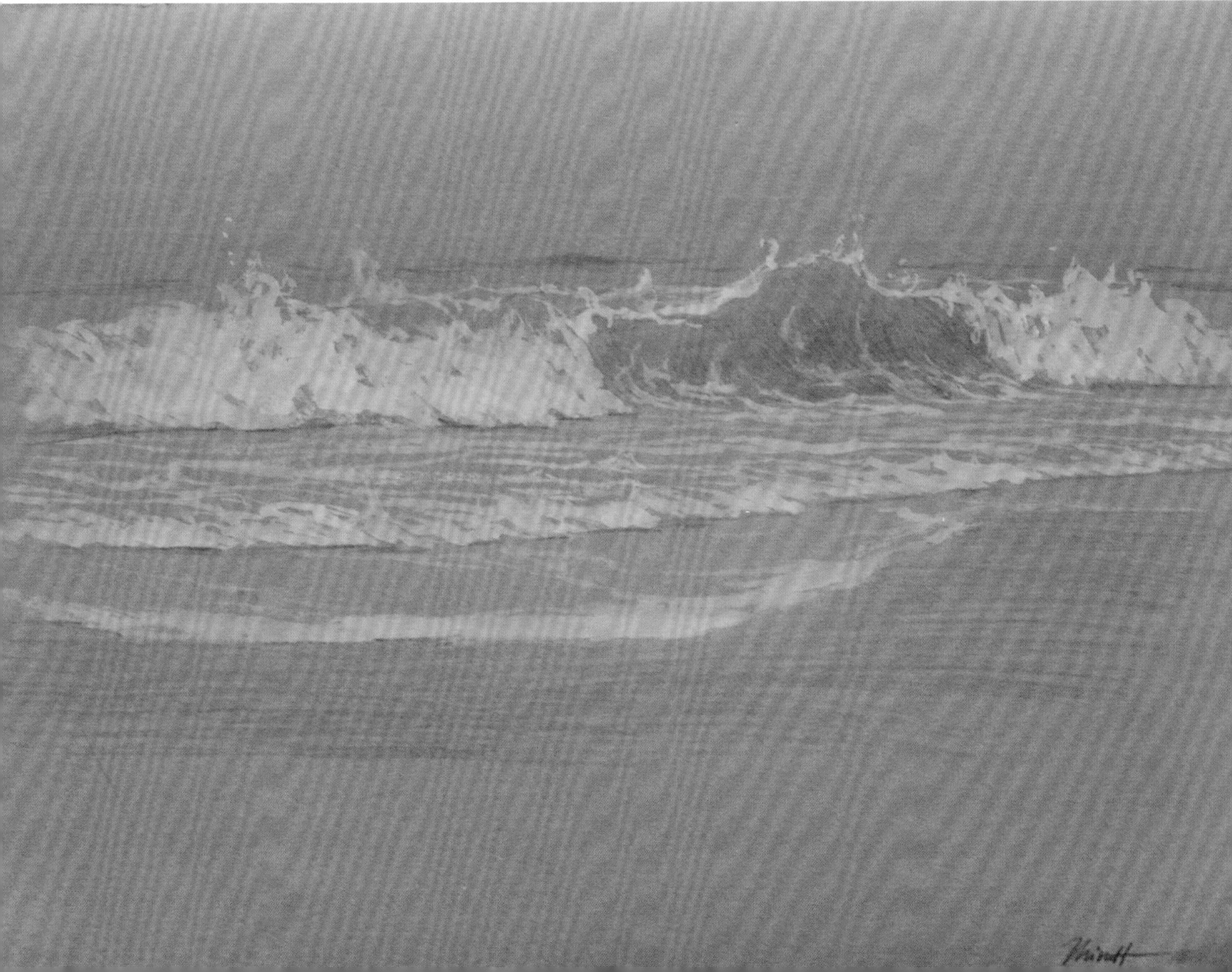

as evidence that you are *already* learning and growing. I've noticed that most seasoned artists actually get excited after they recognize that they have made some dumb mistake. They now have something to *fix*!

My teacher Ted Seth Jacobs combined Asian philosophic perspective with training in Western representational art. In his book *Drawing with an Open Mind*, Jacobs writes:

> In drawing, the best possible teacher in the world and our surest guide—
> perhaps the only true one—is the blank sheet of paper beneath
> our hand. The emptiness of the paper instructs us without bias. It is
> like consciousness with no opinions attached. It is the pure mirror
> of our perceptions.[8]

Jacobs emphasizes nonjudgment when he describes "consciousness with no opinions attached." We often become frustrated when we draw and then *judge*: It's bad! Good! Right! Wrong! To be better at being uncomfortable, what if we drop the judgment and just allow the process to unfold? There is inherent paradox in this advice. If we are striving to draw accurately and build skills, then we must be clear-eyed that there is room for improvement. However, the emotional baggage of constant judgment and evaluation will, in time, grind you to a frozen halt. Your job is not to judge. Your job is to do, to make, to try, let the process unfold, and move on.

Jacobs encourages a mind-set of alert calmness so the movements of eye "flow around the subject like water." He encourages us to relinquish tension and practice a state of "alert receptivity."[9] He believed that cultivating an open mind was *the* essential component of creative learning. Enter the path and allow the process to work upon you. With an open mind, this will happen naturally, as water conquers stone.

When I begin to draw, I find that my lines will reflect this open and alert receptivity—or betray that I am full of a stressed and distracted mind. When I begin, I start with a delicate block of light lines, a vague armature with a built-in margin of error (more on that in Chapter 5). If my lines are light and flexible, they allow for correction and refinement as I work. If my lines get dark, jagged, and emphatic early on, then I am likely to carve in my mistakes and be unable to regain an elegant solution. A calm and attentive mind will arrive at the correct placement far more quickly than a tense one. Like water in your hand, the more you clench to hold it, the more it will slip away.

Molly Judd, *Murmuration*, 2018, charcoal on paper, 23½ x 33 inches (59 x 84 cm). Courtesy of the artist.

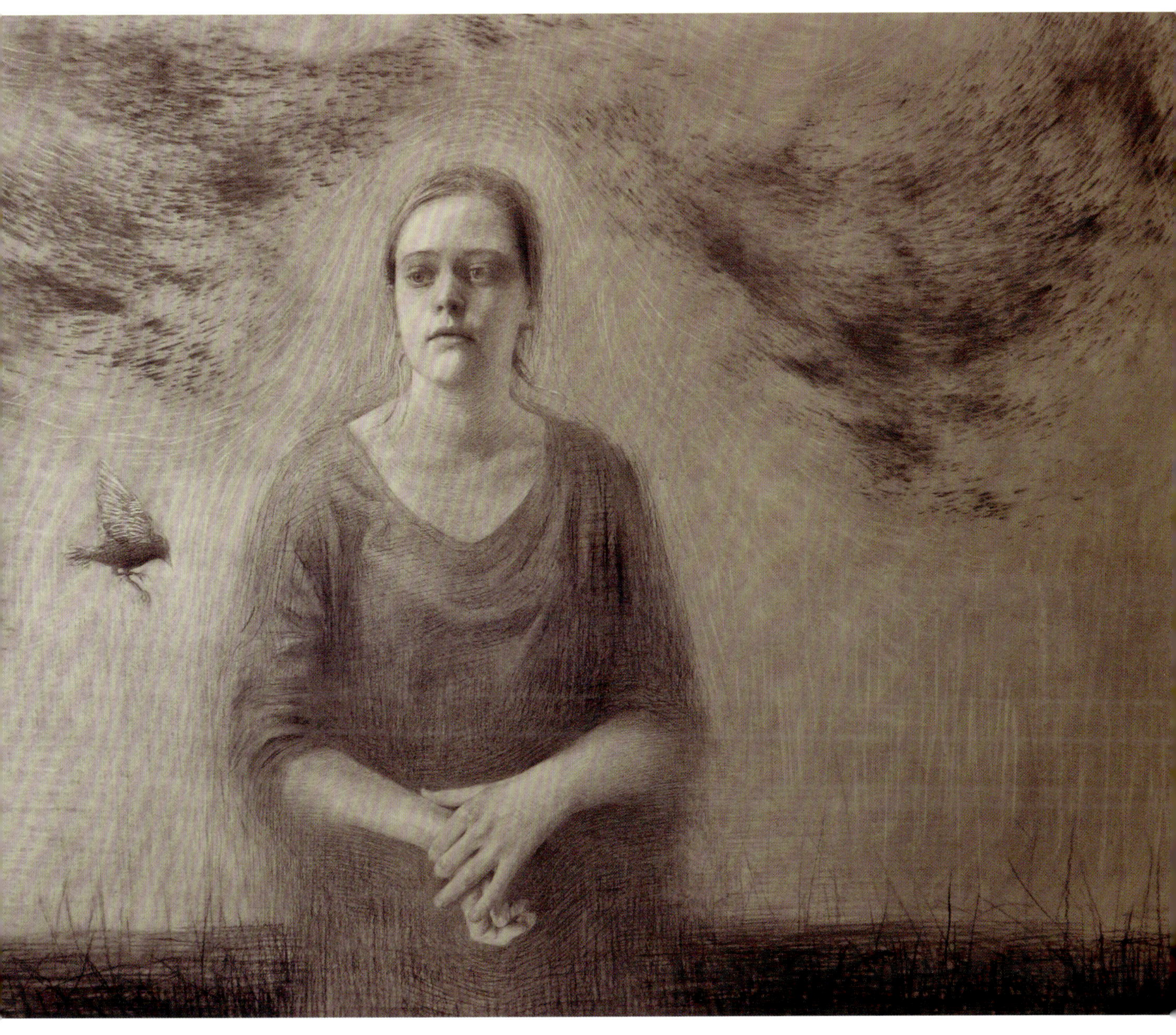

"Like water which can clearly mirror the sky and trees only so long as its surface is undisturbed, the mind can only reflect the true image of the Self when it is tranquil and wholly relaxed."
—INDRA DEVI

4

Creative Compost

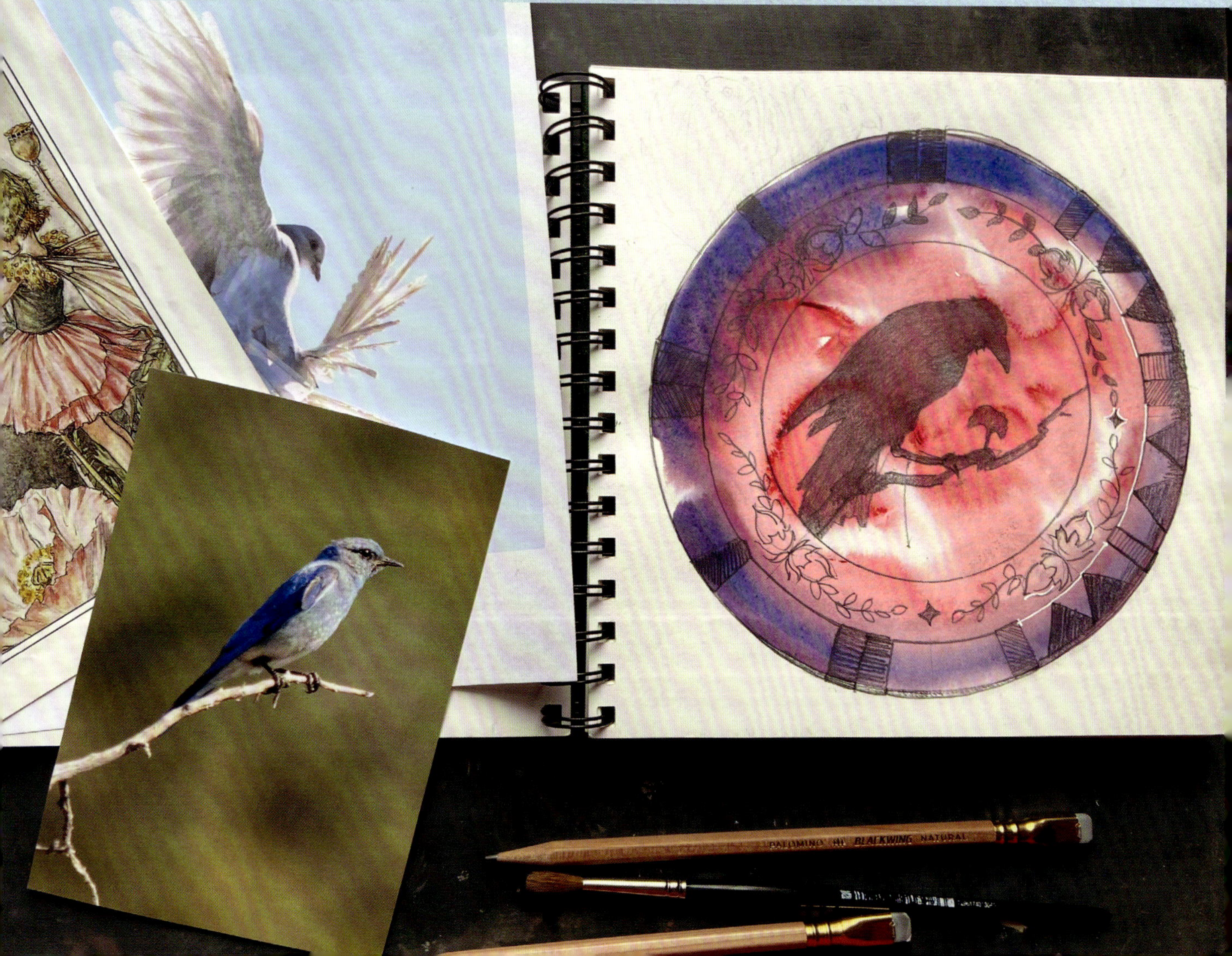

The word *inspiration* comes from the Latin *to breathe in*, suggesting a relationship of one's body to an unsummoned spirit that enters like a gift of grace. I have experienced that blessed state occasionally. But I question that there's a magic ingredient that only some people have—or don't. That's a myth about the creative process.

In reality, creativity can be nurtured. It doesn't typically fly in to perch in our souls at a convenient moment. We have to go out and forage for it, then cherish our findings as a precious resource. Artists learn that inspiration is not a requirement for beginning to work. Instead of waiting for it to appear, we develop practices to summon it. We prepare, work, and trust that inspiration will arise and unfold to our tending.

CULTIVATING INSPIRATION

In Chapter 1, I recommended that you be on the lookout for visual inspiration and make creative foraging a habit. *Creative composting* is the process of gathering ideas for later cultivation. As in forming gardening compost, you must amass scraps of visual materials that through time and intermixing will create a fertile soil for new ideas. Here is my composting method.

I'm always on the lookout for images and concepts that intrigue me. I tear out magazine pictures, cut up brochures and newspapers, and jot down notes and quotes that hit home.

I don't worry about a theme or consistency—if something arrests my eye, sparks a thought, or makes me happy, I keep it.

We live in an age when voluminous images flit past like birds and then disappear into the ether. I may think that an image I see is unforgettable, but after a thousand more images have passed, I wouldn't bet on it. After amassing hundreds of images, I can't remember where I put that delightful postcard or which computer file a photo is in. Personally, I need a slow, easily retrievable analog system.

I print out images I find on the computer and put them with all the other ephemera that I collect into "presentation" or "portfolio" binders with clear plastic sleeves. These inexpensive folders are about 9 × 12 inches, fit

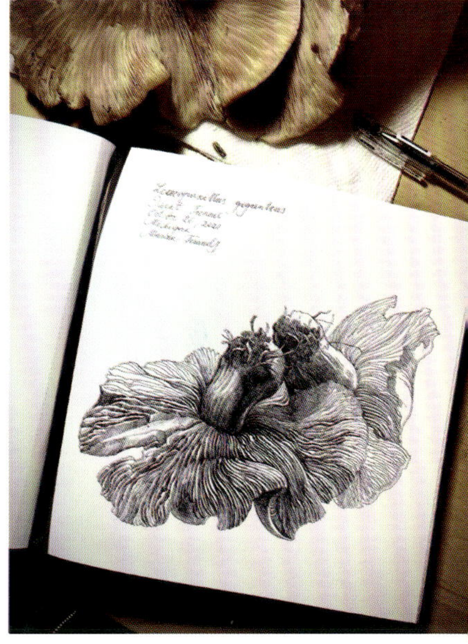

Marina Terauds's creative ritual involves literal foraging. Most days of the year, her practice starts in the woods, where she finds treasure and peace to transform into an ink drawing in her sketchbooks that later gives ideas for more complex etchings and mixed-media work. She says, "These drawings are my daily exercise or workout to keep eyes, hand, and mind in shape. These drawings are an urge and mental rest at the same time."

Above: Marina Terauds, *Leucopaxillus giganteus*, 2021, ink on paper, 8 x 8 inches (20 x 20 cm). Courtesy of the artist.

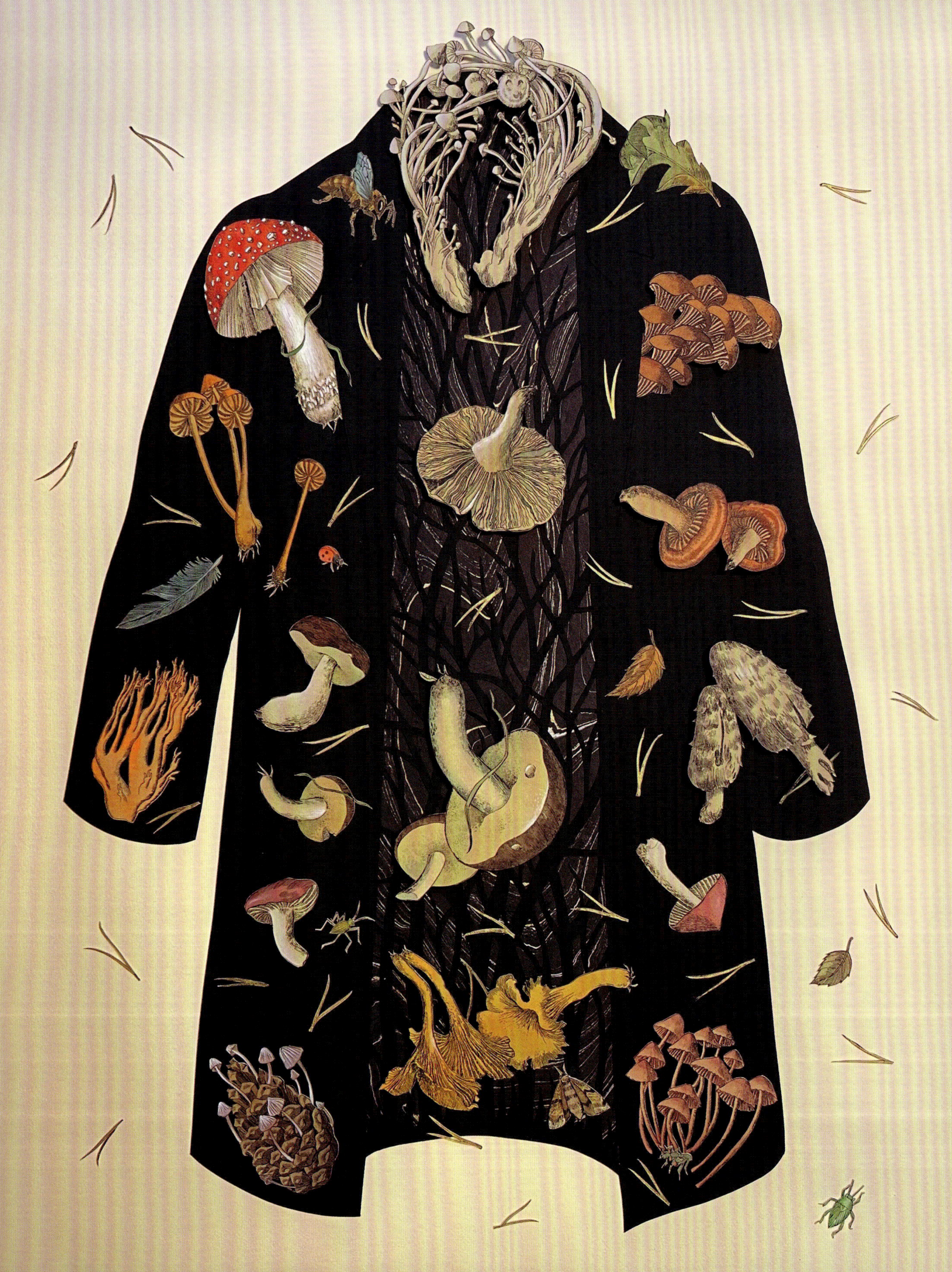

most magazine pages, come in a book of twelve or twenty-four sleeves, and
are easily found at office supply stores. I label the spine of the current
binder "Sourcebook + Year" and keep it on my desk, next to my sketchbook.
I put any loose pictures in the next empty spot, cramming a few into
each sleeve. A cool postcard from my friend's art show? In it goes. It takes
me a year or two to fill and edit one binder.

START SOME CREATIVE COMPOST

First get a portfolio book, then collect the images. Flip through a pile of
magazines and pull out anything that strikes your fancy. Don't overthink it—
more is better. Does a photo of a bowl of tangerines give you joy? Tear it out
along with all pictures of art that you like. Now, make an appointment with
yourself in thirty days (*write* it in your calendar!) to spend twenty minutes
reviewing and editing your compost collection. Repeat this image-gathering
step over the next few weeks to give yourself starting material.

When the pages have accumulated, the reflective and illuminating part
of the process begins. Now that some time has passed, flip through your
folder and see what strikes you about the pictures you saved.

What memories surface about the time you collected it? What makes
you smile? Do you notice any similarities between the images? Look for
repetitions, patterns, and themes. Is it obvious that you have a few favorite
subjects? Are there colors, textures, or aesthetic qualities that repeat?
Perhaps you notice lots of geometric high-contrast shapes. Or maybe lots of
delicate natural forms?

Rearrange your images. Consider grouping by color, graphic quality, or
subject—e.g., winter trees, architectural elements, blue-green shades,
foxes… Are there narrative or stylistic themes that emerge? Do you see
topics prevalent in your world, or connections to art you love? Then consider
why that theme entices. You can use that as a starting point for developing
an image of your own.

Do you notice similarities between your ideas and those of other artists,
as I frequently do? Such *synchronicity* is defined as coincidental occurrences
of events, ideas, or images that arise spontaneously in different places at the
same time. This phenomenon is related to *zeitgeist*, "the spirit of the time":
a common set of ideas that are prevalent in a culture. Artists may work
in similar themes, subjects, and even compositions even when they were not
influenced by direct contact.

Rather than feel discouraged by synchronicity because my idea might
not be as original as I imagined, I feel validated that there is common

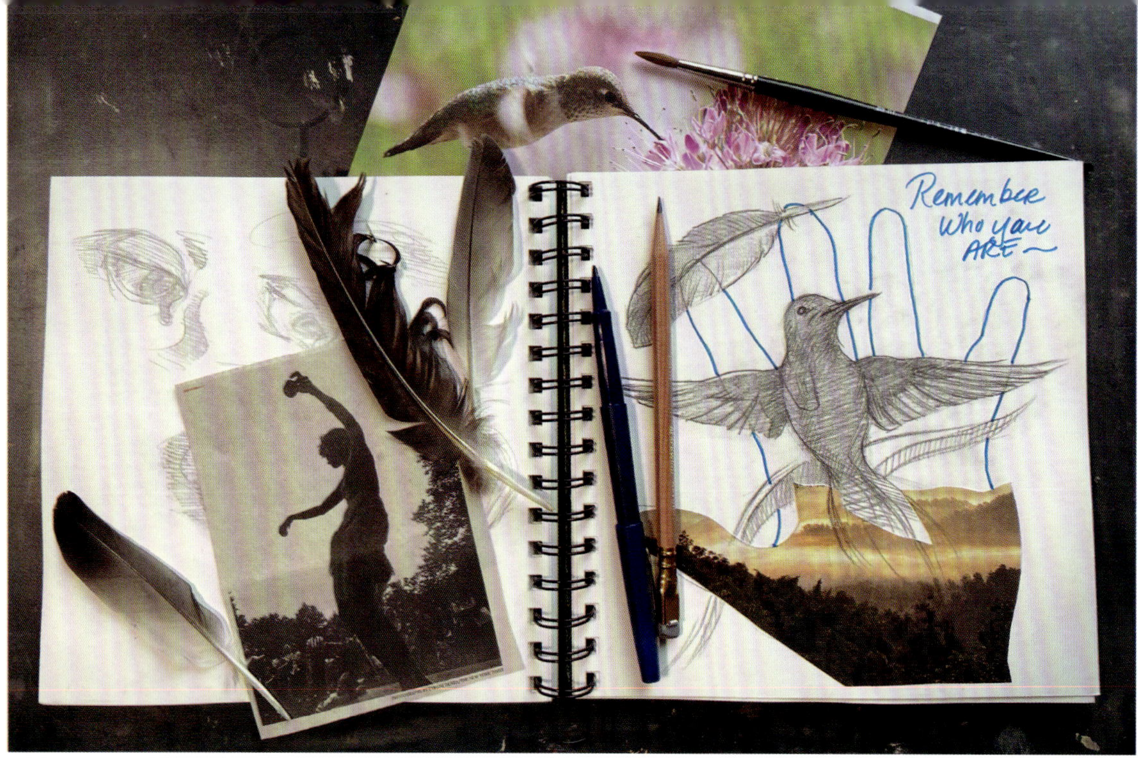

interest and shared language when I see others exploring similar terrain.
I find it encouraging when my particular inspiration seems connected
to a larger whole. On the other hand, if absolutely everyone seems to be
making cyanotypes with wildflowers, maybe you should keep digging for
rarer treasure.

Edit your images, discarding those that no longer inspire. Clutter can be
distracting. Notice your preferences—what is a favorite? What now seems
uninteresting? Toss the boring, but save the odd, confusing, and intrigu-
ing. This collection doesn't take up much space, so don't restrict yourself.
Mystery and enigma can provoke new insights, and some ideas need time
to crystallize. Creativity is essentially making new connections, so embrace
cross-fertilization across disparate and even unexpected points.

Artists can get stuck when we don't have enough variety in our influenc-
es. Throw yourself a curveball by seeking unfamiliar material, a strange
new thing, and intentionally place that into your mix of favorites to see what
new hybrids might spring up.

I have made a dozen of these books over time, and it's fascinating to
revisit what I was gathering ten years ago. Some images mirror my current
interests. Others are reminders of past obsessions and the viewpoint
of a younger self. Looking back at my visual sourcebooks gives me a way to
reflect on the sometimes murky origins of my pictorial ideas.

I love the presentation book with plastic sleeves, as I don't have to do
anything besides tuck the pictures inside and sort them later. A scrapbook

with glue or tape is another workable system, as is a simple pocket folder or large envelope. A digital version of this is a great solution if you are technologically inclined, and there are even apps, programs, and platforms that are designed for this type of image collection, like Pinterest, Evernote, and canva.com.

CREATIVE VISUALIZATION

An axiom of creative compost is the power of visualization to help us achieve our goals, whether as artists or in other parts of our lives such as health, home, friends, or work. Visualization is so essential to human thought that we often cannot understand a new idea if we cannot visualize it first. The process can be imaginative, as an idea pictured in the mind, or concrete, as in a collection of pictures.

When I practice seated meditation, I picture a calm pool of water with a drop hitting the surface that ripples out from the center. Imagining the drop falling and the gentle cadence of ripples helps me focus and settle my emotions. Another example would be imagining my future tomatoes ripe on the vine while I dig a hole for the seeds.

As a visual artist, I get to see the fruits of manifestation over and over again. An idea, a blank canvas, some tubes of paint and brushes, and after some time there is a new thing where there wasn't a thing before. This concrete example has given me great confidence in the principle of visualization and manifestation in all aspects of my life. Did you ever stop to consider how the shirt you are wearing came into existence? How many workers, hours, and ideas were woven together until the moment you slipped it on? Any home you have eaten dinner in, bridge you have walked across, or garden you have strolled through began as an idea in someone's mind.

Imaginative visualization is powerful, but when we make a concrete visualization, it helps even more to manifest our creative goals. For this, I will use my creative compost to make a vision board. A vision board is a collection of images and words gathered in a poster to create a personal and visible reminder of your goals and dreams. Many inspiring thinkers like Deepak Chopra and Oprah Winfrey encourage the use of vision boards as a tool to manifest goals into reality. If you can see it, and maintain your intentions, you can move toward realizing any goal.

A theme of this book is building a creative habit and finding ways to stick with that process over time. Let's create a vision board that will inspire you to keep picking up your pencil. When your vision board is finished, place it where you will see it every day. Mine is sitting right over my drawing desk.

Vision Board

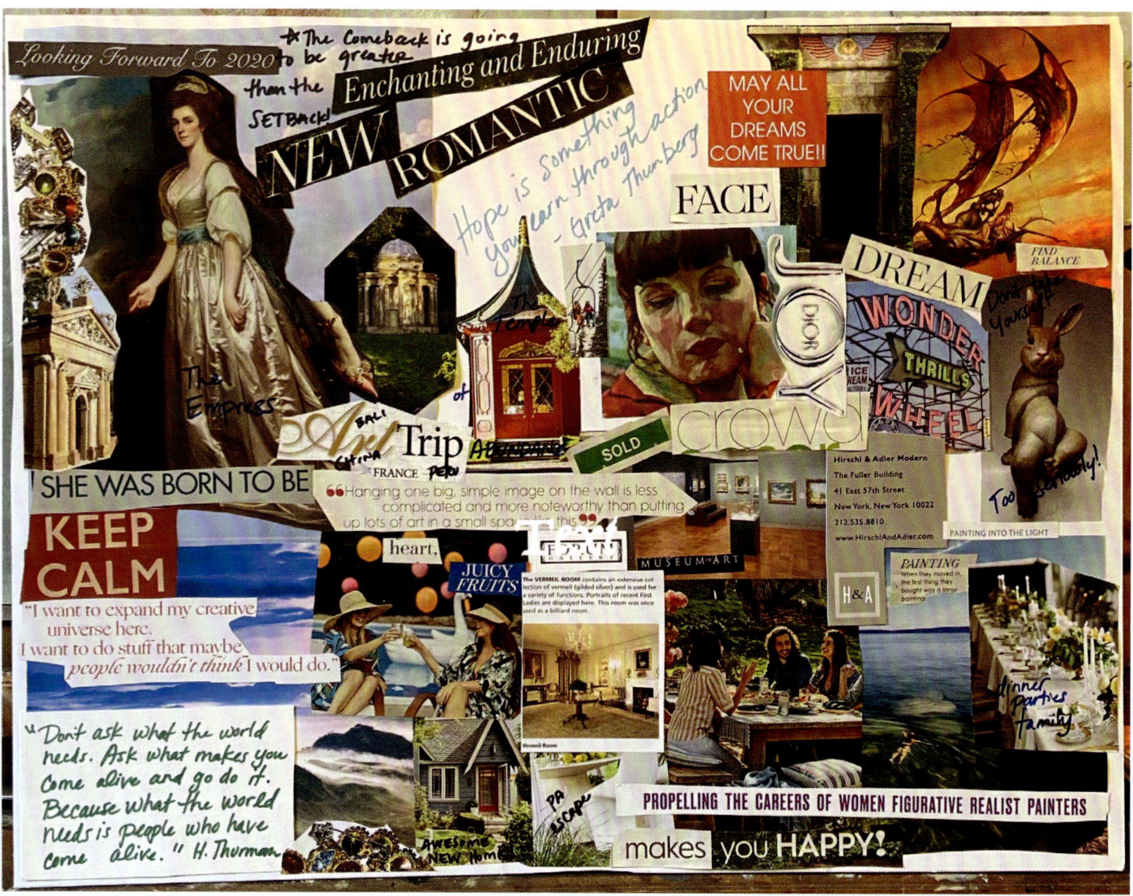

A recent vision board for life and work goals

GATHER YOUR MATERIALS

- White foam-core board, cardboard, or similar, 12 × 18 inches to 24 × 36 inches
- Scissors
- Glue stick
- Creative compost images: magazines, prints, colored papers, stickers, etc.
- Markers or pens for adding your own text

PAUSE AND GET CENTERED

Before you start making your vision board, pause and focus on your intention. Take a deep breath and feel that space between your toes. What qualities do you want to bring into your life with this vision board? As clearly as possible, shape that concept in your mind.

"I AM envisioning __________."
State a creative or personal goal for the next six months.

If a clear focus is elusive, then consider an idea:

"I AM listening and open to what the universe wants to unfold in me here and now…"

GET TO WORK

Now you need pictures and words that connect to your intention. Pull from your creative compost or cut up magazines and newspapers. First gather a good selection of ten to twenty pictures and words. Once you have a good pile, pull some favorites and start to assemble them on your board.

Working intuitively, cut, arrange, and glue. Place larger pictures first and fit smaller ones around. I love adding words and texts that speak to me or direct my aspirations. I will write in specific texts if desired, or add my own symbols or drawings if I can't find a specific image.

AIM FOR PIE IN THE SKY

This is not a place for thinking small or having realistic considerations. This is childlike fairy-tale dreaming, explored with a carefree spirit. Mystery, abstraction, magic, and unrelated elements are all welcome.

NEGATIVITY IS NOT WELCOME

Our minds move quickly from a picture of a new car to "I'll never have the money." Kick that guy out of your party. This is not a strategy meeting—it is a creative exercise that is designed to challenge the normal limits of our ideas of possibility. Allow yourself to dream and visualize as big as you want, and expand from there. The work of nurturing creativity requires boldness and impracticality. Visualization is the key to unlocking doors you never even imagined existed.

HANG IT UP

When your board is complete, it is essential to place it in a highly visible place, and keep it for as long as it serves you. A vision board can start a process of unfolding that may take years to manifest. Looking back, many people realize with delight that something they once imagined has now come into being. Creating a vision board regularly at the new year or your birthday can be a wonderful practice to shape your life and visions. Including a small group of close friends in this project can be nurturing and supportive.

MOOD BOARDS FOR CREATIVE DEVELOPMENT

Another powerful tool for concrete visualization is a mood board, which is similar to a vision board, but it is aimed at aesthetics, image development, and design rather than personal goals. A mood board helps me shape an idea for a painting, particularly when my concept is vague or I want to push in a new direction. It is a tool designers and filmmakers use to develop and communicate a visual aesthetic, and it often incorporates color swatches, textures, and images of environments and costumes.

Are you considering a slick technological design with steel trusses, or a nostalgic landscape with a rustic barn? Even if the artwork you make from the mood board goes off on a tangent or you interpret your mood board abstractly, specific visuals can give you momentum, shape your direction, and help you make choices.

When starting on a new work, I will construct a mood board in the same manner as a vision board, with foam core, scissors, and glue. I hang it on the studio wall to view when I start sketching. My mood board might include paintings or drawings by inspirational masters. I include specific references I might need, perhaps an image of a storm-tossed sea for the background or a specific color combination. Do I want bright pastels, or moody dark tones? I throw in a couple of things that have a feeling or energy I want to translate. I like to add things that seem contradictory, like hot pepper in a sweet stew, to keep things fresh. I prefer a larger board when developing a new body of work, at least 24 × 36 inches, but sometimes I collage a quick small one for a specific artwork on a sketchbook page.

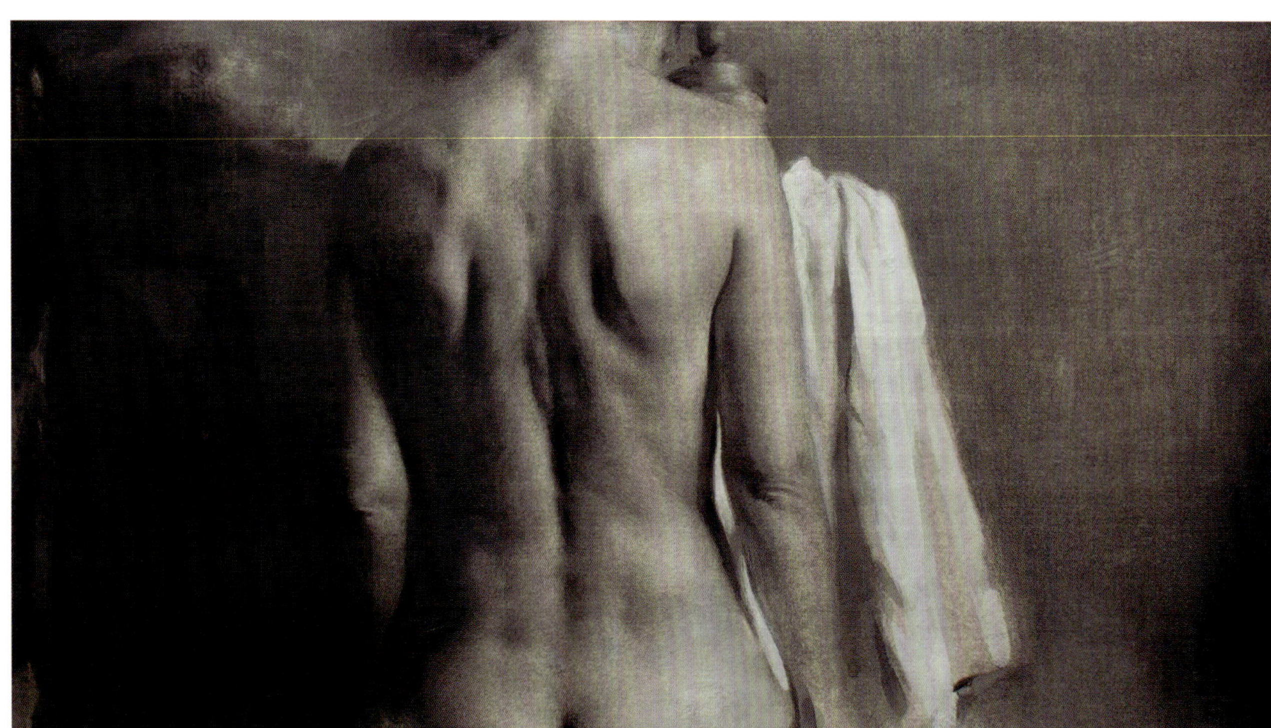

The artist Amaya Gurpide made her whole studio wall into a mood board to inspire an image. All of the moods, textures, and mystery of her creative compost informed her development of this finished work.

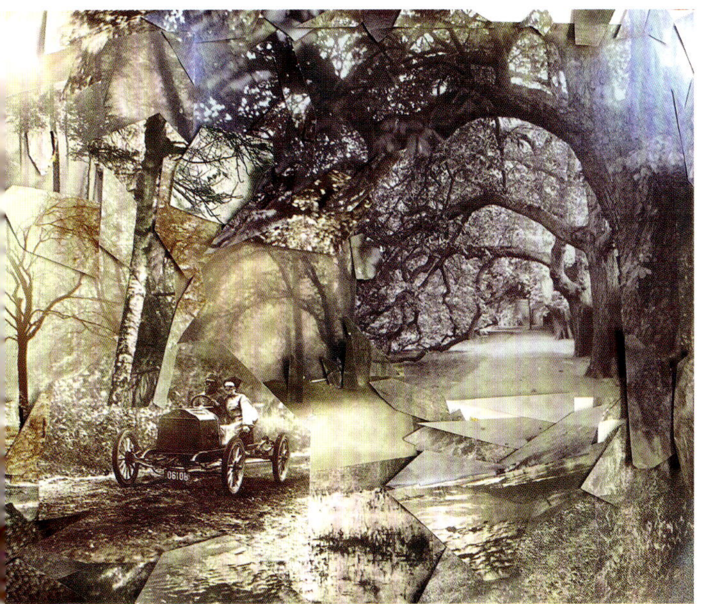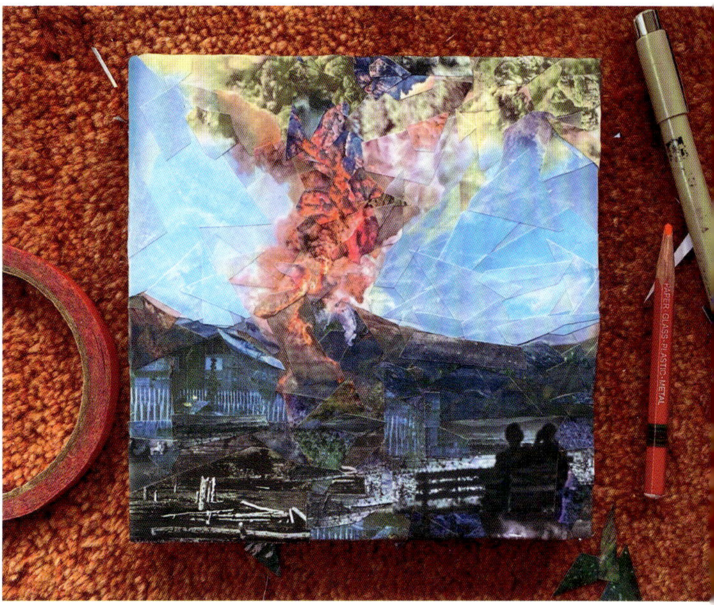

COLLAGE IN ART AND SKETCHBOOKS

With your scissors, glue, pencils, and found illustrations in hand, fill a page with collaged images to generate new ideas. Collage is a type of art made by sticking various different materials such as photographs, paper, or fabrics onto a backing. Artist Alexis Hilliard chooses collage as her primary medium, using abundant creative compost snippets, thematic research, and her own photography. She says that collage "fits my personality. My brain moves quickly, and this allows for fast compositions. It's simple to throw down a couple of images that match or play off each other … and bam! Instant possibilities."[10] Hilliard finds collage an efficient way to develop sketch ideas that might translate well to other mediums, like digital photography or oil sketches.

Creative composting provides endless source material and helps an artist avoid getting stuck in repetitive conceptual and visual ruts.

TIPS ON DRAWING FROM REFERENCE MATERIAL

We have an infinite resource of images on our computers and phones. Need a picture of a green dragonfly? Done. High-resolution, copyright-free images are abundant. In many ways, the problem is too many images, not too few.

Left: Alexis Hilliard, *Untitled (work in progress),* 2021, collage on panel, 9 x 12 inches (23 x 30 cm). Courtesy of the artist.

Right: Alexis Hilliard, *Volcano Study No. 2,* 2020, collage on panel, 6 x 6 inches (15 x 15 cm). Courtesy of the artist.

Opposite, top: Amaya Gurpide's studio wall in 2020. Photo by Amaya Gurpide.

Opposite, bottom: Amaya Gurpide, *Galerna,* 2020, mixed media on paper, 9 x 17 inches (23 x 43 cm). Courtesy of the artist.

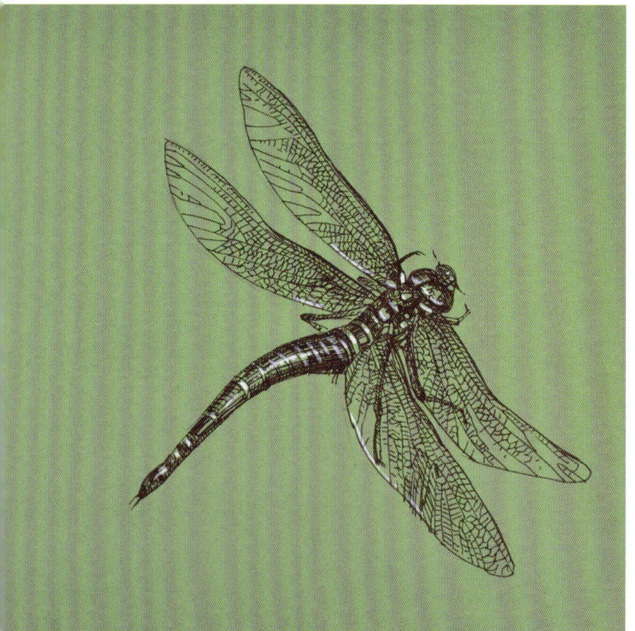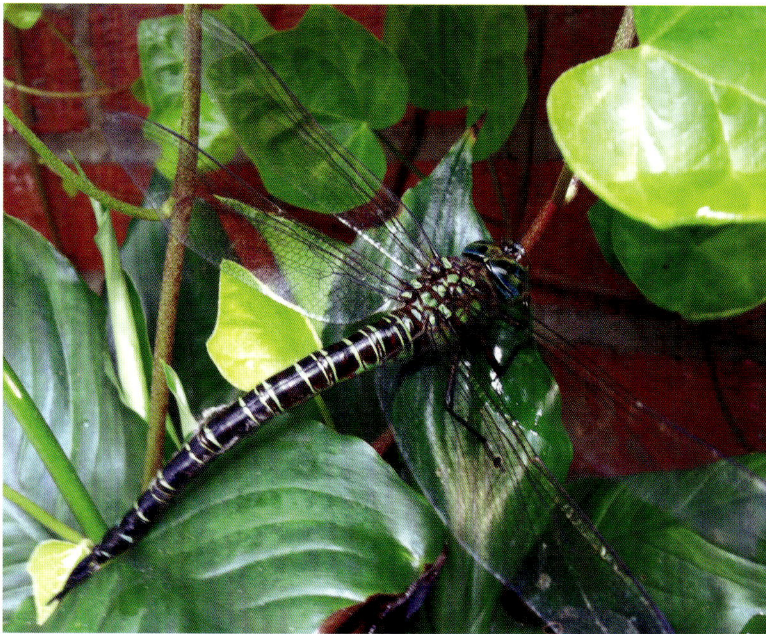

When creating this drawing of a dragonfly, I printed out my photo and made the drawing the same size as the print. This made it easy to measure the wingspan and body.

This is one of the reasons I find creative composting useful for distilling the *one thing* to focus on, given a world with a million possibilities. In this digitally prolific visual age, many artists work directly from a found image on a screen to their sketchbook.

A *special note about copyright*: Artists own the copyright to their images. The person who drew the blue dragonfly or the nature photographer who shot the image owns it. If you want to incorporate someone else's untransformed artwork that you mean to publish, exhibit, or sell, you need permission or a copyright-free image. Type "free stock photos" into your search engine to find copyright-free images.

The adaptation of a found image into a new medium or other significant changes to the original are generally considered fair usage (i.e., copyright-free). There is no concern about incorporating another artist's work into your sketchbook or boards. That's creative fodder for your personal use. Always be respectful and credit or tag the original artist if you share work on social media that incorporates another's creative work.

Here are a few strategies I use when I find an inspiring reference that I want to use to create a new drawing or sketch. To make a close copy, I prefer to work from a print rather than a screen. I find it much easier to translate the shapes from one flat paper to another, especially if they are close to the same size. In this case, you can use your measuring tools (ruler, knitting needle, calipers) to check the proportions one to one.

Consider scale when you work from a reference image. What size is the reference, and what size do you want to make it on your page? Often the image on your screen is much smaller than what you want to make. Changing the size of the visual reference is called *scaling up* (or *scaling down*, if reducing size). Scaling up your visual a little, say 20 to 50 percent, can be done pretty easily.

If you need to scale up your image a lot, say 200 to 300 percent, the process can be more time-consuming. There are two methods I use regularly: the grid method and photocopy enlargement. For the former, make a grid of squares with a ruler on your source image, then make a grid of equal ratio on your large paper.

In photocopy enlargement, I use my local photocopy center to make black-and-white copies to scale, sometimes even taping sheets together or getting a large print. Just inquire about options (this can be inexpensive and very time-saving). For large and detailed works, I want a high-resolution reference for enlargement. Working with too small an image is a recipe for frustration.

To enlarge a drawing with a grid, make a square grid over your original, and an enlarged set of squares the size needed (here it is enlarged from 1" to 2"). Start by plotting all the points that cross the grid lines, and notice any points that hit a corner. Use negative spaces, note proportions, and check angles for accuracy. This can be used to make something very large, like a mural.

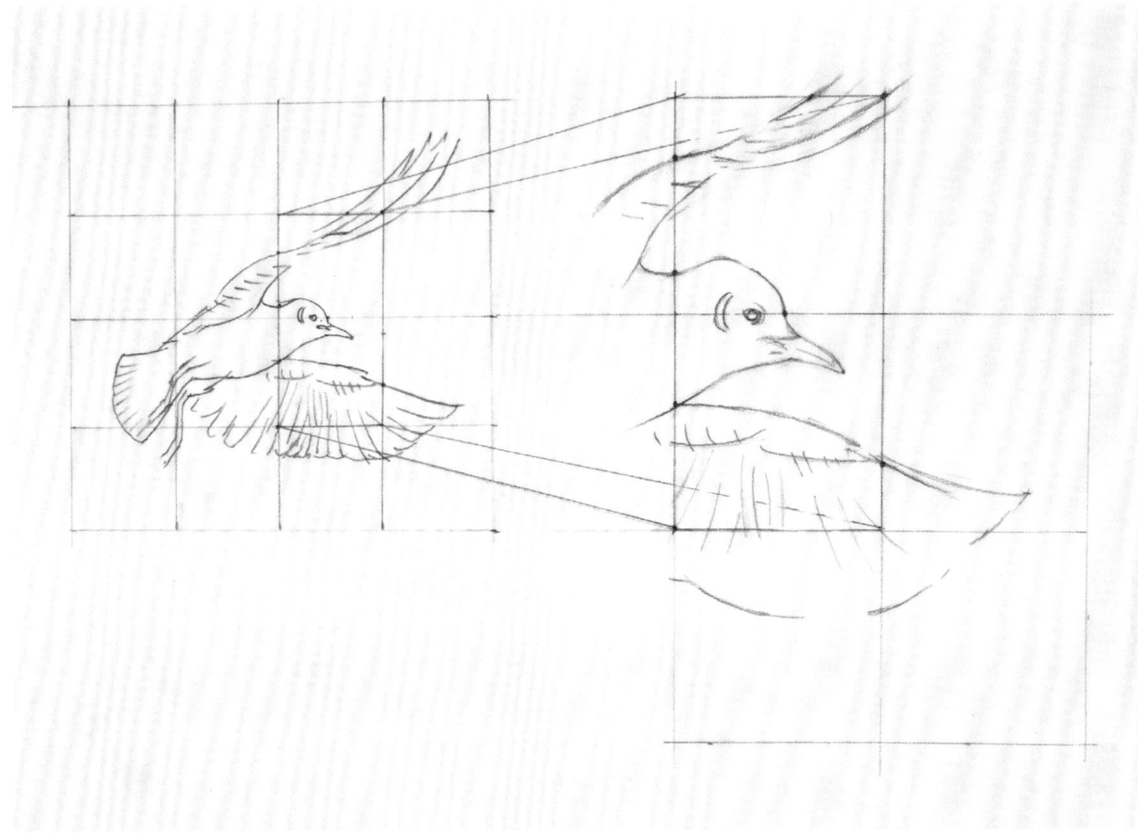

Collage Creative Compost Drawing

This project uses gathered images to make a combined drawing and collage. I use this combination to explore how the images I gathered might grow into a new painting or drawing.

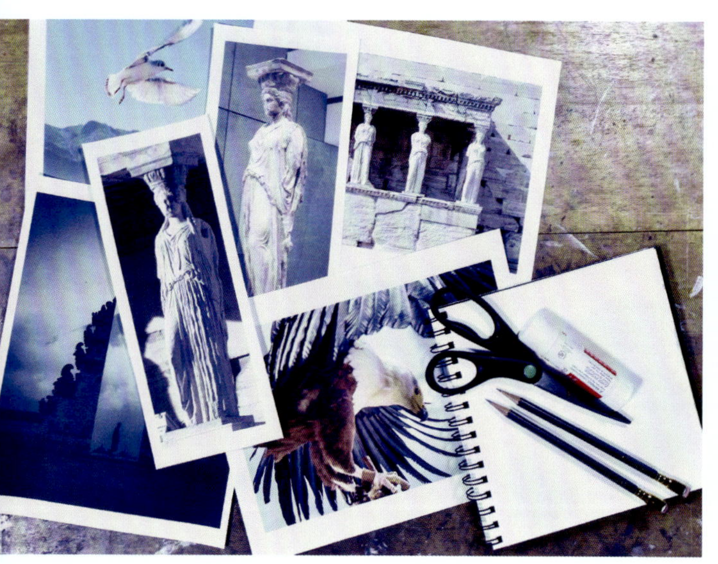

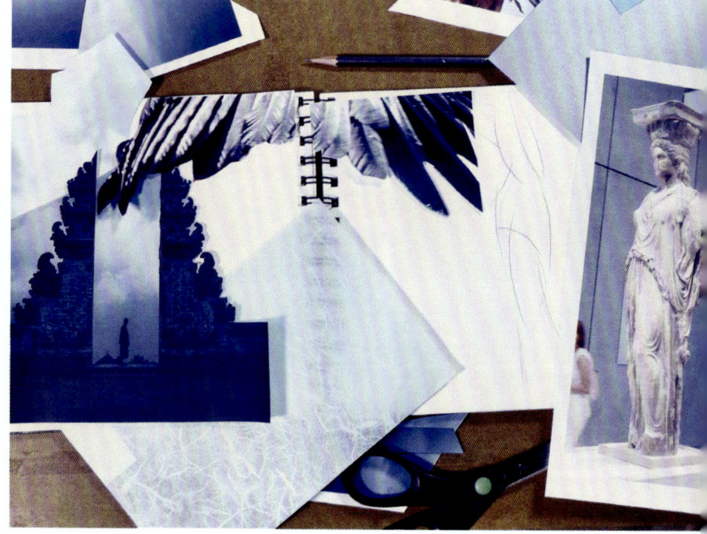

STEP ONE

I selected a favorite subject and primary image from my compost pile—caryatids, which are marble female figures carved into the columns at the Parthenon in Greece. I printed the images on regular copy paper (not photo paper), which is thin and glues flat to the pages of my mixed-media sketchbook. I kept one print to draw from and used the others for collage.

STEP TWO

Next, I decided on a basic placement for my composition, starting with my primary caryatid. I lightly blocked in my drawing to secure a good spot on the paper. Then, I cut out sections of a couple of my favorite prints to place around it. I start with one or two cutouts and add more as needed. Cut, arrange, glue. Repeat until satisfied.

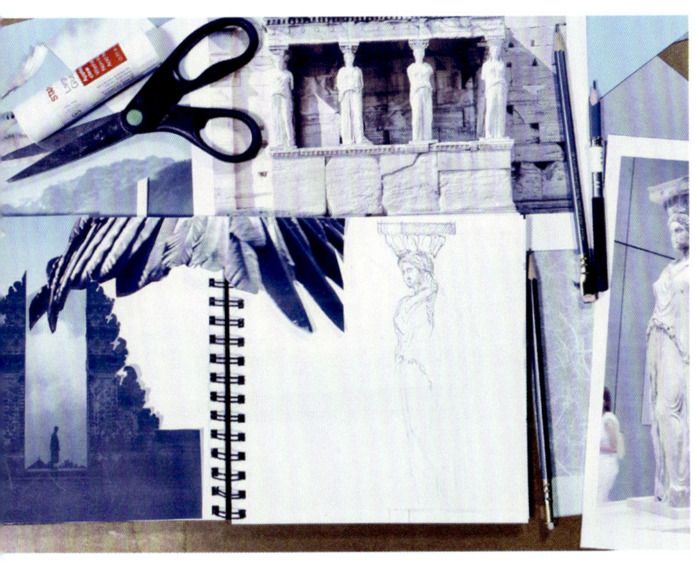

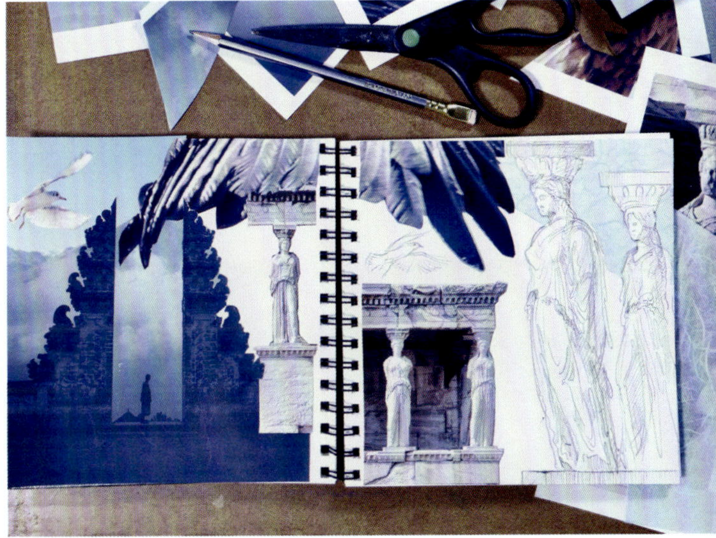

STEP THREE

After my collage images were glued in place, I added the details to my drawing, using contour lines and light cross-hatching to give dimension to the statues.

STEP FOUR

When the drawing was done, I filled up some empty spaces using colored pencil, watercolor, and markers—any mixed media can complete the collage drawing combo.

Collage drawings can be a wonderful seed for a painting—they go quickly and allow for unexpected outcomes that might not be possible through imagination alone. Collage naturally creates a cross-fertilization of images and ideas.

FEEDING YOUR SPIRIT

My guiding principle is that creativity is a practice and inspiration is not an automatic condition. Building a creative habit means *getting* inspired to work and then *staying* inspired to continue on the journey. Just as our bodies need healthy food, our spirits need stock for our creative stores. I want you to engage with art for years to come, so here are some of the things I do to keep motivation flowing.

CREATE A PERSONAL SOURCEBOOK

Above, I detailed my most important tools for cultivating inspiration. Now make your own sourcebook a unique go-to for ideas and reflection. Use vision boards and mood boards to develop specific projects. Keep a small notebook and/or sketchbook handy (like 3½ × 5½ inches) to be ready when ideas strike.

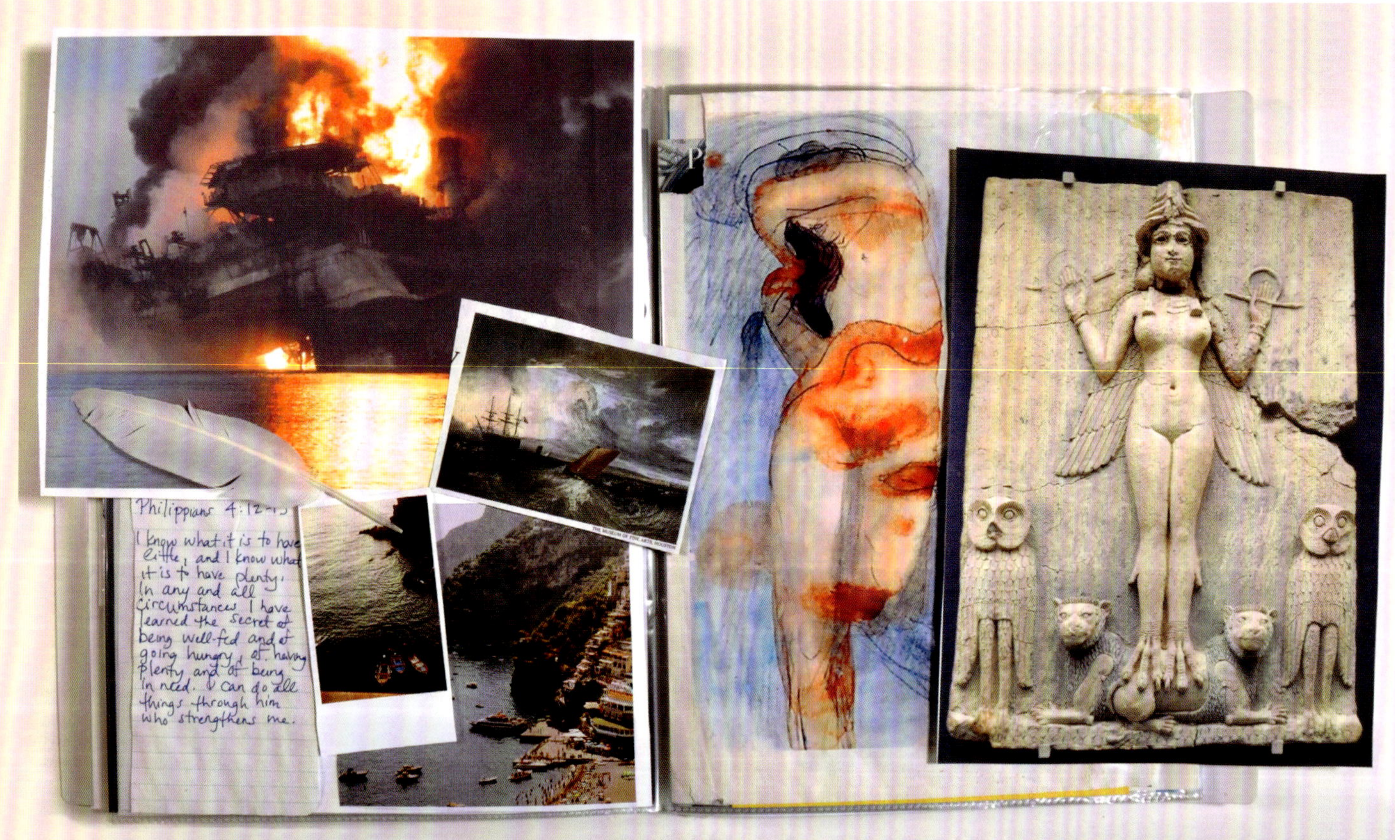

FOLLOW CURIOSITY

We love the romantic fantasy of being swept up in a fever of creativity with an inspired idea. I find that's a rare state of being. Instead of waiting for passion and clarity, pay attention to *curiosity*, which is a friendly and gentle motivator that can lead you down fruitful rabbit holes. Ideas and motivation can accumulate with very small nudges. I can feel insecure when I don't have a big idea and I'm not convinced that my direction is useful or worthy. This insecurity is connected to the myth that great artists are seized with a wonderful idea and simply *must* create in a burst of energy. That's just great for movies about artists. Real life is a lot more boring.

Instead of waiting for a flash of clarity, just walk down the path of curiosity. Trust that your particular interests, from your particular viewpoint, are entirely unique. Put faith in your personal experience and perspective rather than in bolts of lightning. Connect ideas across experiences and disciplines. Over time, you will see individual points of light become a constellation. Your creative compost is your path to the stars.

When I collect, sort, and arrange my gathered images, themes and pictorial ideas emerge.

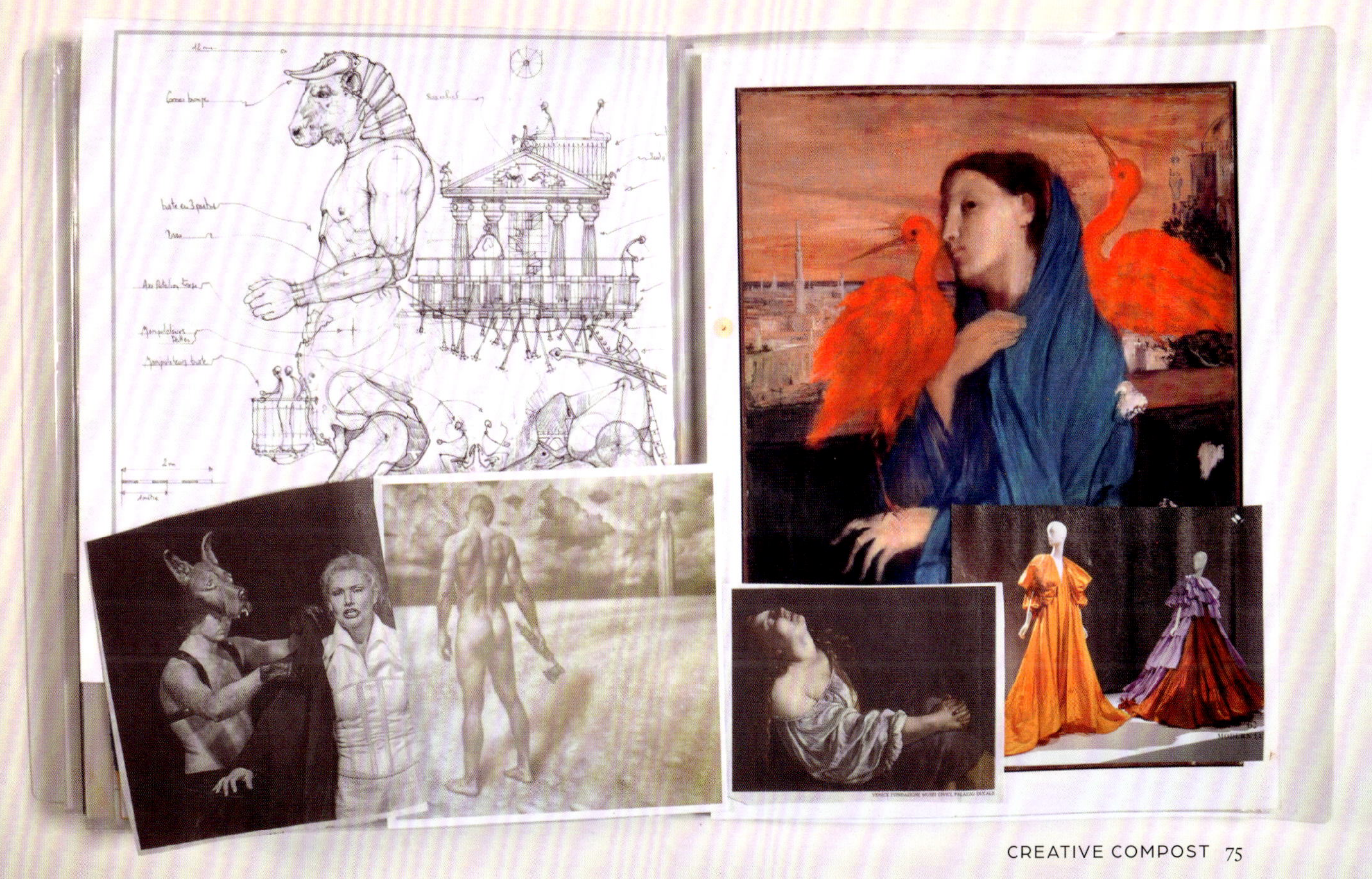

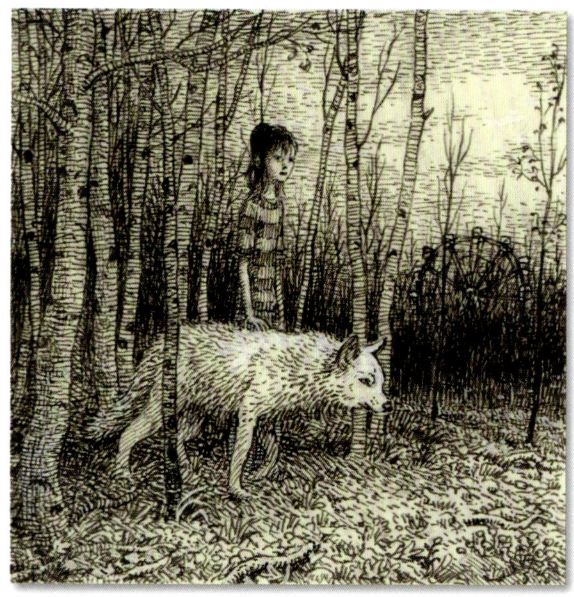

"I dwell in Possibility –
A fairer House than Prose –
More numerous of Windows –
Superior – for Doors –

Of Visitors – the fairest –
For Occupation – This –
The spreading wide my narrow Hands
To gather Paradise –

—EMILY DICKINSON

FILL UP ON AWESOME

As a visual artist, it is obvious that I would find inspiration in pictures. However, creative compost can consist of anything you might experience in the world. I recommend that you expose yourself to *awesome things* of all kinds—not limit yourself within a restricted field. Watch a dance performance, stroll through the woods, or visit an exhibit at the science center. Notice when you stumble on a certain idea multiple times in various places; some ideas seem to pester you until they get your attention. Whether they're poems, radio shows, music, or conversations in a restaurant, the little ideas you encounter become resources. Include notes and text in the clear plastic sleeves. Gathering, sorting, and reflecting on bits of inspiration will build your awareness of your preferences and interests.

A quiet practice of art needs an occasional infusion of energy. Go out and experience things that *move* you on a regular basis. Artists must not forget what it *feels* like to be excited, emotional, inflamed by an inspiring moment. When you have an extraordinary moment, *notice* that precious state—so that you have a bank of emotional memories to tap into and use as a North Star for making art.

KEEP ENCOURAGING NOTES ON HAND

If you have made artworks and shared them with an audience of one or a thousand, it is truly encouraging to hear "Wow! I love it!" I'm as proud of a gold star now as I was in second grade. The positive reaction of a friend, teacher, or total stranger should be saved for a day when you might need some encouragement. I got a postcard from my most beloved and feared graduate school art professor congratulating me on a show. I will save that card forever. When there are long gaps of silence and uncertain outcomes, we need support to continue working. If you have received a positive response to your work, record it and keep it where you can see it over and over again.

TAKE A UNIQUE AND PERSONAL JOURNEY

One of the richest rewards of my practice of creative composting is that I have developed a stronger sense of what makes me unique in a world full of makers. It took me time to discern what subjects and images I prefer and to select a path that feels personal. Early on, you might be quite unsure what subjects you like or why you like them. Trust that insights will distill over time. A lot of work done in the present feels like muddling through and figuring it out as you go. That is our working ground. If you are intentional, reflective, and patient, be assured that veins of gold will become visible and that you will learn about yourself through the creative act.

A sourcebook is a physical manifestation of our individuality. No two people would ever create the same collection. Likewise, your sketchbook and collages will never be like another's. The gift of creativity is that if we trust in the journey, the process will reveal our true natures. This takes the time it takes. Stay engaged and over time your confidence in your creative path will flourish.

5

Orientation Lines

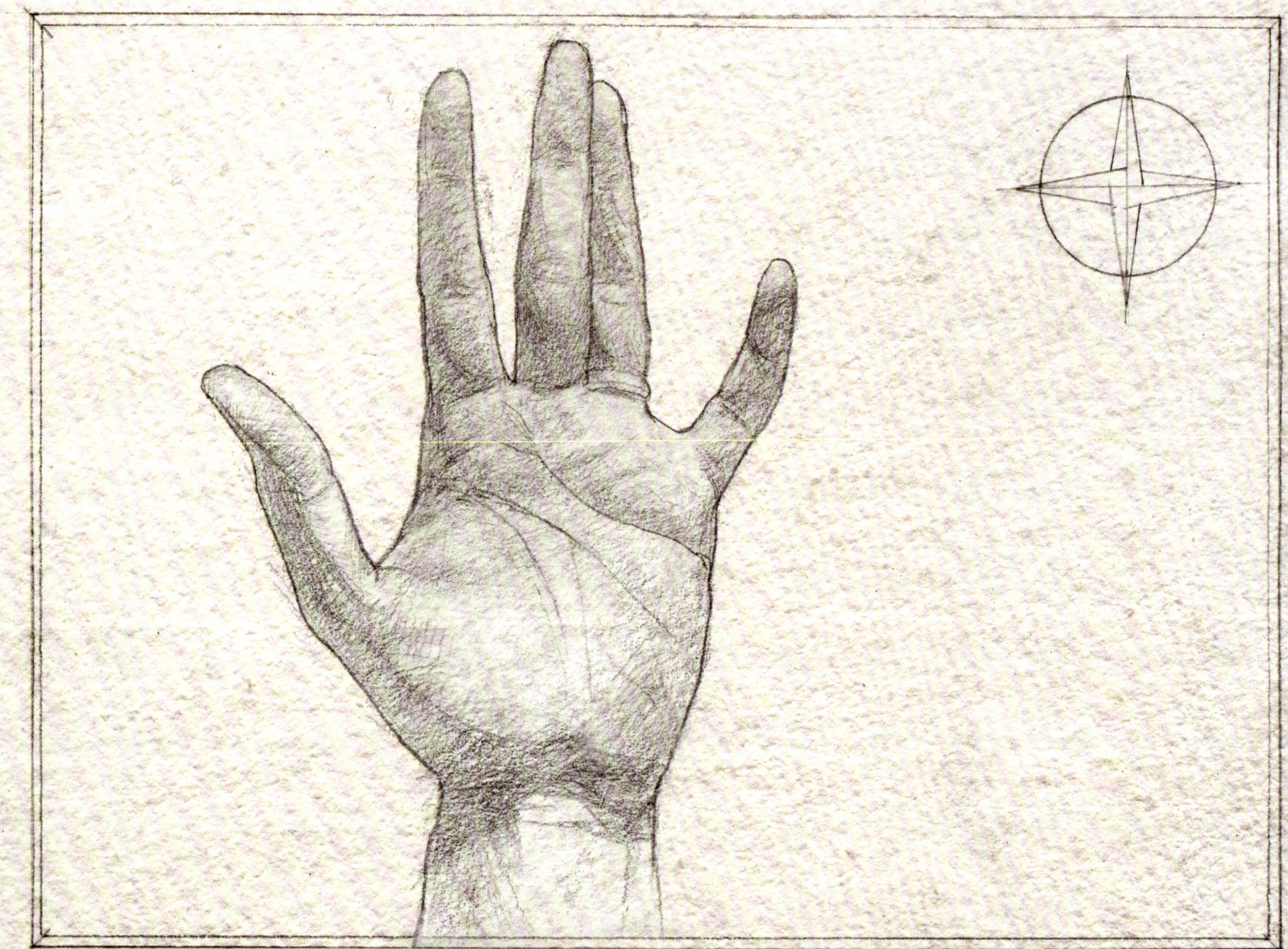

TOOLS FOR FINDING YOUR WAY

In this chapter, I will introduce some tools and techniques that every artist needs to find their way around a drawing. When you start out on a trek, you want to head in the right direction and have a map and compass handy if you get lost. When you begin a new drawing, you may, at first, feel like you don't know which way to start. Let's consider some useful navigational tools for accuracy in drawing.

Before embarking on a finished work, I measure distances, check angles for direction, and triangulate to gauge placement. The visual field of my empty paper is a lot like a new territory. I map out my planned drawing with a light placement and later hone fine details and add shading.

I once watched the artist Alexey Steele give a demo. He seemed to be doing nothing for the first fifteen minutes except vaguely moving his arm around the paper, making practically invisible marks and talking. While I imagined he was floundering, in fact he was patiently observing landmarks, distances, angles, and the interrelationship of points in his visual field and making minute marks. He was making himself a map before he took off on his journey. After this period of looking and notation, he knocked together a killer portrait likeness in another fifteen minutes that seemed to materialize from thin air. The lesson of deliberate patience and planning sunk in: Never rush. As all careful carpenters know—measure twice, cut once.

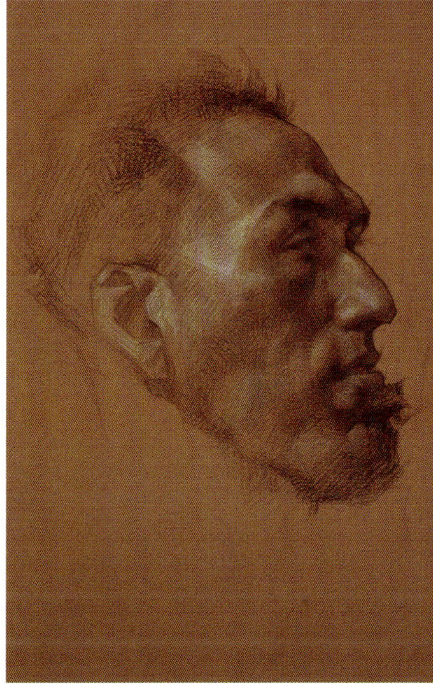

Above: Alexey Steele, *Ricky,* from the My Neighbor series, 2016, sepia Cretacolor on Fabriano soft press paper, 30 x 22 inches (76 x 56 cm). Courtesy of the artist.

BASICS FOR MEASUREMENT

Here are some common errors we encounter in proportion. Humans are pattern-making animals, and these pattern habits can block us from drawing accurately. Our natural tendency is to regularize length and distance: Long and short lines become equalized, and we make things medium instead. Similarly, we underestimate lengths and overestimate widths, making things squat and fat. We focus on the core of a mass and disregard the distal lengths, often running out of room on the page for feet and hands. To draw accurately, you must notice these tendencies and correct your measurements.

Opposite: Patricia Watwood, *Map of My Hand,* 2017, graphite on paper, 6 x 8 inches (15 x 20 cm). Courtesy of the artist.

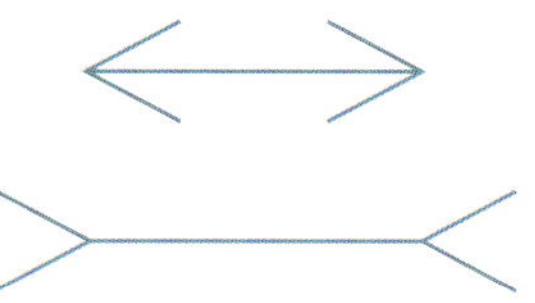

PLUMB LINES AND KNITTING NEEDLES

When you tie a weight to a string and hold it above the earth, the stilled cord—a plumb line—falls in a perfect perpendicular every single time. In a world of shifting terrain and chaotic unknowns, the eternal verity of the plumb line gives us a truth powerful enough to build skyscrapers. The Egyptian pyramids could never have been made without this ancient tool and the universal principle it reveals.

I hold my plumb line in my extended arm. Is the tree trunk I am looking at truly vertical? Which way does it lean and at what point in the trunk does it bend? The plumb line counteracts my natural tendency to make any line that is *almost* vertical into one that is straight up and down.

My second indispensable tool for measuring is a long, skinny knitting needle. Any slender and straight thing will do: a long metal BBQ skewer, a skinny paintbrush. You can use a long pencil in a pinch, but it's a bit short for some work.

I use my needle to measure and look at horizontal relationships. I hold up my needle level, gauging by eye as you would to straighten a picture on the wall. Now, I observe the angle I want to compare. Again, our tendency is to make something that is *slightly* inclined into something level. We need the things in our world to remain stable: Tables must be level so stuff doesn't roll off, and walls plumb to bear the weight of a roof. We unconsciously make our drawings incorrect when we accidentally stick to these perpendiculars. We must develop an awareness of the difference between our latent tendencies

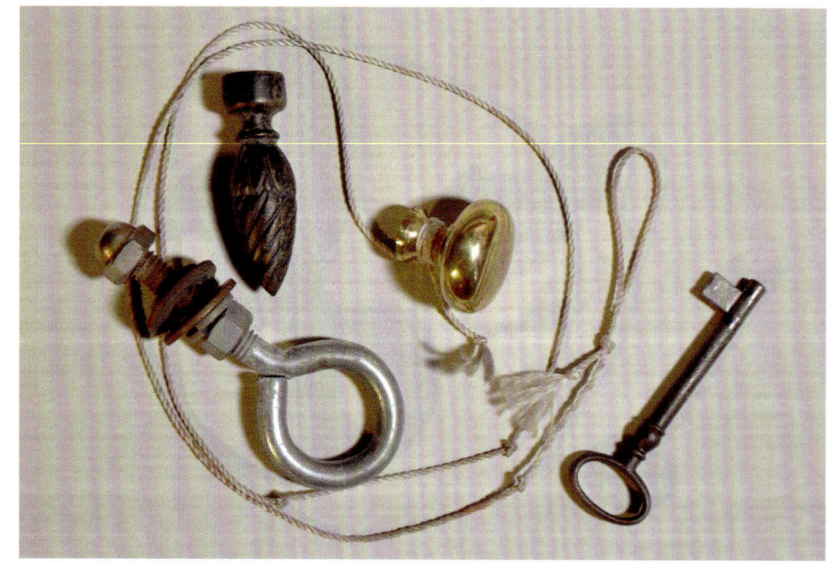

and what is accurate. Through patient discovery, our misperceptions slowly fall away, and we become adept at knowing what we don't know.

COMPASS ROSE

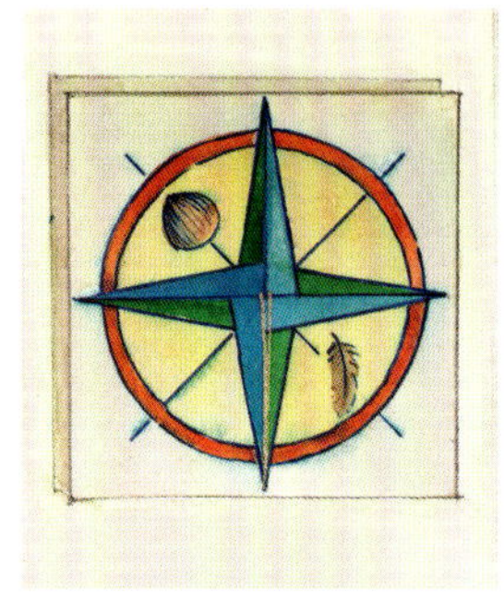

To train your eye, start your next project with a *compass rose*. In the upper corner of your page, use a ruler to draw a perpendicular cross inside a circle. While you are working, check angles with your knitting needle and compare them to the true horizontal and vertical in the rose compass. Typically, beginners have trouble with subtle angles, particularly when they are close to a true vertical or horizontal.

Sometimes folks can inadvertently reverse the angle—it's almost like a kind of dyslexia. A beginner might make a 15-degree angle go to the *left* instead of to the right. If this happens to you, do not be embarrassed! It's actually *very* common. You can easily remedy mistakes by checking angles manually.

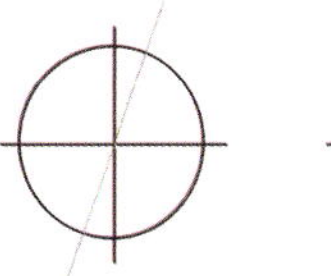
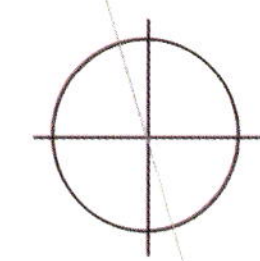

A compass rose helps you see angles. If the angle goes to the right of the centerline by about 15 degrees, a new artist may make the 15–degree angle go to the left instead.

HOW TO MAKE OBSERVATIONAL MEASUREMENTS

Comparative measurement allows you to analyze the proportions of your subject by using one dimension in your visual field to judge another. I check height against width first with my knitting needle. Sit up straight (or stand

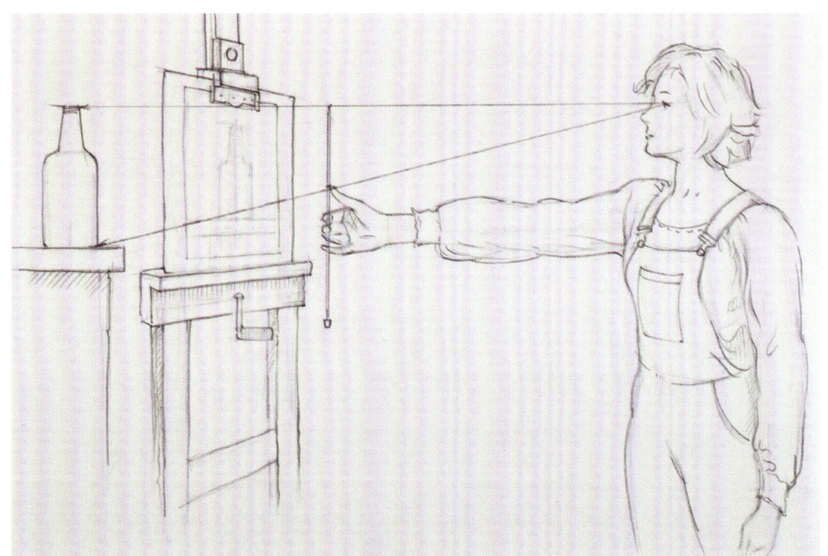

When taking measurements, be sure to hold your arm out straight from the shoulder, and hold the knitting needle perpendicular to the ground. Use the tip of the knitting needle, and mark a spot with your thumb, to take the height of an object.

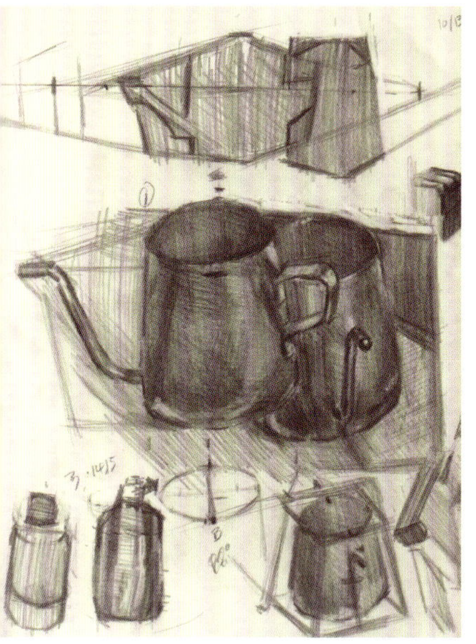

Note how many ways of measuring Steven Johnson II used in this study: comparing height to width, noting the outside shapes, and looking for axes in the ellipses of these everyday objects.

Steven Anthony Johnson II, *Watering Can (Classroom Study 2),* 2020, graphite on paper, 12 x 9½ inches (30 x 24 cm). Courtesy of the artist.

erect) and hold your knitting needle out from your shoulder with your arm straight and your elbow locked. The needle should extend vertically from your hand. Close one eye and align the tip of the needle with the top of the object you wish to measure, switching your eyes back and forth between the object and your tool. Now, use your thumb to mark the bottom of your object.

Don't move your thumb or relax your elbow! You have a height measurement between the tip of your needle and your thumb. Now, rotate your arm and needle 90 degrees, to the horizontal axis of your object. Is it longer or shorter than the vertical axis? By about how much? Sixty percent? Eighty percent? While this measuring system has built-in error from wiggle room and slight shifts of stance, it will focus your attention on these proportions and help train your eye to accuracy.

With practice, you can use comparative measurement to investigate all sorts of proportions—the placement of eyes and mouth on the head, the lengths of limbs, the dimensions of bottles. To help organize a composition of multiple objects, you can measure the spaces between things or the height of a few different objects. When I first learned to draw, I proceeded slowly while I carefully took measurements and trained my eye. Honing your spatial awareness and perceptions of distance takes time, but this essential skill sticks with you.

START WHERE YOU ARE

So far, we have looked at a few different ways to get your pencil moving and break the ice to start a new habit of creativity. To keep your momentum going, let's build some navigation points that can set you off in a good direction.

A common barrier for everyone can be the simple stumper of *what* to draw. You think, "I want to cultivate a drawing practice," but as soon as you open the sketchbook, you have trouble deciding *what* subject to work on. This block to your momentum is called *decision paralysis*, a familiar terror to anyone with a large Chinese restaurant menu who always orders the same thing. With decision paralysis, the curative strategy is:

1. Reject perfection.
2. Accept that you will sometimes make a bad choice.

Good news for artists! Pretty much any bad choice you may make will just end up in the trashcan, where it won't cause anyone harm. Even better,

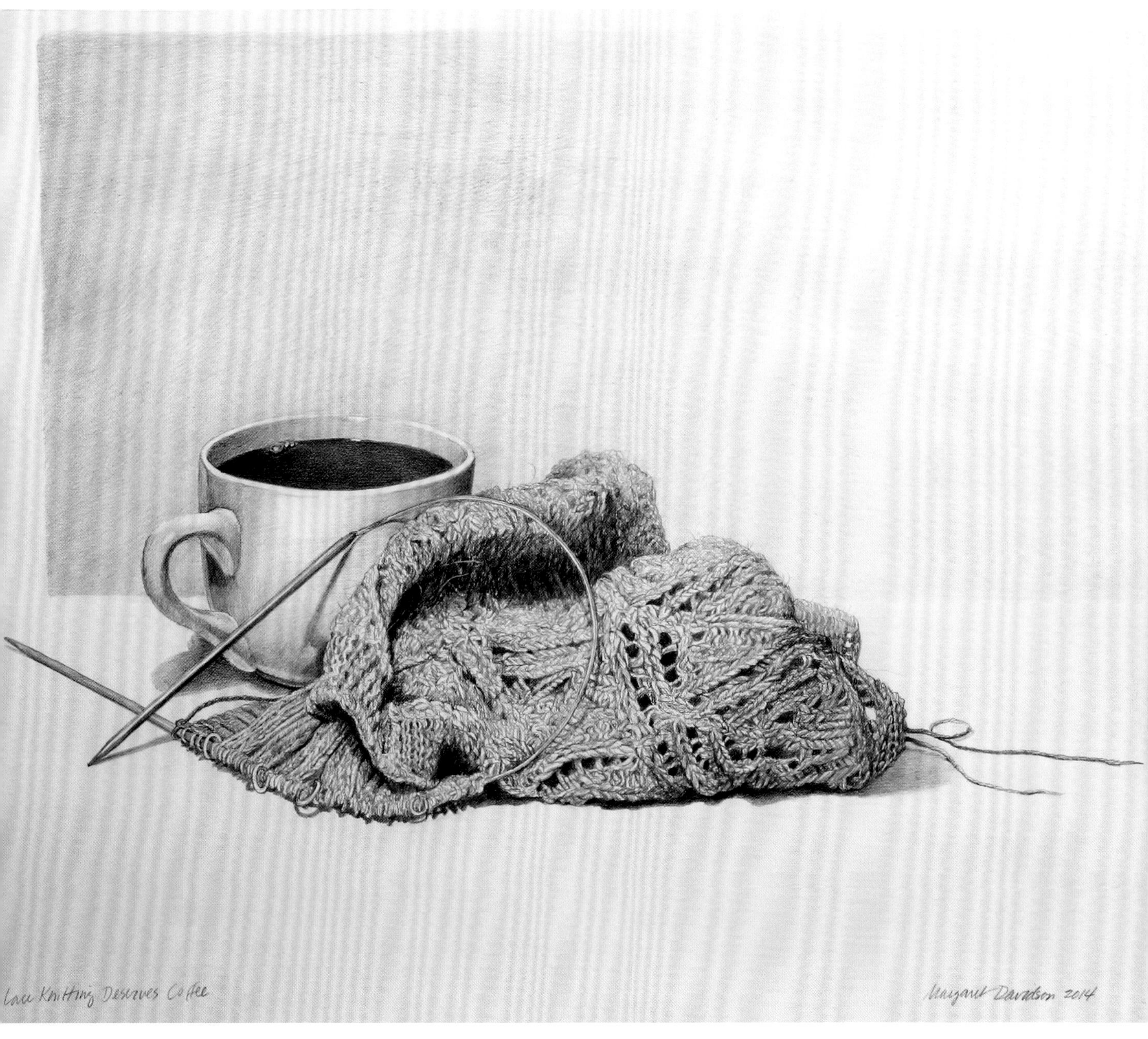

our failures help us grow. You are going to make a mistake. You will waste some time and pursue some dead ends. The sooner you can make peace with this, the better. Make friends with the experience of messing up and restarting. This is the basis on which all artistic developments are built. I am a recovering perfectionist so, with great compassion, I know this is easier said than done.

Margaret Davidson, *Lace Knitting Deserves Coffee*, 2014, graphite on rag paper, 21 x 23 inches (53 x 58 cm). Courtesy of the artist.

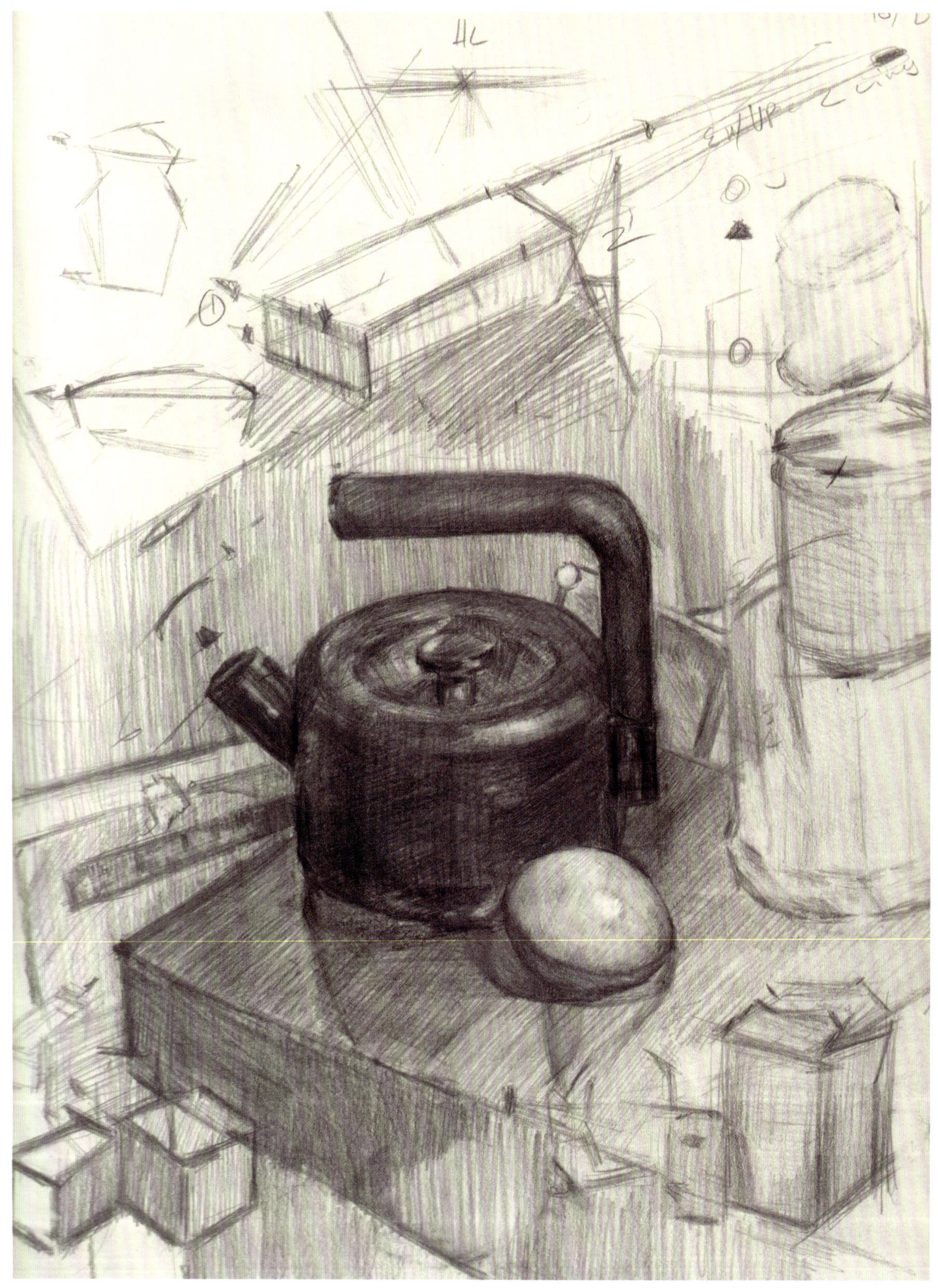

Other artists seem to have cool ideas and endless originality. I just have a blank sketchbook and a cup of cold coffee.

Well, why don't you start where you are?

In their book *Art & Fear*, David Bayles and Ted Orland urge artists to simply learn to work on your work and understand that all other problems are fear in various guises.[11] In this case, my problem of *What to draw?* reveals this underneath: "I don't know how to pick something because I'm not *really* an artist!" Aha! I see you, self-doubt. All right, sit down over there while I consider this cup of cold coffee. Instead of being derailed by self-doubt, I will learn to work on my work.

Absolutely anything that gets you working will aid in the continuing journey of creativity. Without getting up, take a few calm breaths and let your eyes gently explore your space.

I bet there are ten things in your visual field that might serve as a starting point. One thing that visual artists learn to do differently is *notice*. Pay attention with your eyes. Don't just glance hastily—slowly look around and notice where your eye lands. For example, I see a small enameled box my aunt left me, a camera lens, the sunlight hitting Dottie's embroidered pillow, a pair of scissors, a mechanical pencil sharpener—the clutter of my life. But looking again, I notice that each object has its own shape, character, and details that tell a story about a particular moment and place in time.

"Drawing is the artist's most direct and spontaneous expression, a species of writing: it reveals, better than does painting, his true personality."

—EDGAR DEGAS

THREE PROMPTS FOR WHAT TO DRAW

1. Look around you for thirty seconds, and pick something within your space in that time.

2. Flip through a favorite art book and copy a work of art you love.

3. Pull a reference from your creative compost book and make a sketch.

Cold Coffee

I'll use a cup of coffee as my subject in order to demonstrate helpful strategies for starting an observational drawing. The only way to learn to draw is to put pencil to paper, so grab a coffee mug and your sketchbook. You'll be learning three basic skills: placement lines, contour lines, and cross-contour.

STEP ONE

Start drawing with marks for placement by first noting the top, bottom, and left and right of your cup. Guesstimate the height and width of the mug. Do not worry now about whether the proportions are correct.

Make light vertical and horizontal axis lines on your paper that approximate the cup's dimensions. Consider the placement of your lines on the paper and the size you'd like to draw the cup. Want it

larger? Smaller? More to the left? Now is the time to erase and revise your marks.

STEP TWO

Now check proportions by comparing the height and width of the mug to your axis lines and adjust as needed. Tall and skinny or short and fat? Compare each side from the central axis line to check if you've made the cup symmetrical.

Lightly sketch all the lines with delicate marks and use straightish line segments: Several tries and short lines are typical in beginning a drawing.

STEP THREE

Before you go any further, erase any obviously incorrect and unwanted lines, such as the axis guidelines. If your sketch lines are heavy and dark,

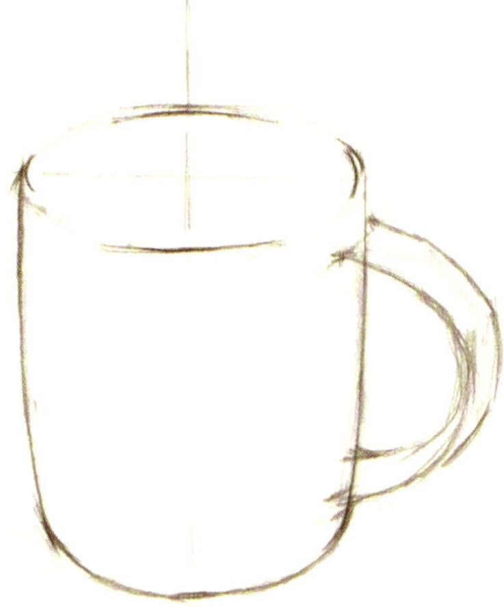

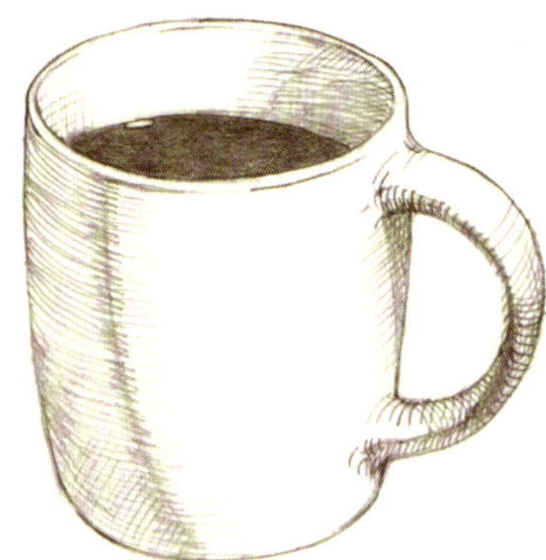

use a flattened kneaded eraser to lightly pat the surface and lift the tone.

Now, using a more assertive line weight, draw the contour lines of the mug on top of your first sketch, making corrections as needed. Create your contours with multiple short lines and stitch these together with careful erasing. You don't have to be able to make a single fluid line.

Use your eraser again to clean away any light sketchy lines and create the illusion that you've made a clean contour all at once.

The rim of the mug, visually an ellipse, is the hardest part. Make very light vertical and horizontal axis lines across the top of the cup. Start the ellipse with the long arcs at the top and bottom on the centerline, gently sweeping the curves toward the edges. Then make short, tightly curved lines at the sides of the cup along the horizontal axis. There are no corners on an ellipse! Connect your line segments and erase to make a smooth line. Remember that the cup has a thickness, so you'll need two concentric ellipses. For a more realistic effect, don't make two complete ellipses, but show the thickness in just a few places.

STEP FOUR

Vary the line weight to make the rim and edges of the mug move in space. A stronger, darker line will capture the viewer's focus and make a line seem to advance. A delicate or more broken line can make the edge appear to recede.

To suggest shading and dimension, try regular hatching lines along the edge of the shadow. Try layering the hatching and cross-contour lines in multiple directions to mimic the curvature of the cup.

For the dark tone of the coffee, lay in an even tone and blend it with your stump.

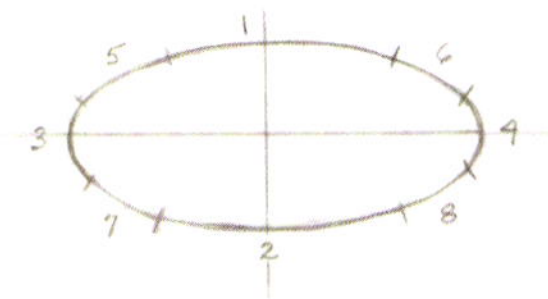

Eight line segments of the ellipse, numbered to show the order in which I build the shape. There are no points or corners on an ellipse!

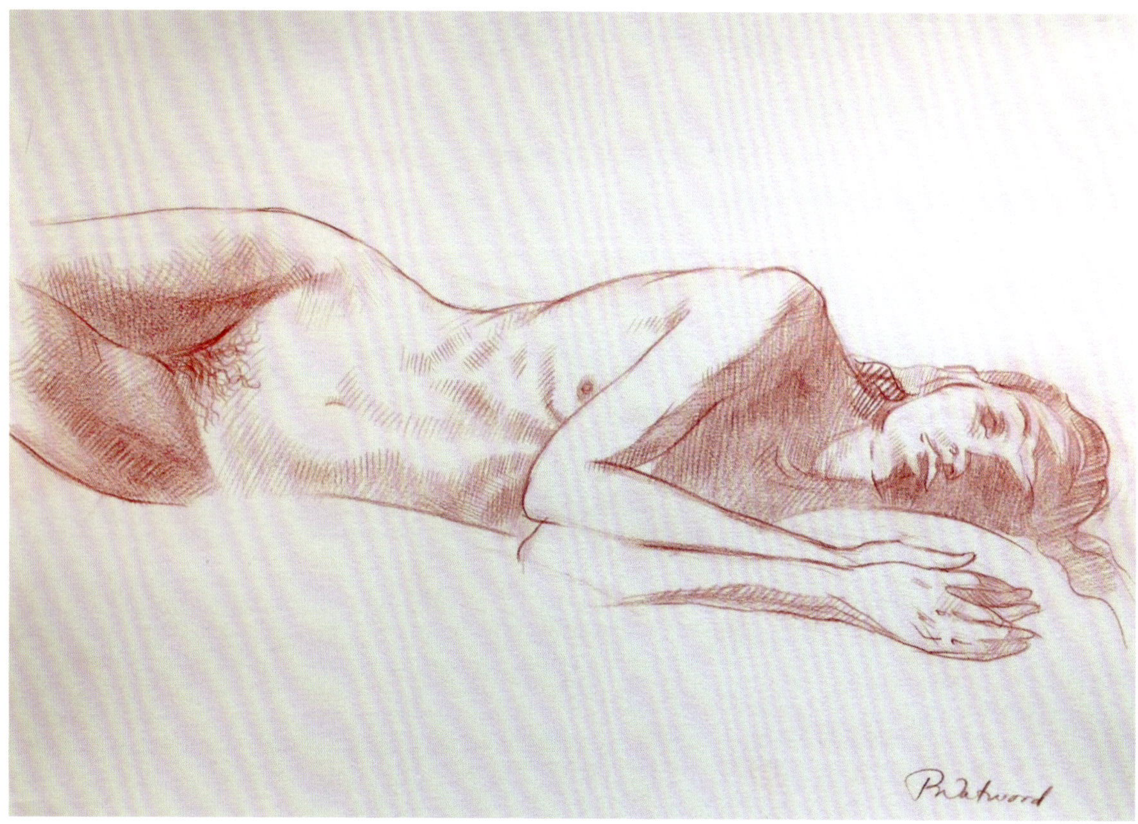

Patricia Watwood, *Figure Sketch,* sanguine colored pencil on gray paper, 11 x 15 inches (28 x 38 cm). Courtesy of the artist.

SKETCHING

For artists, the word *sketch* conveys a state of mind as much as a type of drawing. This mind-set is relaxed, investigatory, and exploratory. The sketch is how I begin when I don't know how to begin. You might expect that as an experienced artist I know what I am doing. I'm afraid not. Instead, I have mastered a set of skills that help me confront new visual information and approach an unknown process. Every time I sketch a figure, as I have done hundreds of times, I encounter a fresh puzzle of *this pose* in *this light* with *this model.* The process of sketching is a path to discover how I might next make a formal work like a finished drawing or painting. Sketching introduces us to the gift of art making. It gives us the capacity to see a world that is infinitely new and endlessly full of discoveries.

The process of drawing is generally built on two stages—the foundational sketch and the finishing graphic elements. Although a finished work may contain no trace of the foundational sketch, know that a trained artist had some armature she used in construction. Dear friend, it's not magic—we cover our tracks.

Even Michelangelo
sometimes ran out of
room for the feet.

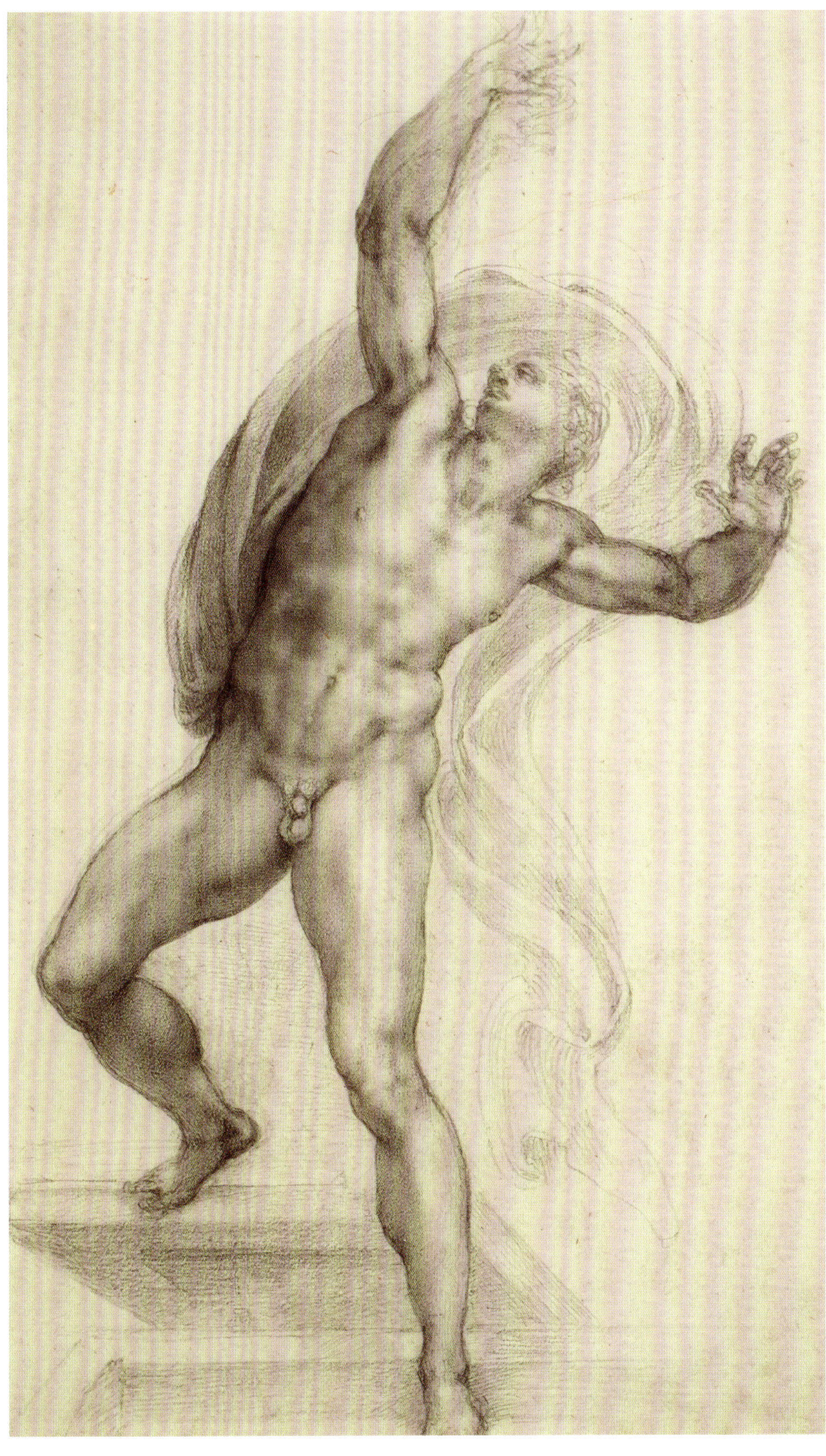

Michelangelo Buonarroti (Italian, 1475–1564), 1532, black chalk on paper, 14½ x 8¾ inches (37 x 22 cm).
Royal Collection Trust, © Her Majesty Queen Elizabeth II.

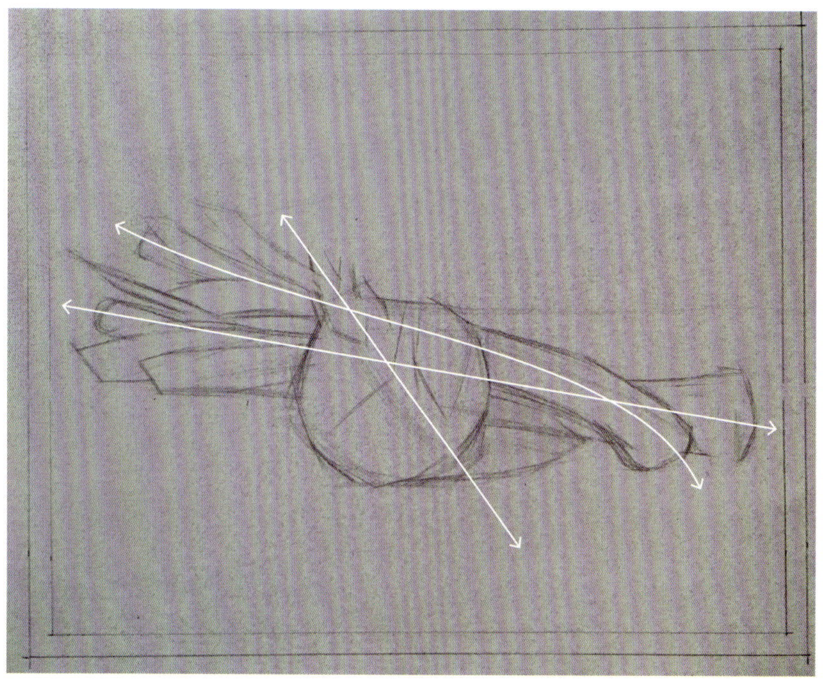

PLANNING PLACEMENT

In sketching the coffee mug, the very first marks you made were for placement. The process of composition began with *where* on the paper and *how big*? For a simple volume like the mug, light marks for the top, bottom, far left, and right of the subject gave you something to build on.

Placement: *Initial marks that plan out the location and size of the object on the page.*

A special note for beginners: There is a problem in drawing that happens to everyone—we start with a placement of one size, but as we work, somehow the drawing tends to grow unintentionally, and we run out of room. To solve this, I like to lightly draw a border around the edges of my page with a margin of about one-half inch (one inch for big sheets). This gives me a bit of wiggle room and strengthens my consciousness of the available space. After you gain experience, you can omit the borders.

In this still life of leeks and an onion, I made a foundation sketch to plan the placement and composition. For an elongated shape like a leek, begin by visualizing the central axis line. Imagine a single line down the center of the volume and draw the axis line where you want it on your paper. Central axis lines are useful for any symmetrical organic form and essential for man-made objects like a bottle. In figure drawing, look for the central axis line of a leg or torso to give you a structural foundation and length on which to build more complex forms.

Central axis lines: *Orientation lines that guide the center and length of an elongated or symmetrical form.*

With my foundation sketch, I sort out problems like placement, angles, proportions, and relationships of things. Once that sketch is set down, I can then begin the stages of creating a detailed drawing.

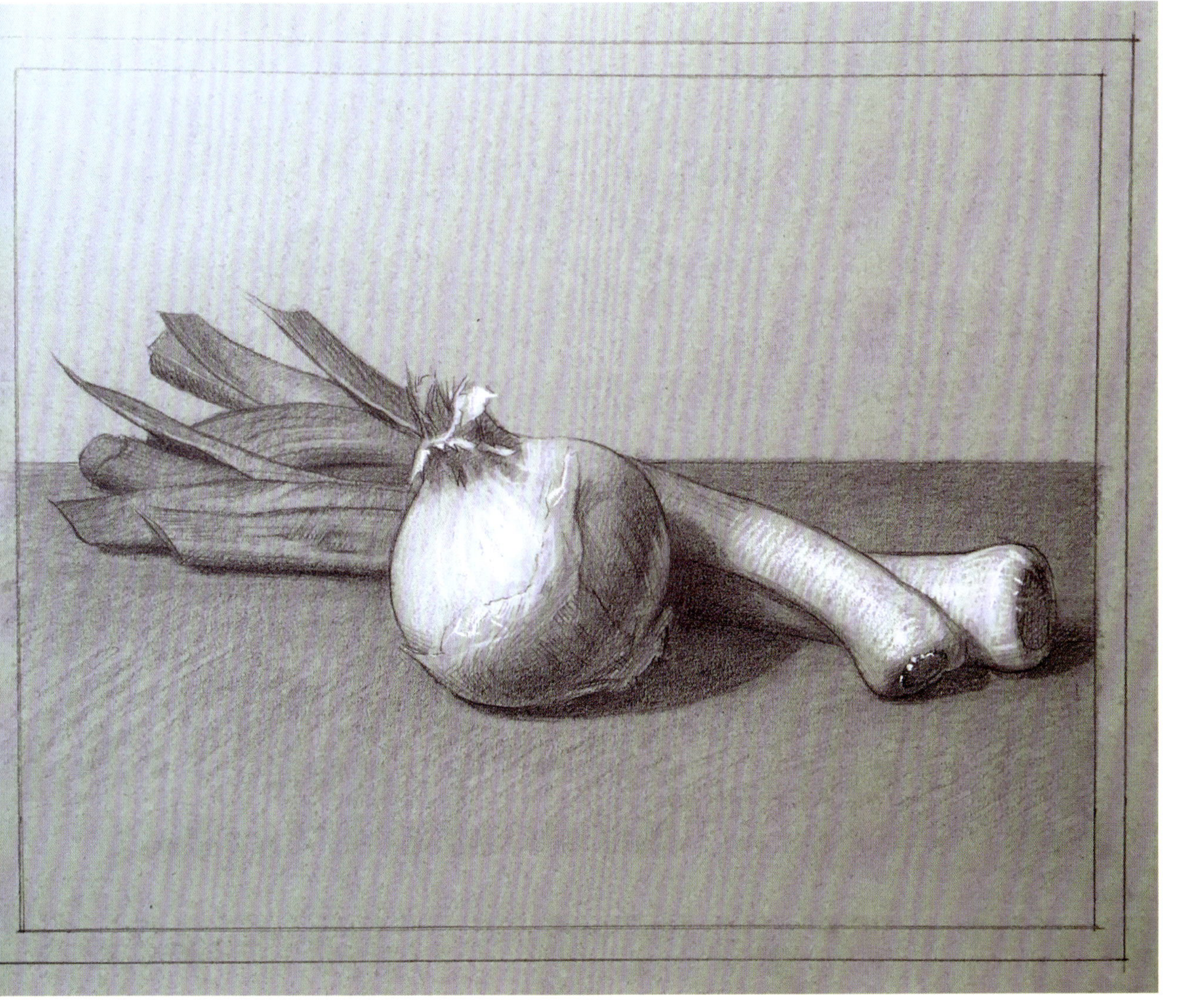

Patricia Watwood, *Leeks and Onion*, 2017, graphite and white pastel on gray paper, 11 x 14 inches (28 x 36 cm). Courtesy of the artist.

TRIANGULATION

One of my favorite tools for orientation when I begin a sketch is *triangulation*. Triangulation checks the angles that connect three different landmarks (easily found visual points on your subject). When you find three points and accurately note the angles that connect them, you find the correct placement of things in relationship to each other. Eventually you will be able to create an overlapping map of two or more triangles, and the correct proportions will fall into place. At any size or distance, triangulation is always a handy guide to keep from feeling lost. (Practice this with the *Draw an Oak Leaf* Project on p. 96).

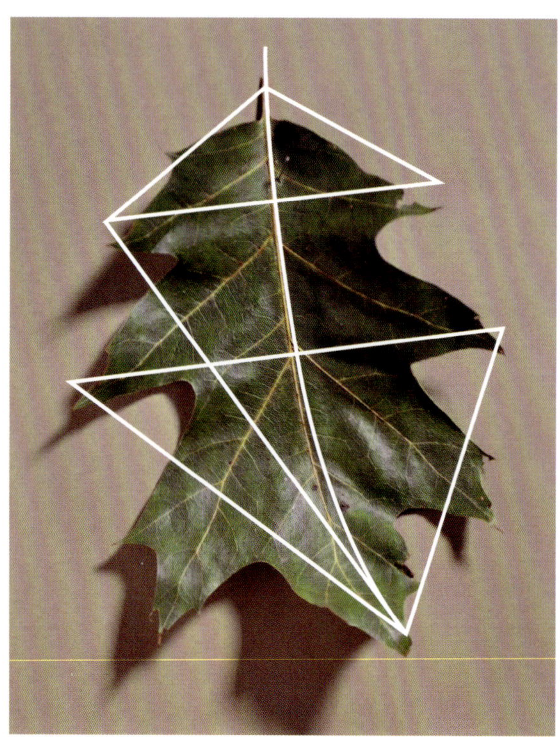
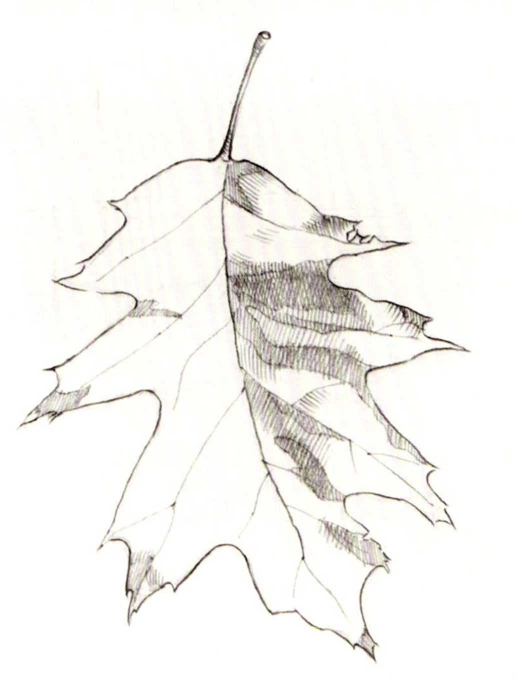

FINDING GEOMETRIC SHAPES

To build our skills at visual literacy, there are a few basic techniques that help us observe with more specificity and organize complex shapes. In the project on pages 53–54, I looked for simple geometric shapes such as the semicircle in the ginkgo leaf. Many organic objects have a substructure of numbers and shapes: three petals or five, a star or a cross. Noting these

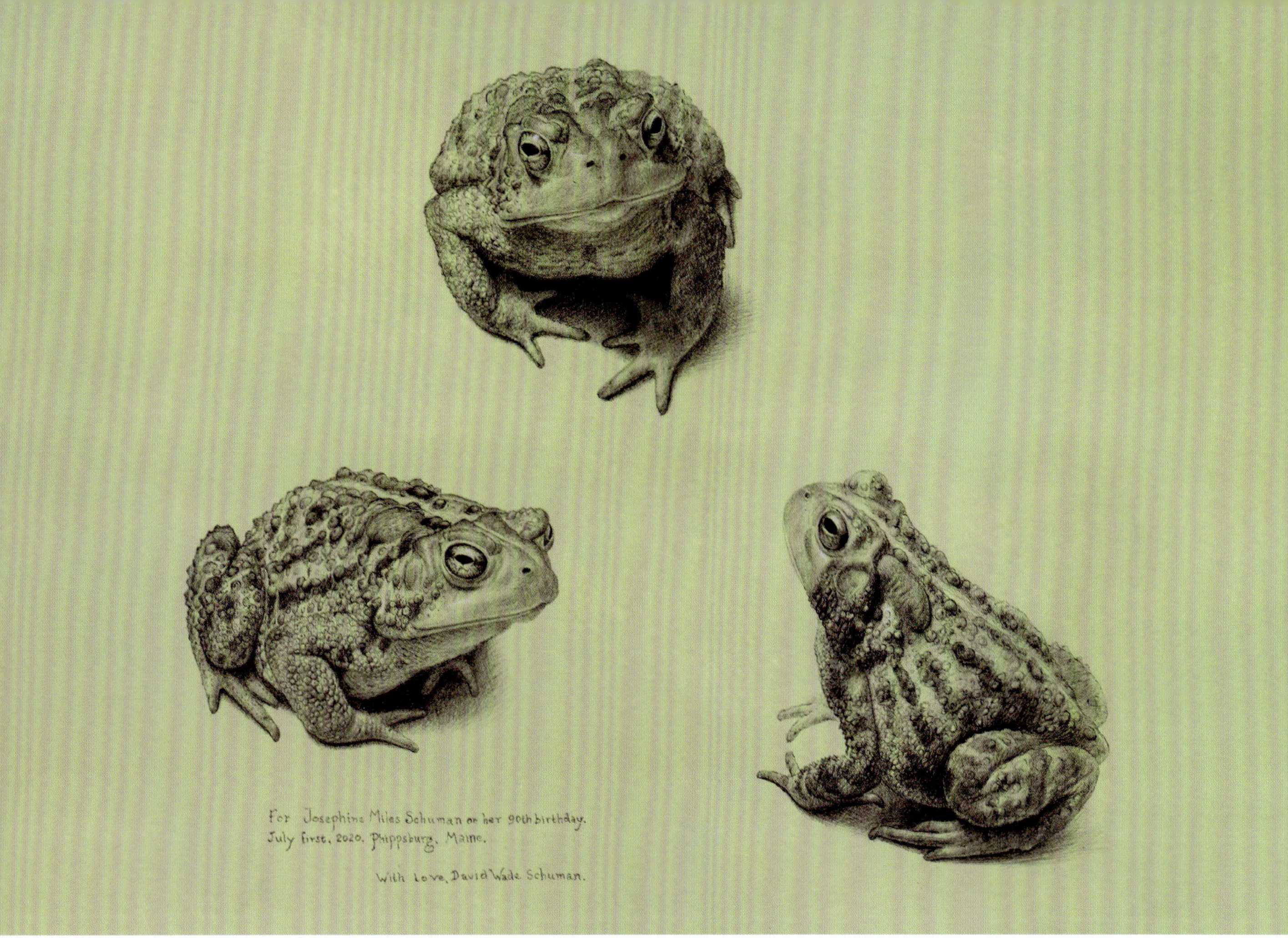

construction patterns saves a lot of time in planning a drawing. When
we look for large relationships, we can use our well-developed sense
of geometric shapes to analyze a form. Triangles, rectangles, squares,
diamonds, circles, ovals—use any of these familiar shapes to help build a
block-in for a drawing.

BLOCK-IN LINES

Block-in is an academic term for the foundation sketch of a drawing in
which the placement, proportions, angles, and shapes of your subject(s) are
mapped using light sketch lines. This is also called *blocking in*.

The block-in is an armature that you create before drawing your
robust lines, shading, and details. It is essential to accuracy in realistic
drawing. Time invested in a good block-in makes subsequent work easier.
The character of the block-in is long, light, and straightish lines, often
with multiple tries, and not firm, specific, or curvilinear lines. When I block

Looking at the outside
shapes of these toads,
I see circles and triangles
that I could use to begin.

Wade Schuman, *Three Toads for
Josephine*, 2020, ballpoint pen on
paper prepared with acrylic,
22 x 18 inches (56 x 46 cm).
Courtesy of the artist.

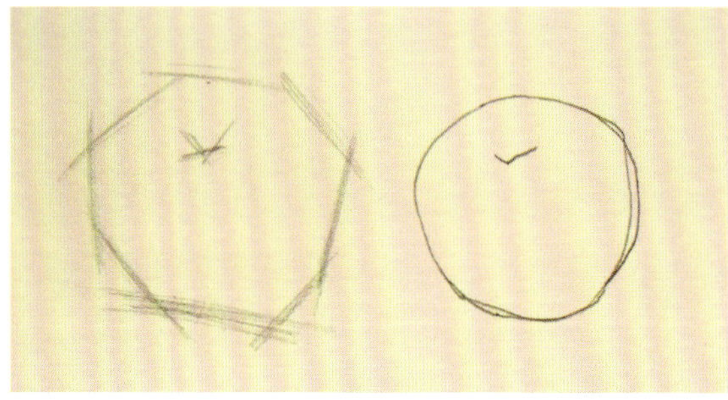

Block–in lines are light, straightish, angular, and inexact. On the left, you see block–in lines mapping out the placement of future contour lines. On the right, I tried to make a continuous contour line without any preliminary planning. The line might be expressive but is less accurate, as even with a trained hand, it is difficult to capture all the inflections of a complex curve in one go.

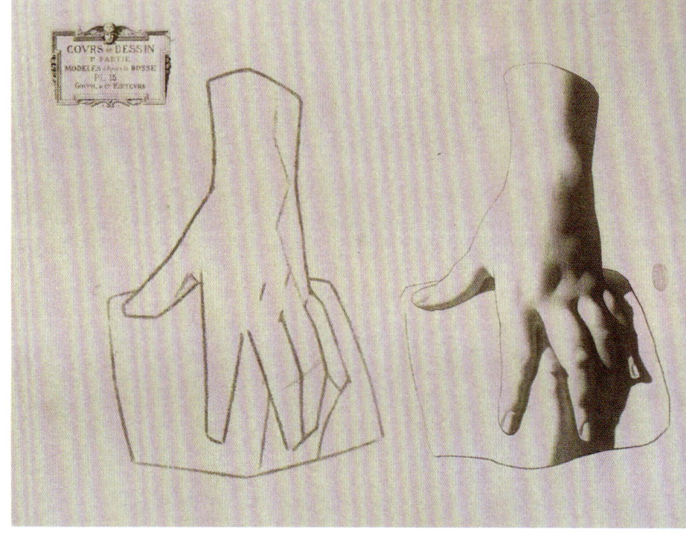

Charles Bargue, Mains, *Main d'une femme pressant son sein,* (Hand of a woman pressing her breast), 1868, lithograph, 24 x 18 inches (60 x 47 cm). Inv. 90.I.1.603 (1). Photo L. Gautier, Mairie de Bordeaux, Musée Goupil. *Note: this image has been rotated and edited to reduce empty space.*

in, I make loose marks and erase generously. I'm not aiming for precise lines, but accuracy within a reasonable margin of error.

The block-in is like the foundation and framing out of a house. It doesn't matter how lovely the plasterwork or marble tiling is on the inside if the framing is all crooked and the foundation isn't sturdy. The block-in stage of your drawing, in light lines, should contain all the proportional, structural, and rhythmic elements you want to include.

This illustration from the nineteenth century is reprinted from the instruction book *Charles Bargue and Jean-Léon Gérôme: Drawing Course.* Many contemporary ateliers (small art schools) still use Bargue plates to teach fundamentals of perceptual drawing and learn Beaux-Arts aesthetics. The plate above shows a simple block-in of a hand that uses long, straight-line segments to plan the placement of the contours for the refined drawing.

When beginning, you'll need to practice simplifying shapes and creating long, delicate lines without bearing down and producing dark marks. As you make multiple corrections, it's natural to make each new line a bit darker. *DON'T!* Be patient with your first efforts. For blocking in, artists will hold their arm out away from the body and draw from the shoulder. This helps make long lines and keeps us looking across big distances. Over time, you'll develop more hand-eye coordination and learn how to sketch lightly in the early stages. Slow down and visualize your intended image and begin the process with openness.

I find this stage useful for taking my emotional temperature while drawing. If I am stressed and hurried, with my muscles tight, it will be very difficult to make a light armature. When I anguish about my drawing going south, my stress will damn the endeavor. I find it essential to straighten up, release my clench, and breathe.

Perhaps you feel that you are not a patient person or can't sit still for ten minutes! Calmness may not come naturally. I want you to know that a creative practice can *change* that. When I was young, I loathed practicing the piano, doing the same thing, badly, over and over. Guess what? I still can't play the piano. However, my commitment to a long-term goal of mastering drawing gave me a way to develop calmness. I did not start out patiently standing at my easel day after day, trying to draw an accurate nude. The practice of drawing changed me slowly over time.

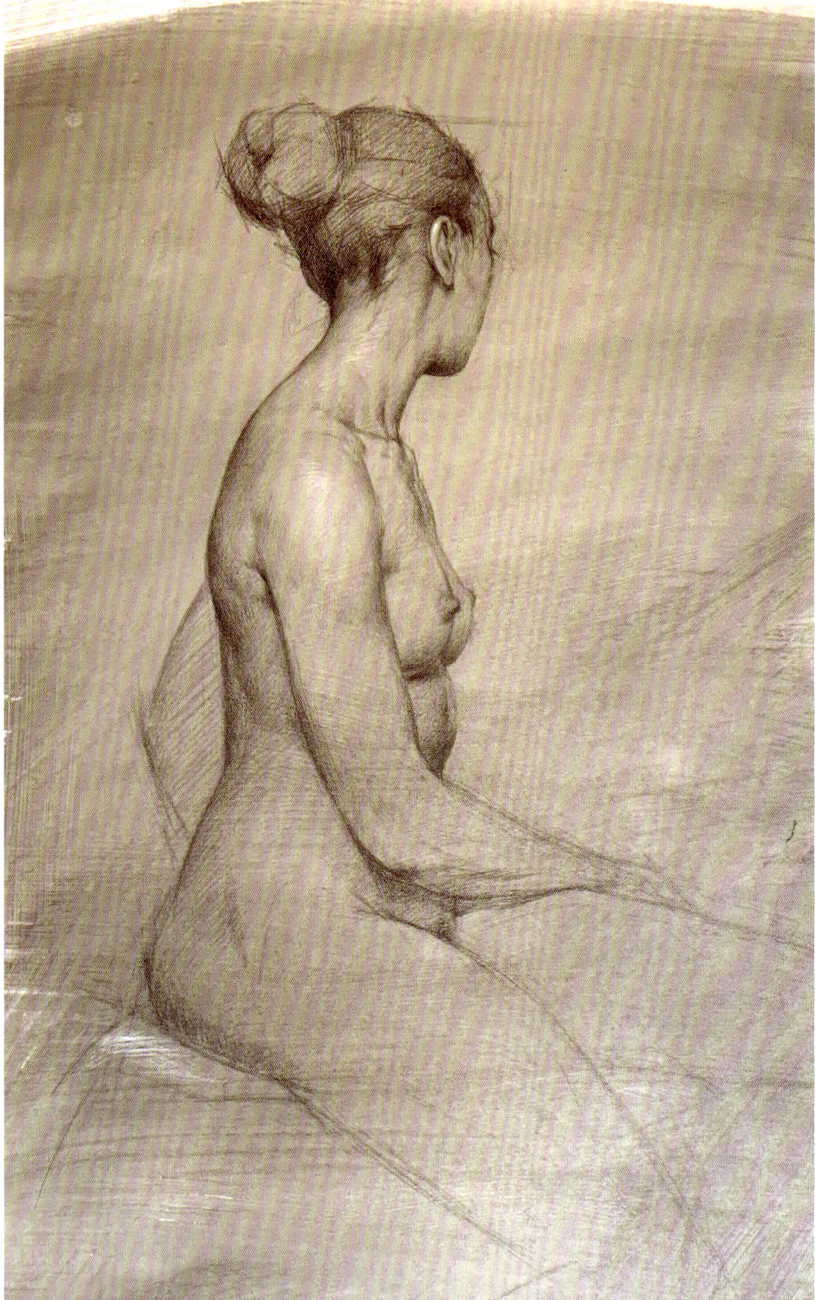

The light lines on the thighs and right arm show the block–in stage of the drawing, while the upper torso and head have been fully resolved on top of the block–in foundation sketch.

Nicole Michelle Tully, *AB (twist),* 2017, graphite and white chalk on paper toned with watercolor, 24 x 18 inches (61 x 46 cm). Courtesy of the artist.

Draw an Oak Leaf

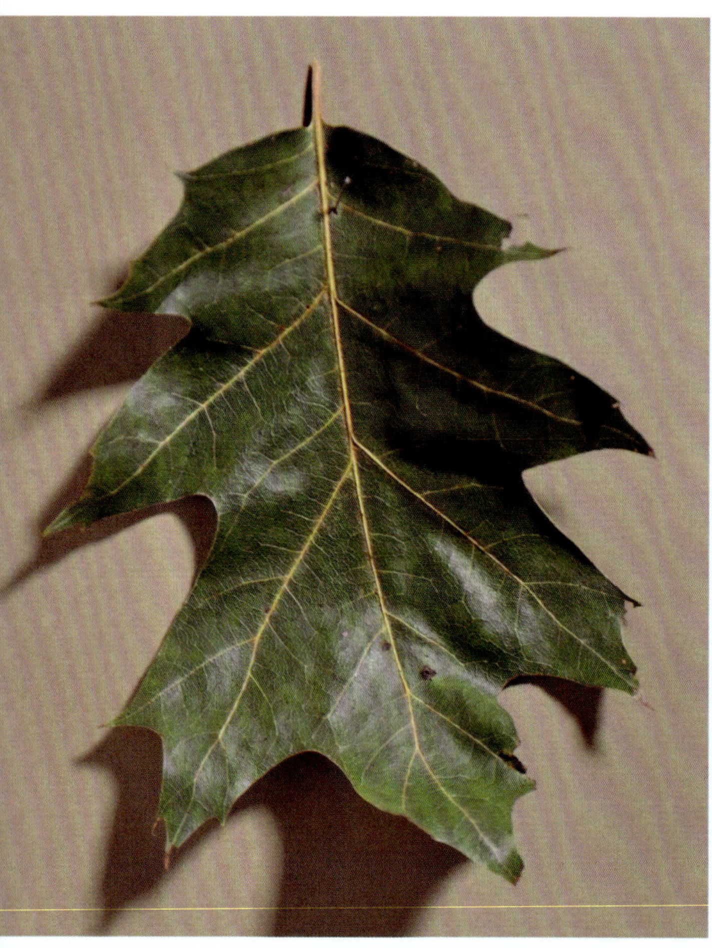

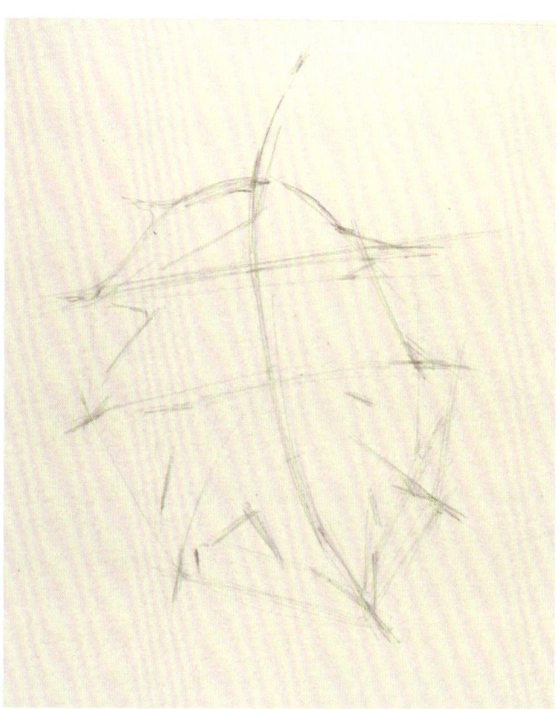

make yourself a small compass rose in the upper corner. Use a ruler to draw a perpendicular cross inside a circle (see p. 81). While you are working, check angles with your knitting needle and compare them to the true horizontal and vertical in the rose compass.

After comparing the true vertical on the compass rose, draw a central axis line for the center vein of the leaf. Make marks for the top, bottom, and sides. Hold up your plumb line to check what point exactly is furthest left or right.

The leaf has seven main points: Look for each as a landmark. Now use long, straight lines across from point to point and around the bottom triangle of points.

In this project, you can practice placement, proportion, measurement, and triangulation. You will learn how to make an initial block-in *underneath*, then a refined contour *on top*.

STEP ONE

Before making any marks, first visualize the drawing you plan to create. How big do you want it? Where should it fit? Make light marks for placement. Next,

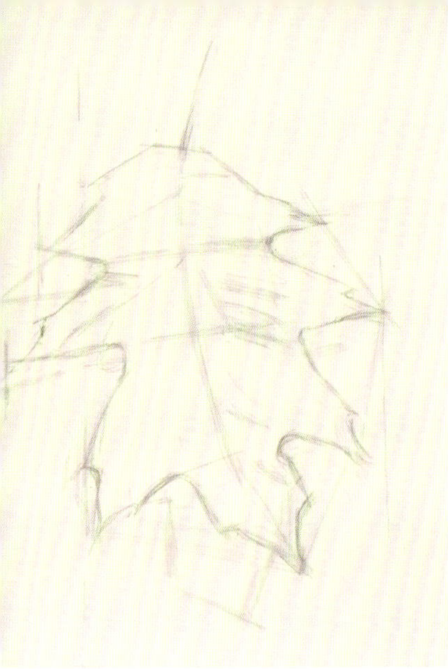 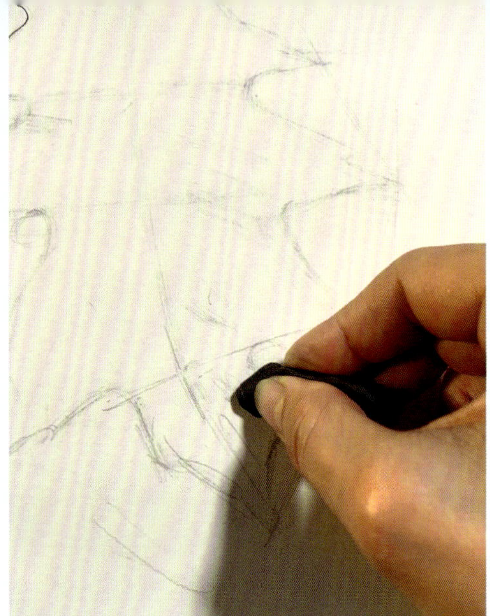 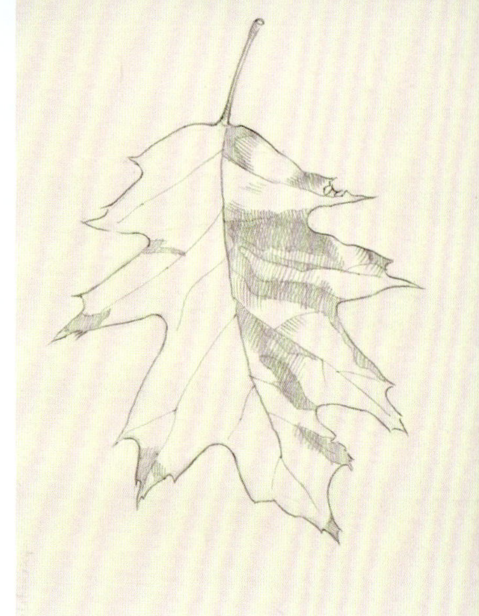

STEP TWO

Measure: Compare the height and width of the leaf with your knitting needle. Are the proportions the same in your drawing? Can you find the halfway point along the central axis of the leaf? How does your midpoint compare? Take the time you need to make adjustments.

Look across two leaf points (at the tip) and compare the angle between the reference and sketch, using your knitting needle or compass rose. Train your eye by moving your focus repeatedly across two points—first on the leaf, then on your drawing.

Triangulate: Look for the leaf point at the bottom and note the relationship to the first two points you checked. What shape triangle do they make on the leaf and on your sketch? Correct so they match. Find another set of three points and check again. Getting all your triangles in agreement can take patience but makes a very accurate placement. See illustration on page 92.

STEP THREE

Develop your block-in by lightly sketching the shapes of the leaf edges. You can use multiple light lines and short segments. Look for the smaller points along the leaf contour, and consider the proportions along a distance to help place them.

You can include interior lines like veins to help you keep track of where you are looking.

Continue to use your knitting needle to check the angles you find along the way. This exercise is full of points to measure and check, and this trains your eye when you take the time to check.

STEP FOUR

Did your block-in lines get a bit messy and dark? No worries: Make a ghost. Just gently rub your flattened kneaded eraser across all the lines. Clean up the junk. Your lines will lighten without being removed completely.

STEP FIVE

With *all that* preparatory work done, make it look like magic by refining sharp contours on top of your map. Follow the edge of the leaf around as if you were navigating a coastline. Start in one spot and make contour lines showing the bends and curves you notice. Work from point to point—find the big ones first and then work out the little bits. Erase away any block-in lines that helped you along the way with your kneaded eraser , shaping it like a bird beak so you can get into the small spaces (see p. 119).

Build up some cross-contour lines, interior veins, and a bit of hatching to give the leaf a rippling surface.

How did your drawing go? I hope you are excited, because you just made a drawing that's much better than you imagined you could produce. Deliberate planning helps you build a solid armature for accurate work. A good block-in stage makes everything go smoothly.

Or what? It's not perfect? Did you feel frustrated that it didn't go as well as you hoped, maybe not as good as the sample? Maybe it took a lot longer than you expected? Well, I can relate to that—I was fretting about mine being good enough to print in this book. Perfectionism is a dogged critical voice that seems bent on ruining our joy in our accomplishments. Most important: You worked on your work. Moreover, you developed techniques that build accurate observations and translated those onto paper.

Your feelings are the raw materials of mindfulness. While they're fresh in your head, take note of your emotional weather. Were you patient? Engrossed? Relaxed? Stymied? Awkward? Harried? All of the above at various points? Were your moods caused by the drawing, or the fight you had with your sister? This flurry of emotions is par for the course when doing creative work. Mindfulness is noticing that flurry while you stay engaged in a project. As you proceed through the lessons in this book, I invite you to reflect regularly on your emotional weather. You'll notice patterns and habits, and over time become familiar with your typical responses while you make art. The goal of mindfulness in our creativity is to notice our feelings both helpful and otherwise, instead of being governed by them.

I'll share more soon on how to quiet the voice of criticism so that you can continue to move forward with equanimity on the path of drawing.

"At age 83, legendary cellist Pablo Casals was asked why he continued to practice four and five hours a day. Casals answered, 'Because I think I am making progress.'"

—LEONARD LYONS

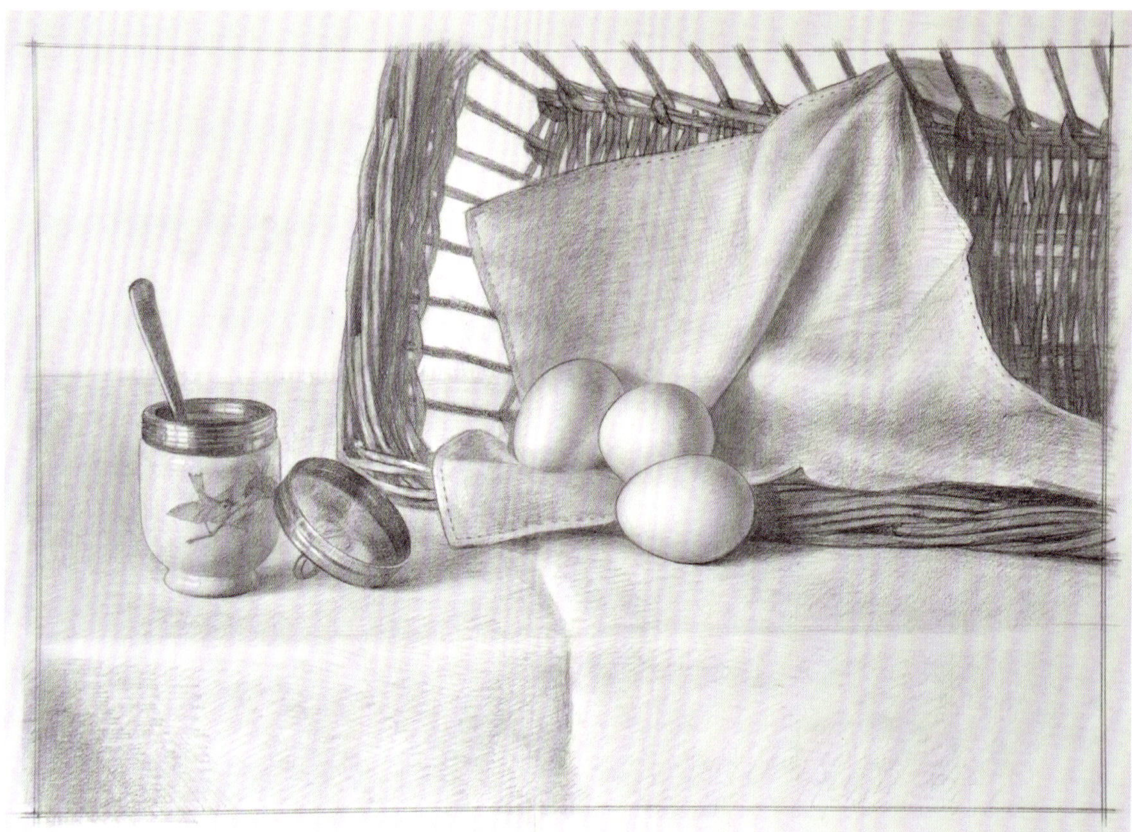

THE ENVELOPE

One of the great challenges in art (and life) is our tendency to miss the forest for the trees. Almost all drawing problems relate to the special challenge of organizing small details within the unified whole. Our eyes tend to focus in, seeing one small area in detail. We must train ourselves to continually look at the big picture and draw the small components to fit properly within the large relationships. In previous projects, we looked carefully at *one thing*, but how do you get to work when you have a *few things* or a complex shape?

One last orientation skill I employ regularly to find my way in a drawing is an *envelope*. The envelope is an irregular shape with three to six sides used to organize the key landmarks of a complex composition or shape. Beginning with the envelope trains our eye to look for the largest possible set of relationships and use that guide as we add the details. I start my figure drawings with an envelope (that's a complicated shape!) and any project that is composed of multiple objects, such as a still life. I find the envelope essential for finding the correct proportions and angles and organizing small details.

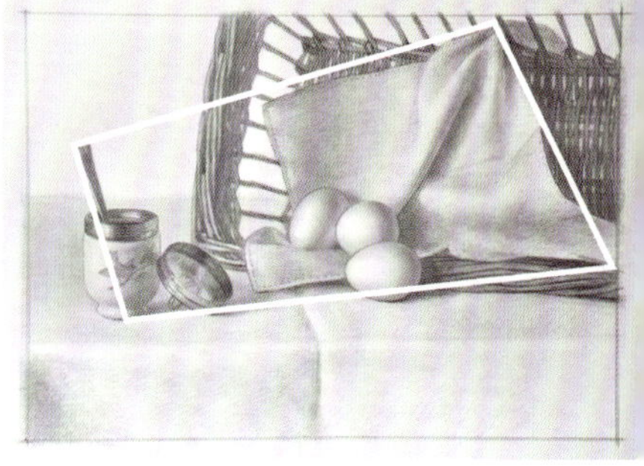

To place a group of objects, look for an envelope—a set of points that frame the objects and help you draw them in relationship to one another and the whole composition.

Patricia Watwood, *Eggs and Basket*, 2011, graphite on paper, 12 x 16 inches (30 x 41 cm). Courtesy of the artist.

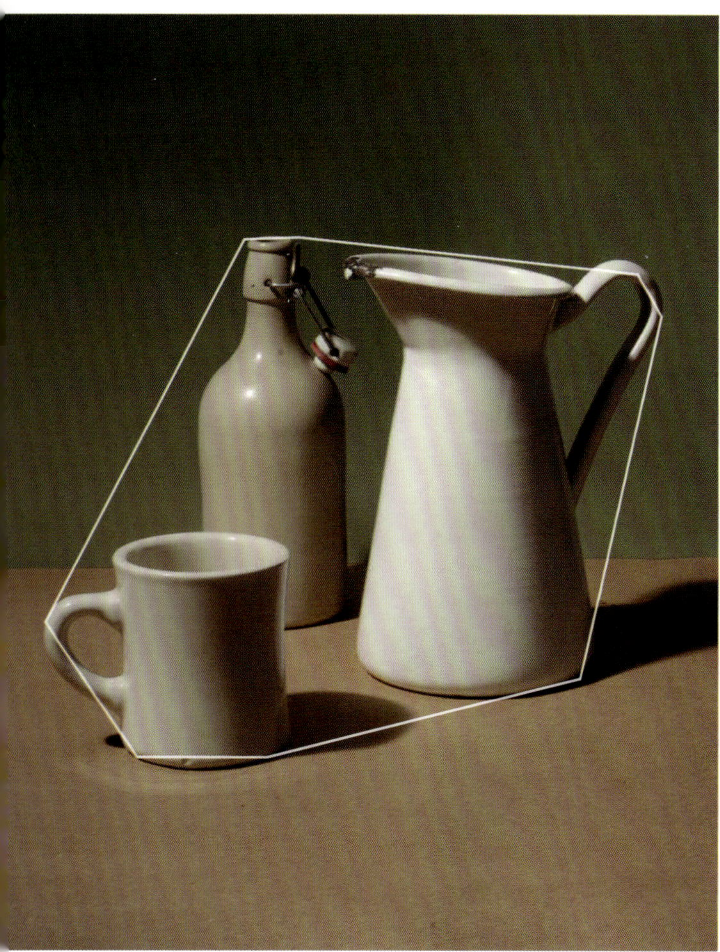

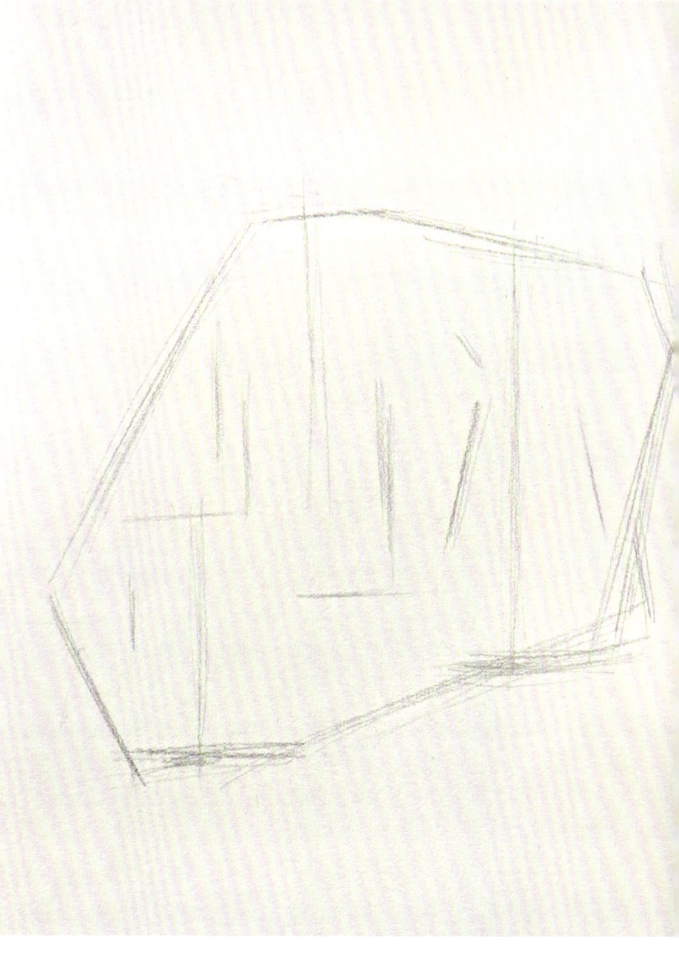

There is a bit of an art to seeing and making the envelope. It is not an exact science, and you will get the knack of using it through some practice and trial and error. In general, look for key positions such as the topmost point and the bottommost point. Then look for strong visual tilts and angles. I will use my knitting needle when I begin to observe these angles accurately. In the drawing *Eggs and Basket* (preceding page), I used the long angle between the bottom of the egg cup and the egg and the angle of the tilt of the spoon. But notice how the egg cup doesn't fit inside the angle I drew down the spoon. Not everything will fit perfectly inside the envelope. Rather, look for major points and large relationships that encompass the subject in general.

Your first tries at an envelope might leave you wondering if you are doing it quite right. With practice, and adding triangulation and measurement, you'll start to develop a sense of what's important and what's

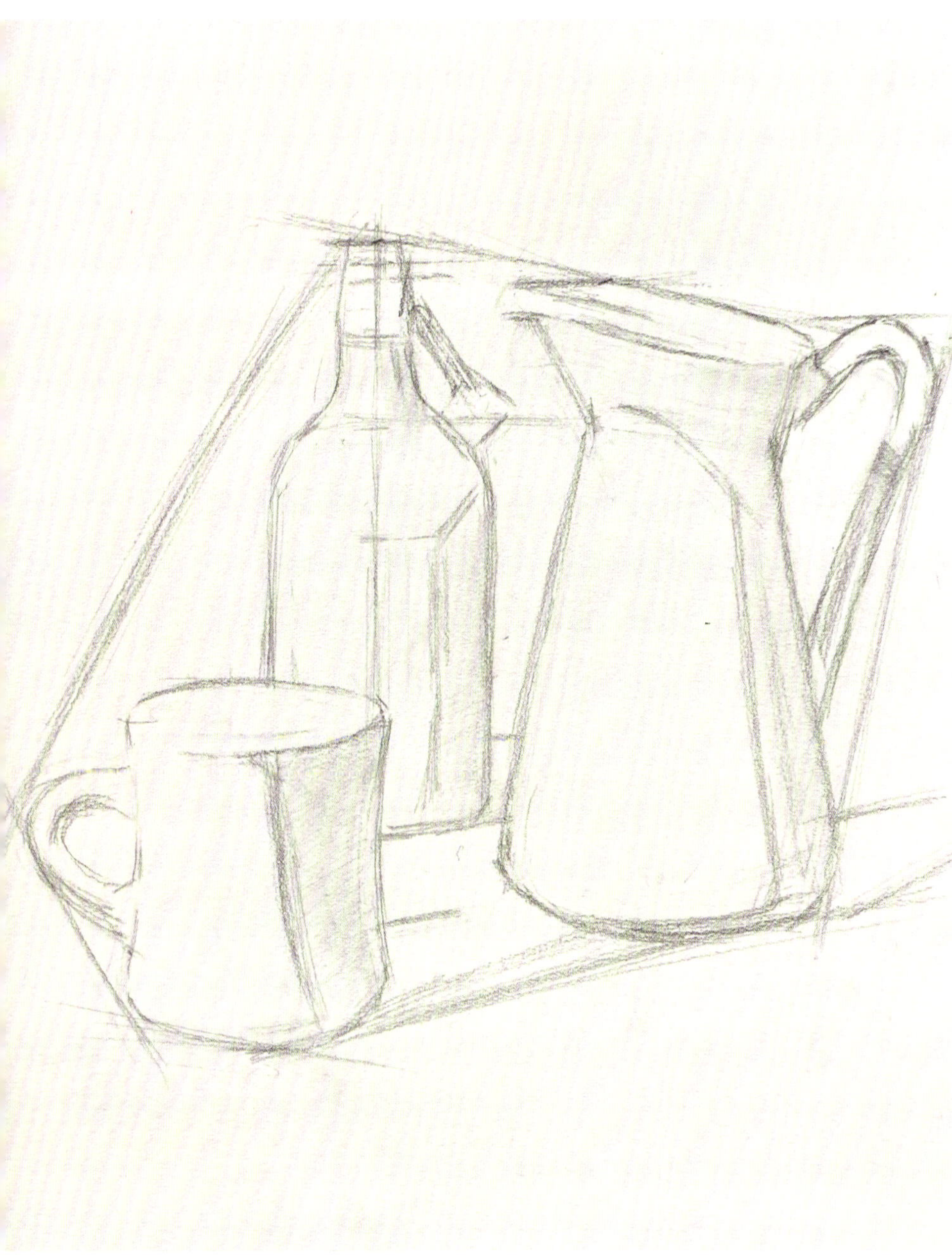

less so, and you'll learn to see the large relationships first. I highly recommend that you persist in exploring this foundational practice. The artist Tony Ryder wrote, "My teacher Ted [Seth Jacobs] said that if we practiced the envelope for a year, we would save ten years of study. I gave it a shot, and two years later, I was teaching figure drawing. In my experience, the practice of the envelope broadens, deepens, and empowers the visual capacity of the mind."[12]

6

Strong Graphic Lines

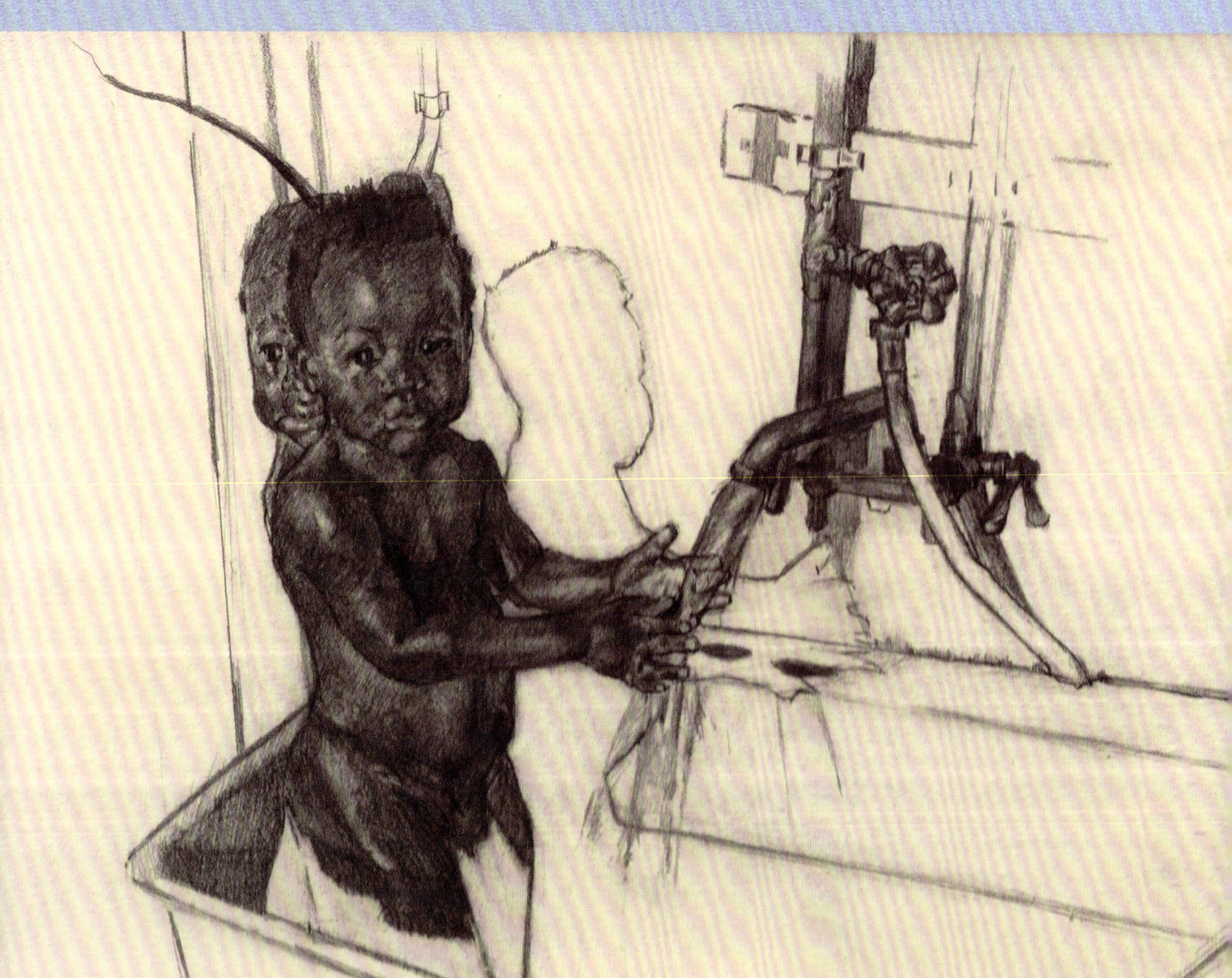

There is a moment of stillness gathered when I touch my pencil to the paper and my eyes, mind, and hand unite in focus. A line can be understood as pulling that instant into a series of moments. If a point is a second, the lines are a record of the pathways of experience on paper. Lines in artwork convey not just graphic information but a record of the state of mind in that experience. Were you exuberant? Quiet? Bold? Shy? Frenetic? Relaxed? Even when we are not conscious of how they do so, our lines express those qualities—and this translation of our experience of emotion into a visual record is the seed of expression.

Let's look at various types of graphic lines that artists use in their work.

Opposite: Steven Anthony Johnson II, *Had I dreams anymore, they would be of a future that I hope you would possess,* 2020, charcoal, graphite, ink and watercolor on mounted paper, 9 x 12 inches (23 x 30 cm). Courtesy of the artist.

CONTOUR LINES

When we think "drawing," the most common idea is a sketch that uses simple outlines to make an image. In art parlance, that outline is called a *contour line*, which defines the outer shape and edges in an object. In simplest terms, this is also the silhouette—the edge that distinguishes the shape of one object from another. The contour of a shape will change depending on your viewpoint of the subject. The contour line is a boundary line that separates the thing from the "not thing" around it. This is also called positive space and negative space in art.

> **Contour:** *The line that defines the edge or shape of an object or form.*

In her portrait drawing at right, Agnes Grochulska articulates contours to define the face, hair, features, and clothing, and she indicates shadows only lightly to shape the graphic impact. She also uses cross-contour lines to describe the surface and interior forms, as we see in the cheeks and forehead.

CROSS-CONTOUR LINES

Often an artist uses linear handling to describe the volume and interior shapes of an object. These lines suggest the surface of the object by mimicking the undulations of the surface with the directions of the line.

Agnes Grochulska, *Liquid Line 1* (detail), 2020, graphite on canvas, 30 x 30 inches (76 x 76 cm). Private collection. Larger image on p. 2.

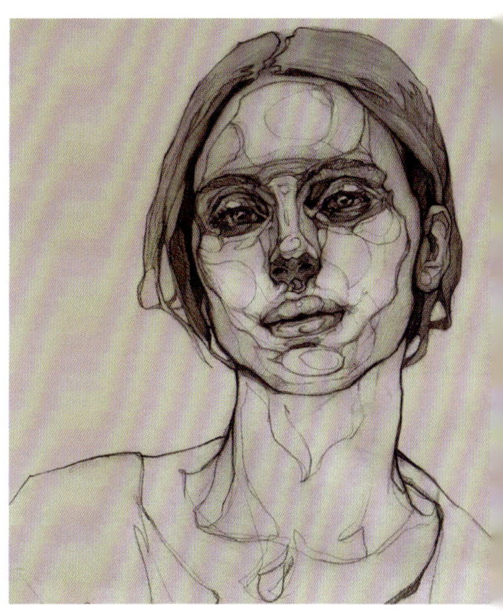

Cross-contour lines can go in multiple directions across a surface, almost like a web.

> **Cross-contour lines:** *Lines that suggest the surface of the object by mimicking the direction the surface moves with the shape of the line. Cross-contour lines can go in multiple directions across a surface, almost like a web.*

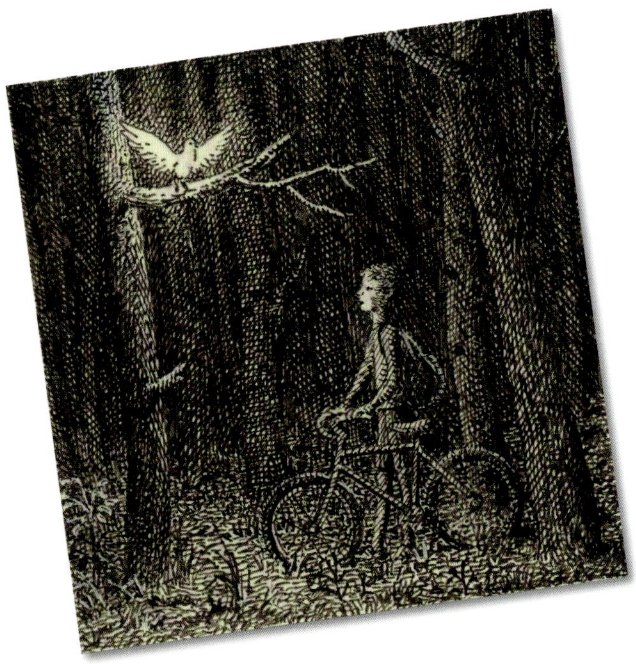

Aron Wiesenfeld, *Post–it Note Drawing #17*, 2021, ink on paper, 3 x 3 inches (7.6 x 7.6 cm). Courtesy of the artist.

GRAPHIC PLAY

The element of play and exploration is essential to creativity. While the structure of regularly scheduled time and discipline to build skills is important, let's not lose sight of the fact that we need *motivation* to do creative work. In her book *The Artist's Way*, author Julia Cameron encourages us to stay connected with our carefree and playful side. "Over an extended period of time, being an artist requires enthusiasm more than discipline." She explains that the artist's self "is actually our child within,"[13] and that it is enthusiasm for play, rather than a duty to work, that entices this child to the creative process.

In developing a practice of creativity, it can be helpful to consider this inner child, and even role-play. You might even invite her to pick out a new toy at the art supply store. Ask her: What sounds like fun to do with scissors and glue? What's your favorite color? We are too quick to lay down silliness and fun in our desire to be taken seriously. Did you grow up hearing this? "When I was a child, I spoke like a child, thought like a child, and reasoned like a child. When I became a man, I gave up my childish ways" (I Corinthians 13:11). My friend, this is not advice for artists. As much as possible, the artist must preserve and protect the spirit of curiosity, adventure, joy, and imagination that came so easily when we were young. Maintaining these qualities is the essence of being young at heart. Playfulness is essential to the continual renewal of creative energy and the experimentation needed to keep your work vital and fresh.

How do we play graphically? Moving beyond doodles and spirals, graphic play is essentially experimenting with linear elements to see where they lead you. Much skill is simply built with repetition and eye-hand coordination—that is a form of graphic play. Play is trying different materials: a glitter blue gel pen, white pen on black paper, or a gold paint pen. My artist child is getting excited just thinking of these options. The idea of working in marker or ink may seem intimidating. Once upon a time, you may have climbed on a bike for the first time, and after some (terrifying) struggle, found yourself flying. A marker is a lot less scary than falling off a bike—so channel that brave child and make some strong graphic imperfect lines.

Agnes Grochulska, *Sketchbook: Sleeping Mookie*, 2018, ink on paper, 9 x 12 inches (23 x 30 cm). Courtesy of the artist.

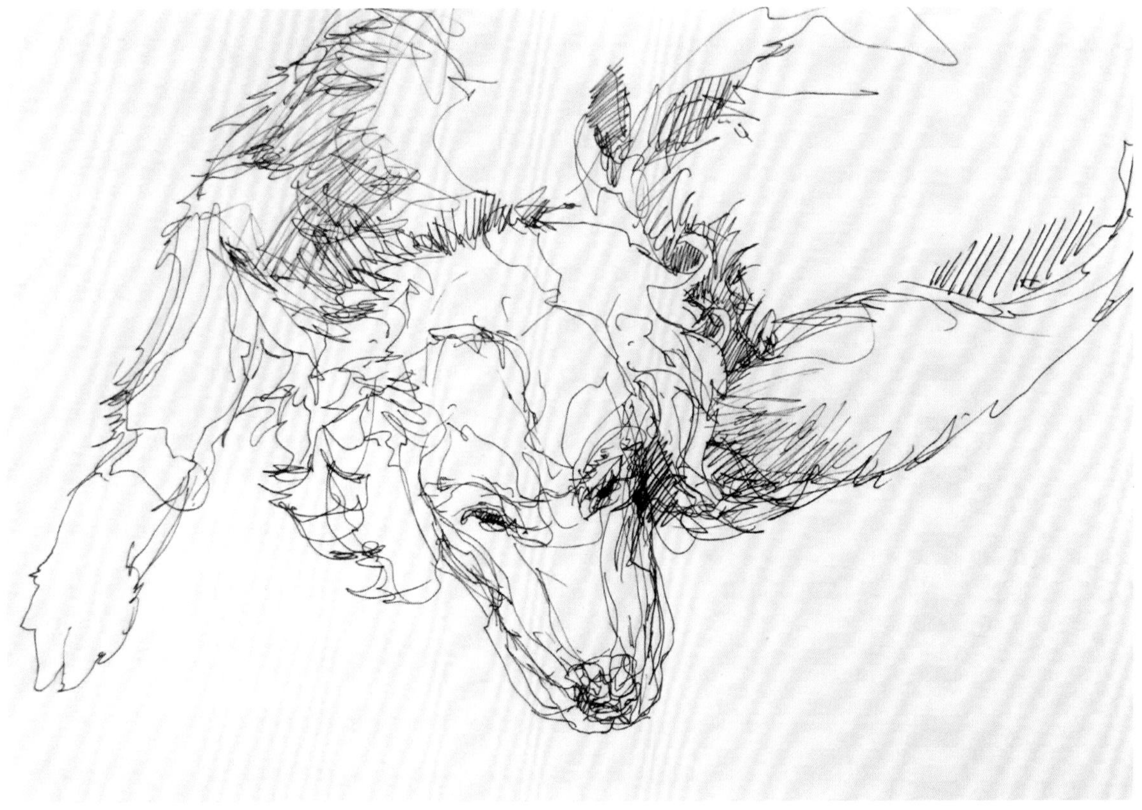

BLIND CONTOUR DRAWING

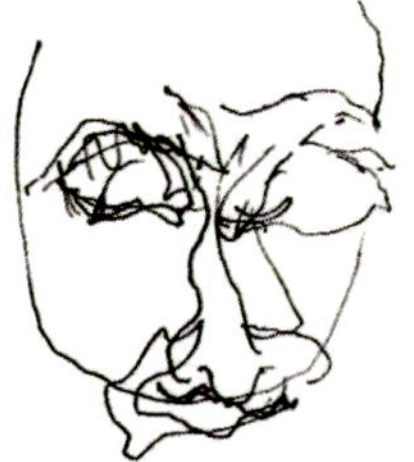

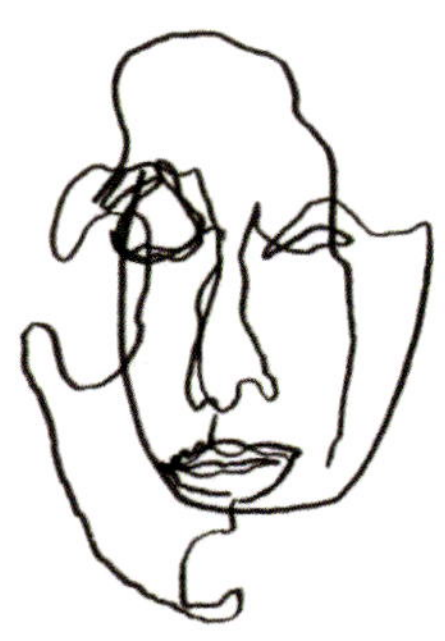

There is a popular type of art school exercise called a "blind contour drawing." To make these, you let your eye follow along the linear edges and parts of, say, a face, and you draw by moving your pencil or marker in a continuous line on the paper without looking at the page. This is fun, and it helps you to observe lines and edges carefully. A great way to break the creative ice, blind contour drawings can be hilarious if you take turns with a friend. The results are sometimes comical, if Picasso-esque, and show how attention to the contour without a planned and measured framework can yield expressive but inaccurate results. Grab a marker and a friend or mirror and try this yourself!

An experienced artist who can deftly craft a well-proportioned linear drawing has trained her eye to plan out the correct placement, even if the process omits, obscures, or erases the preliminary guidance. Often, we find a wonderful free and playful quality to a linear contour. In this sketchbook pigeon, artist Agnes Grochulska uses a lighthearted hand in exploring the

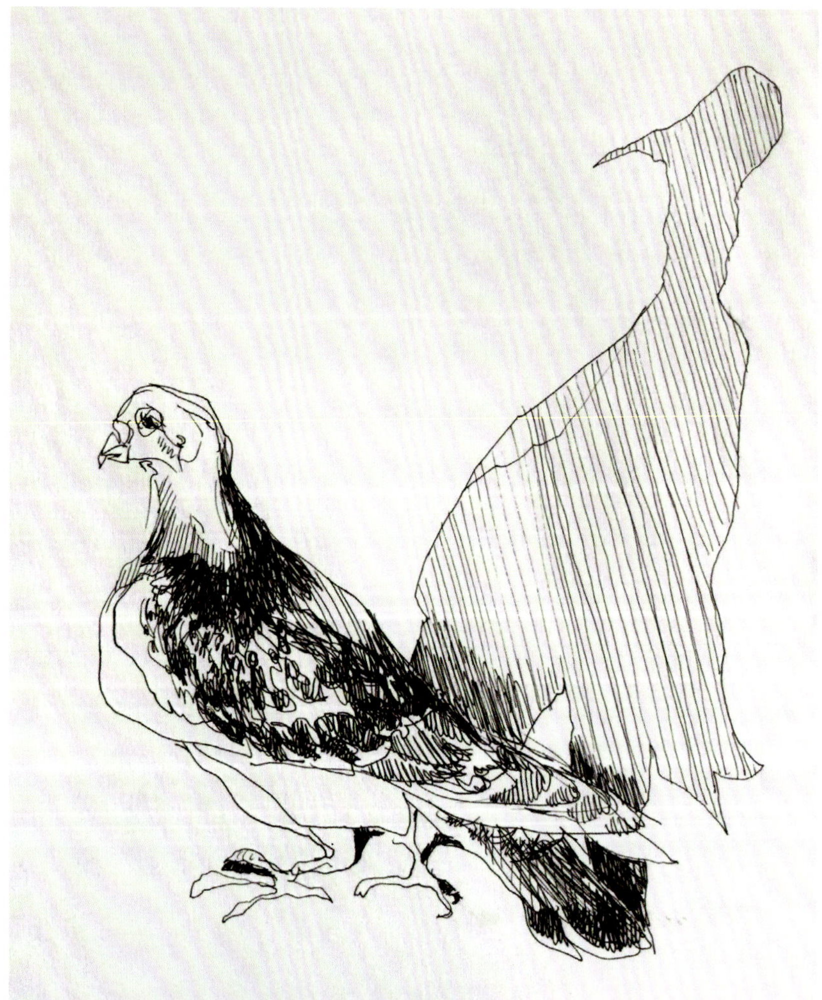

Beaux Watwood, *Blind Contour Drawings of Willa,* 2020, ink on paper, 8 x 10 inches (20 x 25 cm). Courtesy of the artist.

Agnes Grochulska, *Sketchbook: City Pigeons,* 2018, ink on paper, 9 x 12 inches (23 x 30 cm). Courtesy of the artist.

contours and interior markings of the feathers, while the playful linear definition around the cast shadow adds a comic character to her bird.

When drawing in ink, the line is inescapable. The artist Austin Uzor embraces this challenge by using atmospheric gestural lines to create a sense of space and energy. Instead of using a strong contour line, he has first lightly marked the boundaries of shape and then built up a density of darker tones with cross-hatching. This approach of layering lines and hatching to make shapes allows for changes and corrections to become hidden under the dense layers. Instead of being limited by the tyranny of ink, Uzor's technique transforms lines into a new graphic language.

Below, left: Austin Uzor, *Untitled 2,* 2020, Ballpoint pen on paper, 12 x 8½ inches (30 x 22 cm). Courtesy of the artist.

Austin Uzor, *Untitled,* 2020, ballpoint pen on paper, 12 x 8½ inches (30 x 22 cm). Courtesy of the artist.

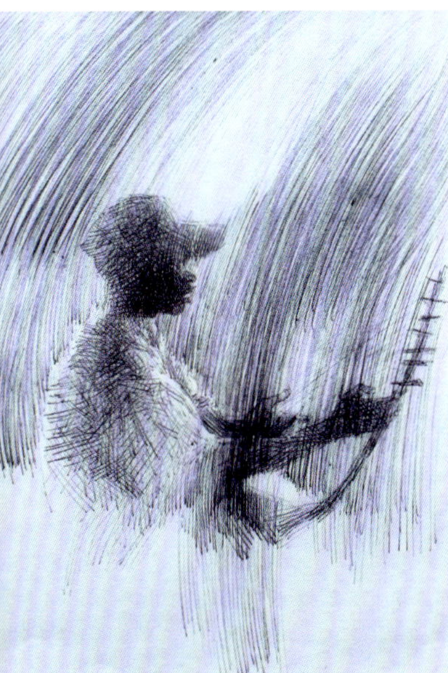

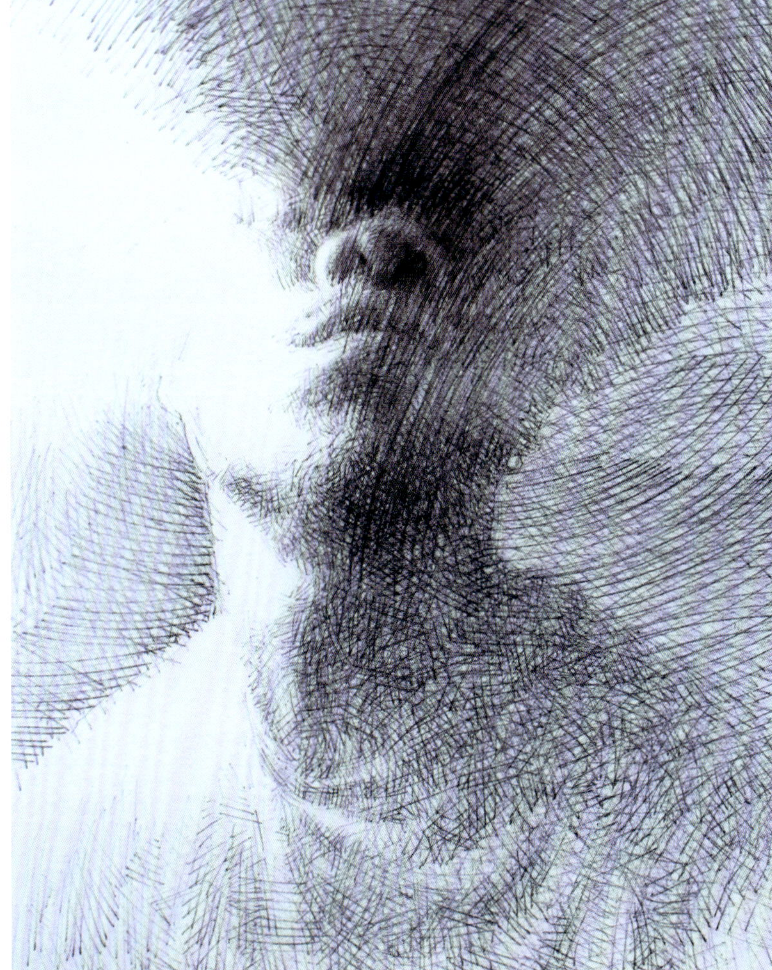

FINDING JOY IN UNEXPECTED PLACES

Another childlike quality that can unlock new creative paths is the lovely ability kids have to make a playhouse of any random set of oddballs. A cardboard box and a cupboard of forgotten junk is enough material for most youngsters to embark on a mission of construction and imagination. How can we model those young people's skills as adventurers? After all those years of walking around shiny, hushed museums where we get yelled at for touching anything, art can feel highbrow and rarefied. A wonderful way to break open that "no fun" zone is with a project I call "What's in your junk drawer?"

Come on, I know you have a junk drawer—or at least a zipper pocket of forgotten treasures in your backpack. Crack it open and look at what's inside. Pull out five or six items, and let's make a drawing. Looking in the least likely place to find something useful and beautiful might be the perfect way to accidentally discover new creative ideas. Even your junk drawer is unique.

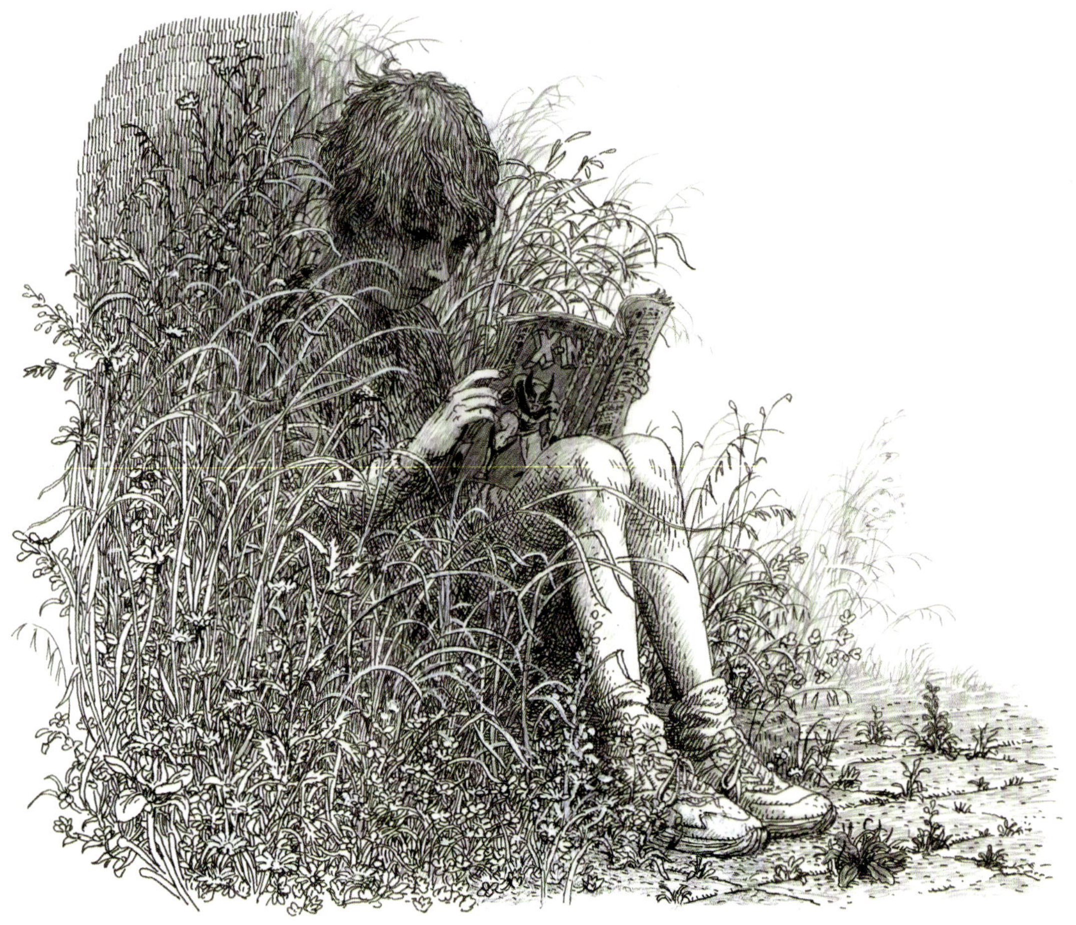

Aron Wiesenfeld, *Reading X-Men*, 2020, ink and graphite on paper, 11 x 14 inches (28 x 36 cm). Courtesy of the artist.

What's in Your Junk Drawer?

The elements selected for this demo are all man-made objects that have symmetrical shapes and many straight edges. These will be useful for exploring lines and graphic play. If you want to gauge your accuracy in proportions, you can use a ruler to check your spacing and lengths or to help with long straight lines.

STEP ONE

Before drawing, lay out the junk drawer items in a shape and with spacing that fits your sketchbook. Make a linear border to emphasize the composition edges and create the style of a technical drawing. Set your objects flat on a table and look down at them, making the composition a "plan view."

Focus on proportion and spacing: Using long axis lines to set up the placement of each item, compare the heights and widths of each piece. You can use a ruler or knitting needle to look across from object to object. Try doing everything by eye first, and then check with a ruler if it seems out of whack.

Next, rough in a block-in shape of each piece, looking for geometric shapes, like rectangles, circles, and triangles.

STEP TWO

With the placement planned with the block-in, now focus on one item at a time and refine the contours. Erase block-in lines you don't need.

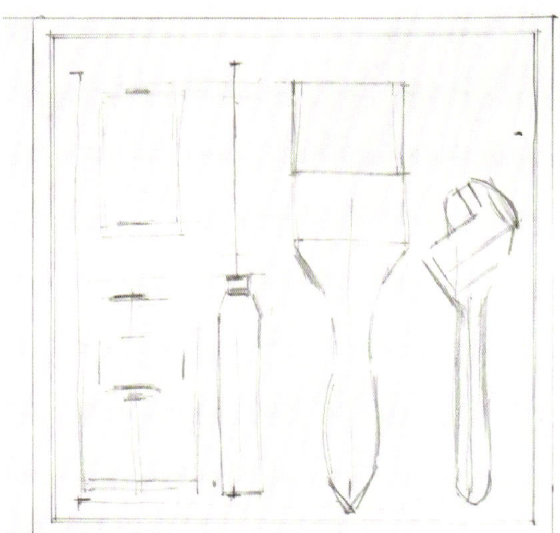

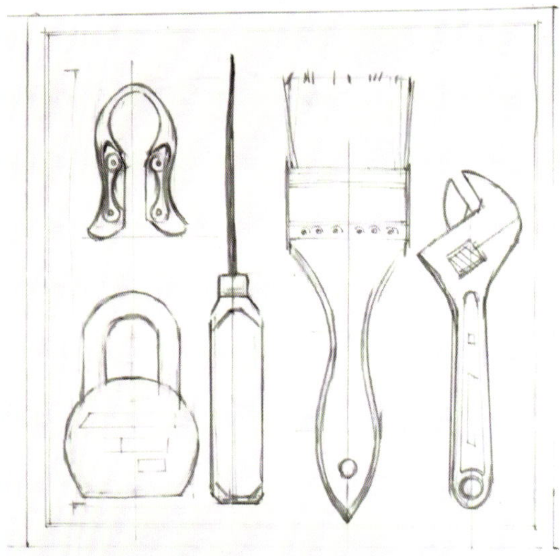

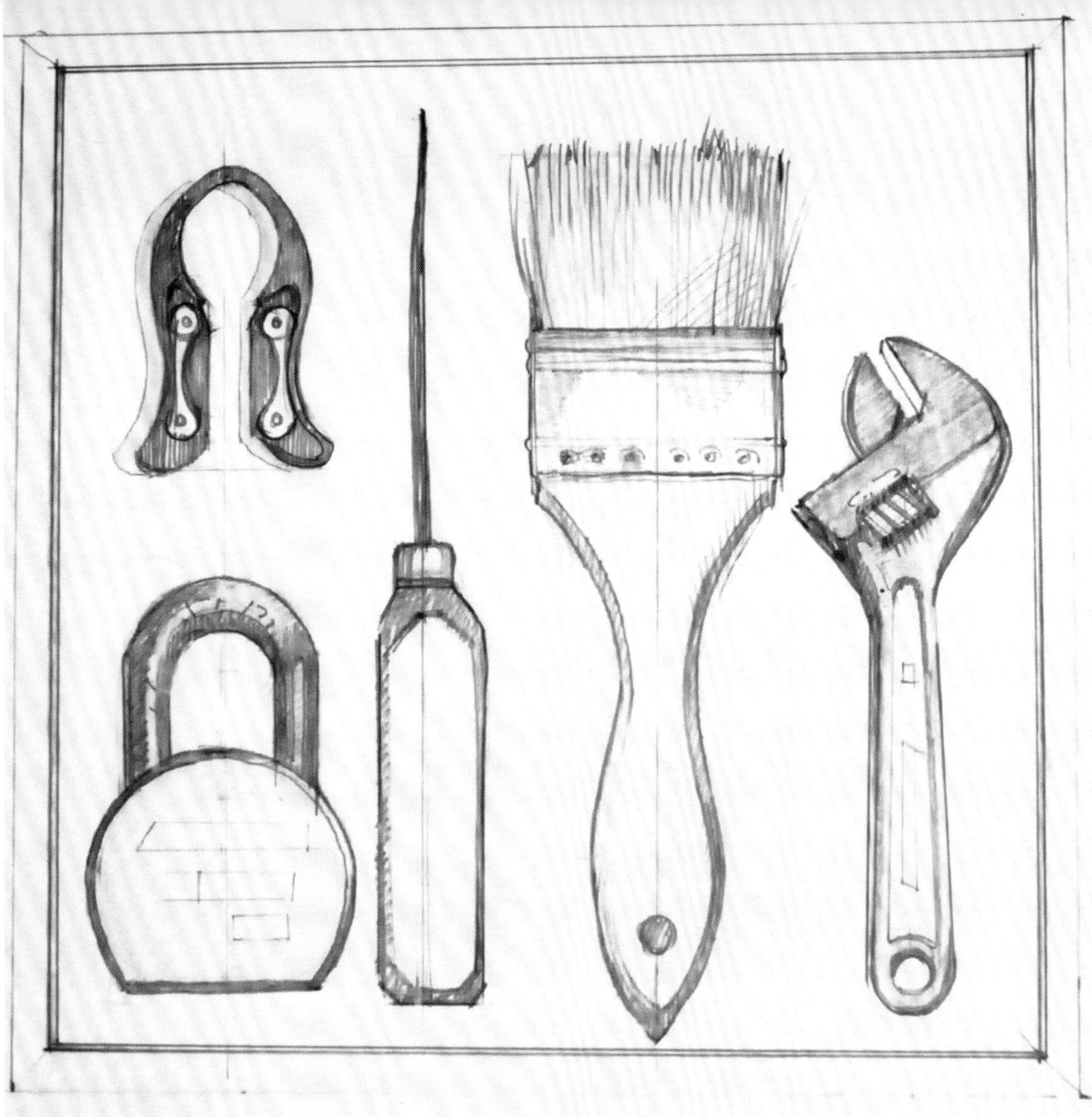

Man-made objects have many symmetries. Draw a centerline down the brush with a ruler and measure for the widest and narrowest points.

Explore various line weights and use darker lines for the exterior contours and lighter lines for interior shapes.

STEP THREE

Add graphic variety by darkening some of the shapes and planes. The shading at the edges gives a sense of thickness to the items. I hatch in tone and then blend with a stump to make a smooth gray. Light feathery lines suggest the bristles, and dark lines mimic the sharpness of that ominous ice pick.

Did your imagination start to roam free while you concentrated on these overlooked objects? A crescent wrench starts to seem like a dinosaur head and a rusty ice pick reminds me of making ice cream in my grandmother's garage. Associations of texture and shape can send your mind on an imaginative journey to unexpected places. These are the childish ways we must cherish and protect our creativity.

POSITIVE AND NEGATIVE SPACE

This diagram shows many different negative and positive spaces I looked for while creating the demo for the next project, *Drawing Bottles* (p. 117). Holding a ruler horizontally at the top of the middle bottle, I can see how much empty space is above the left one. On the ground plane, horizontal lines help me correctly distance each bottle from the bottom edge. Looking at the negative spaces between the bottles (and imagining the bottle where it disappears behind) helps me space them out. By looking carefully at both the proportions of the positive shapes (the bottles) and the negative spaces around them, I more easily fit various objects in the right relationship in the composition.

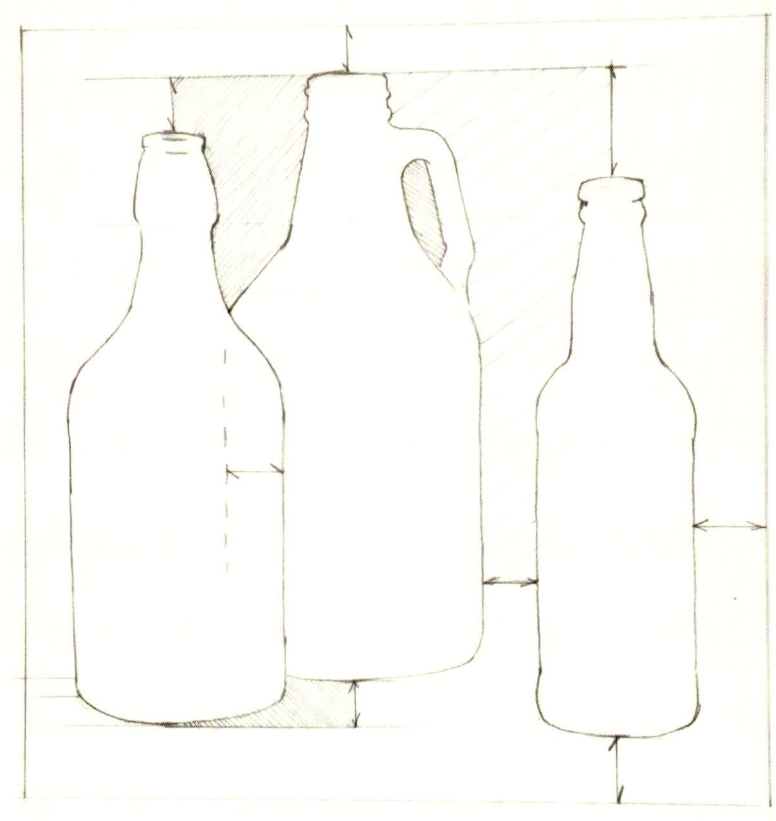

To learn to use negative and positive space, find three different bottles and set them up on a table nearby, spacing them apart. Can you see the spaces between the bottles, and on the table around them? Artists learn to see both the bottles and the spaces as flat shapes, and use them gauge proportion and spatial relationship. Our next project, on p. 117, will build this skill.

LINE WEIGHT

To develop more masterful drawing, pay special attention to two things: line weight and the use of overlaps. Both of these techniques are essential for

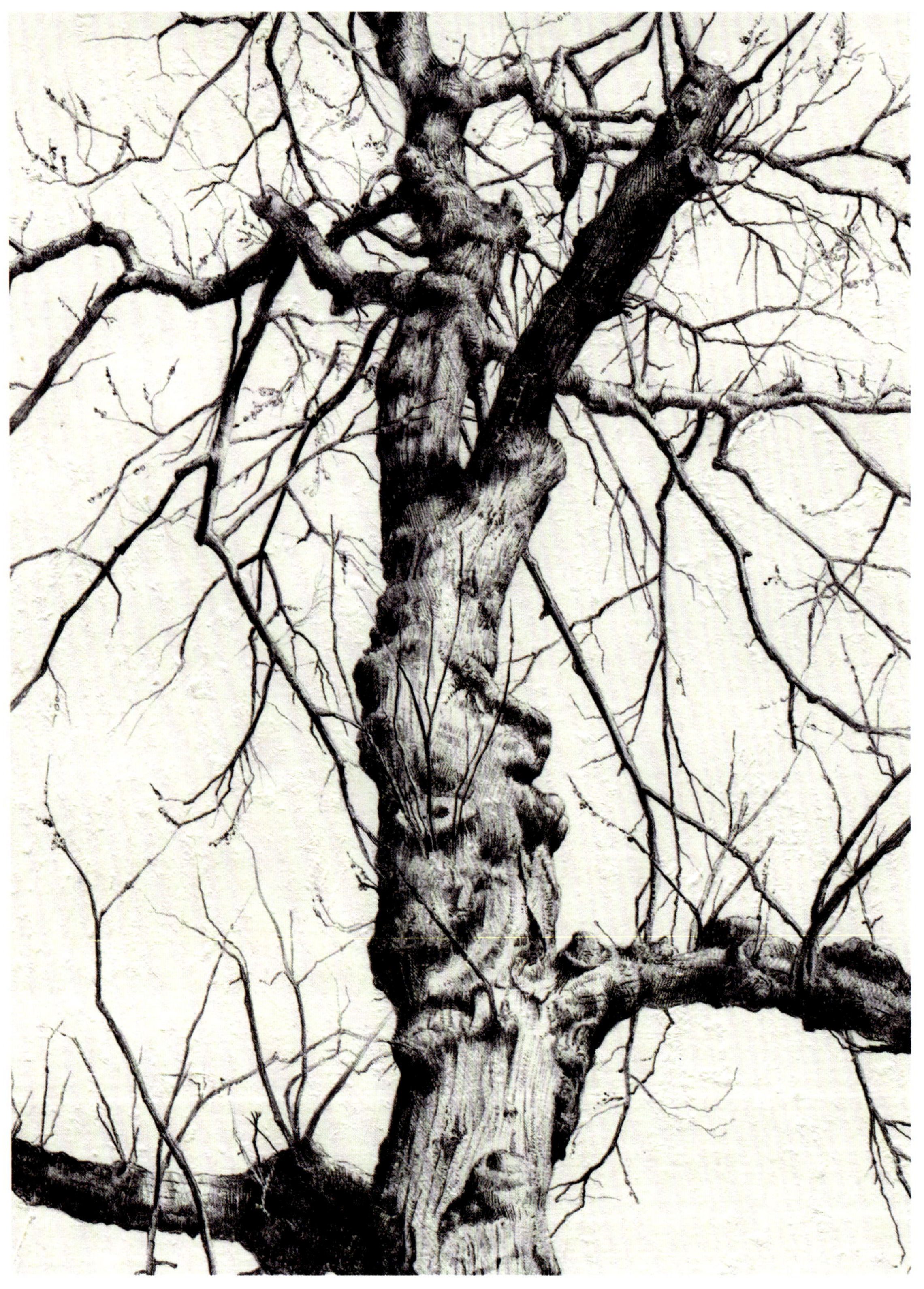

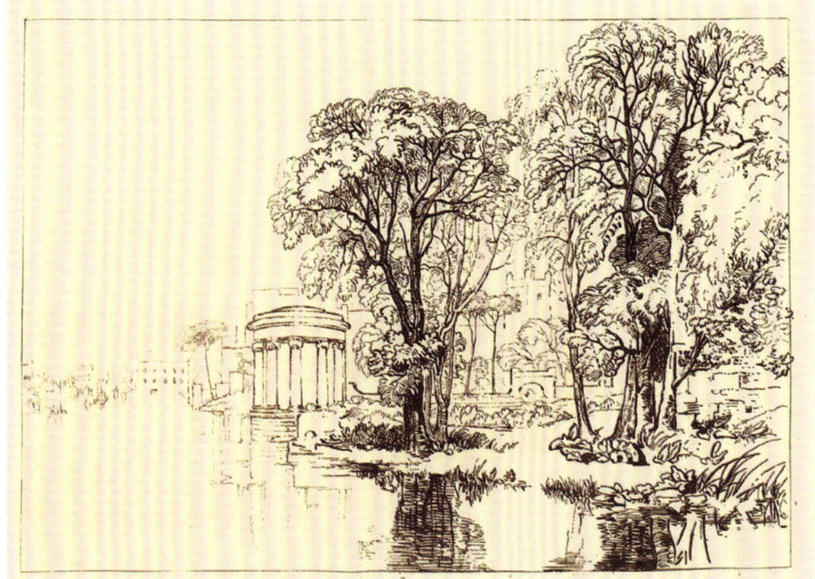

helping to define space, showing the artist's organization of one form from another, and creating a pleasing graphic style that leads the eye around a drawing. With the "Hit the Dot" exercise (p. 38), you started to build some manual dexterity and control in varying line weight. Let's consider how to use that variety of line to useful effect.

First, a dark, single line draws the eye to that particular edge of a form and tends to stand out. A strong line conveys energy that is confident, emphatic, and accents the two-dimensional quality of the paper and material. In Marina Terauds's dynamic *Dandelion* (next page), the use of line pulls our eye out to each point of the composition, where the jagged and complicated contours slow us down to dwell on the leaf shape. The fine single lines for the roots trail off and evoke delicate tendrils. The lines of each plant stem make an exuberant firework of shape that arrests the eye.

A delicate line speaks with more reserve, like a poetic whisper. Dark lines tend to advance. Light lines tend to recede. This alone can help your drawing take on an element of pictorial space. *Atmospheric perspective* in art is created by using darker values and more contrast in objects closer to the viewer, and lighter lines with less contrast the farther away objects fall in space. A common mistake for beginners is to make all the lines dark and overworked as they search for a correct contour. This ends up flattening forms and making the overall graphic image clumsy. Begin delicately, and make conscious choices about where to place an assertive line for spatial or design emphasis.

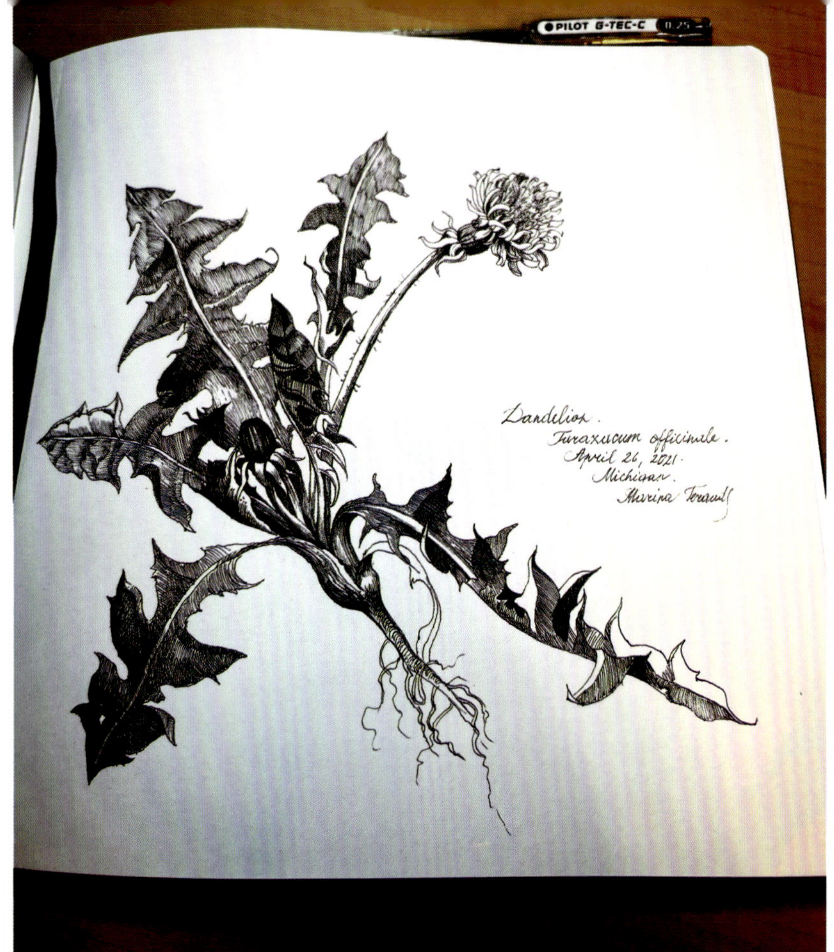

Line weights show what objects are in front and what is receding away from your eye in space. In the delicate drawing of a hyacinth, at right, artist Andrew S. Conklin paid patient attention to how the various leaves are arranged in space as shown through line weight, overlapping contours, and erasure of hidden bits. Darker accent lines draw the eye to the central blossom and bulb. Often an artist will begin this spatial organization by drawing all the lines in, then strengthen lines they want to keep and erase parts that are hidden. Slow down and pay special attention to where one contour disappears behind another form.

TANGENT AND OVERLAPPING LINES

A special note about the effect of lines that run tangent: Try to avoid places in your drawing composition where the lines curve up next to each other and "kiss" without overlapping. In the two-dimensional realm of your paper, these tangent lines both draw the eye strongly and will "attach" to each other graphically; they also tend to flatten out the image on the surface of

the paper. Unless you are making a specific *choice* to create a visual effect
with a tangent line, it generally works best to have the lines more clearly
cut across one another. Watch out for unintentional tangent lines for better
composition and spatial relationships.

On the other hand, the careful use of overlap in contours can really
improve the sense of space and placement. Clear overlaps help one form
project clearly in front of another. Always look to see what things are forward
and what goes back, and carefully erase stray marks that cross into the form
in front.

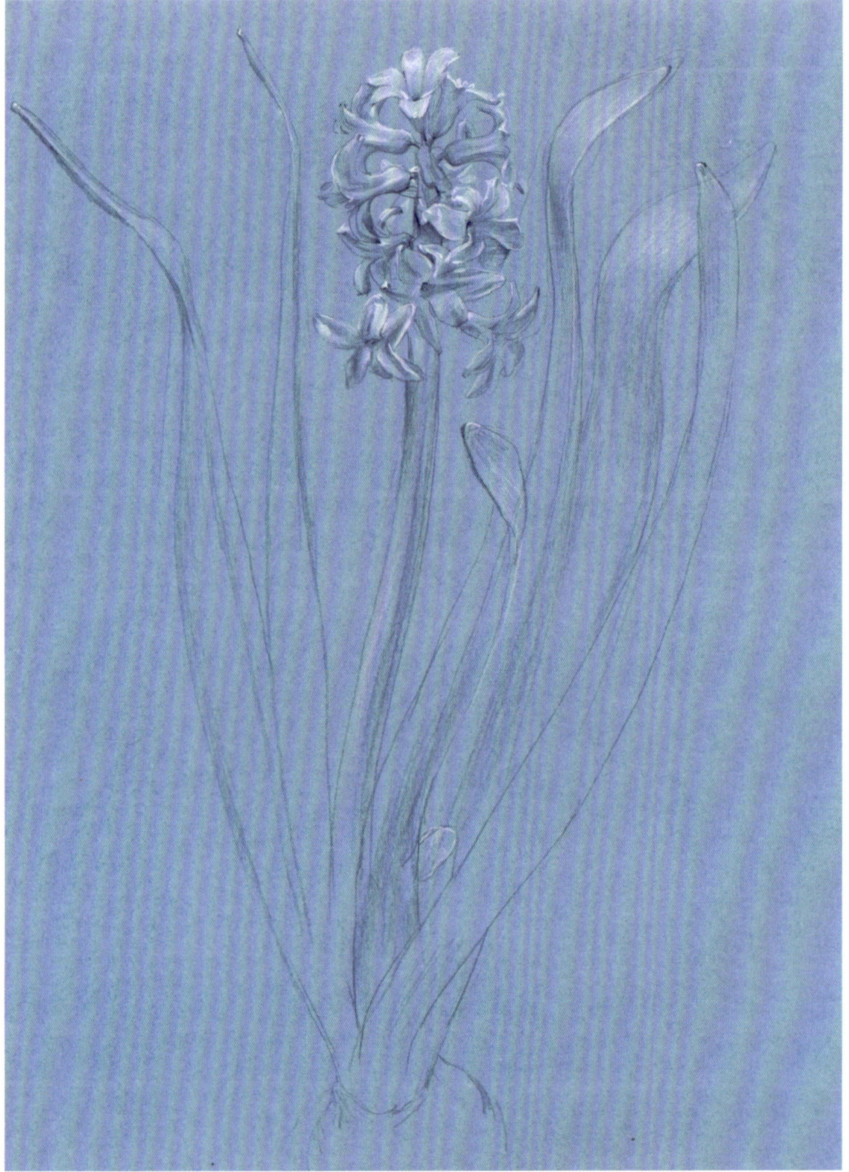

Delicate lines and careful
overlaps show which leaves
come in front of or behind
others.

Andrew S. Conklin, *Hyacinth,* 2006,
colored pencil on blue stationery
paper, 12 x 9 inches (30 x 23 cm).
Courtesy of the artist.

The mastery of line quality comes to you through practice and repetition. Even when you know exactly what kind of line you want to create, it can take time to get your hand and pencil to cooperate. I love pencil precisely because it allows me to try and try again. First, notice how successful artists use different lines and strive to imitate techniques you like. Then, practice and repeat—your hand and pencil will in time follow exactly the path you have chosen.

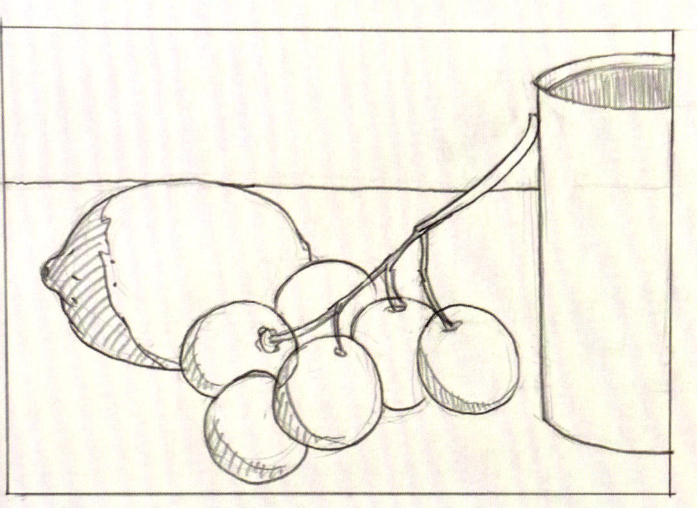

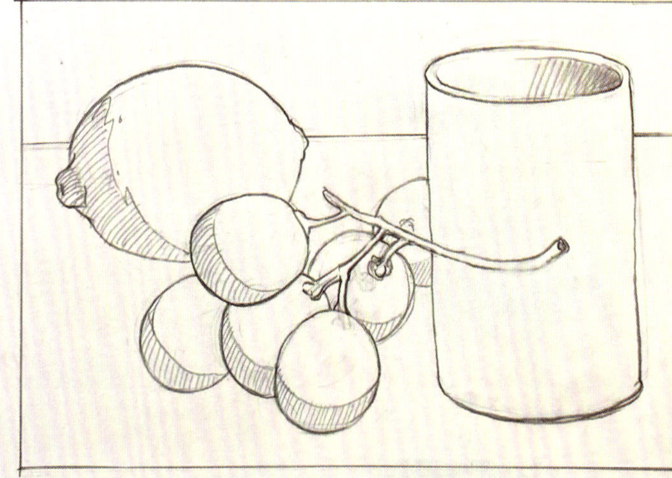

This diagram shows some of the problems we can have with unintentional tangent lines. At left, there are several errors in composition and drawing that make the space ambiguous:

1. The tabletop and lemon "kiss," making the table line appear to attach to the lemon instead of lying behind it.

2. The main stem of the grapes touches up against the cup. Is it in front? Behind? Accidental tangent lines make elements attach and appear flat.

3. The overlapping lines of the grapes and stems are confused.

4. The cup, because it is bisected, makes a strange composition shape and clings to the side of the rectangle picture frame. Cropping an object can be done, if carefully, but bisecting an object makes an odd visual choice, and tends to draw focus.

5. The ellipse at the top of the cup has a corner, which distorts the shape of the cylinder.

The image above at right shows choices that make the composition better and the spacing clear:

1. Arrange your objects to avoid tangents that kiss.

2. Make clear overlaps that show one shape as being in front of another (or with distance between).

3. Carefully erase (as in grapes and stem) or add a contour line to show when one part crosses in front, and what is connected.

4. Placing the whole cup in the composition clarifies the pictorial space around it.

5. The edges of the cup's ellipse curve tightly around, but never come to a point.

Drawing Bottles

For your next drawing, set up three different bottles and work from observation. This project starts with an envelope and focuses on line weight, the use of overlap, and positive and negative space. I'll also show you how to use tools to create symmetrical contours in geometric forms. I recommend you set up three bottles, ideally of slightly different shapes, and make this drawing from direct observation. Set one in front so there's a spatial overlap.

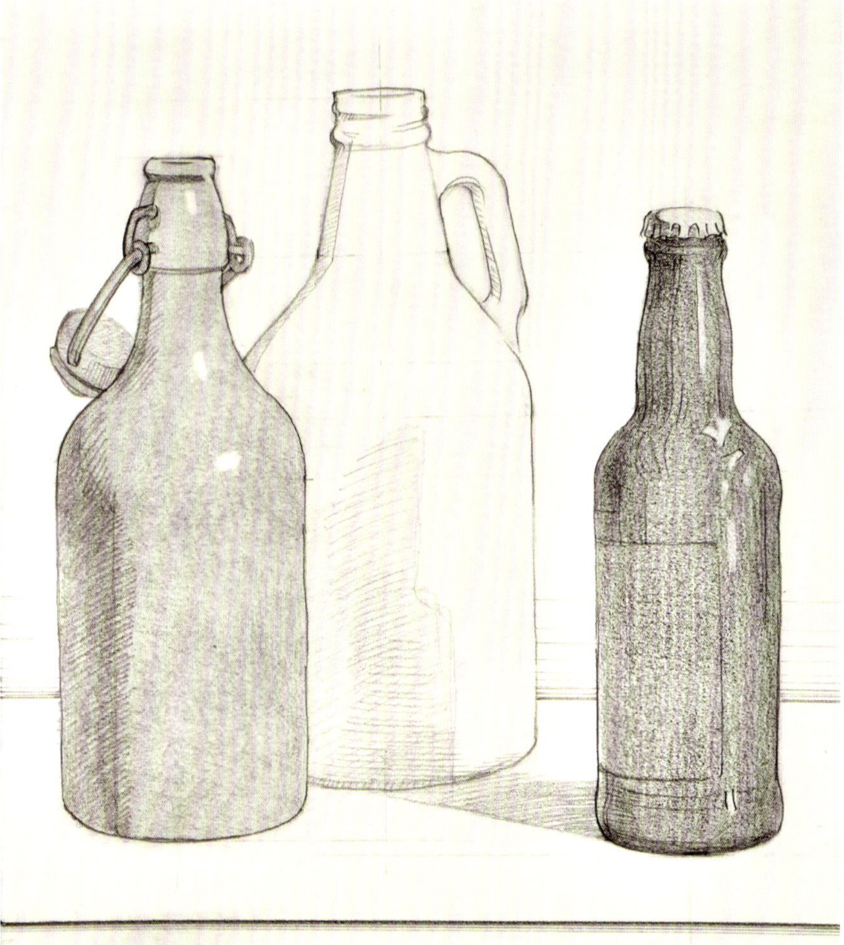

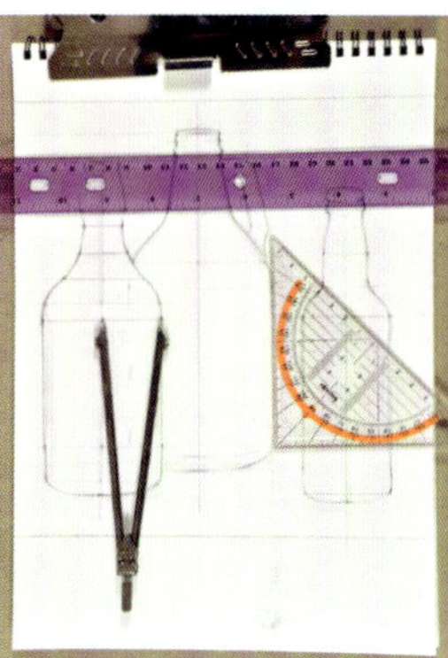

To help create symmetry in drawings of man-made objects, I often use a ruler, a triangle, and calipers or a compass. For this project, you need a 12-inch ruler.

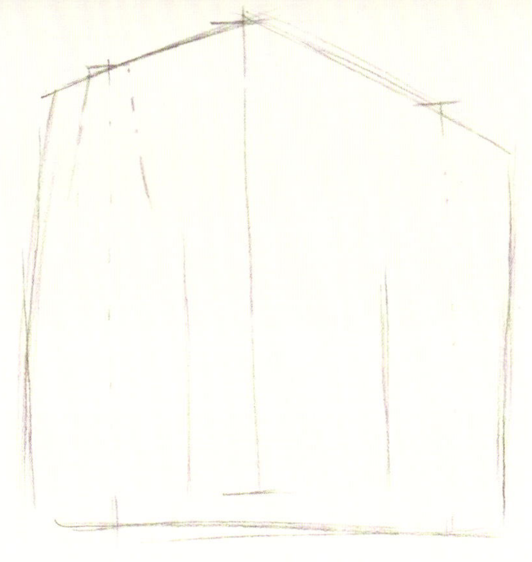

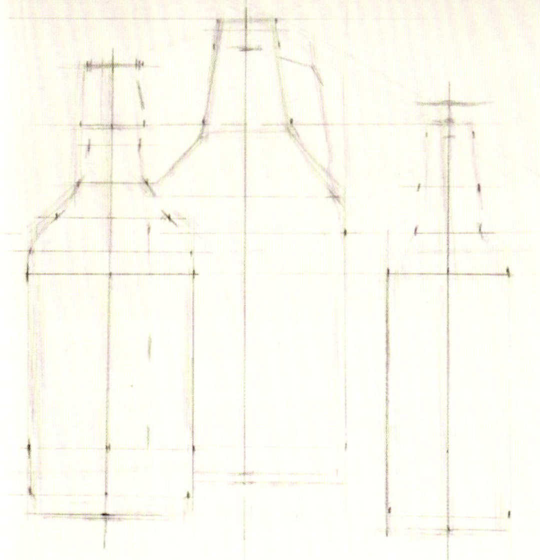

STEP ONE

With light block-in lines, start with vertical axes. Next, create an envelope around all three bottles to see them first as a group. Look at the proportions of height to width and in relationship to the other bottles to build accuracy.

Look at the negative spaces between the bottles and around the edges of your composition (refer to the diagram on p. 111 for guidance). Measure the negative spaces and note the angles of the empty shapes to help you avoid mistakes.

STEP TWO

Once you have eyeballed a placement, do some careful comparative measuring. I measured the height to width and held my ruler horizontally across the tops and bottoms of the bottles. Look for negative and positive spaces for good spacing and accurate shapes.

Now use a ruler to draw a perpendicular vertical centerline. Then use a ruler or calipers (that's a tool like a compass), to make sure that each side of the bottle is equidistant from the centerline. I always measure carefully from the centerline on symmetrical objects.

Next, use a ruler to make horizontal guidelines across the bottle—at the top, bottom, and at the points of inflection (changes in direction) along the curves. Measure symmetrical points along each horizontal. Take your time and make as many guidelines as you feel will be useful.

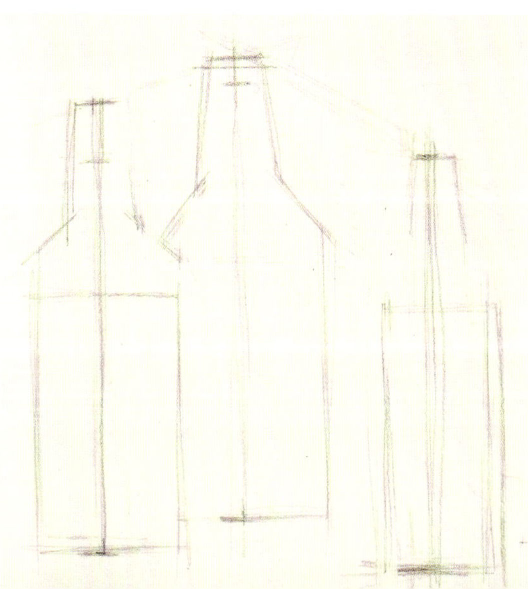

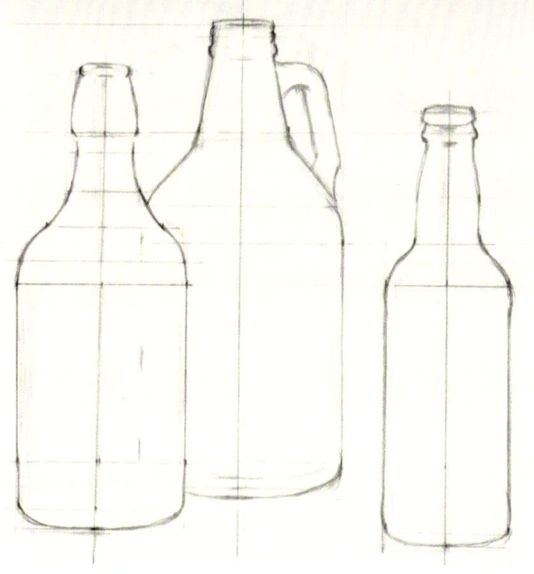

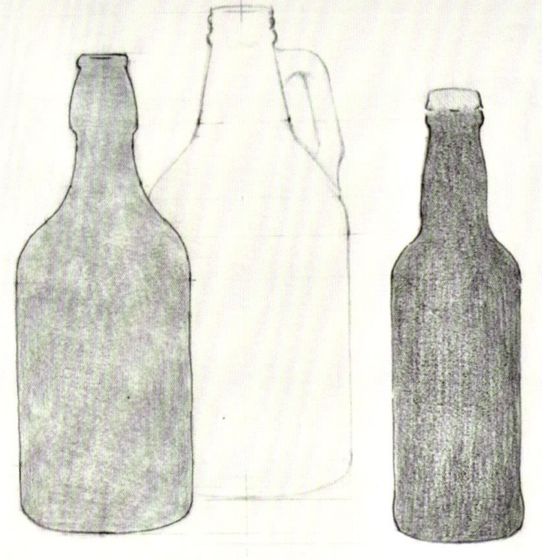

STEP THREE

Measurements done, you are ready to craft your contour lines. Erase the loose block-in lines and sharpen lines point to point on each side of all the bottles to make symmetrical and regular silhouettes. Use the ruler for the long straight sides.

Consider line weight and overlaps: Where a bottle is closer to you, use a stronger line. Where it is disappearing behind, let up a bit. Be sure to notice where one object overlaps another, and erase away when one object is covered. The contour lines in the bottle in front will go all the way around the silhouette and connect—that's called a closed contour. The edges of the bottles in back are not seen all the way around.

STEP FOUR

The light lines of the center bottle naturally make it recede in space. Use a stump and kneaded eraser to even out the shading (see below). The darker values will advance, and heavy lines at the base add a sense of the weight of the bottles on the table.

To finish the drawing, add more linear details, like the bottle stopper, cap, and threading at the top. I made heavier lines on the metal wire of the stopper to show what curves in front and light lines and hatching where I wanted details to recede (see the finished project drawing on p. 117).

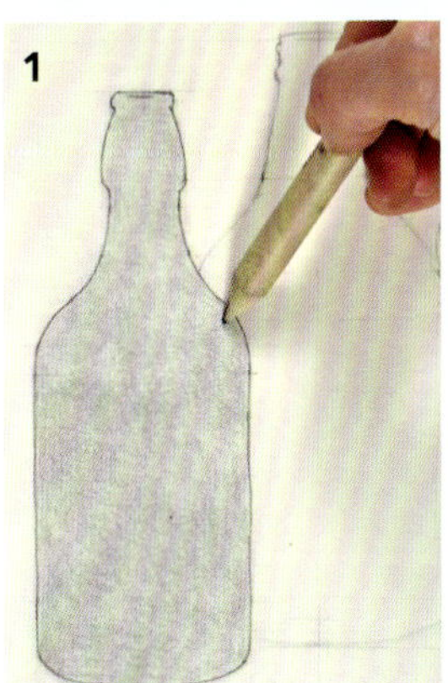

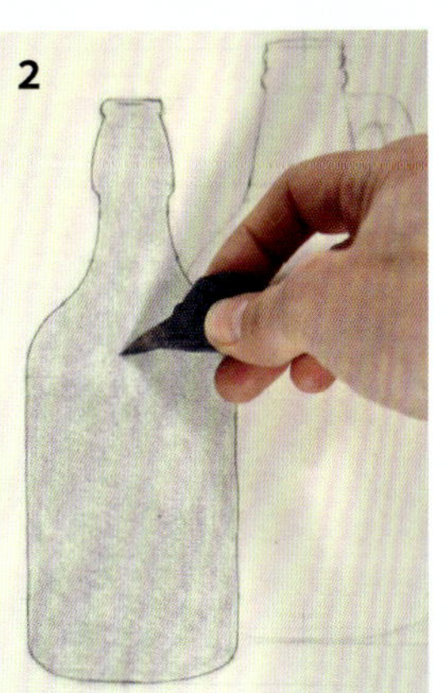

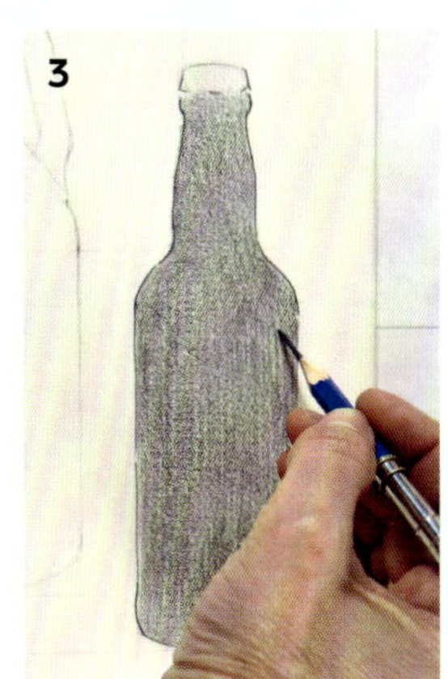

SKILLS FOR FINE DETAIL

1. Gently use a blending stump to even the tone of the graphite.

2. Roll your kneaded eraser into a point (a "bird beak") to pull out small spots that are too dark.

3. Use a finely pointed pencil to darken small spaces that are uneven.

7

The Shadow's Edge

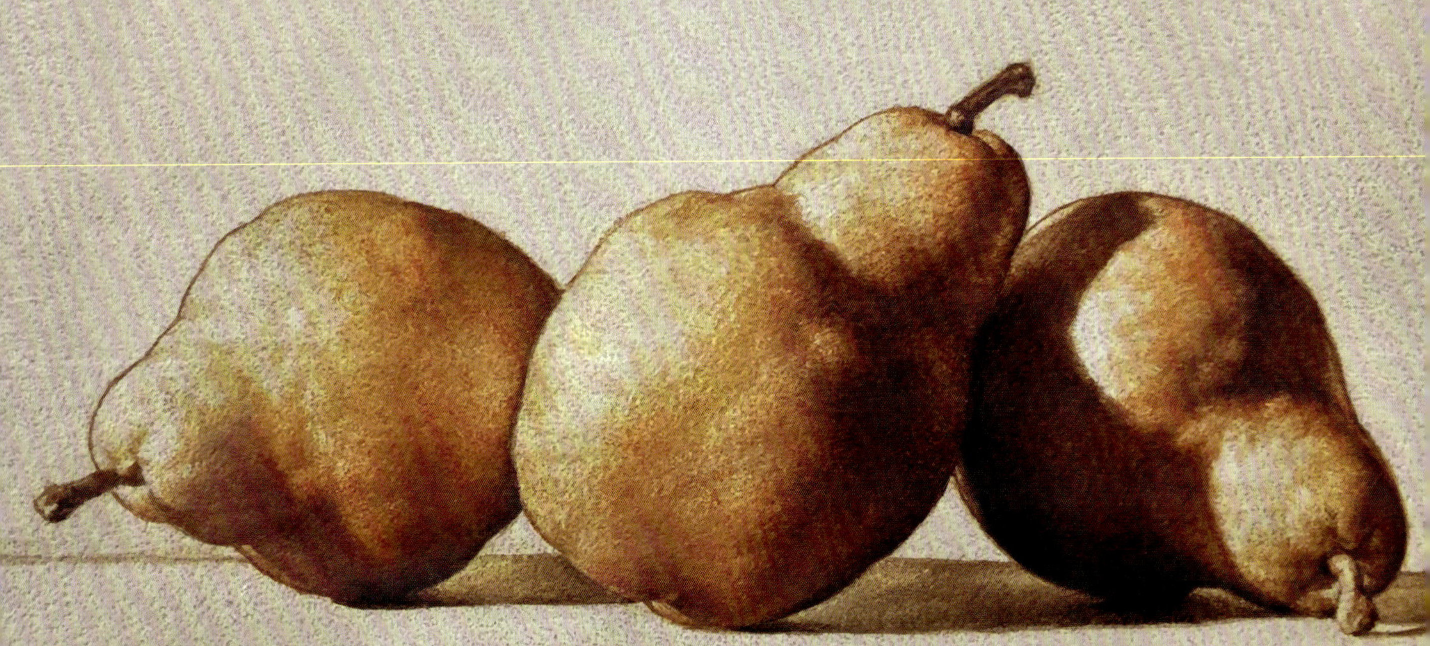

—RAINER MARIA RILKE

THE LANGUAGE OF LIGHT AND FORM

In the universe of realistic drawing, both casual viewers and connoisseurs greatly appreciate an artist's ability to create an illusion of three-dimensional form. It looks like magic to see the semblance of volume and space on a flat piece of paper. We know that we are looking at a two-dimensional graphic arrangement, but we are also sensing weight, volume, and sculptural relief. I believe there is something deeply satisfying when we experience these oppositions at the same time.

To understand how this alchemy happens, we enter into the language of form, value, plane, and light. An artist in atelier training can spend years investigating the subtleties of light playing on various surfaces, such as how muscles rippling over the ribcage shape the skin. However, the essential principles of light and form are incredibly simple. When you understand the terminology and learn what to look for, you can easily unlock a rich set of tools for better drawing.

VALUE

In the artist's vocabulary, *value* is the lightness or darkness of what we observe. Everything in the world that we look at can be perceived in terms of value—the blue sky, the white snow, the black soot in the fireplace. We use our materials in an organized arrangement of light and dark values to a particular graphic end. Moreover, we learn to translate color into value.

The color *blue*, for example, can refer to many different values, such as the pale blue of the midday's far horizon or the deep indigo of twilight. We learn that each color has a *value* independent of its *hue*. *Hue*, in artist's terminology, means the color "name"—like green, blue, or orange.

Hue: *The name of a color.*

The range of values in drawing is limited when compared to our experience looking at the world. From sunlight glaring off the water at the

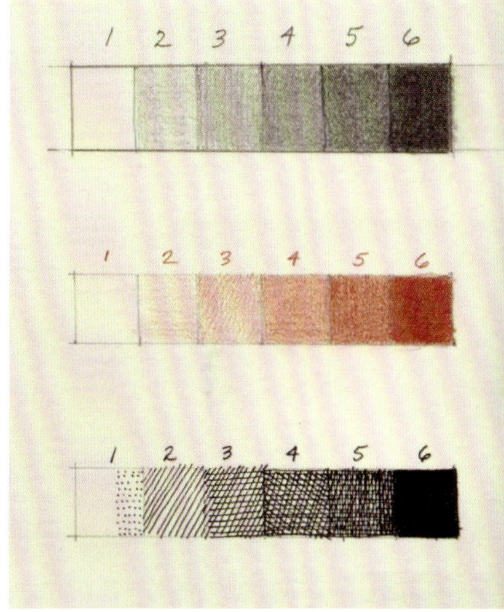

This series of value step scales shows how each material has its own potential range of lightness and darkness. Top is graphite, middle is sanguine colored pencil, and at bottom, ink pen.

Opposite: Anthony Ryder, *Triplets,* 2020, oil on panel, 8 x 12 inches (20 x 30 cm). Courtesy of the artist.

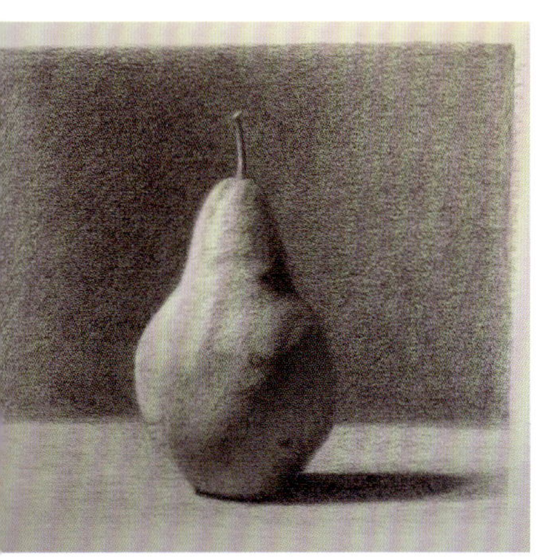

Sonya Gilbert, *Pear in Graphite*, 2021, graphite on paper, 6⅜ x 7¼ inches (16 x 18 cm). Courtesy of the artist.

beach to the black at the bottom of a deep well, our eyes can see infinitely more than our pencil can capture. We must use our available materials to make a graphic interpretation of what we see in life, often reducing the world to a gray scale, like a black-and-white photograph. We cannot express color when using pencil or charcoal, for instance. We learn to prioritize value and form over hue in the limited expressive language of drawing. Our ability to differentiate among local color, value, plane, and light will contribute to our creating elegant drawings with a convincing sense of form.

The pencils and papers we draw with themselves possess value. Is your sketchbook paper a bright white or a bit ivory? It certainly isn't as white as snow in sunlight. The graphite pencil you use will make a dark charcoal gray that can be metallic and shiny if layered and burnished. Perhaps you have a charcoal pencil that will make a very matte black line, but it won't be as black as a drop of India ink. There are *sanguine* pencils in dark reds and *sepia* pencils in warm browns, each coming in a variety of colors and formulas.

Value step scale: *A string of shades arranged in even increments to show the full range from lightest light to the darkest dark in a given material.*

Edmond Rochat, *Sketch for a String in a Maze,* 2017, graphite on paper, 5 x 7 inches (12.7 x 17.8 cm). Graphite on paper. Courtesy of the artist.

Note how much of Edmond Rochat's drawing falls into mid–value and dark tones (values 3–6). The lightest lights are few and saved for key details. This results in a strong sense of light.

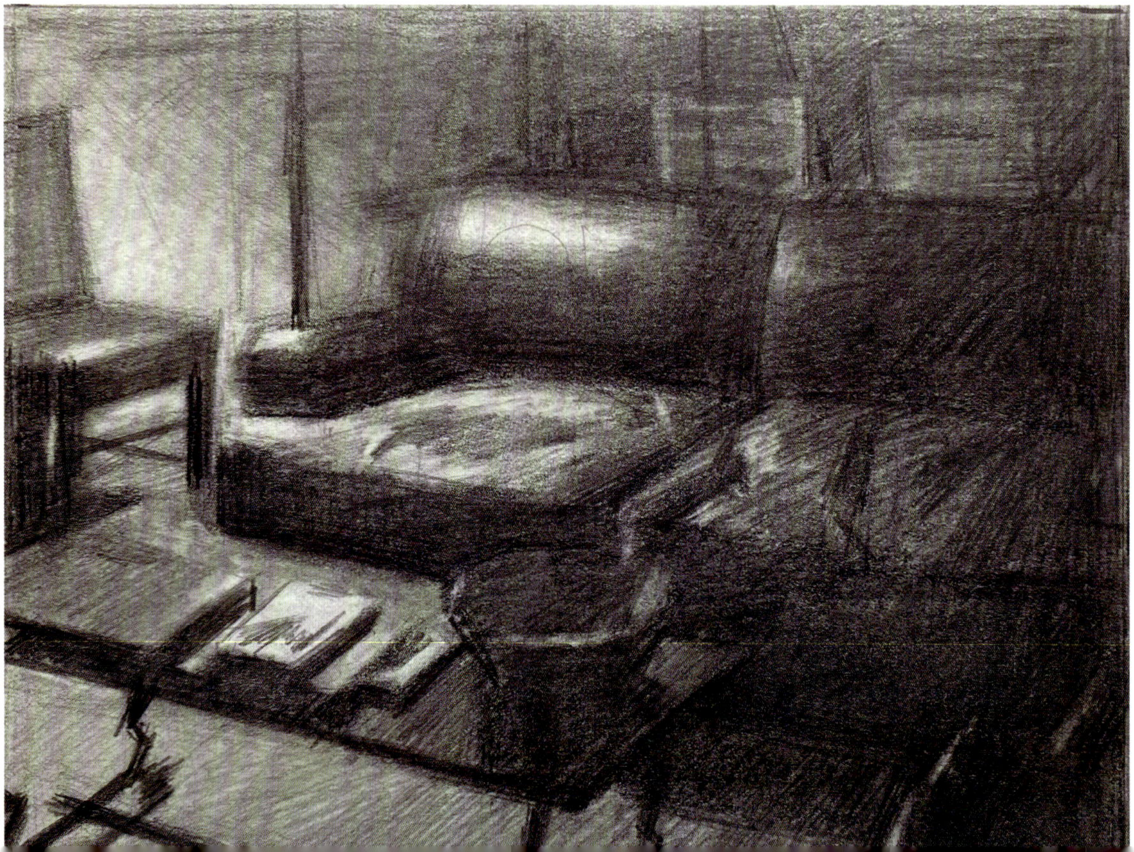

Value Step Scale

There are so many lovely materials for drawing, each possessing its own qualities and intrinsic value range. Silverpoint is a historic material that makes light, delicate lines, which can never be as dark as lines done in compressed charcoal. This does not make one material better than the other. Rather, you must first understand the possible range of values you can create with your chosen materials, then learn to organize that range of values to their optimum graphic potential. My favorite way to get to know the possible range of my chosen drawing tool is to make a *value step scale*—a string of shades arranged from light to dark in even increments—that shows the full range available in a given material.

Begin with a single pencil and white paper.

STEP ONE

Make a long, skinny rectangle that's about 1 inch. Divide that long rectangle in half, and then each half into thirds, making six even squares, labeled "1" through "6" at the top.

First, shade boxes four through six with an even midtone of graphite. You can build up the tone with one or two layers, and you can use the blending stump and kneaded eraser to even it out.

STEP TWO

Shade in box six, layering the pencil over several times to make it as dark as you can. Blend the tone with your stump between layers. Use the sharp point of the pencil to fill in any white spaces. Make the box as dark as you can without damaging or

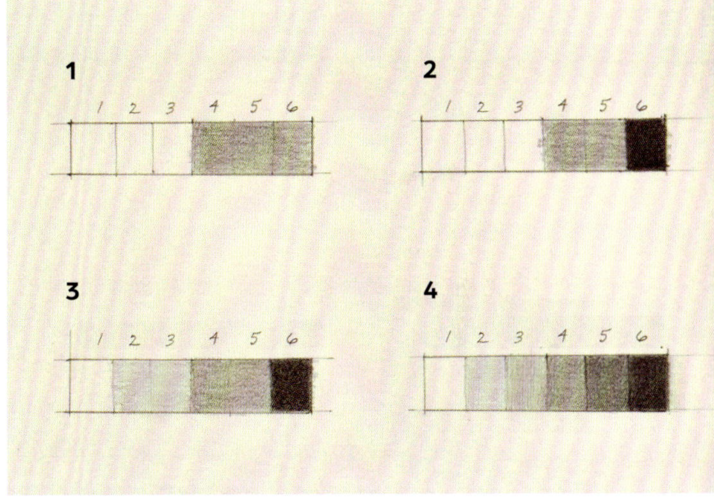

burnishing the paper. By carefully filling in the spaces and using the stump, your tone will become more uniform, dark, and even. Don't underestimate how dark you can make a drawing.

STEP THREE

Next, shade in boxes two and three using a delicate and even graphite. Be sure to keep your pencil sharp.

STEP FOUR

Now, darken the shading in boxes three and five. Adjust the shading in each box to get incremental steps in value from the lightest possible—the white of the paper in box one—to the darkest possible in box six. You may need to adjust the values you initially laid in for boxes two and four. Blend, erase, and layer the shades with a fine point and kneaded eraser to get the boxes toned as evenly as possible.

This simple exercise may have turned out to be harder than it looked, but it is time well spent building simple shading skills. The point of the exercise is to learn what the pencil can do and gain control of even shading in regular steps. The biggest challenge is making each block of value change in even increments, like a regular flight of stairs. To check if the steps are even, focus on a set of three blocks by covering up the rest. Does the block in the middle seem lighter than the one to the right and darker than the one to the left in equal measure? Analyze each step this way, and discover how light or dark to make each step. The most common mistake is to make the entire series too light, particularly boxes five and six. When we don't use the full potential range of our materials, subtle shading becomes even more difficult. Don't be afraid of the dark! Another common mistake is uneven shading in the square. Practice layering gradually with a sharpened pencil, and use your kneaded eraser rolled to a point to gradually darken and lighten little spots. Don't bear down and score the paper.

I recommend that you make a value step scale whenever you start with new materials. If you are using several different graphite pencils, make a step scale to plan where you will use each pencil. For example, I typically use a range of HB (slightly hard graphite) to 3B (soft graphite) pencils, with HB in box two and 3B in box six, the darkest dark. If you are working with ink, use hatching and cross-hatching to make gradually darkening squares. Try stippling with little dots or dashes for the lightest values. You might even experiment with a step scale using half steps if your medium gets quite dark. But remember that it is not the number of possible values that makes the best drawing, but the elegant organization of the values.

ORGANIZING VALUES TO CREATE FORM

Once we have explored the full range of values available to us with our tools, we can organize these values to create form. Artists create form by grouping values of light and dark tones in their chosen media to make an illusion of light, shadow, and dimension.

There is a distinction between value simply meant as relative lightness and darkness and value used to create form. A value has an absolute, even

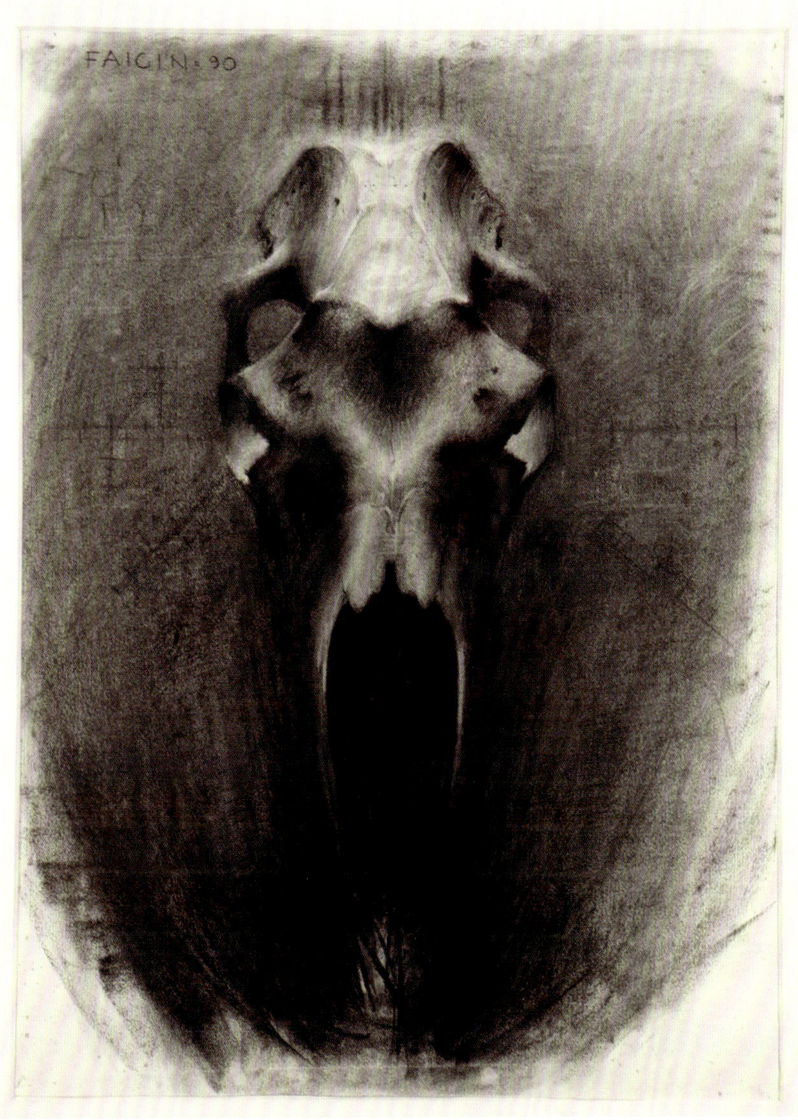

Gary Faigin uses a full range of value, from the white of the paper in the highlights to the darkest black in the interior crevices of the skull. Charcoal, with its dramatic grays and blacks, makes strong graphic impact and rich shadows. In life, the skull was a bone white. Notice how much dark tone Faigin uses to create form on the subject. He has interpreted the pale skull with a full range of values in charcoal for a dramatic effect.

Gary Faigin, *Moose Skull Study #4*, 1990, charcoal on paper, 30 x 22 inches (76 x 56 cm). Courtesy of the artist.

mathematical, identity—a 15 percent or 85 percent gray, for instance. We *arrange* those values to create form by placing the 15 percent gray in the light mass and the 85 percent gray in the shadows. While value can be analyzed somewhat systematically, rendering form requires understanding the principles of light.

You might draw an egg or an eggplant, two rounded oblong forms with very different *local colors*. An egg is white (in value terms, light); an eggplant is purple (in value terms, dark). To create form, the illusion of dimension, don't pay much attention to the local color (which graphite can't well express). Instead, consider the value as related to the *direction of the light*

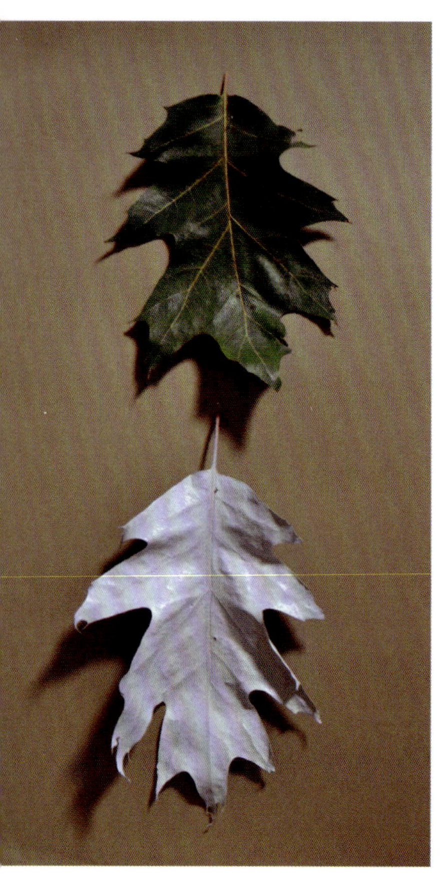

By painting the bottom leaf white, I am able to see and understand the difference between form and local color.

source. Imagine that everything in the world has been spray-painted white. For beginners, select objects for drawing with a light local color and a simple surface such as an egg, green pear, golden apple, or butternut squash. For now, avoid deeply colored, shiny, and variegated surfaces, which hold special challenges.

In the photo at left, the bottom leaf has been spray-painted white. This makes it easy to see and understand the difference between form and local color. In drawing, our ability to express local color is limited, so I prioritize form.

To add confusion to the vocabulary around values, the words *light* and *dark* have multiple connotations. The term *light* can be used to describe the hue (a pale color) of a value (the illuminated side of a form) or the light source itself. Imagine sunshine falling on that eggplant. The local color, purple, has a dark value, but the vegetable still has a bright (lit) side and a dark (shadow) side. To create three-dimensional form in realist drawing, artists learn to prioritize the shading that results from the light falling on their subjects rather than the values of local color. In drawing, you can *suggest* lighter and darker colors like the white egg or purple eggplant— but if you want the illusion of volume, you must focus on rendering light and shadow and not hue.

In art pedagogy, yet more befuddlement arises from the myriad systems of numbering and vocabulary used to teach the same material. Acknowledging the variety, I'll attempt to lay out a simple and clear set of definitions to introduce this area of artistic study. I continue to use the six-step value scale I learned from artist Gary Faigin, my earliest teacher. Six steps are easy to learn and remember, well-suited to the limited value range of drawing materials, and easily divided into half-steps when you need more subtle distinctions.

BASIC VOCABULARY OF FORM

To create the illusion of a three-dimensional object, we use values to *model* or *render* form. These terms denote the shading in subtle gradations of value in order to make the illusion of a rounded form on a flat surface. This is achieved by showing which parts of our subject face toward or away from the light. I will be using the terminology of value to define the specific relationships of the subject to the *light source*, not to local color.

The most important observations to discern: What do we see that faces the light? What parts are in shadow? We look for the light shape and the shadow shape to plan our modeling.

Let's organize the six-step scale into values we'll use to render form. Values 1–3 are light values (illuminated areas), and values 4–6 are shadow values:

1. Highlight
2. Light mass
3. Dark light
4. Shadow mass
5. Terminator or core shadow
6. Accent shadow—the darkest dark in your range

The conical arrow shows the direction of the light source. On the sphere, the side facing the light is the light shape. The shadow shape is comprised of form shadow and the cast shadow. The numbers show the arrangement of the six values on a curved form.

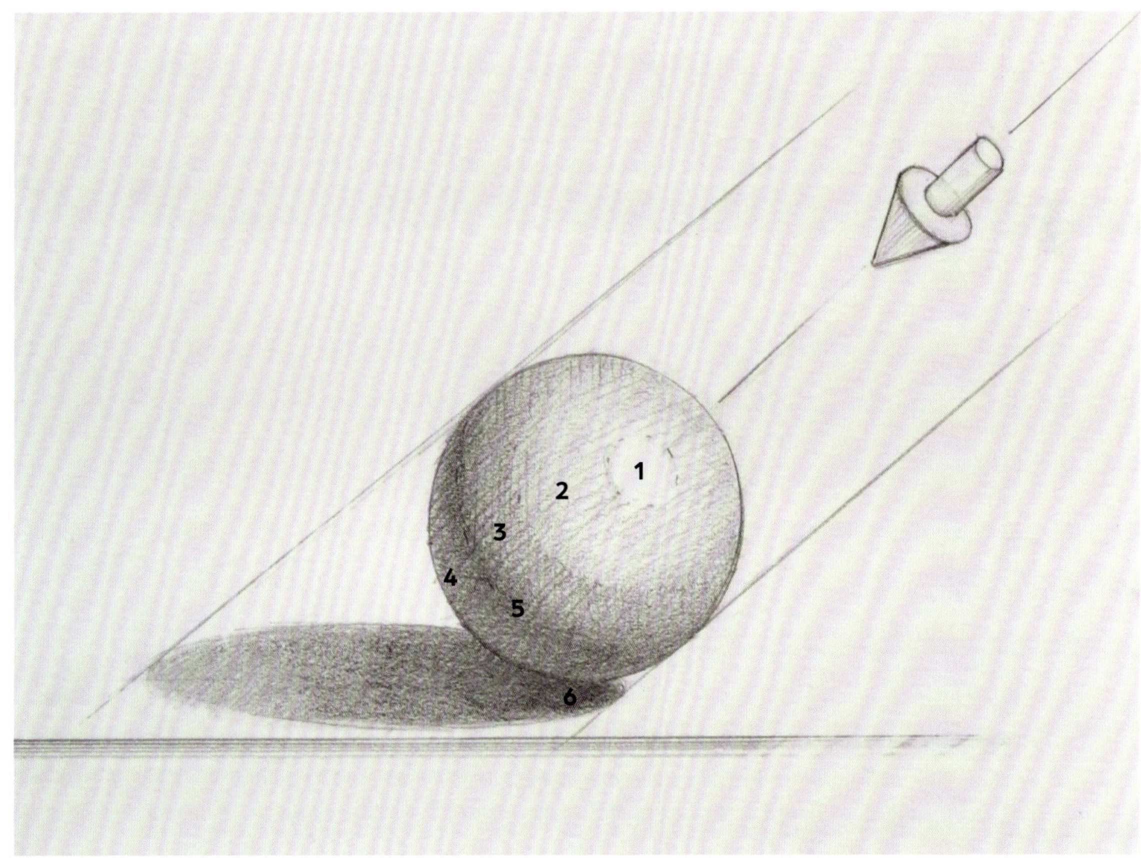

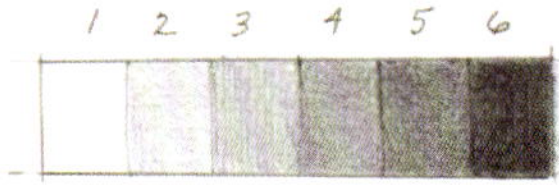

DEFINING TERMS

Highlight: *The lightest spot on a form. The highlight is the reflection of the light source as it bounces off your subject to your eye. Its quality is determined by the surface of the object—a shiny apple will have a bright highlight and a fuzzy peach will have a barely visible one.* Value 1 on our six-step scale

Light mass: *The part of the subject that is illuminated by the light source.* Value 2

Dark light: *The area of the light mass where it darkens as it approaches the terminator.* Values 3–4

Terminator: *The boundary between the light and shadow on a form; i.e. the form shadow edge. This is the point on the form where the light (from a single light source) no longer touches the object and falls past it.* Value 5

Form shadow: *The part of the subject not illuminated by the primary light source; the part of the form in shadow.* Value 5

Reflected light: *Part of the form shadow where ambient light brightens the value of the shadow as it curves away from the terminator. Ambient and reflected lights are secondary light sources, like reflected light bouncing off the table or other small lights in the room.* Value 4

Cast shadow: *The shadow created by the form when the subject blocks the primary light source.* Values 4–5

Accent shadow: *The darkest part of the shadow, where there is no ambient or reflected light.* Value 6

KEY PRINCIPLES OF LIGHT

There are a few key principles to help our perceptions of light and form. It almost seems too obvious to say, but remember that everything that is visible to us is seen because it is illuminated by a light source. The light rays emanate from the source—the sun, a lamp—in a straight line and then bounce off the subject to our retina. From the Renaissance to today, artists have studied form using a *single* light source, ideally a north-facing

Opposite: Note how the marvelous control of value shows various local colors and surfaces. The lightest parts in the skin are still darker than the highlights on the metal jewelry. The hair masses have a light shape and shadow shape, though they are handled in a dark key.

Michael Meadors, *Crescendo*, 2017, graphite and water–soluble crayon on paper, 8 x 6 inches (20 x 15 cm). Courtesy of the artist.

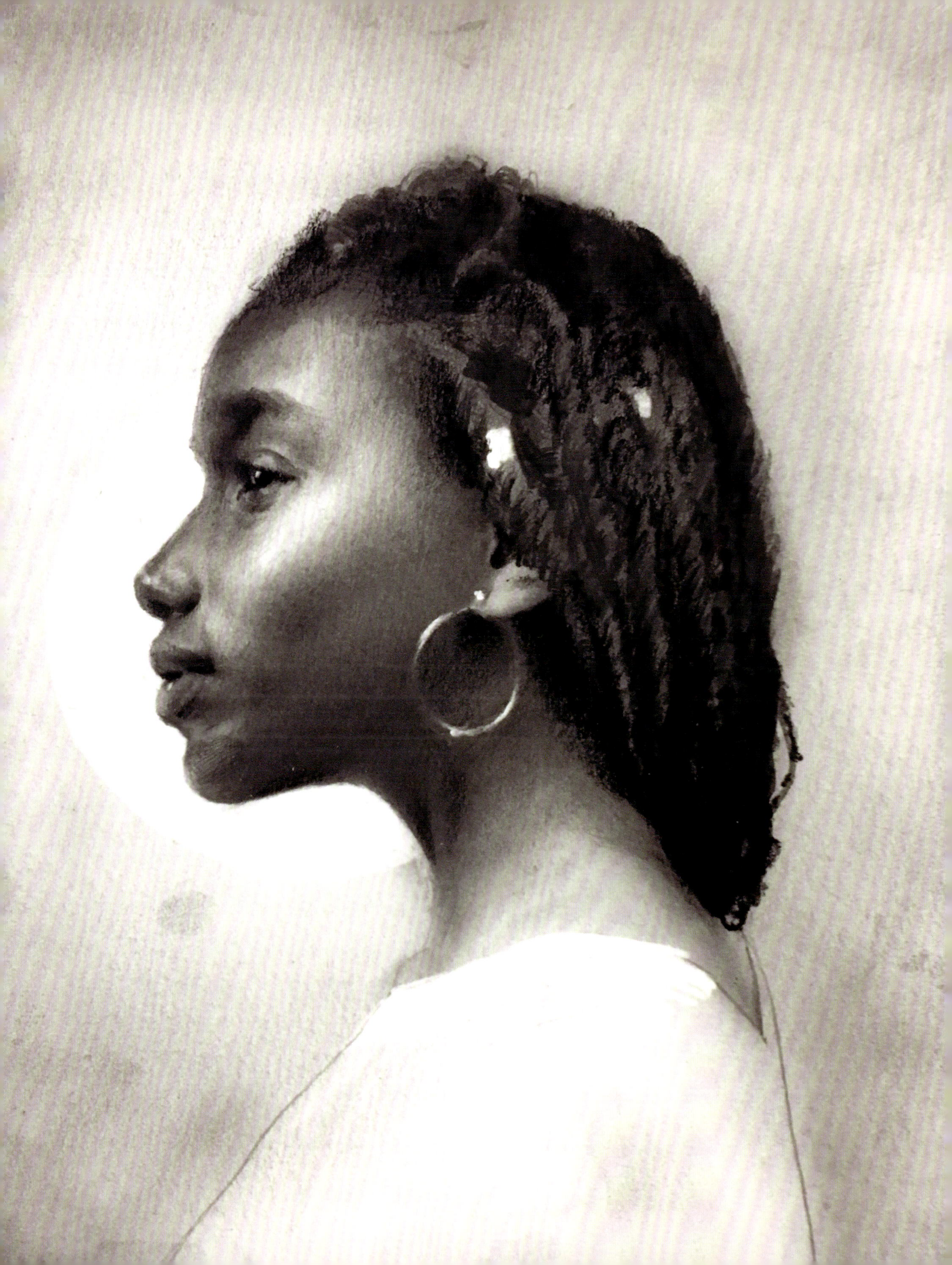

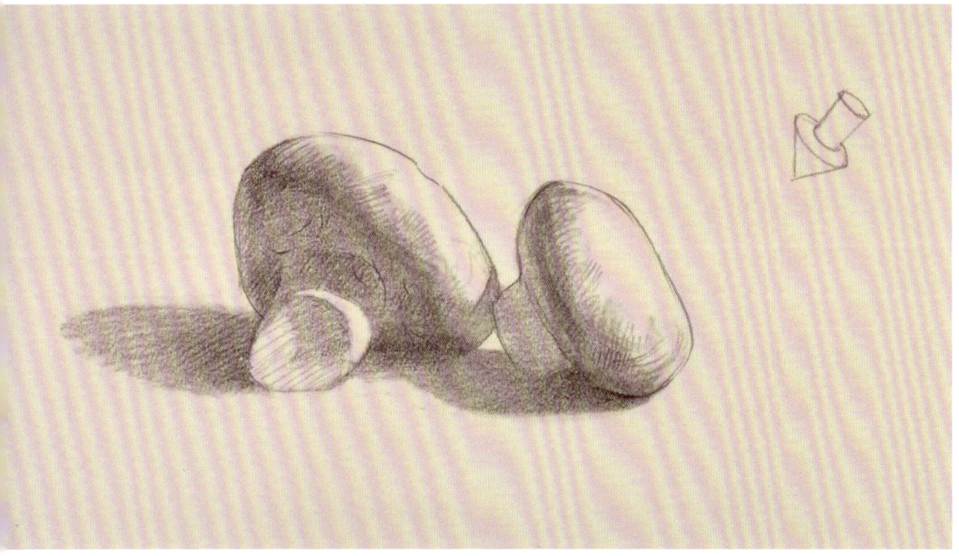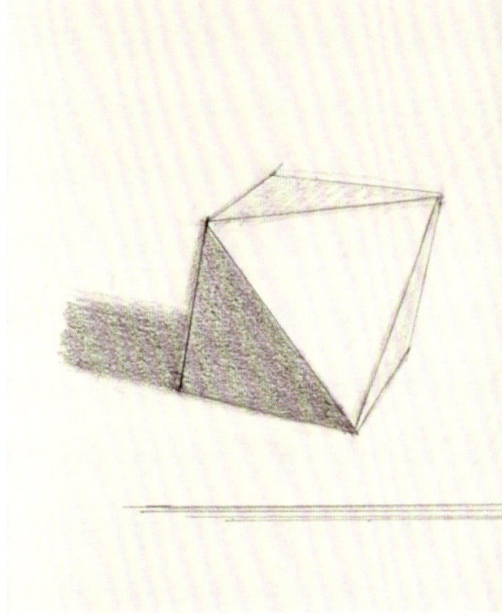

window or skylight. Today, we have so many different electric light sources in our homes that artists will block secondary light sources and use only a strong primary light on their subject. This helps them create images that are convincingly three-dimensional. Ultimately, artists may choose a composition using various lighting conditions. However, when working in a realist mode, artists typically master a single light source first.

In the sphere diagram on p. 127, the light source is coming from the upper right, positioned toward the front of the object. This creates a large light mass on the right side and a crescent-shaped shadow on the left. This is called *three-quarter light* (75 percent of the object in the light mass, 25 percent in the shadow). This particular angle and placement of the light source is very useful to beginners learning about form, and I recommend it for drawing study. The line that shows the border between the light and shadow is the *terminator*. The terminator gets its name from astronomy, not science fiction. For astronomers, it is the point on the surface of a planetary orb at which the rays from the sun no longer kiss the surface. If you are standing on Earth and the sun is overhead, you are in the light mass. If it is dark, you are on the shadow side of Earth from the sun. If it is sunset, you are experiencing the beauty of the terminator, where light is about to stop intersecting with your eyeballs. The concave curve of the crescent moon defines the terminator of the waxing or waning sphere.

On rounded objects, the terminator is a zone where the light gradually falls off as the form curves. When a form curves smoothly, the values *must* darken gradually both *into* the terminator and *past* it. This gentle gradation says "round" to our eyes. Contrarily, on an angular solid, such as a cube, the terminator will be seen as a hard line that denotes a change of plane. The quality of the terminator—soft, wide, vague, or sharp—is always determined by the kind of light and the nature of the form that the light falls upon.

The terminator describes the form of the subject more than any other part of a drawing. I call it the *third contour*. Aided by the contour lines that describe either side of the silhouette of a form, the terminator defines the third dimension of a mass. Even with very little shading, one can say a lot about shape and mass by focusing on these three lines: two outer contours and the terminator.

In the drawing at right, the candlestick has two contours on each edge that show the shape. The terminator is the third contour that shows the dimension. The third contour also shows the edge from the point of view of the light, where it no longer touches the object and falls past it.

THE TECHNOLOGY OF A SINGLE LIGHT SOURCE

The photo at top left on the following page shows a pear set up for drawing with a strong light source making a clear shadow shape. The box blocks ambient light from the shadows, which make shadow edges harder to see.

One essential component to realist drawing is good lighting. Why does that matter so much? Look around you in whatever space you are in right now—how many different light sources do you see? From my desk, I can see a desk lamp, three bulbs overhead in a fixture on the ceiling, and a window. Every single one of those is *light sources* creates a light and shadow pattern. It is characteristic of a modern building that the ambient light might be quite bright, but sometimes our broad and diffuse light sources make drawing more difficult. In art school, we learn to use one strong light source for our work, because this creates a specific condition that is very useful for drawing. With a strong single light, we see two essential components: the shape of the object itself by seeing the *contours* (or edges), and the dimension of the object by observing how light falls and describes the *form* (the three-dimensional character) with light and shadow.

LIGHT REVEALS FORM

How do you perceive the difference between a circle and a basketball? Bear with me; this stupid question helps us gain an insight. You know the difference between a circle and a sphere because your brain perceives the dimensionality of the volume of the sphere. How does the brain do that? The eye's sensitive rods and cones interpret the way light gradually

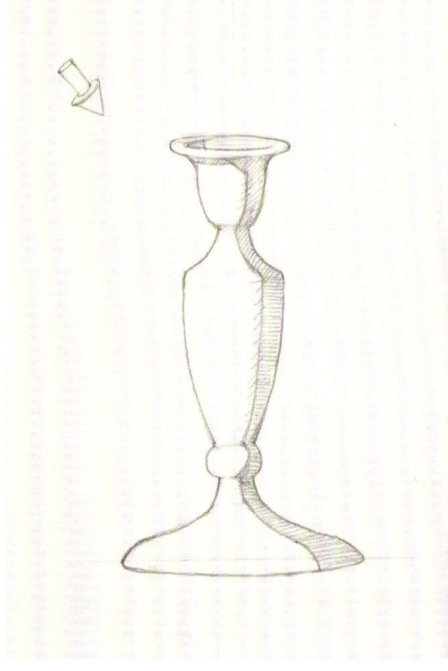

The candlestick has two contours on each edge that show the shape. The terminator is the third contour that shows the dimension. The third contour also shows the edge from the point of view of the light, where it no longer touches the object and falls past it.

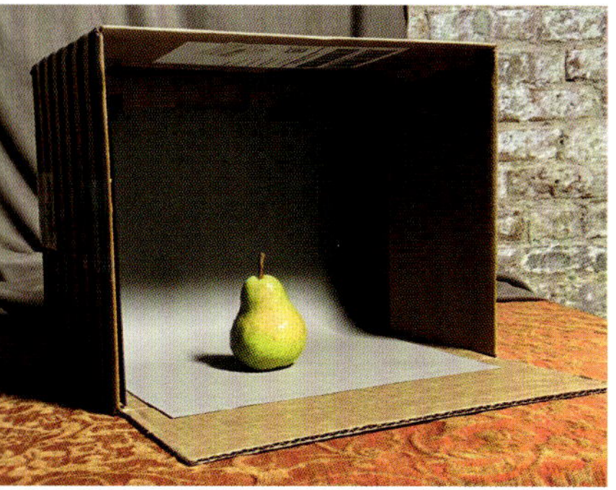

This pear is set up for drawing with a strong light source making a clear shadow shape. The box blocks ambient light from the shadows, which make shadow edges harder to see.

diminishes on the object and reads the shape of the shadow. With this data, the brain comprehends the roundness of the form. We don't even need to be conscious of this process. Learning to draw is, in part, learning to comprehend what our brains unconsciously sense.

The use of good lighting to reveal and create the illusion of form was an important innovation in creating realistic art. Drawing with a single light source was a technical innovation of the fifteenth century, a time in which the rigors of scientific inquiry were directed at the nature of perception in studio practice. Artists like Leonardo da Vinci discerned that light rays—from the sun or a candle—*always* fall in a straight line, predictably and universally. They strike the objects you observe, bounce off, and travel to your retina, creating the phenomenon of vision. Understanding this action of light made it possible for artists to understand, predict, and then re-create the illusion of light in art.

The technology of a single light source was like going from mono to stereo for visual artists. From any single point of view, you perceive the shape of an object. When you add light, you can see the image from two angles simultaneously. What? How is that possible? You see the silhouette from your fixed point of view. The light "sees" the shape from another point of view. (If you looked from the point of view of the lightbulb, you'd see a different silhouette, right?) By combining the artist's point of view with the light's point of view, you get two different sets of information about the volume of a sphere at the same time. And thus, you can perceive and then render the volume of a form.

DIAGRAM THE LIGHT DIRECTION

When I sit down to draw from life, the first thing I look for is the light condition on my subject. I want to know: Where is the light source relative to my subject and to me? How bright is it? Can I see a shadow shape and a highlight? On my drawing, I use a conical arrow to record the direction of the light and keep it constantly in mind.

MAKE A CONICAL ARROW

Learning to make one of these diagrams will help you start conceptualizing light direction and form.

- Start with a simple line showing the direction of the light.
- Next, try to describe the spatial orientation of the light by using a cone and cylinder. Is the light straight above? Or close to you and just a bit to the side?

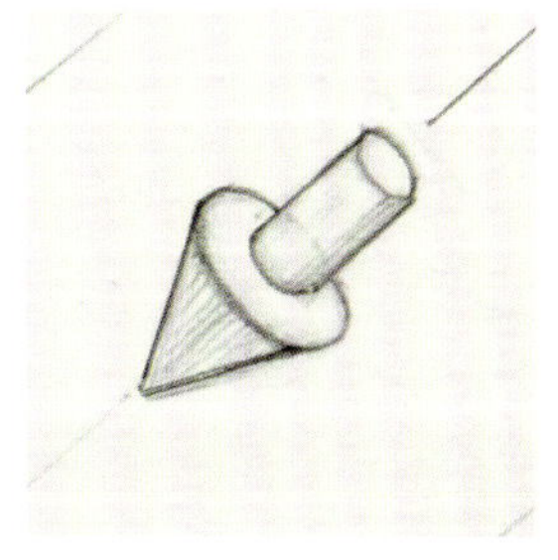

Draw a Pear with Light and Shadow

To help you observe light and shadow in this project, I want you to set up a pear with controlled lighting and a neutral background. We will make a drawing that looks dimensional by applying graphite in a simple arrangement of six values.

SETTING UP

The best way to learn these concepts is to work from direct observation. Select a pear or similar piece of fruit with a light, solid color. Avoid striped or boldly multicolored fruit. Set up your pear in an open, lined carton on a table a few feet away from you. The box creates a neutral space that eliminates light bouncing from multiple sources. Direct one strong desk, clip, or window light at your pear to create a large light shape and a narrow shadow shape—*a three-quarter light*. The key to success is to be able to see a clear shadow edge and a highlight. If you can't see these, there are probably too many ambient lights. Look carefully: Does the pear cast multiple shadows? If so, turn off extra lights and nest the pear deeper inside the cardboard box, or try a brighter bulb in your lamp. Take the time you need to set this up correctly, as it will help the lessons of the project sink in.

STEP ONE

To begin, make placement marks and a basic block-in: check the ratio of height to width, look for the central axis line, and block-in line segments.

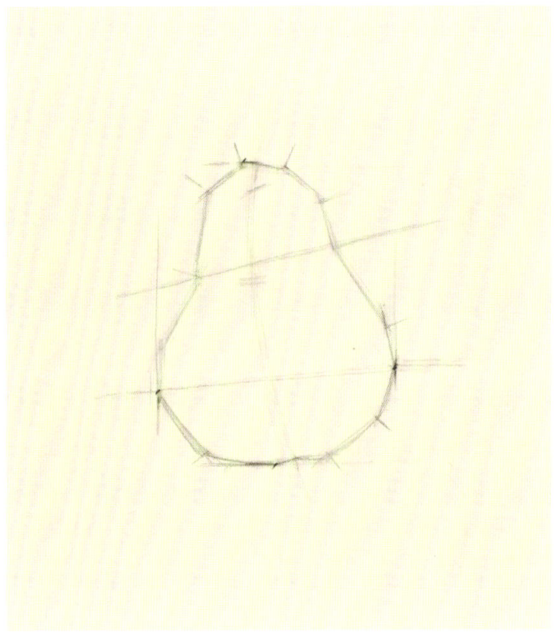

Look for landmarks across the neck and widest points of the pear, and check the tilts and angles of the contour.

STEP TWO

Block in the shadow shape by drawing the terminator. Note the subtle irregularities of the shadow edge that reveal the organic form. Next, make a value step scale on your page to plan your value range. (For instructions, see p. 123).

STEP THREE

To develop the dark values, create an even tone matching value 4 across the entire shadow shape on

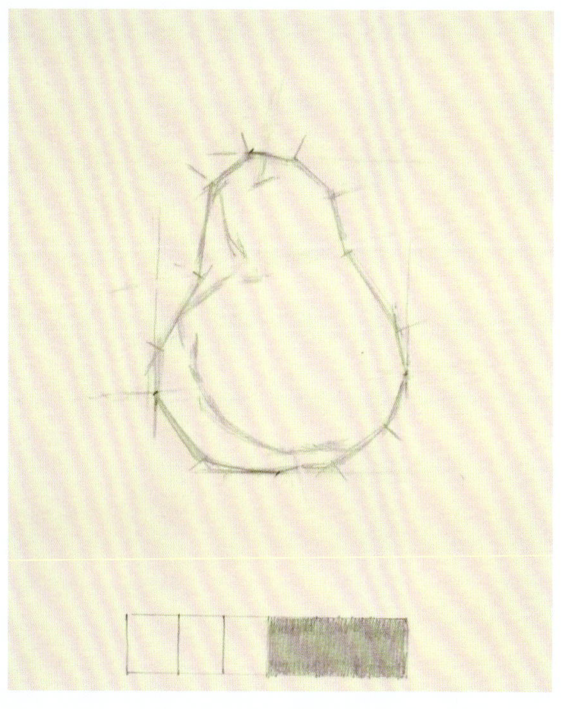

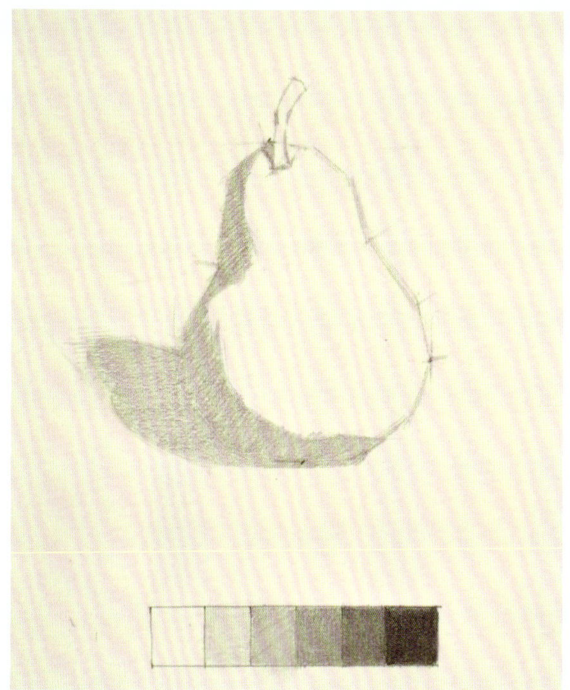

your drawing. Sketch the shape of the cast shadow, also at value 4. You have now separated the pear into a light shape and a shadow shape. The pear is a gently rounded form, so each value blends gradually into the next. Starting at the terminator, crosshatch over the shadow edge to soften it. The value of the terminator will get darker to value 5.

Now, model the dark light to values 3–4 and blend into the shadow by crosshatching and layering value. Keep your modeling simple; all the shadows are values 4–6.

Within the cast shadow, create an accent shadow of value 6 where the pear sits on the table. The far edges of the cast shadow should remain lighter and softer; try feathering it out with some hatching lines.

STEP FOUR

Now it's time to use the top values on your scale to create roundness and detail in the light mass. First

darken the edge of the pear to value 3 along the light side to suggest a rounded contour.

Use delicate shading in value 2 to shape the lights. Leave value 1, the white paper, for the highlights. All the lights should be values 1–3.

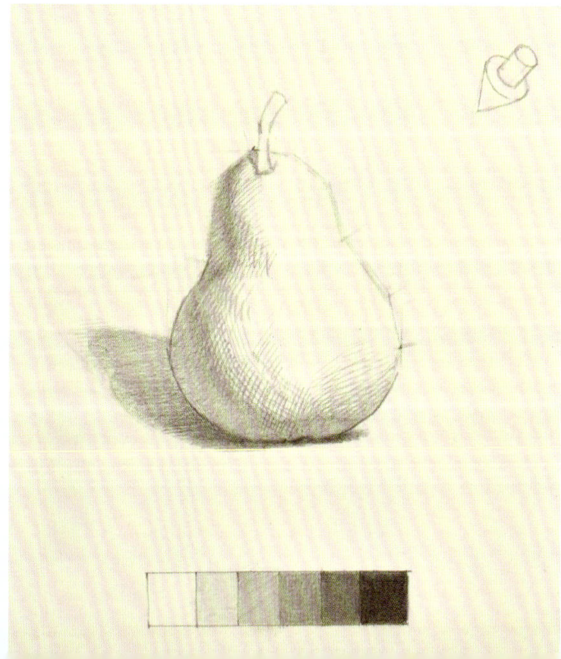

KEEP LIGHTS AND DARKS UNIFIED

Consider this systematic approach to the pear as a template for placing values in relationship to each other, but not as strict guidance. When you understand how value and form can work together, you will have great freedom to modify the range and materials that you choose. Not all beautiful drawings use the full range of white to black values. Instead, they possess a clear organization of light and shadow to control the values used.

The most important principle to remember is to keep the lights and shadows unified. In school, I learned "The lightest light in the dark is darker than the darkest dark in the light." Kind of a maddening koan, but it makes sense when you figure it out. (The inverse is also true: The darkest dark in the light is lighter than the lightest light in the dark.) A common mistake is to make too many value changes in the shadows. When you make the reflected light too light (say, value 3), it destroys the unity of the form. Make all the shadow shapes dark and simple and keep the reflected light very subtle. Another common mistake is that the more detail you add in the light areas, the more you make spots in the light mass too dark (say, value 4). Keep the lights all value 3 and up.

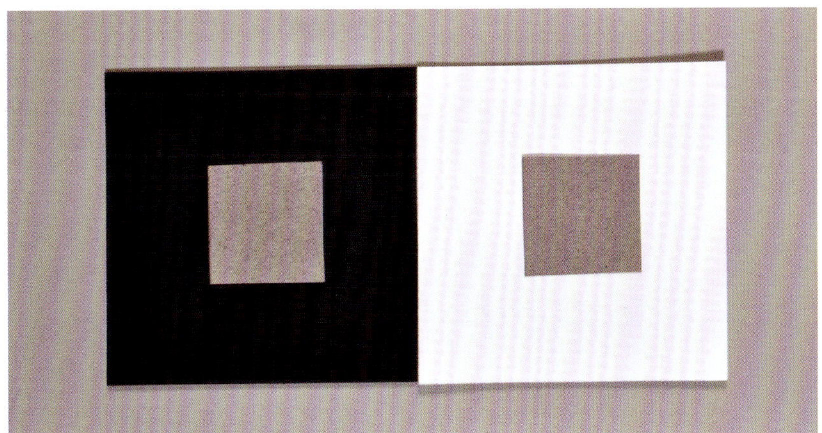

We see shapes and notice contrast better than we can judge value. We always see value in relationship to the other tones around it. This image shows the phe–nomenon of simultaneous contrast. The gray square of paper in the center looks dark on the white square and looks light on the black square. The gray middle square is exactly the same.

OPTICAL ILLUSIONS AND CONTRAST

We see some things very clearly and others ineffectively. We can spot a wolf at a great distance, examine the delicate wings of a bee, read volumes of text, and accurately match a paint swatch. However, there are things that we rarely see with acute specificity. We are not good at detecting subtle shifts of light in the middle of a brightly lit form (like that pear), or the way values darken across a stretch of wall as it gets further from the light. (Our brains just say "white wall.") We are bad at judging the color and value of two different spots if they are not adjacent to each other. We tend to attribute great authority to what we see "with our very own eyes." Be wary and remember that our perceptions can falter. The pleasure of an optical illusion is the dissonance between believing what we see and then realizing we've been duped. As artists, be ever mindful of the gap between seeing and knowing.

The pear exercise offers a classic example of an optical challenge. When we set a bright object such as a green pear against a neutral or dark background, we see a vibrant contrast at the edge on the light side (see project on pgs. 133–134). Because of the vivid contrast, it is nearly impossible to see how the values darken at the light edge of the pear. This is an optical illusion. Our eyes register contrast more readily than small shifts in value. The brightest part of the pear is not at the edge but in the middle of the light mass at the highlight, where the surface of the pear most directly faces the light. Instead of leaving the edge very bright, darken the edges to make the pear curve around.

In this poetic drawing of a plaster cast, Sadie Valeri adds white chalk to model the light shapes on dark gray paper. In the shadow shape, she adds sepia pencil to deepen the accent shadows. Clearly organizing your media into light and shadow values makes a drawing unified and elegant.

Sadie J. Valeri, *Bird Cast Study,* 2022, pastel pencil on toned paper, 10 x 8 inches (25 x 20 cm). Courtesy of the artist.

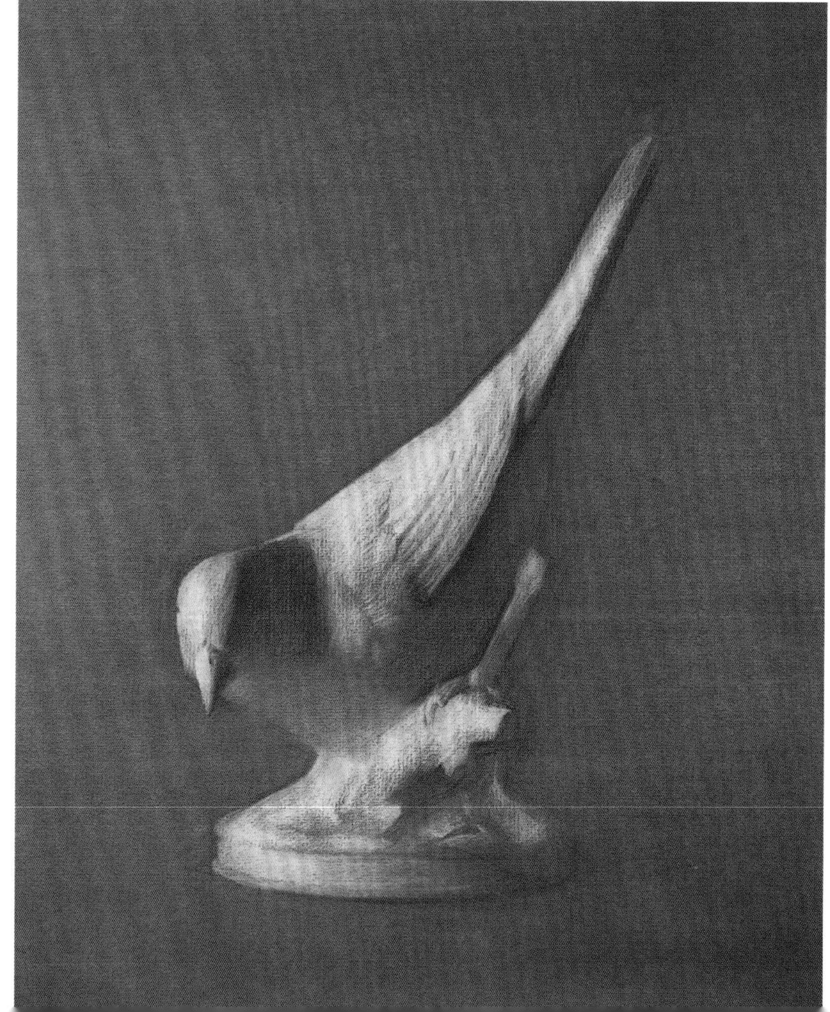

Shell Drawing on Toned Paper

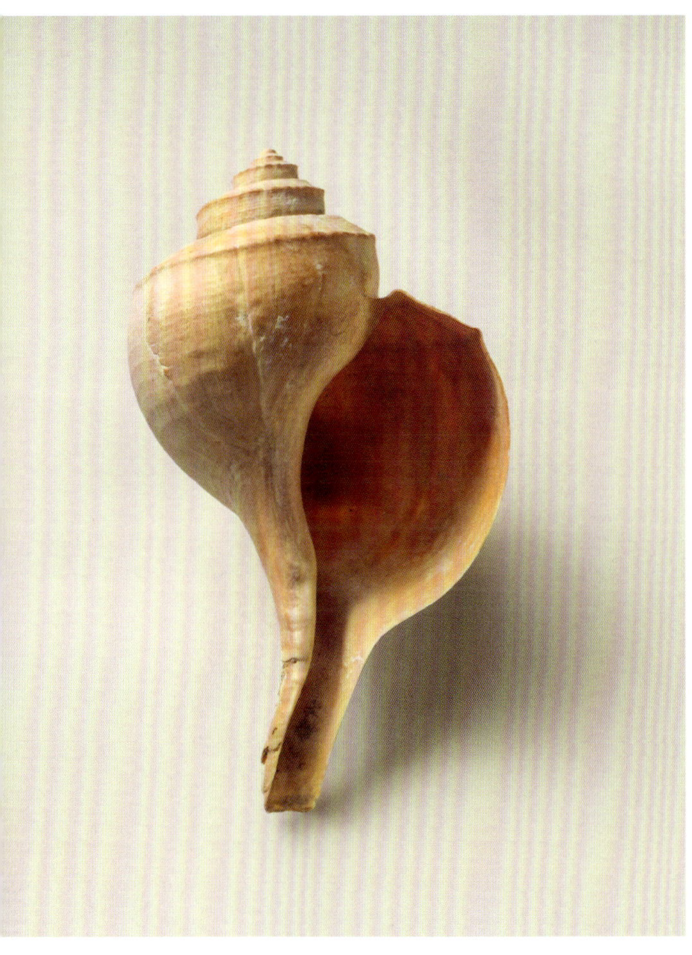

Photo by Stefan Hagen

For this project, I worked from life, setting up a seashell with a single light source. This variation uses toned paper. In Chapter 8, I share techniques for making a watercolor wash on mixed-media paper. This is a perfect project for such a prepared

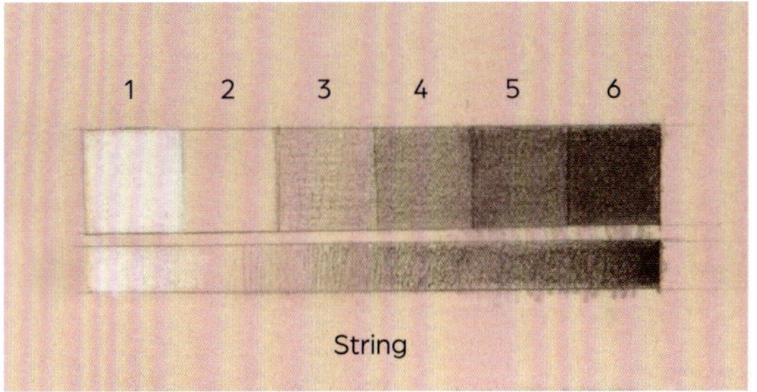

paper. Otherwise, there are many wonderful colored papers available for purchase in single sheets at an art supply store.

First, we will learn to understand the value of the paper by creating a value step scale. Next, we will create a drawing in graphite and add white colored pencil for the highlights.

STEP ONE

Each kind of toned paper has its own intrinsic value, so first make a value step scale on your new paper and drawing media.

Here, you see that the value of my paper fits into the value 2 box. For lighter values, add white, and for darker values, build up the graphite. If you have a darker paper, the value might fit in the value 3 box, so you would use more white, lightly at first in the value 2 box, and layered for full brightness in the value 1 box. Below the step scale is a *string*: a quick way to discover the possible range of values in your materials.

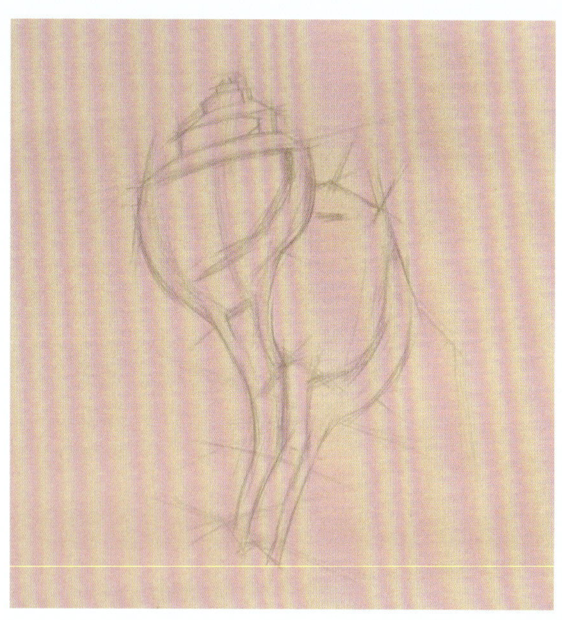

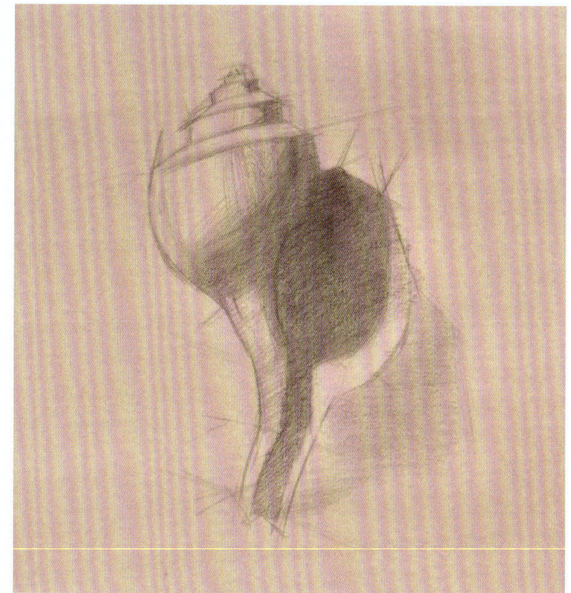

STEP TWO

Block in the contours and use comparative measurement to check the proportions.

Block in the terminator to plan the light shape and shadow shape.

STEP THREE

Shade in the shadow shapes with HB and 3B pencils, to values 4–6. In this drawing, I left the cast shadow pale and deepened the values in the shell to make it stand out from the background.

Be sure to make the shadows dark enough and blend and hatch the tone evenly. Minimize any reflected light and suggest it only subtly.

STEP FOUR

Add details in the light shape, using the HB pencil for value 3 where the form turns into the shadow. Let the paper remain in value 2.

Add delicate highlights for value 1 using a white colored pencil (like Prismacolor) or a white pastel pencil (like Pitt Pastel). Do *not* mix the graphite and the white pencils, or it will become grayed and muddy.

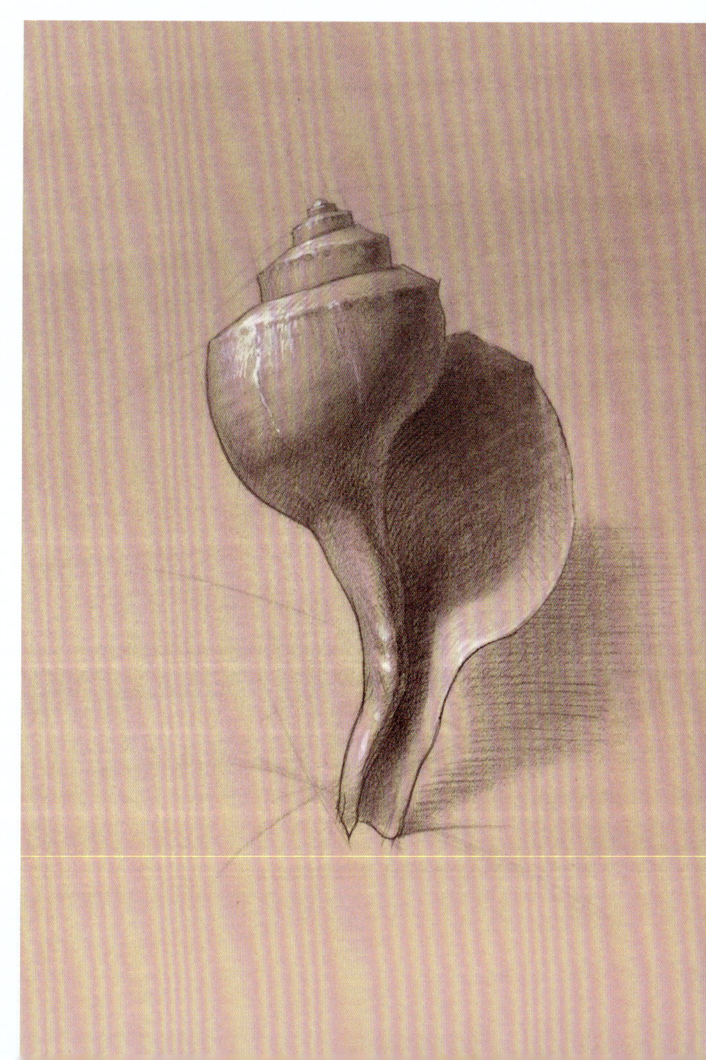

ARTISTIC SUPERPOWER

Can you visualize a sphere? A globe on a table at school? A translucent sphere covered in meridian lines? This is the spatial visual imagination. To render form, an artist must first observe carefully and also develop a mental conceptualization of the direction of the light and plane of the subject. The ability to accurately draw the two-dimensional shapes (as in *block-in* and *contour*) while concurrently visualizing a three-dimensional form is your "artistic superpower." The path of drawing leads to the refinement of this subtle mental capacity.

Early in our art studies, we focused on learning to see what is really before us, examining details, contours, and colors. These lessons in modeling with values help build our powers to create form with graphite and paper. After cultivating observational skills, the next stage is to build the spatial visual imagination and conceptualize form. The spatial imagination is like magic. The eye and mind together make it possible to draw and paint not just what you see, but what no one else can see—the stuff of dreams and imagination.

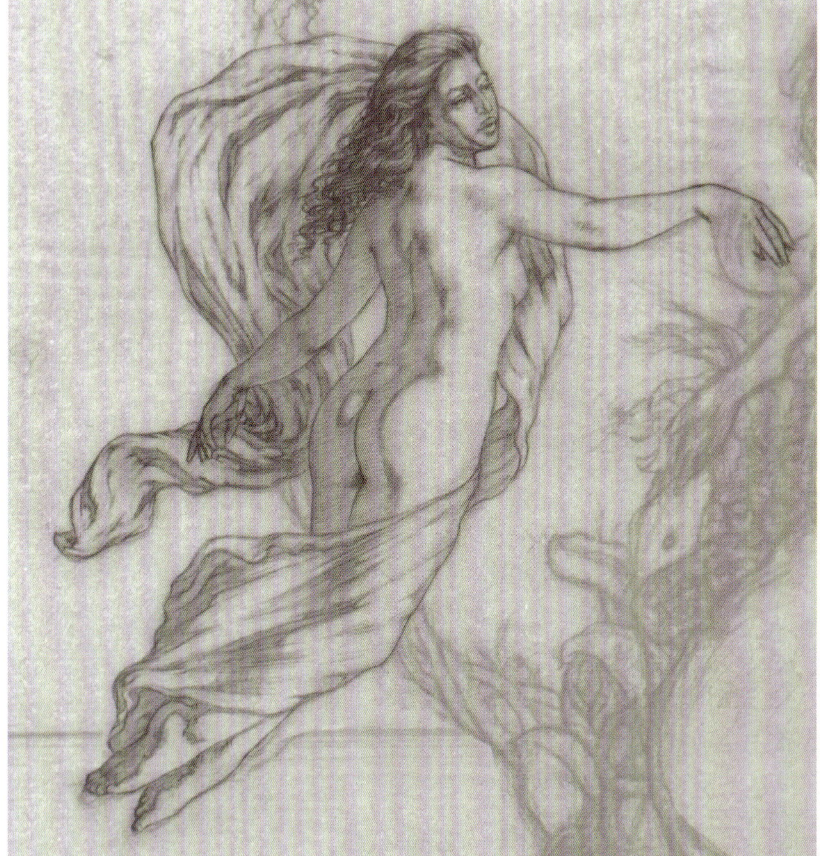

Tenaya Sims, *Drawing Study for Birth of Venus,* 2014, graphite on tracing paper, 16 x 16 inches (41 x 41 cm). Courtesy of the artist.

8

New Paths in Color

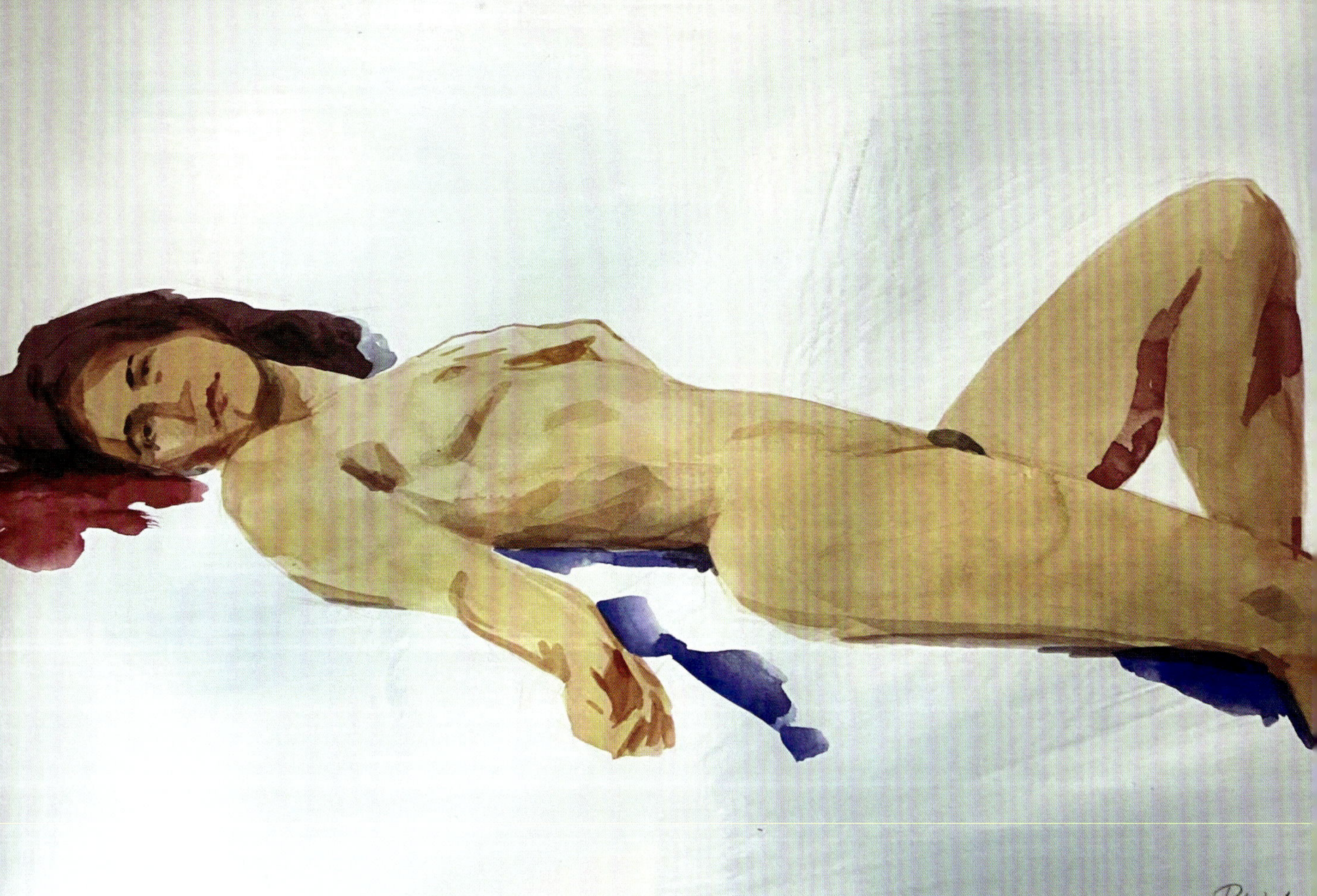

A paradox of art practice is that the seeds of boredom lie within the
comfort of ritual. We repeat processes to build our competence and master
skills that were once hard to pull off. But repetition eventually leads to
stagnation, with the inevitable next step of dropping the practice. We must
combine comforting practices with playful, enthusiastic discoveries. Writer
Julia Cameron recommends: "Enthusiasm (from the Greek, 'filled with God')
is an ongoing energy supply tapped into the flow of life itself. Enthusiasm is
grounded in play, not work."[14] To keep the fire of our practice alive, we need
to prioritize pleasure and maybe a bit of chaos.

A healthy balance between serious and playful practice is key to continued artistic growth. The "serious" practice keeps me learning and building
skills. The "play" keeps me wanting to return again and again. I add watercol-
or and other media to my sketchbook practice when I need to reconnect with
the *joy* of art. These simple additions keep my creative energy light-footed
and fresh precisely because they are unpredictable. What's going to happen?
I don't know! My sketches are not intended for the public eye. In this space
of free play, I intentionally detach from the certainty of a fixed outcome.
Here, I create art as a simple expression of my experience, not a product.

Opposite: Patricia Watwood,
Mackenzie, 2019, watercolor on
paper, 15 x 22 inches (38 x 56 cm).
Courtesy of the artist.

SIMPLE WAYS TO BEGIN WITH WATERCOLOR

Consider starting with one color of paint. One day in the studio, I will make
a quick wash of color for the simple pleasure of watching the pigments
swirl on the page. That colored page might sit for months, waiting for a new
drawing to top it. It's a reminder to the future me: "Hey, I started something
for you here. Why don't you add a drawing?" Yet another way to disrupt the
fear of the blank page.

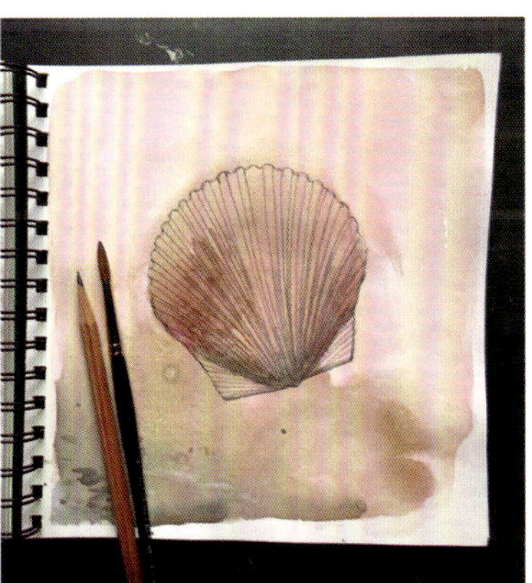

Left: Here's a watercolor
wash, applied somewhat
playfully, with just one color.

Right: This shell drawing
shows a simple watercolor
wash with a graphite drawing
on top.

Watercolor Circle Washes

Note: This project will create a unique page you'll use for a project in Chapter 10.

This project combines elements of exploration, intuition, and imagination. Watercolor is a unique medium, as the pigments make unpredictable effects as they flow together with water. Over time, you'll become familiar with the beautiful ways that watercolors float and bleed. I find their interaction with water mesmerizing, and this simple project quickly gets me lost in my work.

Trace a circle with pencil on sturdy mixed-media or watercolor paper using a 5- to 8-inch plastic container lid, plate, or stencil.

Pick two colors (here I used Alizarin Crimson and Winsor Blue) and squeeze a bit of each on a palette or ceramic plate. Taking a three-quarter-inch mop brush, clean water, and a few paper towels, make two puddles of paint by diluting each color separately.

With a clean three-quarter-inch oval wash brush (which has both a large belly and a decent point),

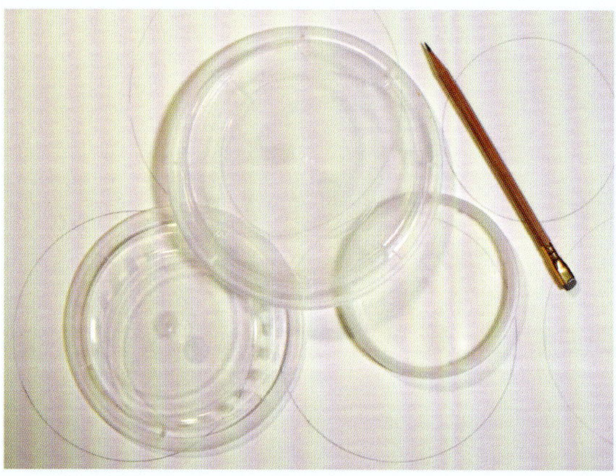

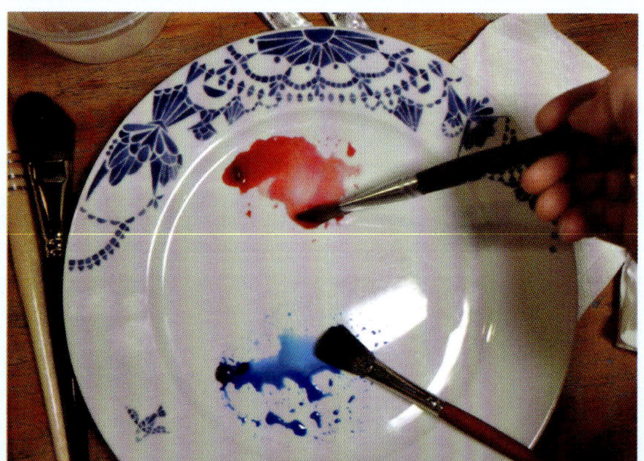

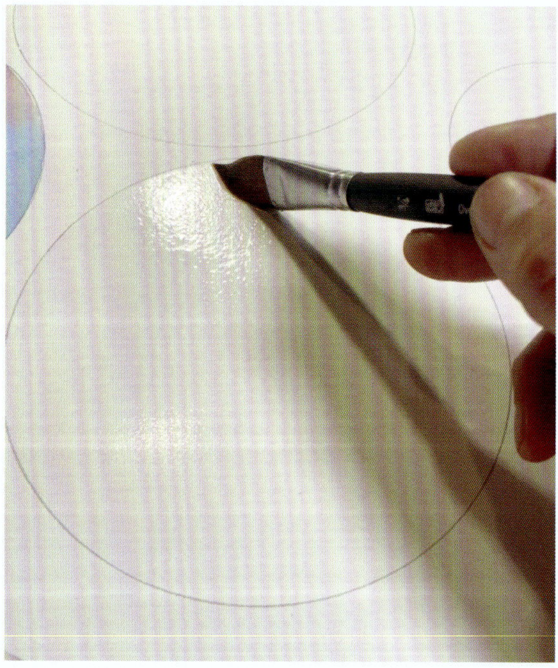

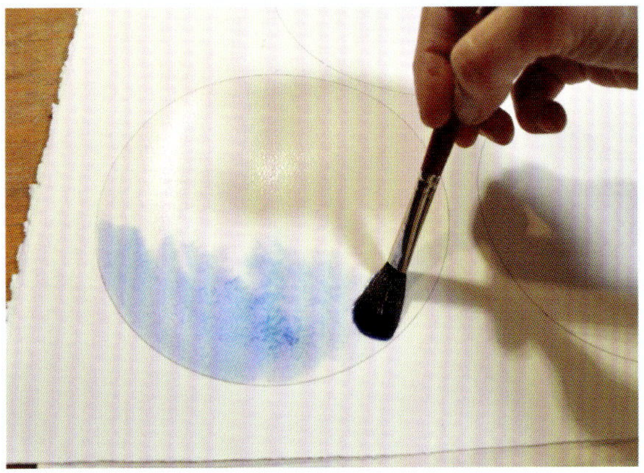

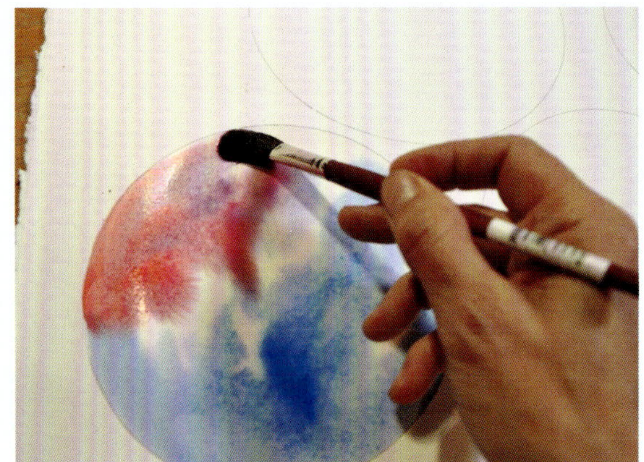

mop a layer of clear water onto the circle. Don't worry about crossing over the pencil lines.

Working quickly, while the whole circle is still wet, load a brush with one color and swirl it onto part of the circle. Notice how the color pulls and floats into the wet paper.

Rinse your brush and load it up with the second color. Fill in the circle by swirling the two colors together in the wet wash. Don't be shy of bold color. Vivid puddles can be thrilling, and also dry lighter.

You can use a clean brush or a rolled piece of paper towel to lift out color and manipulate drifting puddles as you like. Watch how the pigments move, and enjoy the beauty of their interaction with water. These circles take only a few minutes— try various colors and lose yourself in the visual joy without expectation of great results.

Let the paper dry completely. If it warps a bit, you can flatten it under a drawing board topped with a few heavy books. (Caution: Thin paper will not flatten.)

Once the paper is dry, use a pencil, marker, or other medium to top the wash with a drawing. The colors

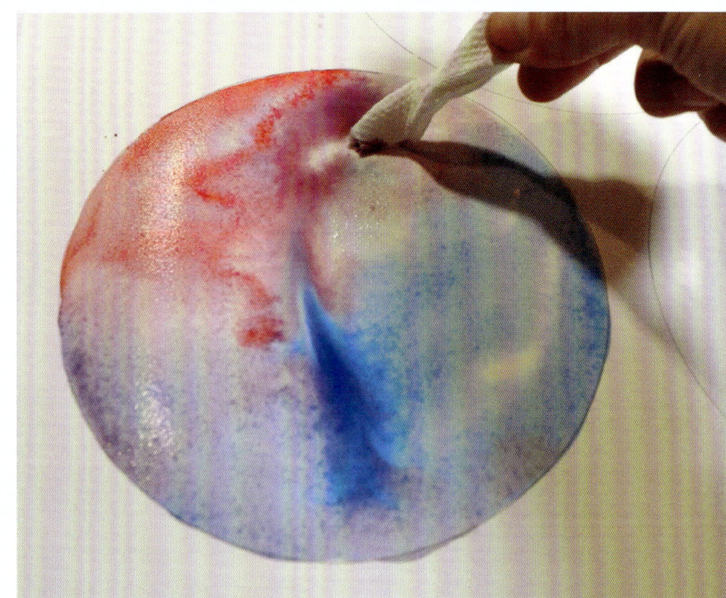

I create watercolor circles and washes in my mixed-media sketchbook and add a drawing (here, drawn from imagination, in ink) at a later time.

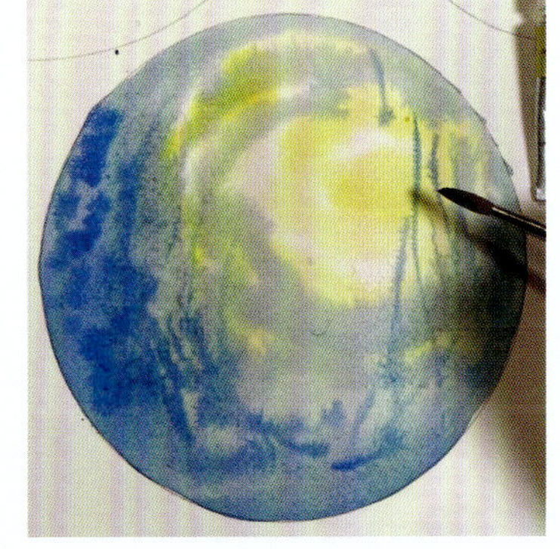

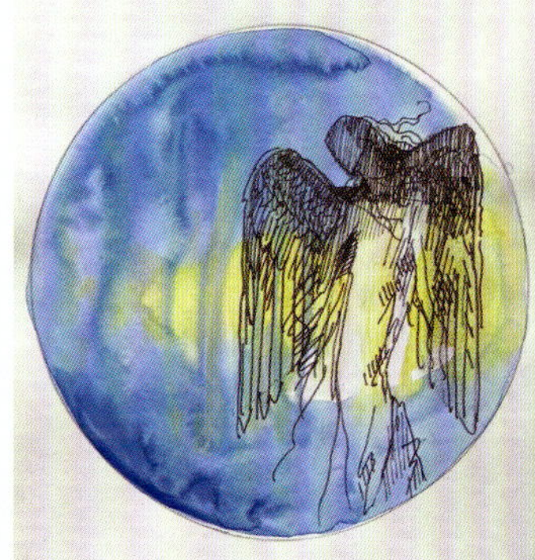

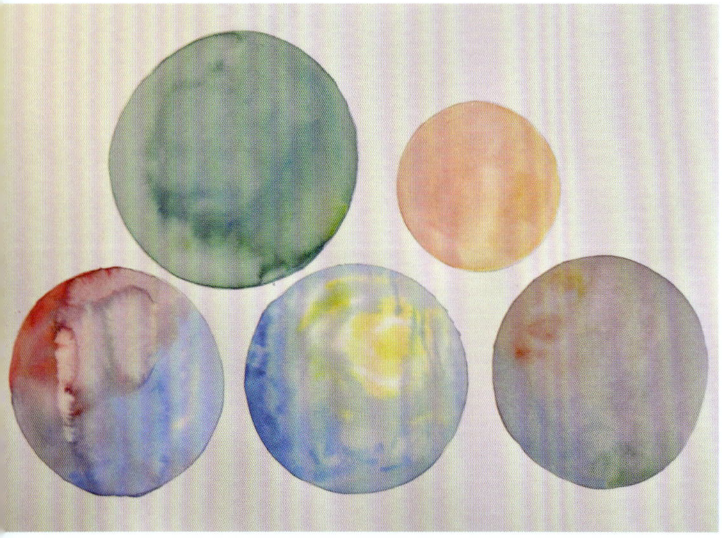

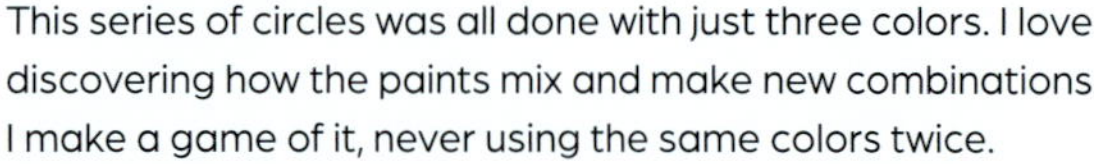

This series of circles was all done with just three colors. I love discovering how the paints mix and make new combinations. I make a game of it, never using the same colors twice.

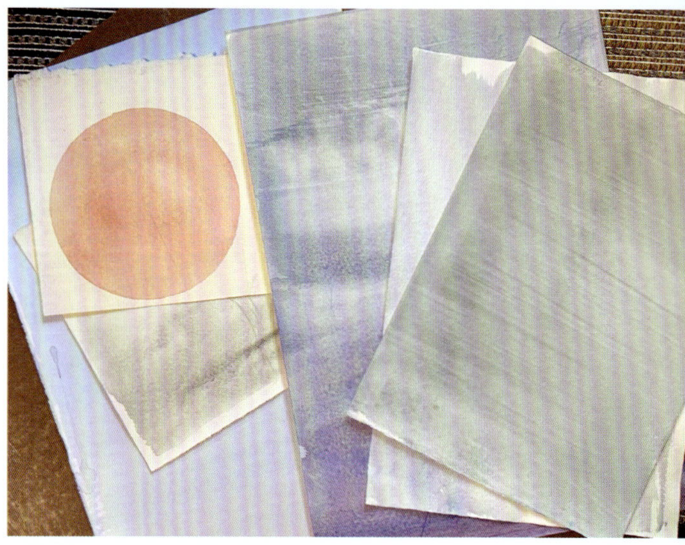

These papers are prepared with simple watercolor washes to create a unique surface for a drawing.

and shapes created in the watercolor circle can suggest an image that emerges unconsciously. Should your imagination be sparked by the swirling forms, take note and enjoy the journey.

HOW TO MAKE A ONE-COLOR WASH

Use your mixed-media sketchbook or a sheet of thick mixed-media or watercolor paper, like Arches Aquarelle or Fabriano Artistico 140 lb. hot press watercolor paper (use a full, half, or quarter sheet).

With a large mop brush, prepare a large puddle of color on a ceramic plate or palette. One color, like Payne's gray, ultramarine blue, or burnt umber, will make a good general-purpose tone. I will often mix two colors, like indanthrone blue and alizarin crimson, to make a mixed violet or other unique hue.

With a wide wash brush (like a 2-inch hake brush), wet the entire page with clean water.

Working quickly, pick up a load of colored wash from your puddle with the wide wash brush and lay it on the wet paper in long, wide bands. Tone the whole page in one direction, picking up more color as needed from your puddle of paint. To even the tone, cross the strokes a second time in the perpendicular direction.

Let the tone be a bit darker than you think you want it. It will fade when it dries.

To make the tone more textured, try sprinkling part of the page with salt, or flick the page with a spray of droplets of watercolor or wet paint. I like to add more irregular touches of paint around the edges and leave the center smooth.

Lay the paper flat to dry.

When your papers are dry, press them under a drawing board with a heavy weight to flatten them out, and store for later use.

LEARNING ABOUT COLOR WITH A LIMITED PALETTE

It is easy to get overwhelmed with new colors and materials, so instead I recommend starting with just a few. The watercolor artist Thomas W Schaller uses a simple palette for travel and gets gorgeous colorful results. The sketch below includes French Ochre, Burnt Sienna Light, Burnt Sienna, Cobalt Teal Blue, and French Ultramarine. Schaller's colors have poetic names, and they are traditional pigments that artists have used for many centuries. Essentially, they are good old-fashioned reds, yellow, and blues. Any secondary colors like orange and green are mixed. When limiting your palette, there will be some vivid hues of fuchsia and apple green that may be a bit hard to match, but I find that what I lose in precise hue, I gain in overall harmony. When we build our palette from a few primaries, the secondary and neutral mixtures all seem to go together like a chic piece of interior design instead of a crazy clown car of clashing colors. A small tube can cost five to seven dollars and lasts me a year or more. You can adapt

In this travel sketch, Thomas Schaller creates harmonious tonal relationships out of two dominant colors: a rosy orange, and its complement, bluegreen. Simplifying color in this way can create unity from complex visual data.

Thomas W Schaller, *Dock–Giudecca*, 2019, watercolor on paper, 9 x 12 inches (25 x 30 cm). Courtesy of the artist.

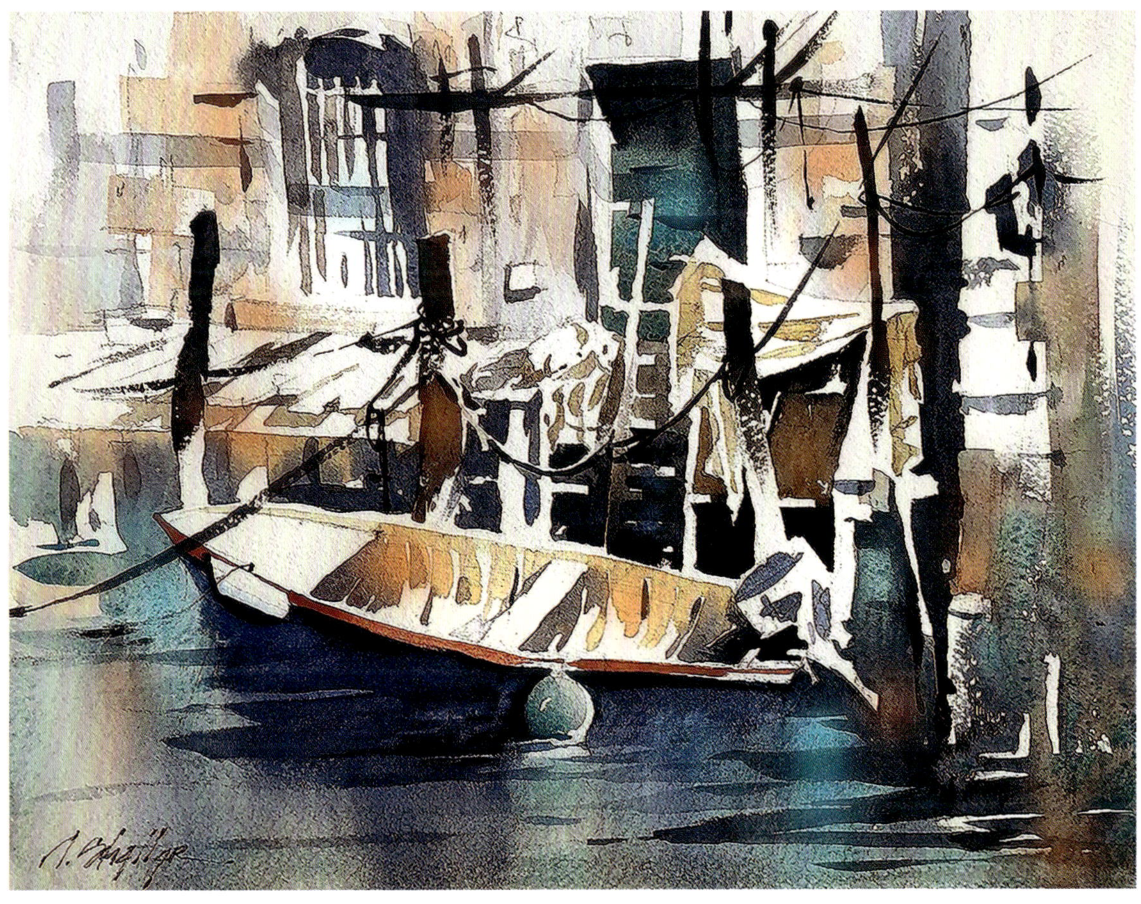

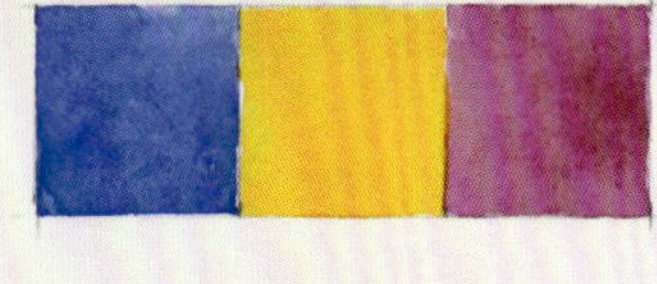

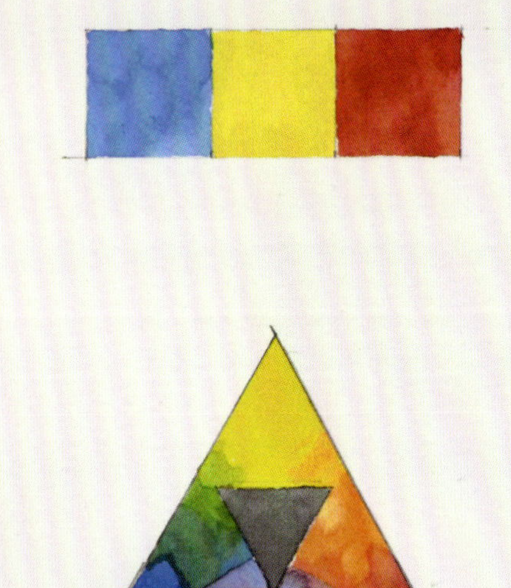

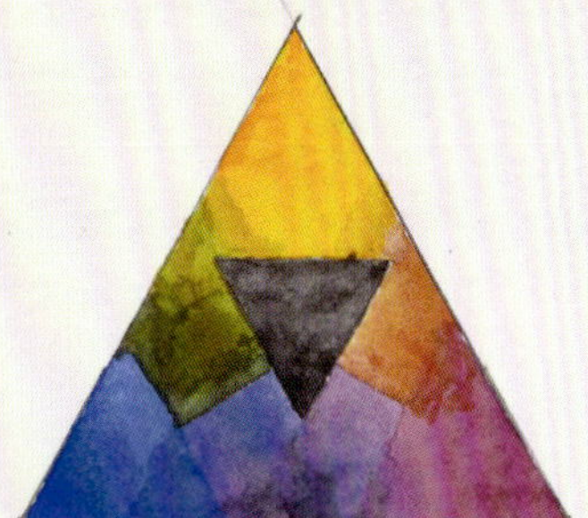

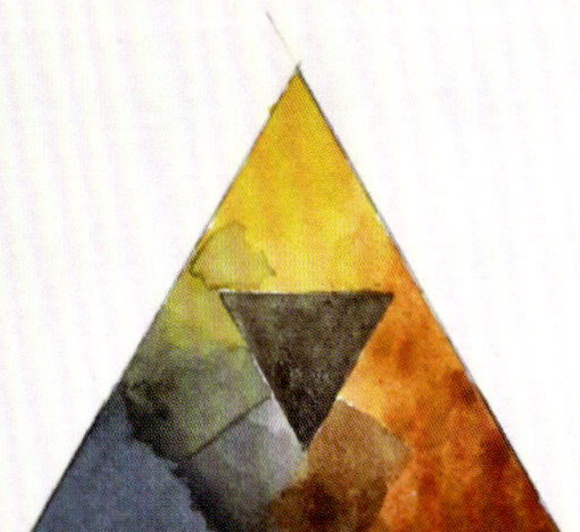

Palette One: Basic Primaries
Winsor Blue (red shade) PB15*
Winsor Yellow PY154
Alizarin Crimson PR83

Palette Two: Vibrant Combos
Ultramarine Blue PB29
Cadmium Yellow Deep PY37
Quinacridone Magenta PV19

Palette Three: Earth Tones
Payne's Gray PB15, PBk6, PV19
Yellow Ochre PY43
Burnt Sienna PB

*Note: Every color has a universally used code number for pigments. Paint makers may give a red a name like "magic rose," but if you know the pigment number, you know exactly what it is and can match across manufacturers; i.e., PB: "Pigment Blue" and 15: Phthalocyanine (see the Color of Art Pigment Database at artiscreation.com). Natural pigment shades vary. Good paint makers print this info on the label.

the ideas here with many media—acrylics, gouache, markers, colored pencils. Start with three colors and build out when you discover a material you love.

When artists use a restricted set of colors, we call it a *limited palette*. The elegance of using a small number of paints is beneficial for several reasons:

- It's affordable to start with just a few tubes of paint.
- We learn how to get the greatest range out of a single color.
- We gain intimate knowledge of a color's properties—the hue, texture, strength, and character in mixtures.

This sampler shows three pairs of different limited palettes. The first two bars are variations on saturated (strongly colored) primary colors. The triangles illustrate the mixing of these primaries into secondary colors. In the center of each triangle is a "mixed neutral"—a gray made with all three colors. The third triangle of colors uses natural pigments in duller hues, that are great for skin tones and earth colors.

On his travels in Cuba, Thomas Schaller made a fading ruin into a

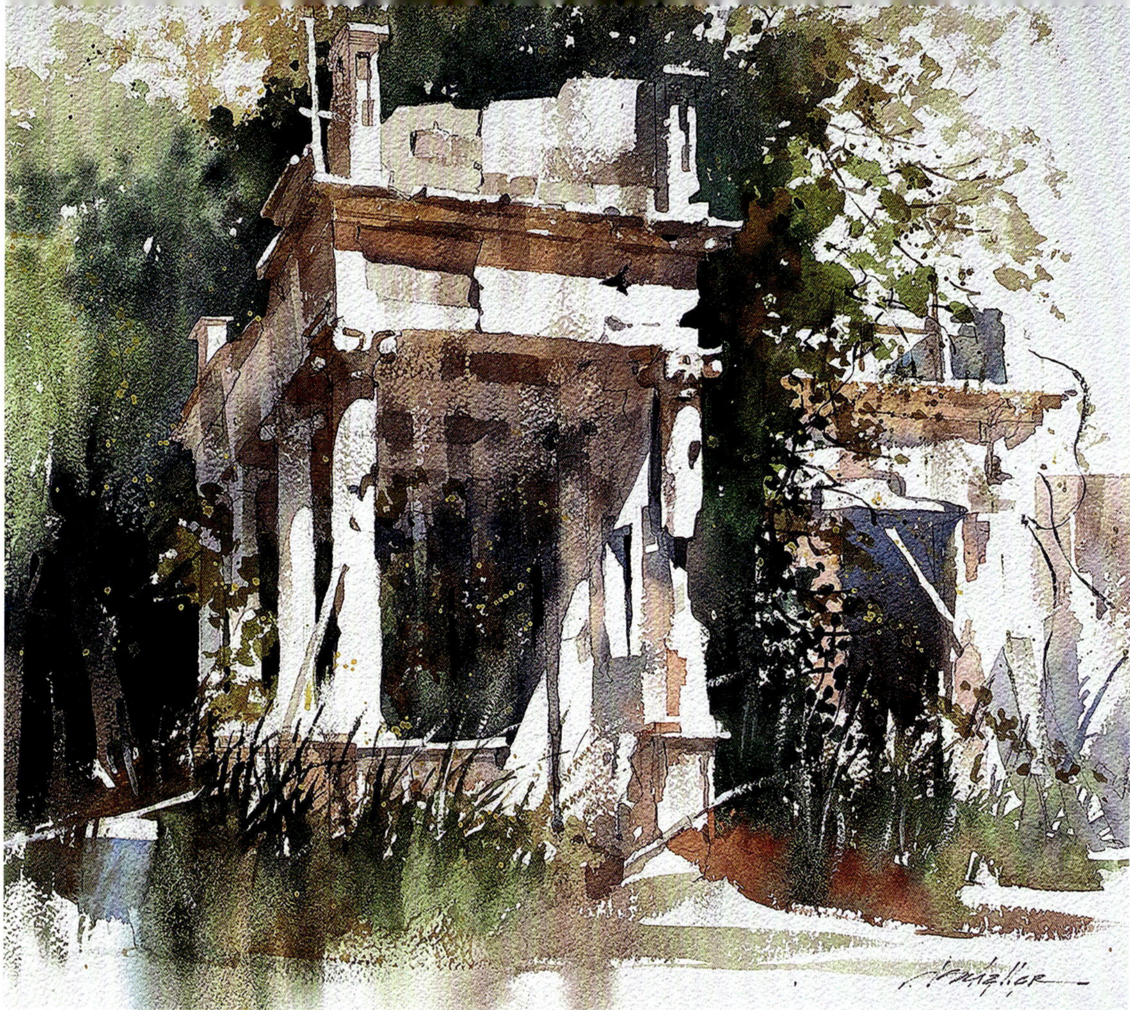

majestic testimony of contrasting light and dynamic color in *Still Standing–Havana*. Notice how Schaller uses warm sienna in the shadow of the stone, and cool green and blues in the deep shadows surrounding the bright white stone. Attention to complementary tones, and shifts of warm to cool make the lighting effect vibrant. Another example is the intermixture of green grasses into the red earth tones at the base of the colonnade. When you allow the colors to intermix visually on the page, you can create lush neutrals instead of muddy browns. When experimenting with a limited palette, avoid making the tones too similar and neutral, and instead explore the full possible range of hues you can create with three paints.

Thomas Schaller's limited palette used here: French Ochre, Burnt Sienna Light, Serpentine Green, Jadeite Green, Ultramarine Blue.

Thomas W Schaller, *Still Standing— Havana*, 2019, watercolor on paper, 14 x 14 inches. (36 x 36 cm). Courtesy of the artist.

More ideas for three–color palettes:

Yellow Ochre	Indian Yellow	Yellow Ochre
Ivory Black	Prussian Blue	Cerulean Blue
Cadmium Red Light	Venetian Red	Cadmium Red Light

Intuitive Explorations in Color

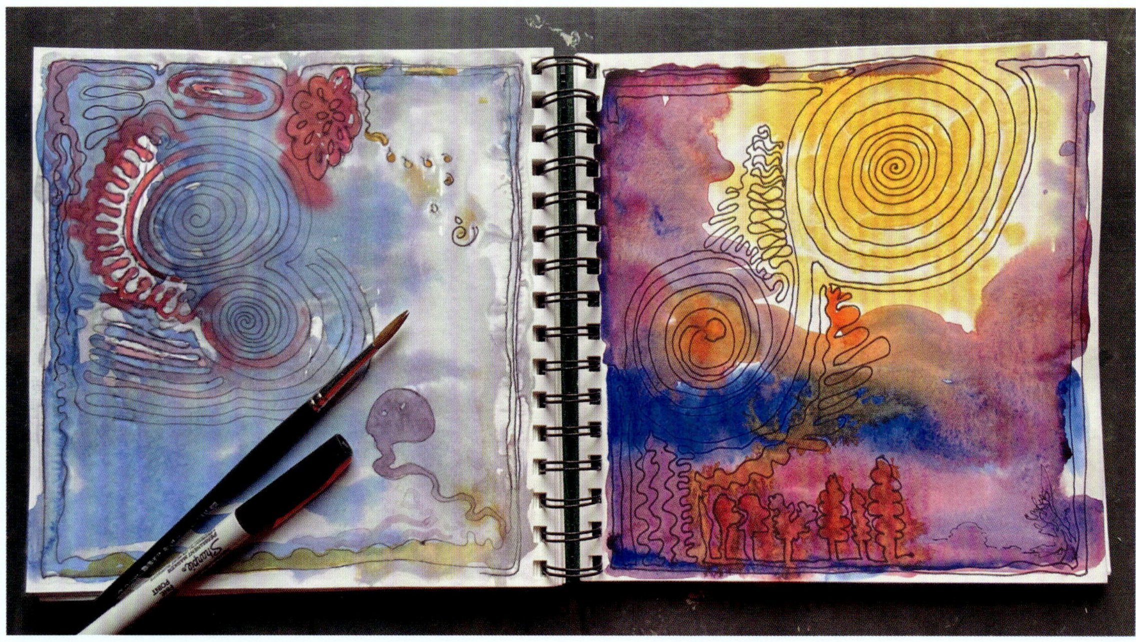

To explore a limited palette, this project begins with an imaginative abstract drawing in pen and layers watercolor puddles and washes on top.

The sketchbook image above shows an easy, intuitive way to begin playing with color.

Use a fine-point permanent marker (waterproof, such as a Sharpie or Micron pen) and sturdy watercolor paper.

This is a centering practice that will bring you to an attentive connection with the page, using your intuition. Start at a random point on the paper. Move your hand in any shape or direction according to these two rules:

1. Do not cross over another line.
2. Do not lift the pen from the paper.

Using a limited palette of three colors, add washes and shapes to your drawing. You might "see" forms and wish to define them more with color. Or your image may be entirely abstract, so follow your intuition about picking colors or passages. Freely experiment with drippy bleeds and overlapping tones, and use highly saturated washes for rich, bold colors. Shhh…sometimes I add more marker.

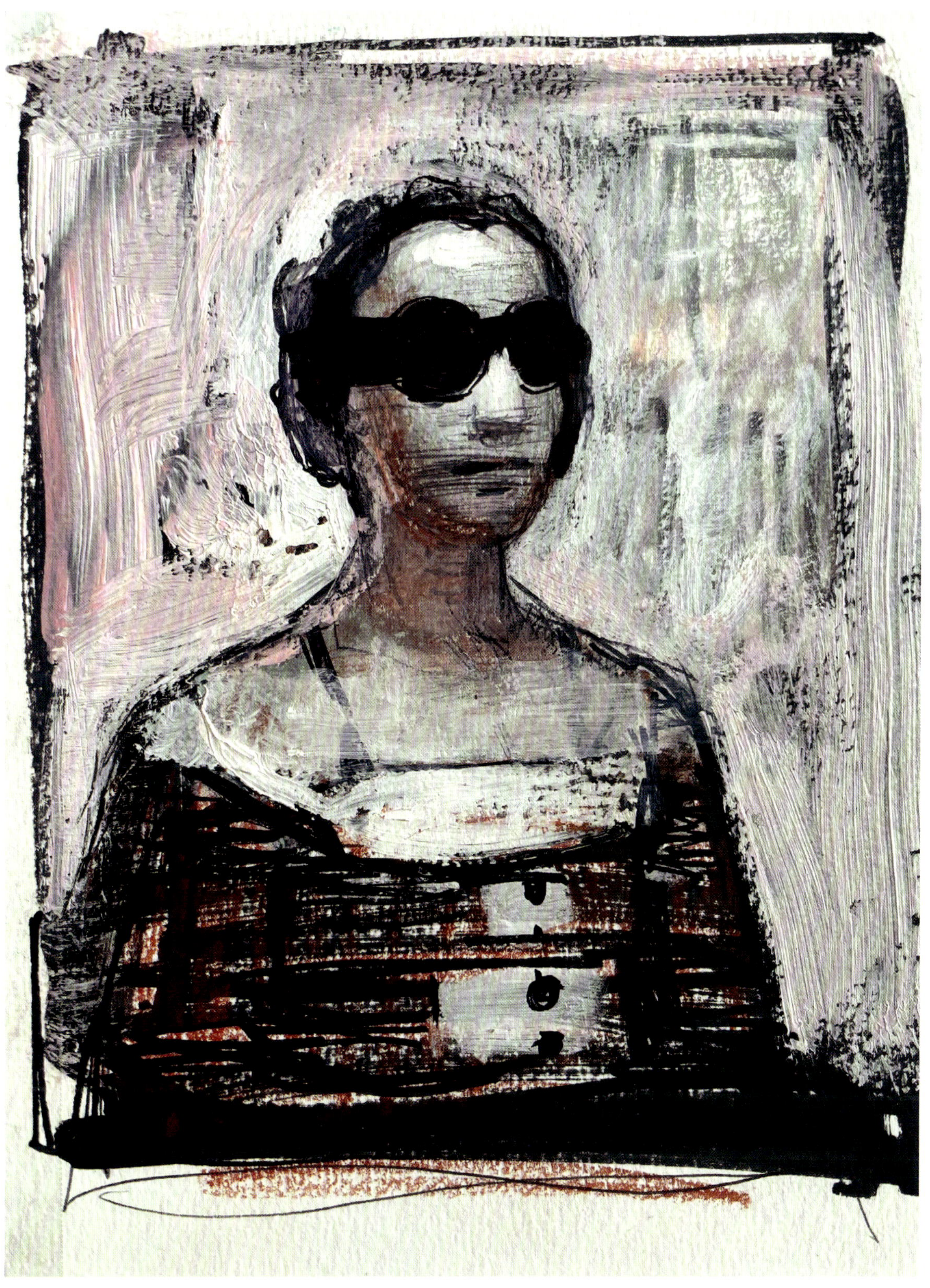

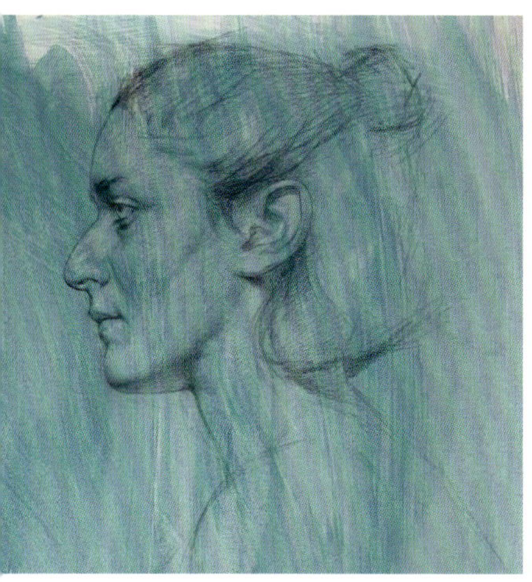

Above: The relaxed modern chroma in the background updates a classical profile.

Nicole Michelle Tully, *JM on Green* (detail), 2018, graphite and white chalk on paper toned with watercolor, 12 x 9 inches (30 x 23 cm). Courtesy of the artist.

IDEAS FOR MIXED MEDIA

There are so many delightful tools for adding color and variety to your sketchbook. You are *not* too old for glitter gel pens. The artist Janet A. Cook's favorite implements include opaque white Sakura Gelly Roll gel pens, which can be used to draw on darker colors or make corrections on white paper. She also likes colorful Pigma Micron pens with archival inks, which come in dozens of colors including neons. They resist fading and bleeding and freely mix with watercolor.

In her portrait sketch *Rachel in Yellow* (opposite), Cook's playful yellow pen stopped me in my tracks. A *yellow* marker for a portrait? With this color choice, the sitter becomes radiant with inner energy. Cook explains, "I started using pen and ink because I was dismayed to find that carrying my sketchbook around could smudge my pencil sketches. I find pen and ink helps me make better decisions about proportion, and there is less room for mistakes." The graphic boldness of markers and pens can make a quick project on paper feel complete.

Below: Nicolas Sanchez, *Azulito*, 2015, colored ballpoint pen on paper, 8 x 10 inches (20 x 25 cm). Courtesy of the artist.

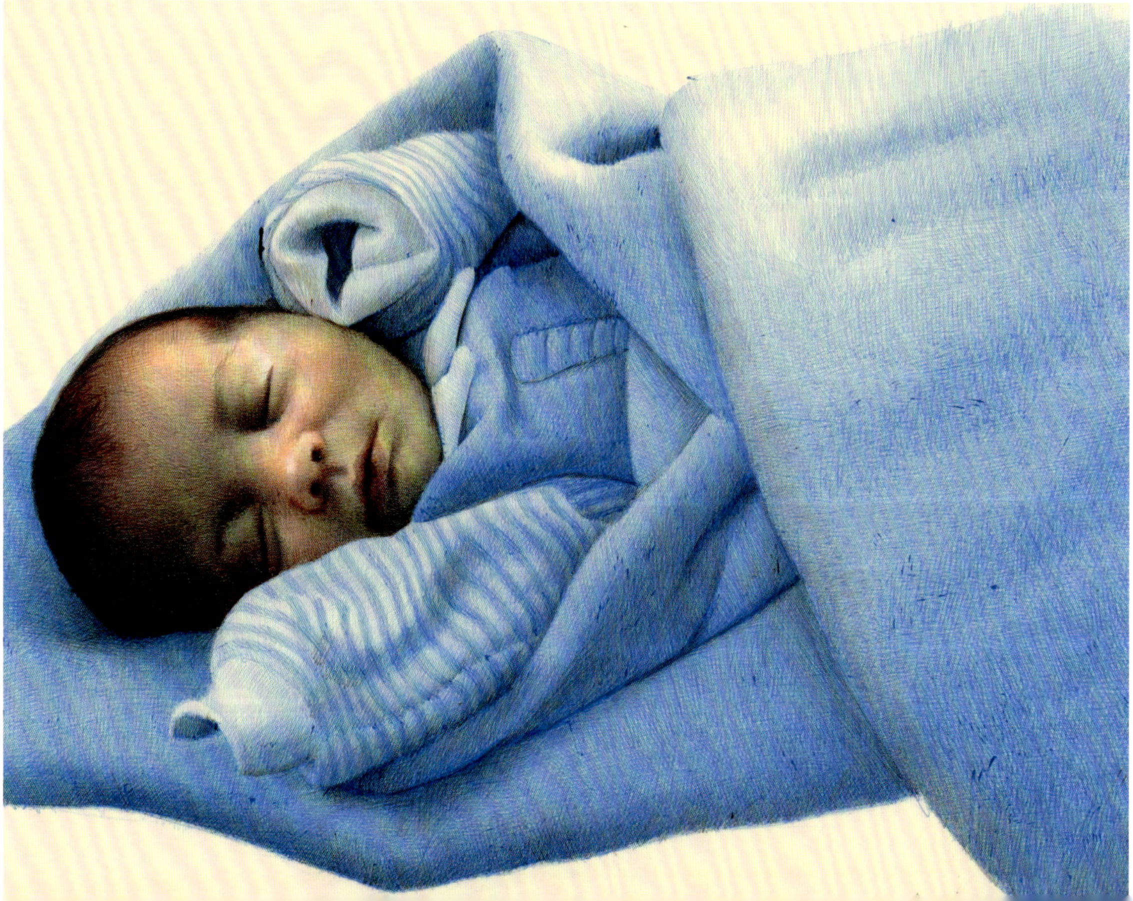

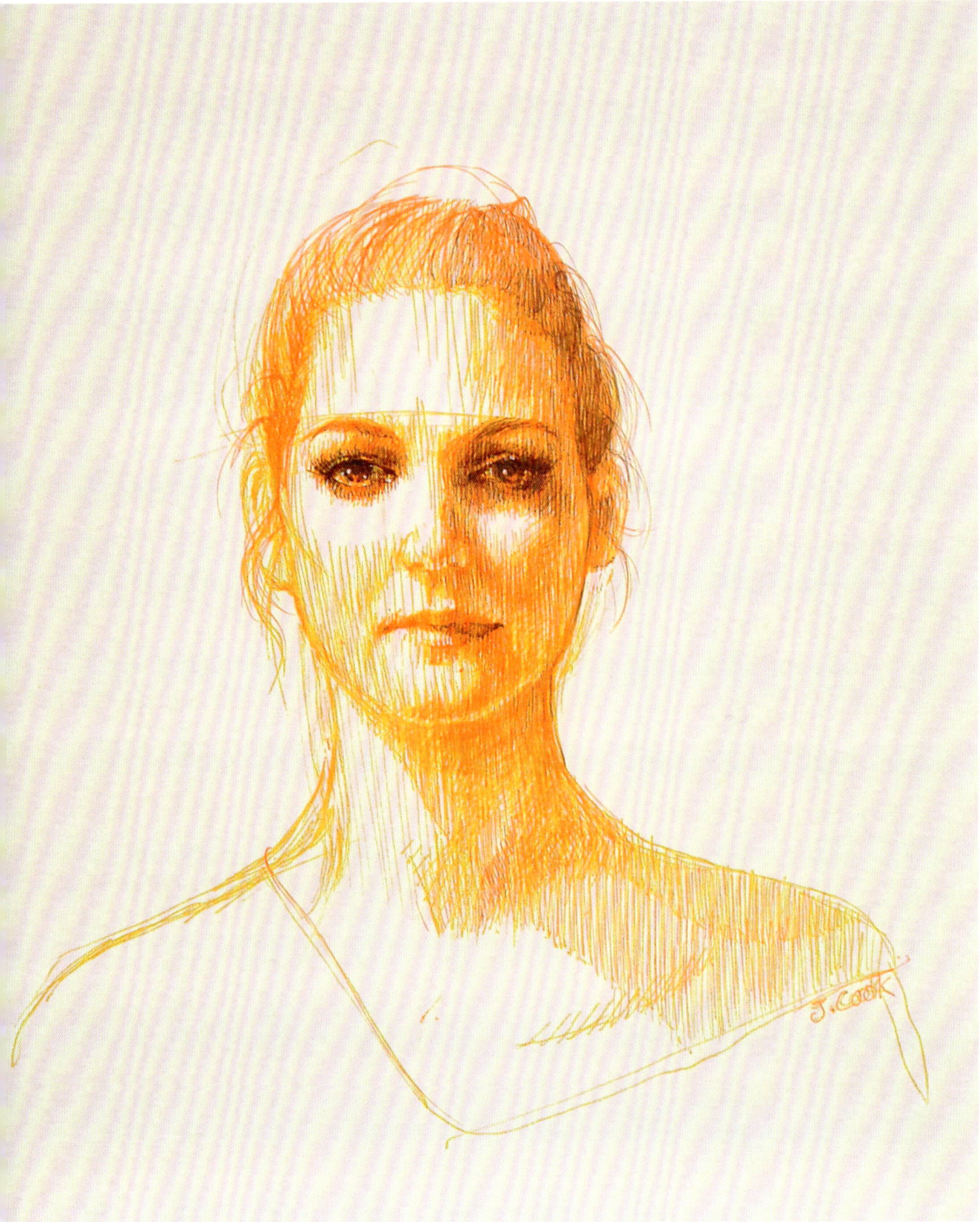

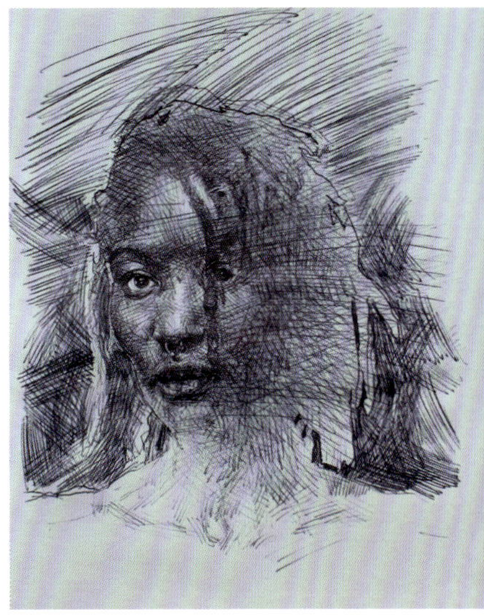

Artists submerge errors
and placement marks in a
network of dynamic lines.

Above: Austin Uzor, *Untitled*,
2020, ballpoint pen on paper, 12 x
8½ inches (30 x 22 cm). Courtesy
of the artist.

Left: Janet A. Cook, *Rachel in
Yellow*, 2018, Pigma Micron pen on
paper, 10 x 8 inches (25 x 20 cm).
Courtesy of the artist

Using markers and pens forces a commitment to your lines, and errors
must be embraced or hidden within a network of other lines. Working in pen
or marker can significantly improve your graphic work, pushing you to be
more intentional, specific, and controlled in your use of line. When you are
first starting, the permanence of the marks can be daunting. Embrace the
chaos for a moment and make four or five quick works with a nonerasable
drawing tool before you decide how you like the effects.

Page 149: Brooks Frederick, *Pink
Punk*, 2021, graphite, charcoal,
chalk, Sharpie markers, gesso, and
acrylic on paper, 8½ x 5½ inches
(22 x 14 cm). Courtesy of the artist.

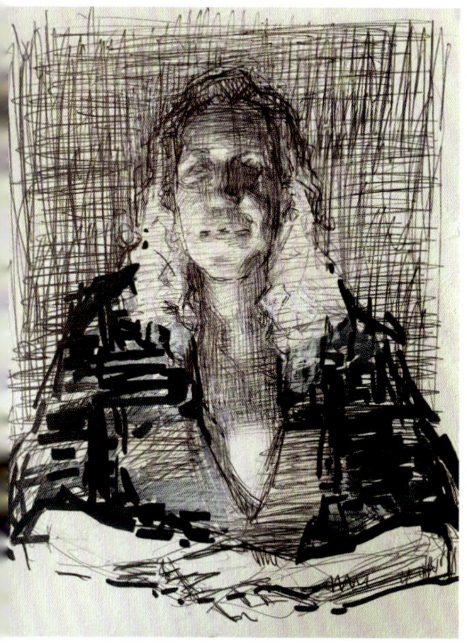

Too often, we get attached to our first idea and move forward with a composition solely because we've worked on it for a long time. Instead, make multiple sketches, fast and loose, which allow you to try visual ideas without getting bogged down in corrections and perfections. This process cultivates detachment and leads to more surprising and innovative choices.

Artist Brooks Frederick uses mixed media in his myriad fast sketches. Working quickly—sometimes in only five or ten minutes—Frederick intentionally changes his materials; for example, switching to a bold neon pen or a quirky new substrate such as Yupo paper (a plastic drawing sheet). "Childlike materials put me in a less self-conscious place," Frederick notes. He starts with a thought—"I've never done an academic drawing with a Sharpie"—and picks up a marker to see where it leads. Some solutions require fresh innovations with your tools. By trusting in a process of exploration and disruption, Frederick unearths new visual ideas and stays enthusiastic about his drawing practice.

Brooks Frederick, *Jess in a Robe*, 2020, ballpoint pen and chalk on paper, 8½ x 5½ inches (22 x 14 cm). Collection of the artist.

Right: Brooks Frederick (upper right image is collaboration with Craig Banholzer), *Life Studies*, 2021, mixed media on various papers, 12 x 9 inches (30 x 23 cm) and 11 x 14 inches (28 x 36 cm). Courtesy of the artists.

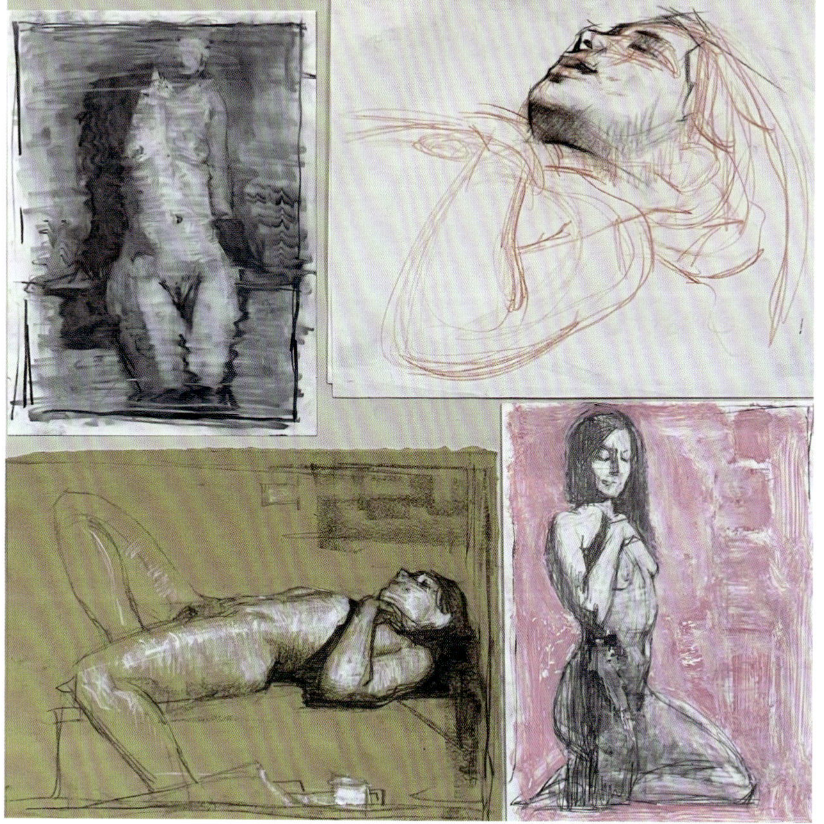

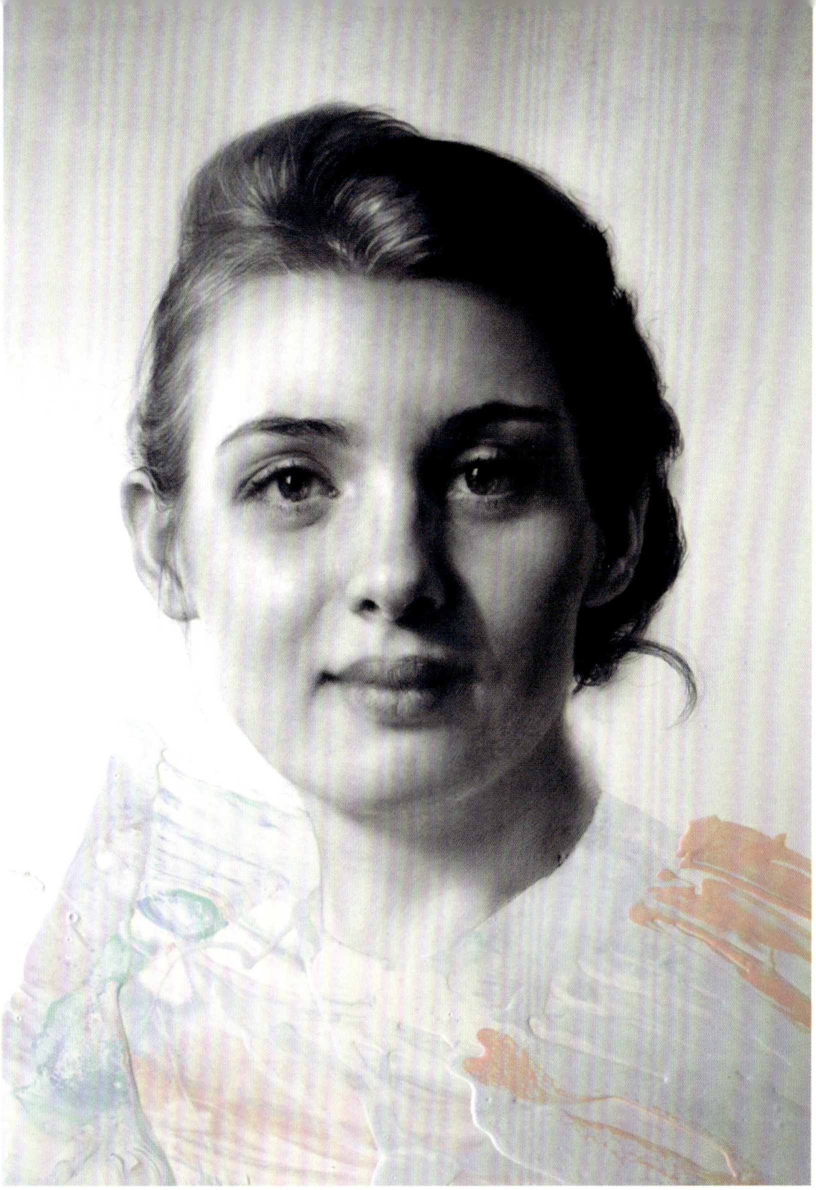

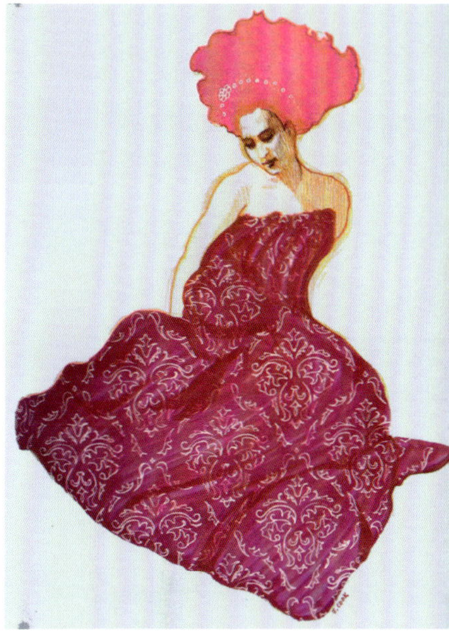

The life drawings by Brooks Frederick and Craig Banholzer (opposite) show a variety of combos you might play with to mix up your game.

1. Sharpie, eraser, and colorless blender on Yupo paper
2. Red sanguine and compressed charcoal on Strathmore paper
3. Compressed and vine charcoal and white gouache on tan BFK Rives paper
4. Graphite, marker, and acrylic paint on mixed-media paper

The use of stencils might seem like cheating, but professional artists are game to employ them in their graphic work. Ornate patterns are visually alluring, and mixing in stencils opens another door for ideas. They are widely available at art and craft supply stores and online.

MIXED-MEDIA PAPERS

Tools that artists often mix into a sketchbook include colored pencils, markers, gouache, acrylic paints, inks, and collage. A mixed-media sketchbook is designed to handle many materials, including wet water washes and glues, without wrinkling or tearing, and has thick enough pages that most markers will not bleed through. Papers are marketed by weight with a pound (lb.) or grams per square meter (gsm) designation that tells you how thick it is. For a sturdy mixed-media book that won't warp or bleed with wet materials, look for 90–140 lb. (160–260 gms). For loose sheets, I buy 140-lb. (252 gsm) paper.

I prefer a spiral-bound book that lays completely flat. I like sizes 6 × 9 inches to 9 × 12 inches, either square or rectangular format.

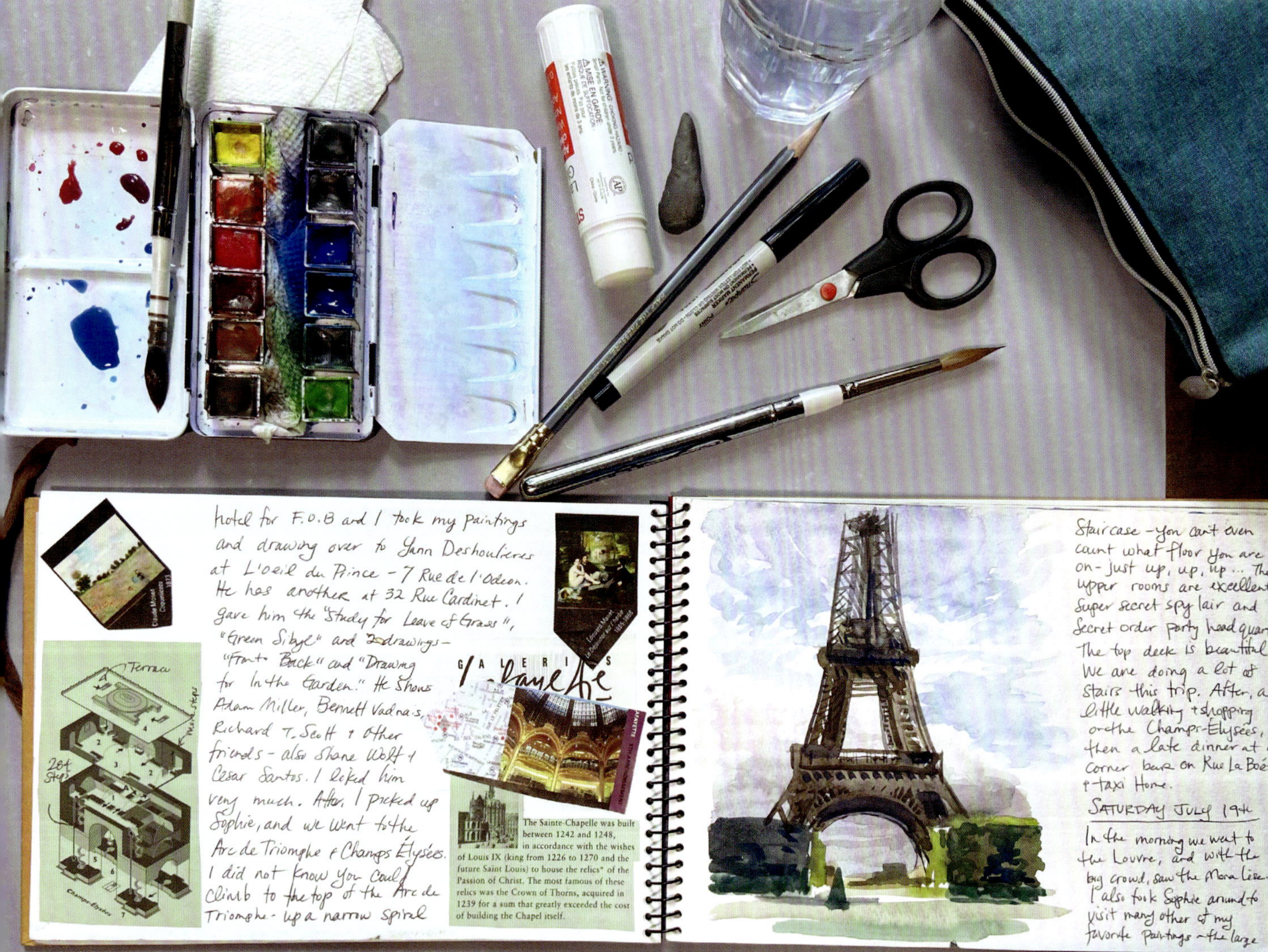

HOW TO BUILD A TRAVEL SKETCHBOOK KIT

When I travel, I carry my small sketchbook along with a pouch for water-colors, brushes, pencils, a couple of waterproof markers, and erasers. I also bring a pair of tiny scissors and a glue stick. I love to collect ephemera from the places I visit, like ticket stubs, brochures, menus, receipts, and even food wrappers. When I go, I'll pack a sturdy transparent plastic envelope that's useful for papers collected along the way. I'll cut and glue them into my sketchbook, along with travel notes and lists of yummy things I got to eat. Spending FOB time (that's *feet on bed*) working on my sketchbook gives me time to rest and cherish the experiences of the day. Nothing helps you remember the smells, air, light, and feelings like sitting down to sketch or add to your book in a special location. All of these visuals leave me with strong memories of my travels and are a far better souvenir than a T-shirt.

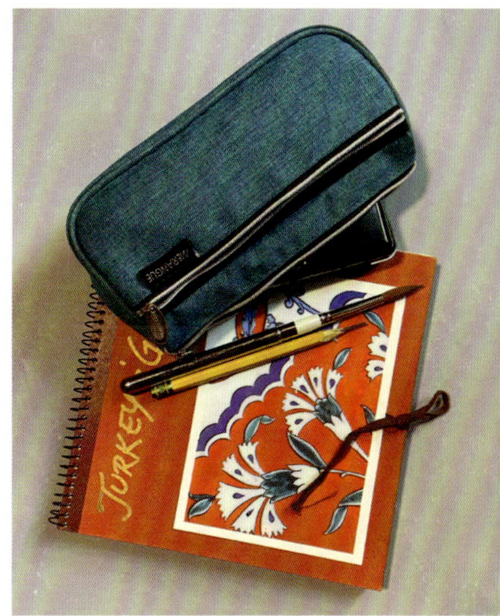

WHAT'S IN MY KIT

Mixed-media sketchbook (6 × 9 inches or 8 × 8 inches), with tie or elastic closure

Translucent plastic envelope with closure in 6 × 9-inch or letter size, for gathering ephemera

Two pencils with built-in erasers

Fine-point Sharpie permanent marker

Blue Rollerball pen

Small scissors (about 4 inches long)

Small glue stick

Small piece of kneaded eraser

Small piece of sandpaper (about 2 × 3 inches) and a single-edged razor blade (for sharpening pencils)

Three to four short-handled watercolor brushes, including:

- One small, pointy sable-type round
- One medium sable-type round
- One wash/mop brush ½ inch across or more

For travel

Rosemary & Co, watercolor travel brushes:

- R10 Pocket Golden Synthetic Pointed Size 8
- R3 Pocket Pure Kolinsky Sable Pointed Size 10

Two to three paper towels, cut into half sheets

Water bottle

6–10 oz. plastic cup (or find on site)

Fabric zippered carrying case for these items

Plastic folding watercolor palette and three tubes of watercolors

Four tubes of watercolors, .17 oz./5 ml (the following are Winsor & Newton colors, but Sennelier and other brands also work well)

- Winsor Yellow PY154
- Alizarin Crimson PR83
- Winsor Blue (red shade) PB15:1
- Burnt Sienna PBr7

For a complete set, try the Sennelier travel watercolor palette, Metal Pocket Case Set "A" of 12

Leaf Drawing with Watercolor

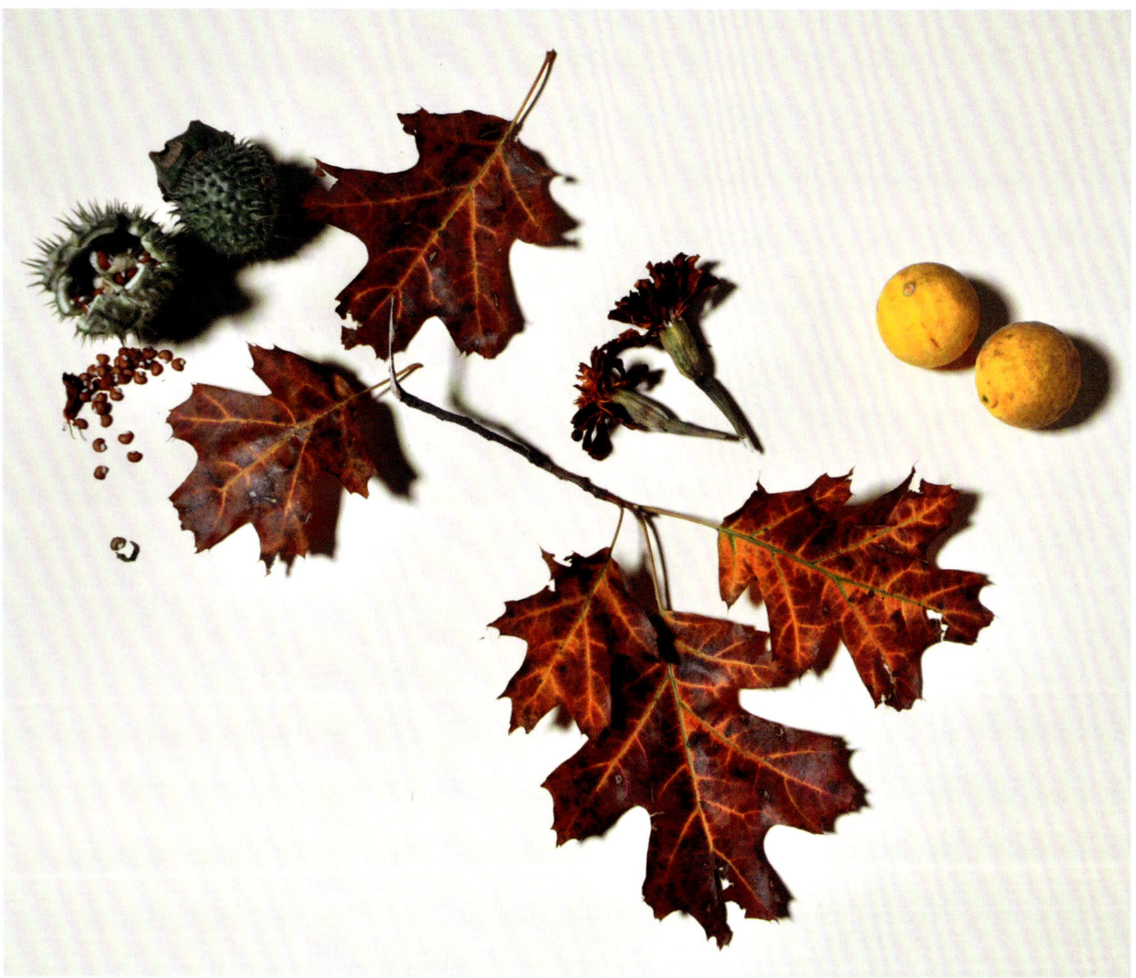

This project adds watercolor to a Gathering From Nature project, as shown on page 53.

STEP ONE

On an 11 × 14-inch sheet of 140-lb. hot-press watercolor paper, I first created a light drawing in pencil using an envelope and block-in and then refined the contours, as we did in the Oak Leaf project.

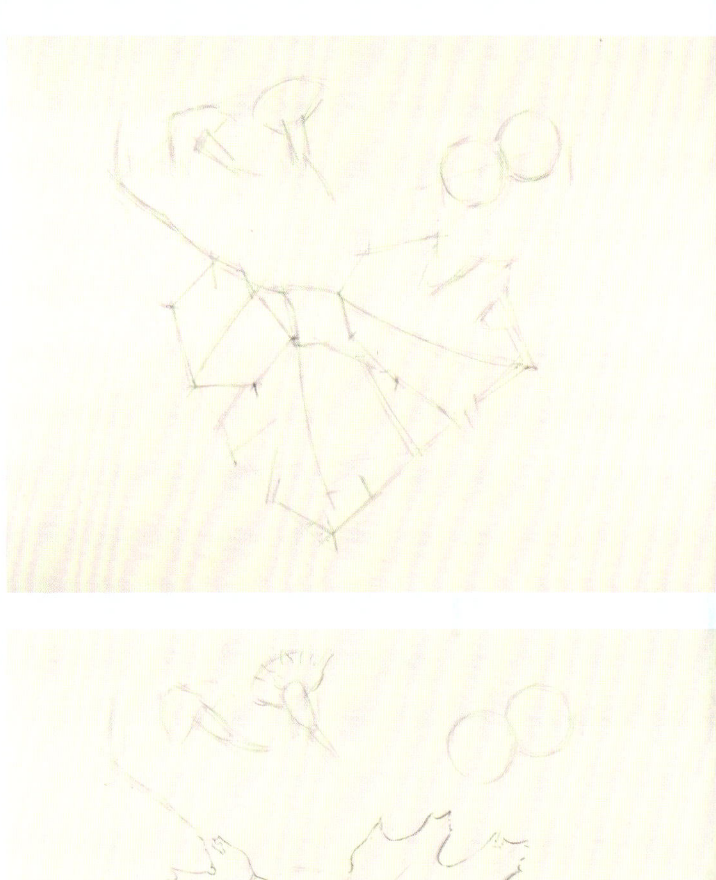

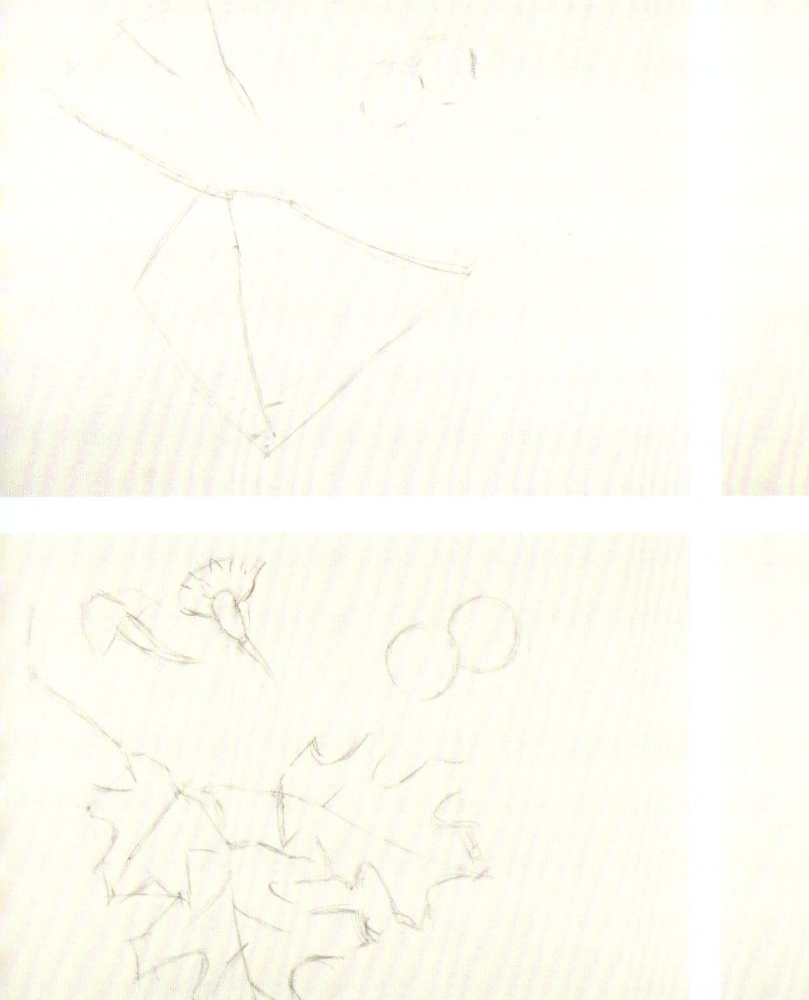

STEP TWO

Get your painting materials ready.

Watercolors:
- · Winsor Yellow PY154
- · Alizarin Crimson PR83
- · Winsor Blue (red shade) PB15

Brushes:
- · 1 small pointy sable-type round
- · 1 medium sable-type round
- · 1 wash / mop brush ½ inch across or more

White plate for a palette

Paper towels

Two 8–20 oz. containers of water:
- · one for rinsing brushes, one for clean water

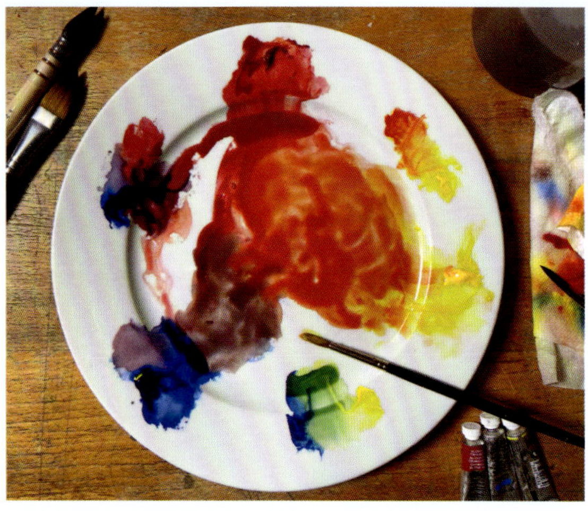

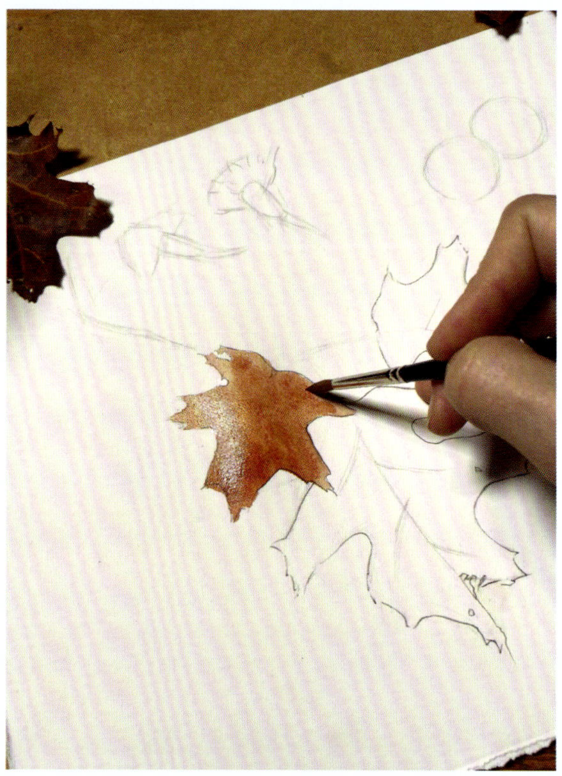

Use a simple dinner plate for your palette and put the primary colors (red, yellow, blue) along the edge in a triangle. A neutral color is created when your mixtures include all three colors. Autumn leaves, with their streaks and earth tones, are a perfect subject to explore mixed neutral colors. The oak leaves in my setup are predominantly dark orange. The orange is made by mixing the red and yellow, then adding a touch of blue to darken and neutralize the hue.

STEP THREE

Start with the smallest leaf, and do one at a time to get the swing of things. First, brush the whole leaf with clean water with your medium pointy brush, letting it puddle on the surface a bit. Follow the contour lines at the edges of the leaf. Work quickly and use enough water so that the whole leaf will be wet at the same time.

Now, dip your brush into the puddle of mixed color and drop the brush down in the middle of the wet leaf. You will immediately see the color spread to wherever the paper is wet. Push the brush around a bit to the edges and the whole leaf will fill with the wash. Play with dropping in more paint to darken and vary the tones.

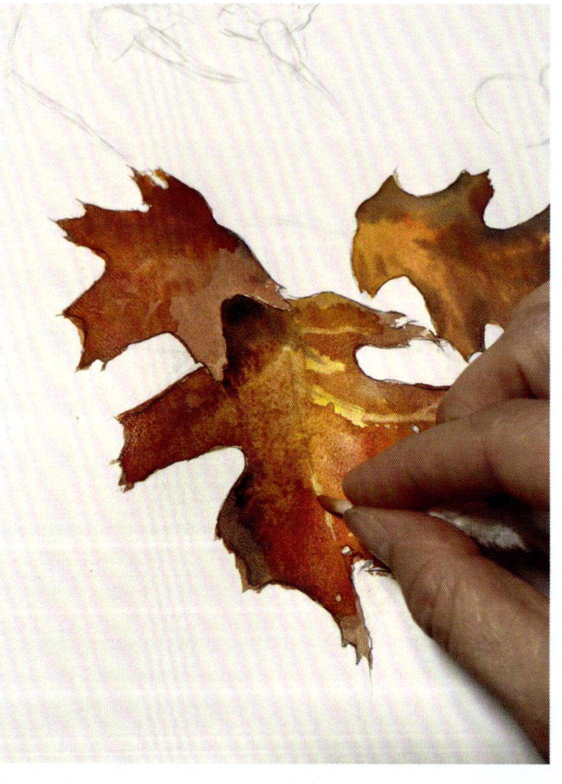

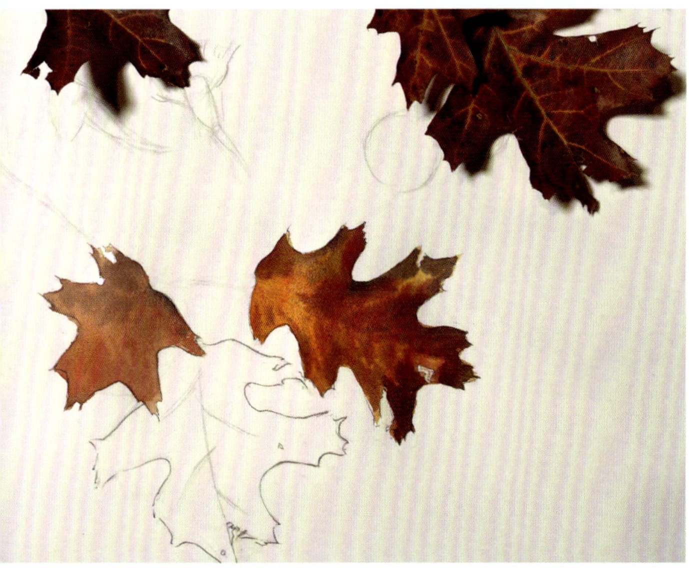

Darkening colors in a puddle.

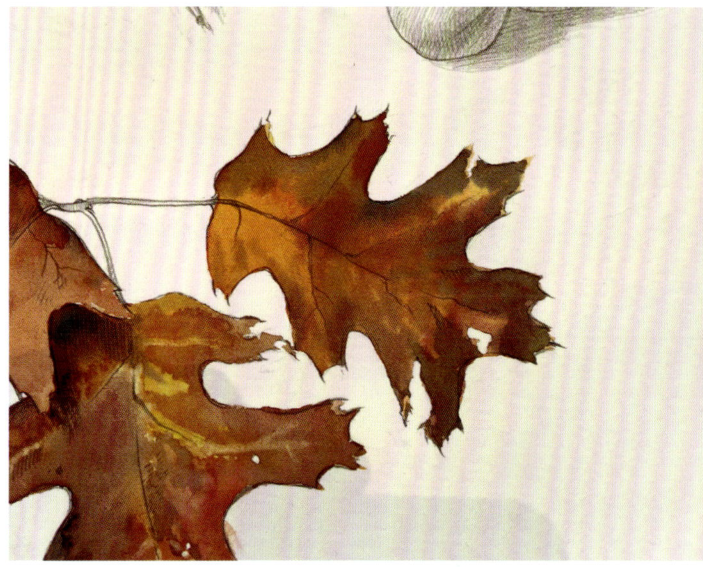

Adding pencil detail after the area is dry.

To make lighter veins, use a little piece of paper towel rolled to a point. While the paint is damp, touch it with the paper towel to remove color in the center vein. The variegated orangey brown of the leaf is very forgiving. Even if the colors and shapes are different from the leaf you are rendering, the harmonious colors and effects of the watercolor are delightful.

I worked on one leaf at a time and let them dry so that the edges stayed sharp. To create more detail, I let the first wash dry, then repeated the process on top to add a darker color. On the second leaf, I started with a bright orange, and the second pass had more dark brown.

STEP FOUR

When the watercolor was completely dry, I finished the drawing using a sharp pencil to add delicate details like the central vein lines. If your watercolor strayed over the edges, simply redraw the pencil lines at the new edge. I drew in other the botanicals

after painting the leaves. Since watercolor can get messy, it's easy to screw it up. By saving the rest of the drawing for later, I had less at stake when I started swinging around a wet brush.

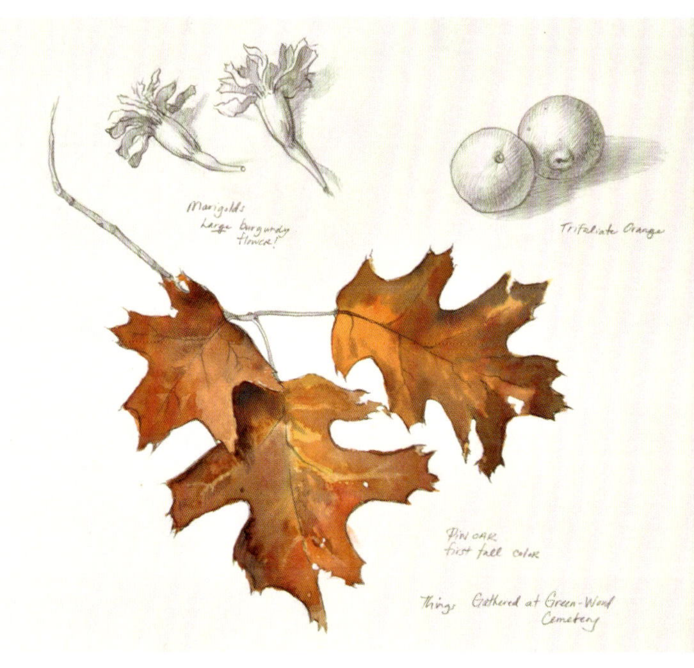

9

Monsters and Mandalas

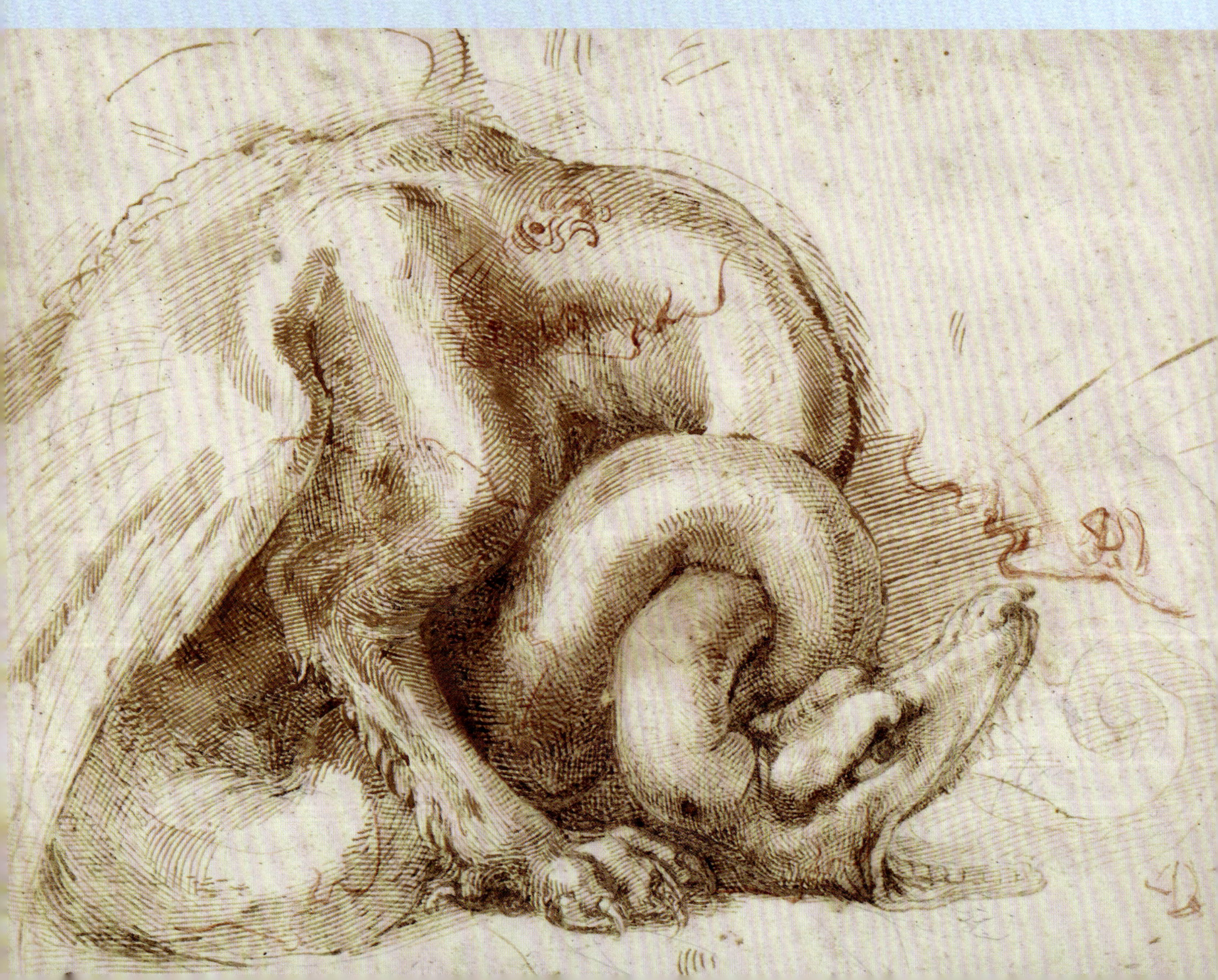

I would like to introduce you to my monster, Nigel (at right).

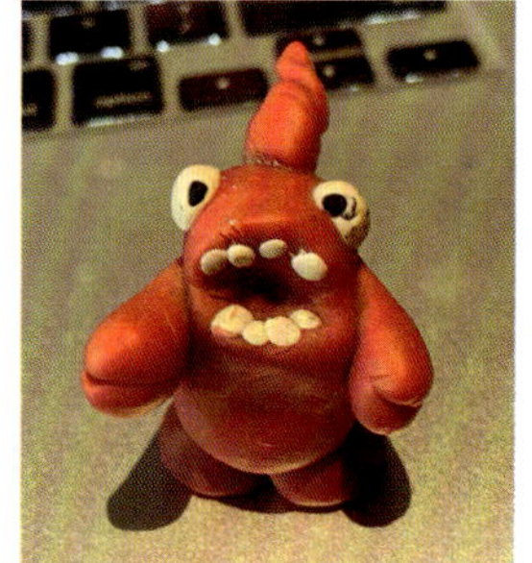

He has a place of honor on my desk and was sculpted by a young artist, Beaux Watwood, as a gift. Keeping Nigel nearby helps me remember to keep my negative thoughts right-sized.

Nigel looks small and harmlessly cute, but once he gets inside my brain, he's a demon of destruction. He marauds around, saying things like, "This is SOOOOO stupid! You can't even draw! I can't believe you're so bad after all this time. You are *never* going to make this work!" At turns snarky, worldly, mocking, or belittling, Nigel's voice booms with authority, and I cringe as if I'm in the principal's office.

Julia Cameron calls the negative voice the Censor.[15] Elizabeth Gilbert simply calls it Fear.[16] The monster's message is ubiquitous. Stop. Don't. You can't. It's terrible.

Hold up. Let me ask you: Where did the monster in your head get all that *authority*? There you were, happily bumping along making art, and suddenly he rolls in to slam you down, and you think, "Oh, well, I guess he's right! I *am* terrible!"

Stop right there and question the legitimacy of this blustering brute. Scary, intimidating, loud, and obnoxious, sure. But *right*? In fact, the negative voice is not based in reality, however much it might pretend to be the voice of reason. First and foremost, work to reject the inner voice of negativity as a knowledgeable authority. Bold, clamoring voices are usually grasping for power they shouldn't hold. The calm, quiet, and hopeful voice is far more likely to guide you forward successfully. Mindfulness about the complex interactions of your thoughts and emotions can teach you to see that scary monster as an annoying troublesome demon that pesters but does not derail.

I've accepted Nigel as a regular companion, but I don't let him do permanent damage when he's on a rampage. In order to hold on to my creative practice, I've learned strategies to tame and manage my monster.

Michelangelo Buonarroti (Italian, 1475–1564), *Dragon and Other Sketches,* 1524–25, pen and brown ink over black chalk on paper, 10 x 13¼ inches (25 x 34 cm). Collection of Ashmolean Museum, University of Oxford.

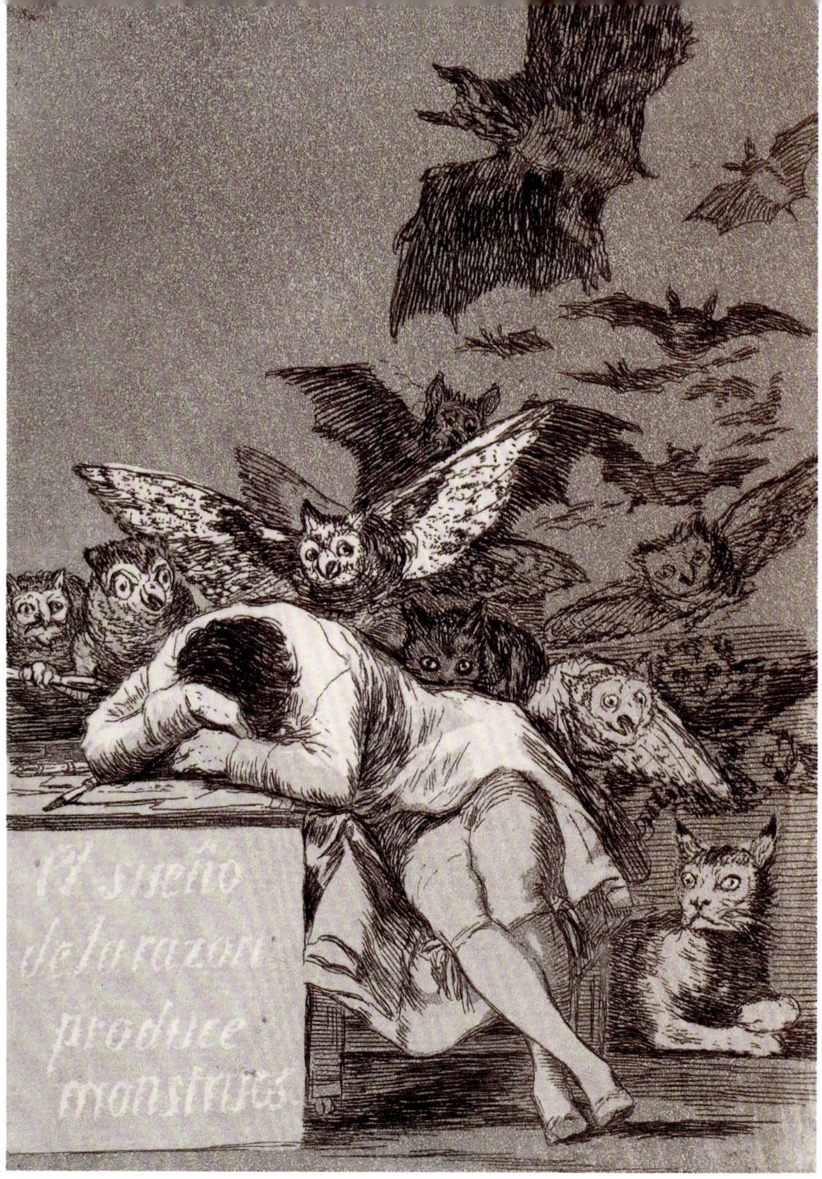

Francisco José de Goya y Lucientes (Spanish, 1746–1828), *The Sleep of Reason Produces Monsters (No. 43)* (from Los Caprichos), 1799, etching with aquatint on paper, 7½ x 5¾ inches (19 x 15 cm).

MEET THE MONSTERS

This is a partial list of horrible "monsters" that many creatives battle in the quest for art. While it is more comfortable to avoid peering into the darkness, when we name and identify the shape and contours of the negative thoughts that plague us, we are well on our way to understanding how to get past them.

"Our capacity for wholeheartedness can never be greater than our willingness to be brokenhearted."

—BRENÉ BROWN

FEAR OF JUDGMENT

There's my grad school professor blaring, "Does not meet standards. F!" My biggest monsters are fear of judgment and fear of looking stupid. These twins of insecurity basically threaten that if I make X, *they* will judge it bad and consider me stupid for thinking it was good. *They* are a vague and unfriendly imagined public who tell me that I'm not *really* an artist and don't have the magic whatever-it-takes to become one.

Obviously, my monster reasons, the safest thing to do would be to hide, never show anything to anyone. But because I am trying to make my way as a visual artist, such hiding is clearly not a viable solution.

IMPOSTER SYNDROME

If you've had the exam dream, where you show up naked for a test, you can probably relate to the imposter syndrome—the fear that you are not as knowledgeable, prepared, or competent as you think you are or need to be. At any moment you will be exposed as an imposter pretending to be an expert (the opposite condition is overconfidence, labeled the Dunning-Kruger effect).

PERFECTIONISM

This monster argues that if it's not perfect, it's not good enough: "You'd better do X more things, read X more books, redo this X more times." Our perfectionism can drain the exuberance and vivacity out of almost any fine thing. I've learned that as an artist, it is better to be wrong than to be boring.

FEAR OF ATTACK (MONSTERS UNDER THE BED)

This monster rings the alarm anytime we start to explore the path not taken and try a new thing. This beast fears the unknown, the unexplored, dark corners. Is it safe? What if it's horrible? You'd better stay where you know exactly what will happen (which is nothing).

FEAR OF MISPERCEPTION AND EXCLUSION

I grew up in the Midwest, where there's a strong cultural worry about standing out from the crowd. As an artist, I've had to develop muscles to let my eccentric side out. I can't tell you how often I've imagined that people will think I'm weird if I...

- sit on the floor of the coat room and draw.
- wander around the grocery store picking up every squash and dragon fruit looking for a subject.
- squat on the sidewalk looking at a dead bird.

- ask if I can take the turkey carcass home.
- draw their picture on the subway.

Sadly, some of us live in spaces where being different can be dangerous. It's a terrible experience to feel excluded or isolated because you are apart from the mainstream. But there are creatives and unconventional thinkers everywhere. When following a path of creativity, trust that along the way you will find others who share your joys and experiences and treasure your uniqueness.

SHAME

Brené Brown, who researches shame, found that 85 percent of the people she surveyed had a strong memory of someone (often a teacher!) making

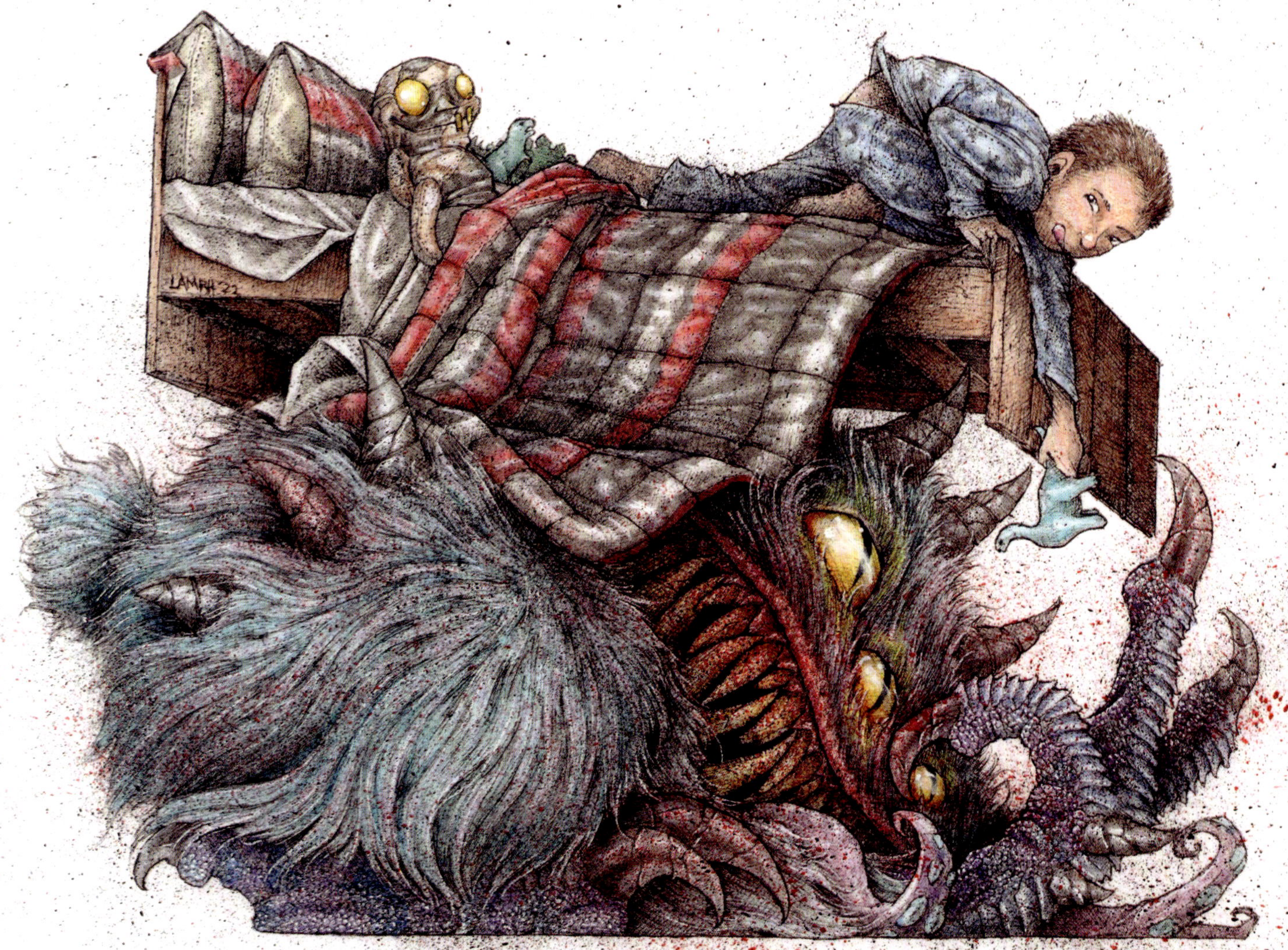

a disparaging comment about their youthful singing voice, art, or other talent.[17] This early experience can be so shaming that it can permanently squelch a creative aspiration. Shame comes from the fear of disconnection—it boils down to, if you do X, everyone will think you do not belong in the group. Shame can be paralyzing.

BEFRIENDING YOUR MONSTER

Our instincts scream, "*Slay* the monster!" In fact, we cannot simply destroy or suppress the parts of ourselves that we don't like. The healthier path is to be wholehearted and integrate our fears and negative thoughts into a negotiated balance. Instead of pretending it's all sunshine and roses, we can acknowledge the monsters we journey with as intrinsic to the complexity and richness of our human experience. The key to monster cohabitation is to recognize, externalize, normalize, and neutralize.

RECOGNIZE

Become familiar with your Big Bad. Instead of shutting the door tight, probe into the fear and ask yourself, What is the worst thing that could happen if this fear came to life?

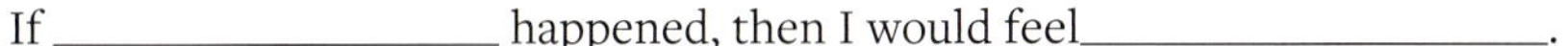

If _____________________ happened, then I would feel_____________________.

Repeat this questioning a few times so you can stare down the creature at the bottom.

EXTERNALIZE

Negative feelings arise from within. Mindfulness allows us to acknowledge that fears and negative thoughts arise yet also depart. I hear the familiar voice of negativity and also understand that it is just one voice, one moment, one feeling, in a larger landscape that makes up my emotional experience.

Externalize the negativity by separating "I did" statements from "I am" statements. Our language is powerful. When we say "I am," we make a statement about our intrinsic nature or ability. When we say "I did," we acknowledge a specific action, not a state of being. Failures help us learn on our journey. But don't internalize them and give them a home to stay.

Say: I did *mess up that drawing*.
Not: I am *bad at drawing*.

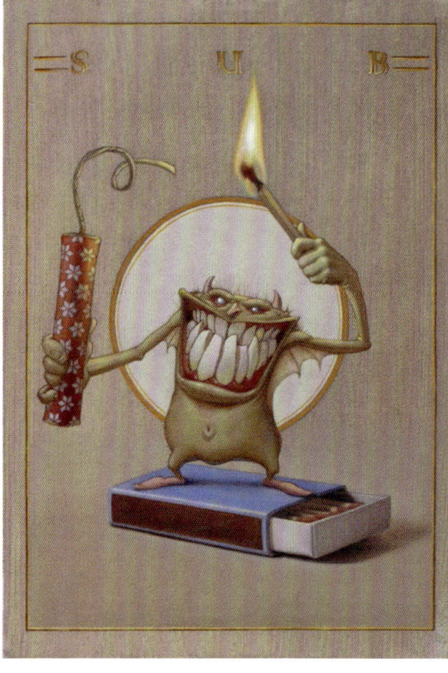

Tony Curanaj, *SUB*, 2017, oil on board, 7 x 5 inches (18 x 13 cm). Courtesy of the artist.

Opposite: Tyler Lamph, *Monster*, 2022, ink, marker, gel pen, and watercolor on paper, 4 x 5 inches (10 x 13 cm). Courtesy of the artist.

NORMALIZE

Our feelings can confuse us into thinking that we are isolated and unique in our experiences of negative thoughts. Honey, everyone has a monster. Never compare your insides to someone else's outsides. Some smooth and stylish artists brim with enthusiasm and confidence. Good for them, but I suspect it's well-polished showmanship and years of practice. A true monster master will never tell you, "I never had to deal with any of those struggles." They will say, "I've had to battle all those bastards. Let me tell you what helped."

NEUTRALIZE

This activity has two parts. First, downsize the demon. Though it seems big and scary, it's actually pretty small. Next, accept your monster as a traveler on your journey. All parts of us serve various purposes, and this imp really just wants to protect you from getting hurt. So, tell him that you heard, thank you, but now it's time for him to sit down quietly so you can work. As Elizabeth Gilbert notes in her book *Big Magic: Creative Living beyond Fear*, fear has to go along on the road trip of creativity with you, but never, ever let him drive.[18] Backseat only.

Most of these monsters are actually very similar. They morph and change disguises to continually evade your mastery. They can be hybrid chimeras. Over time and in various stages of life, you might find your emotional landscape has new demons you never had to deal with before.

A PRIVATE BUBBLE

Where do you feel safe?

Creating a bubble of safety while doing creative work can be essential to nurturing growth. While artists may aspire to a spacious and airy skylit studio, they often find that the most productive work can happen in more personal, even constrained, spaces—in your room. On your bed. In the bathroom. In the cabinet under the stairs. In the basement, the attic, the barn. Comfort is not as important as a sense of safety and privacy. We need freedom from intruding eyes whether they are enthusiastic or judgmental. The beginning forays into art can be like fragile seedlings that wither quickly under examination.

If you are feeling stuck, maybe the best way to move forward is to change your setting. Take your sketchbook into a small space where you can nurture little ideas in your own time and way. Inside your house or out, find a place where you feel safe and undisturbed and guard your creative time.

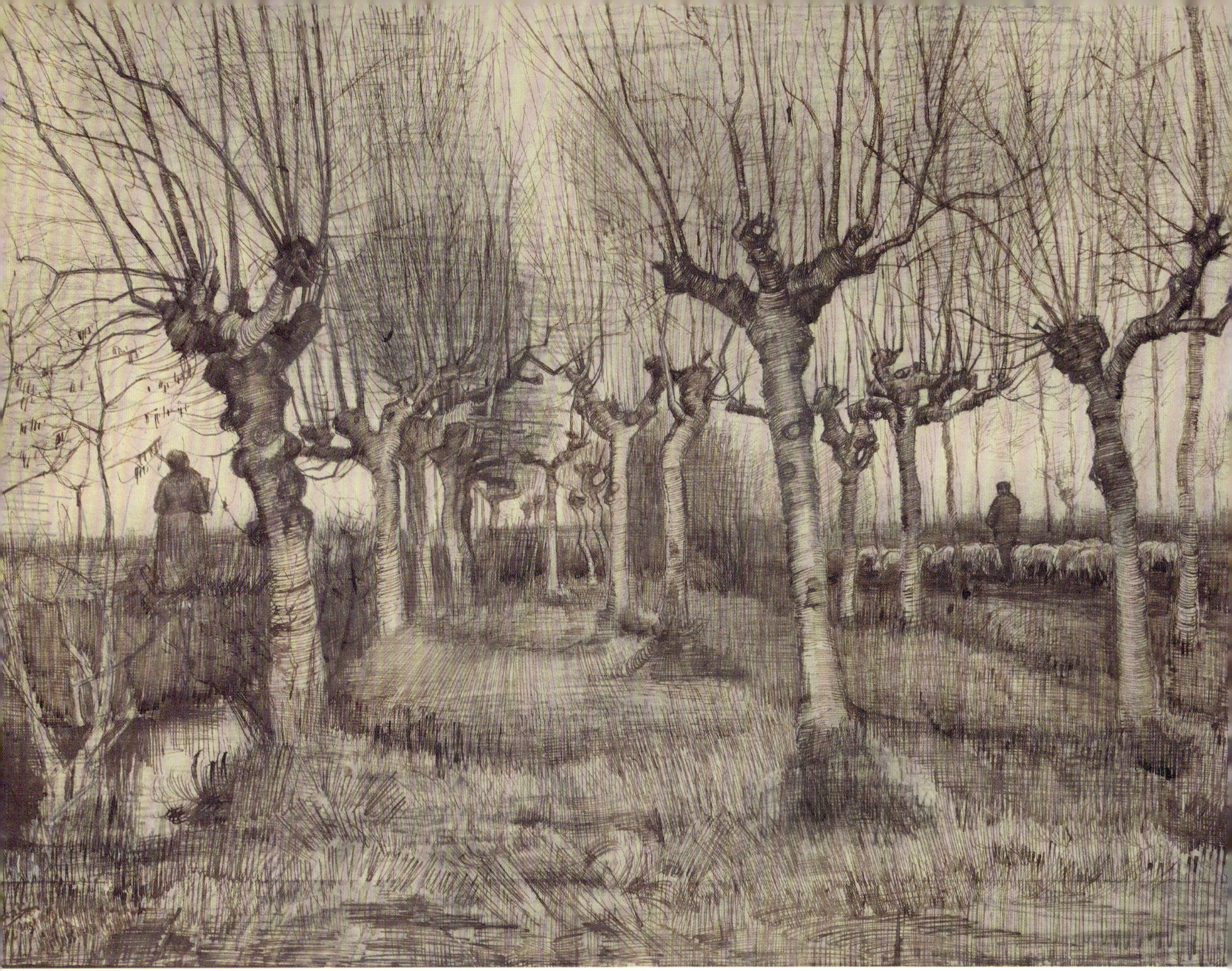

> *"In spite of everything, I shall rise again. I will take up my pencil, which I have forsaken in my great discouragement, and I will go on with my drawing."*
>
> –VINCENT VAN GOGH

EVERYDAY DISCOURAGEMENT

The first time I read that quote by Vincent van Gogh, I felt deep empathy. I imagined him throwing his pencil and sketchbook across the room and walking out, despairing of ever attaining his dreams. How many days passed before he picked up his pencil again?

Vincent van Gogh (Dutch, 1853–1890), *Pollard Birches*, 1884, pencil, pen, and ink and watercolor on paper, 15½ x 21¼ inches (39 x 54 cm). Courtesy of the Van Gogh Museum, Amsterdam (Vincent van Gogh Foundation).

Now, Van Gogh is a highly celebrated artist, but in his time, he endured rejection and untreated mental illness. He was famously plagued by negative thoughts. However, if we see Van Gogh's artistic production as the double-sided coin of an unstable mind, we do creativity and mental health a disservice. Van Gogh's talent survived despite his terrible struggles with mental illness, not because of them. We would all be richer had he survived to make more art. Do not make the mistake of conflating dysregulated and unhealthy mental conditions with creativity, or that jagged word *genius*. Creativity flourishes best with a healthy mind and spirit.

Do you have a margin of time, or is your day crammed with stresses and time pressures?

Have you slept enough?

Have you eaten enough?

Do you feel safe?

Have you taken your medication?

Have you had time to deal with tough feelings and experiences and process them?

Why am I spending so much time writing about mental health in a book about drawing? Because in all my years of teaching and making art, I've come to understand that the reasons people fail to continue with their creative work has nothing to do with techniques or training. It is the internal monsters that stop us from journeying onward.

When we work on drawing, for better or worse, we are left alone with our thoughts. This can be a wonderful gift when your thoughts gently wander and sift, allowing new ideas to bubble up. However, too often we find that all the quiet and solitude leave us undistracted from an unfriendly and stressed-out mind.

Perhaps you find making art to be a completely happy space, with bright colors and sweet pastimes. If that's you—Godspeed, skip ahead! But for many of us, creativity is darn scary. Why is the blank page paralyzing? The unfinished manuscript? The box of paints? Every budding artist I know who has traveled this road for a while, with a fragile flame burning inside to make some really good art, will understand what I'm talking about here.

All I can say is—I hear you. I've been there. In my experience, it actually doesn't stop being scary. Here's the gift—consider your creativity like a gym where you can work out your muscles of bravery and self-examination. Find yourself alone but not lonely, with your thoughts relaxed and directed toward work, not racing around at the nine hundred other things you "should" do.

We face monsters in every arena of life. By embracing these struggles with our creativity, we learn to gently and mindfully work through them. In time, we can then learn to manage these negative thoughts and fears in other areas of our lives that might be way scarier than graphite and paper. Let drawing teach you to examine your terrain of emotions and find stepping-stones forward. Mindfulness through our creative process helps us to evolve in all aspects of our lives.

Patricia Watwood, *Keep Breathing,* 2018, graphite, ink, and watercolor on paper, 8 x 10 inches (20 x 25 cm). Courtesy of the artist. Text by Joanna Macy and Chris Johnstone.[19]

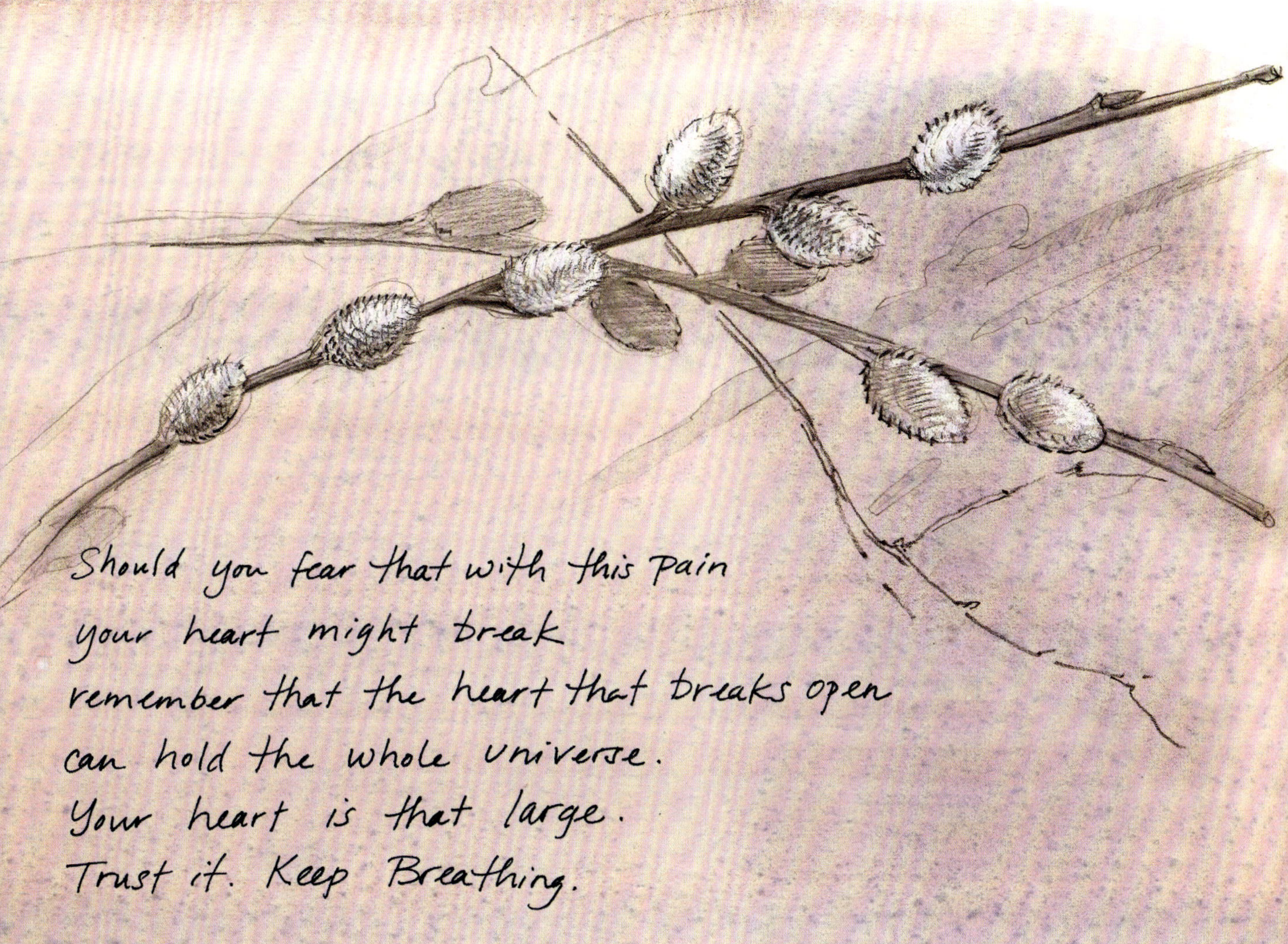

Draw Your Monster

PREPARING

First, you will spend some time examining your
monster in the light, to get a good look at it. Then
you'll make a representation of your monster, which
will help you get acquainted and neutralize its
paralyzing power.

Before drawing, reflect on your most familiar
demons. Consider the triggers that throw you off
track and identify one or two primary monsters.

- My key anxiety around art is…
- The negative voice I hear in my head most
  often says…

Sometimes monsters disguise themselves.
Underneath "I never have enough time" might be
"Your art is not a priority" or "You're going to fail."
Peel back the layers to find the Big Bad. If this is
intimidating, light a candle to create a safe space and
invoke a sense of protection.

The psychologist Carl Jung called this *shadow
work*. He described the shadow as those aspects of
the personality that we choose to reject and repress.
We all have parts of ourselves that we don't like—*or
that we think society won't like*—so we push those
parts down into our unconscious. Jung called this
collection of repressed aspects of our identity our
shadow self. Importantly, he taught that if the shadow
self is not understood—made conscious and inte-
grated—it makes us, and our communities, unwell.

START TO DRAW

As a child, did you ever scribble on the wall with a
marker? Admit it, you probably did. That creative

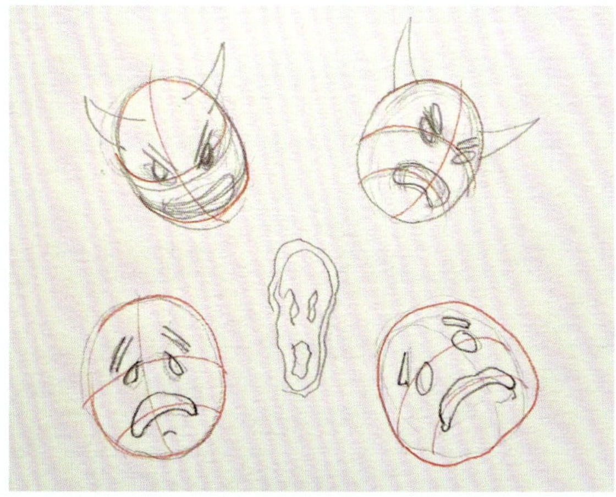

mischief probably pissed off your mom but didn't do
any lasting damage. Channel that feeling while you
draw this monster. The energy you are going for is
rebel child with a gleeful twinkle in your eye.

Scary monsters can have a lot of anger. The key
to an angry face is to have the eyebrows angled
down over the eyes toward the nose. For a woeful
monster, make the eyebrows angle down toward
the ears. Lower the corners of the mouth to make a
scowl or frown.

STEP ONE

Start with a light pencil to begin the head and body
shapes. Work at a small scale so you can go
quickly and outpace your demon. Get the sketch
done before the sleeping dragon wakes up. What
is the dominant emotion for your monster? Anger?
Sadness? Anxiety? Next, the mouth—large and
gaping with scary teeth or miserable with drooping
lips? Gradually darken the lines that capture the
spirit of your monster.

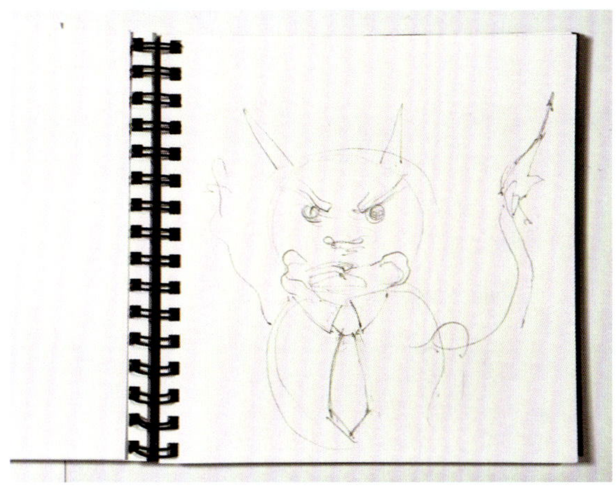 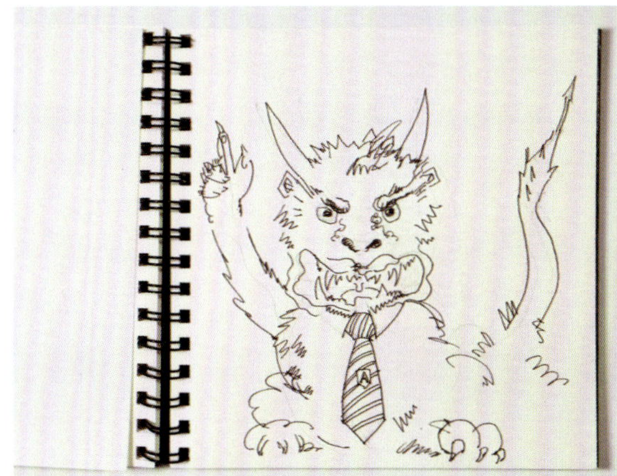

STEP TWO

Once you have some guidelines, switch to a pen or marker. Permanent and aggressive marks will be more effective in taking it down. Ignore mess-ups. Just keep scribbling and redrawing the parts you like. The demon perfectionism will try to tell you you're doing it all wrong, but it doesn't know what it's talking about. Any messy scribbly parts just add to your armor of humor and disruption.

STEP THREE

Finish the drawing with some details and throw in some color if you like. Anything a mischievous kid would like is on board.

I recommend you spend a little time on this project. Start with doodles and explore various angry eyes and howling mouths. Consider symbols for the triggers that trip you up. As you are working, a conversation with the drawing can guide you to get to know your monster better. My monster, for example, is very judgmental and has a lot of highly educated opinions that it's sure will stop me. He tries to use his loud mouth and booming voice to intimidate me into sitting quietly in a corner, and he slashes at my hopes with his jagged swinging tail. I'd say this to him: "You may sound big and scary, but you don't have my best interests at heart."

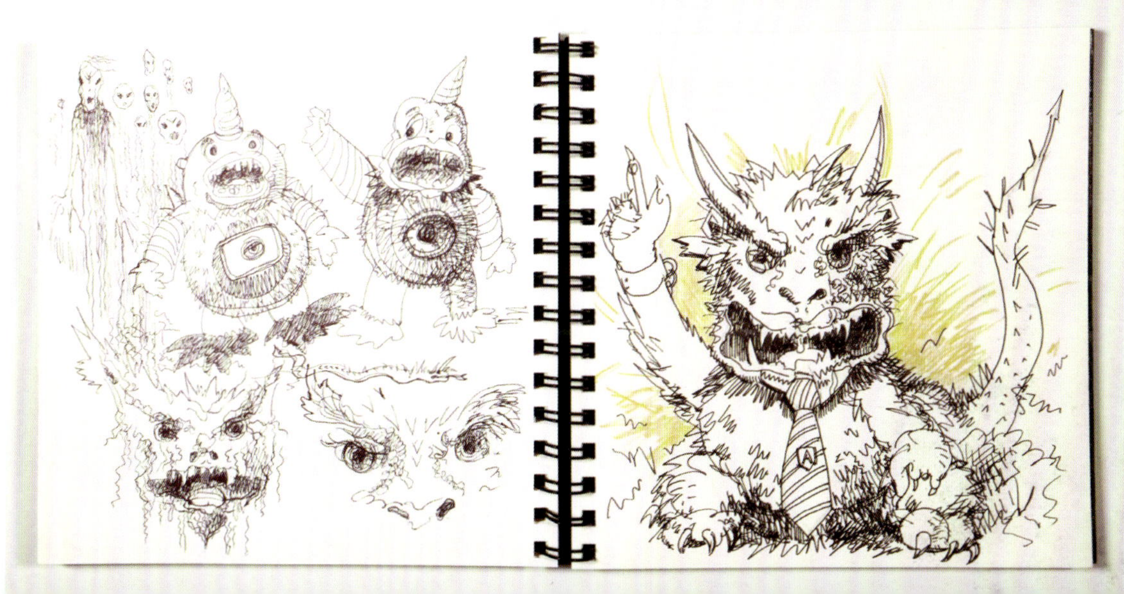

WORKING FROM IMAGINATION

To work from one's imagination—the vast unexplored and murky territory of the mind—is exploring the unknown. The landscape of your inner mind is territory that no one else on Earth can discover. What's in there? Is it wondrous? Interesting? Terrifying? Beautiful? When an artist is able to manifest a personal vision to share for others to experience—this is the expanding edge of our collective consciousness. To peer bravely into the interior of the mind and bring it forth as an image is the magic of world-building. Novels, video games, movies, and plays all begin from the path that travels through the artist's imagination. Exploring this territory through drawing strengthens our ability to visualize and express our singular vision.

Eager for adventure, we quickly discover that the threshold guardian of the landscape of the mind is the blank page. Working without a visual

Tony Curanaj, *A Flower for Maxfield Sketch,* 2021, graphite, red pencil, and white chalk on paper, 15 x 18 inches (38 x 46 cm). Courtesy of the artist.

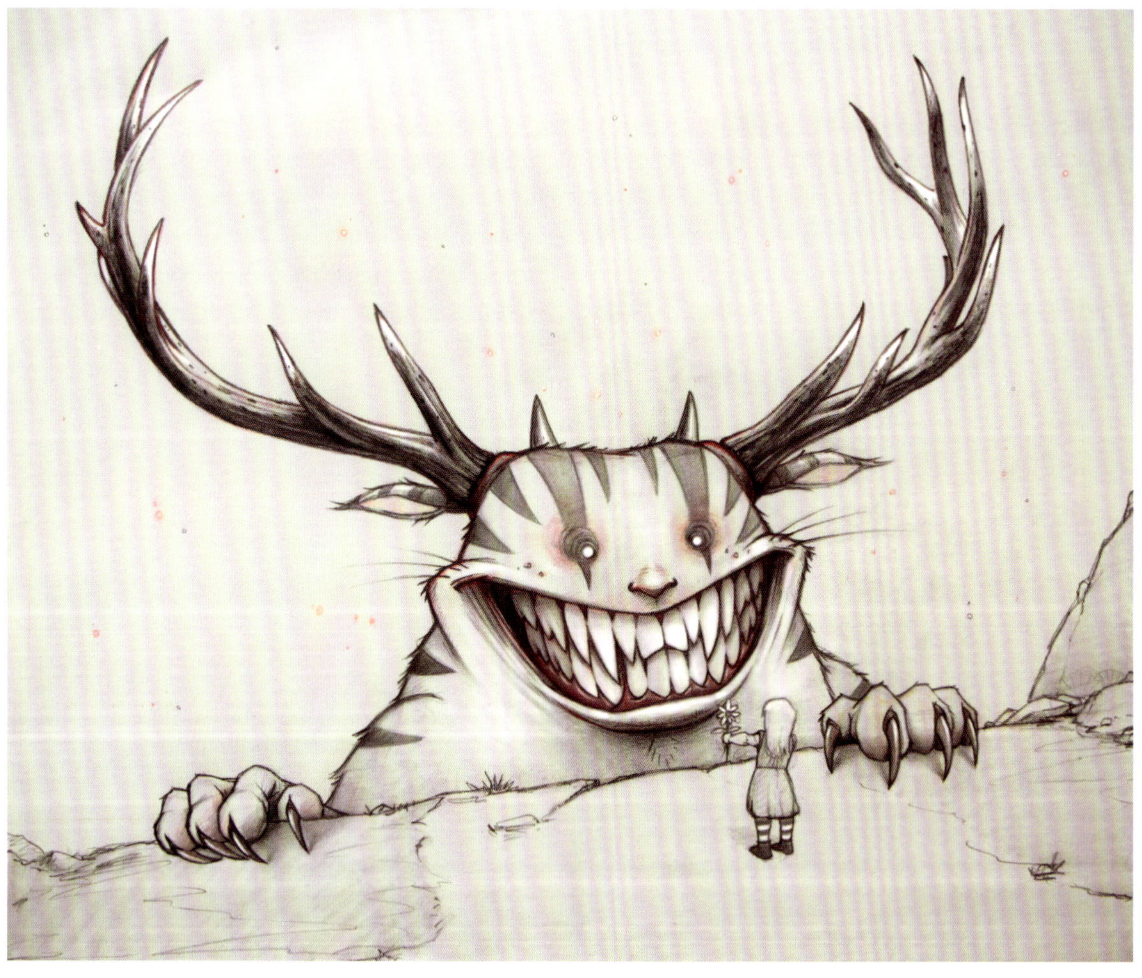

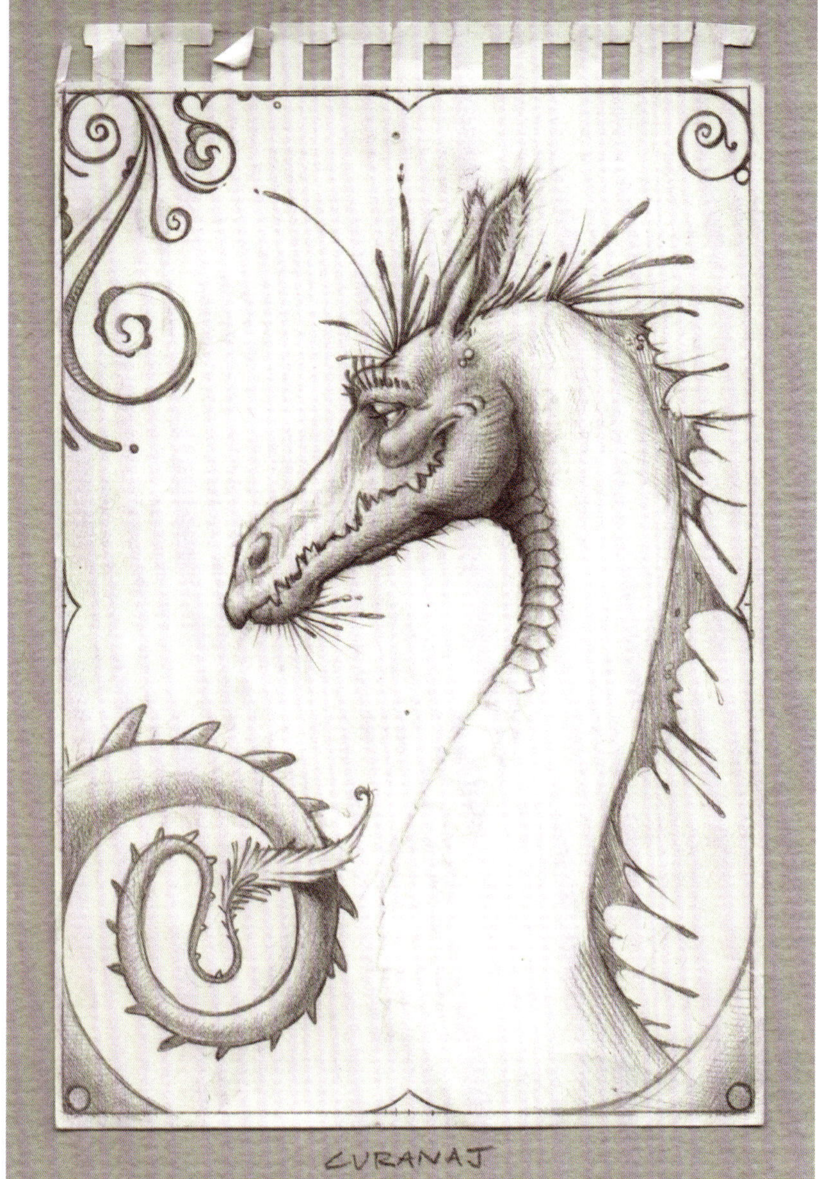

Tony Curanaj, *Dragon*, 2007, graphite on paper, 6 x 4 inches (15 x 10 cm). Courtesy of the artist.

reference, we cannot say, "Is it right? Is it wrong?" If there's nothing to look at, how do I know? Where do I start? The blank page stands guard at the gates of the mind. How can you pass through? I suggest you create a chimera as one way to unlock your interior unknown.

INVENTING CHIMERAS

A chimera is a mythical creature made from parts of various animals. This subject is a marvelous starting point for an imaginative drawing. Lately, I've been obsessed with dragons and have studied how artists through the ages have portrayed them. I notice that they take myriad fragments—let's

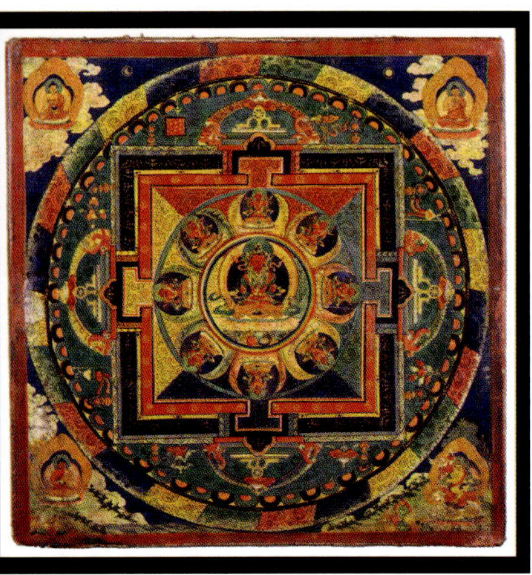

Above: 19th-Century Tibetan School, *Mandala of Amitayus,* c. 1800, paint on wood, 12¼ x 12¼ inches (31 x 31 cm).

say the head of a dog or an antelope, the neck and scales of an iguana, the feet and talons of an eagle, and the wings of a bat. Each segment can be sourced from nature.

To conquer the blank page, begin building a new creature out of found parts using published images for details. Once you have drawn a few chimeras in this way, you will be able to improvise your own variations.

Another springboard for imaginative work is mashing a few familiar ideas into a whimsical narrative; for example, a frog and toad at a tea party. When we were young, these magical worlds came very easily, but as we grow more self-conscious and out of practice, we must regain that childlike spirit through intentional creative exercise.

Tony Curanaj has built a chimera with some familiar traits: the antlers of a deer, a Cheshire Cat of a face, tabby stripes, and claws (see p. 172). Adding small horns and little ears, he mashes up the conventional and adds the magic stroke of changing scales with an enormous snaggly smile in front of a very small girl. With humor and affection, the artist has taken small bits of familiar things to complete the story of making friends with your monster.

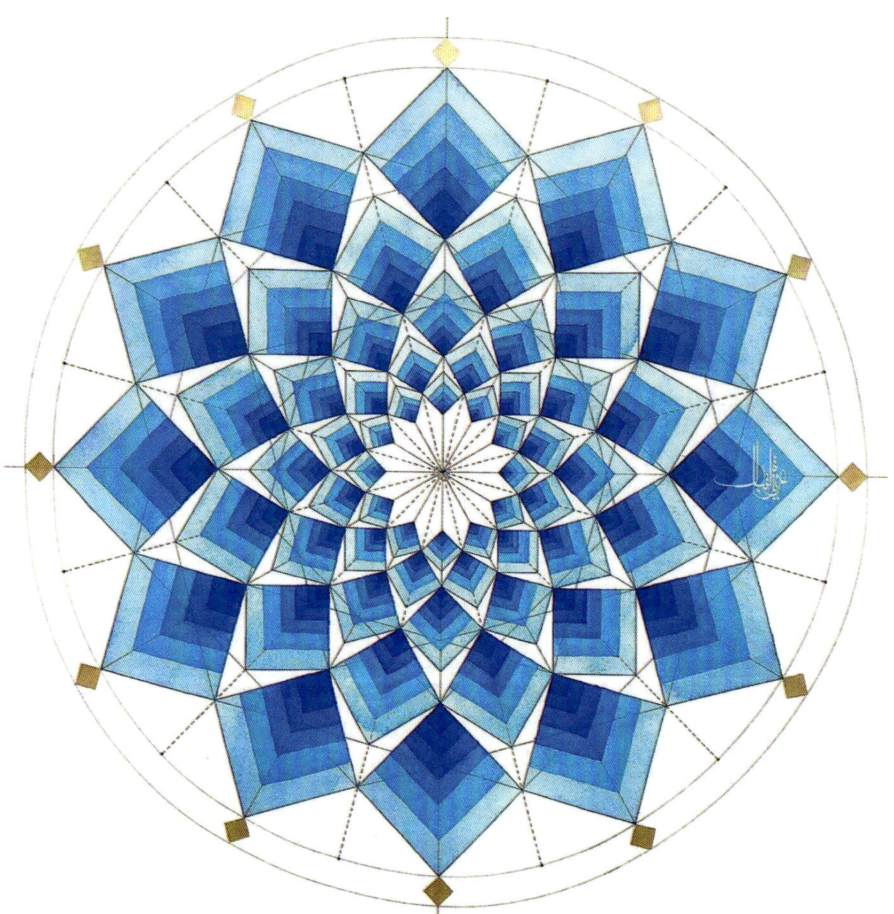

Right: Aziza Iqbal, *Ithna Ashr, Blue,* 2019, ink and 22-karat gold on paper, 15¾ x 15¾ inches (40 x 40 cm). Courtesy of the artist.

MANDALAS

In our next project, I'll share a template to create a mandala drawing. A mandala is a circular geometric design for spiritual reflection, found in Buddhist, Hindu, and other cultures. The colors, designs, and symbols each represent various emotions and wisdoms to help a seeker grow toward spiritual enlightenment. Adapting this concept, this project starts with simple patterns and small doodles to warm up to drawing freehand an imaginative element in the center. If you need a magic shield to take on your adventure, what kind of image could you create to protect you?

Below: Aziza Iqbal, *Whirling Dervish 01,* 2020, ink on paper, 9 x 9 inches (29 x 29 cm). Courtesy of the artist.

Right: Patricia Watwood, *Imagination Mandala,* 2019, watercolor and pencil on paper, 8 x 8 inches (20 x 20 cm). Courtesy of the artist.

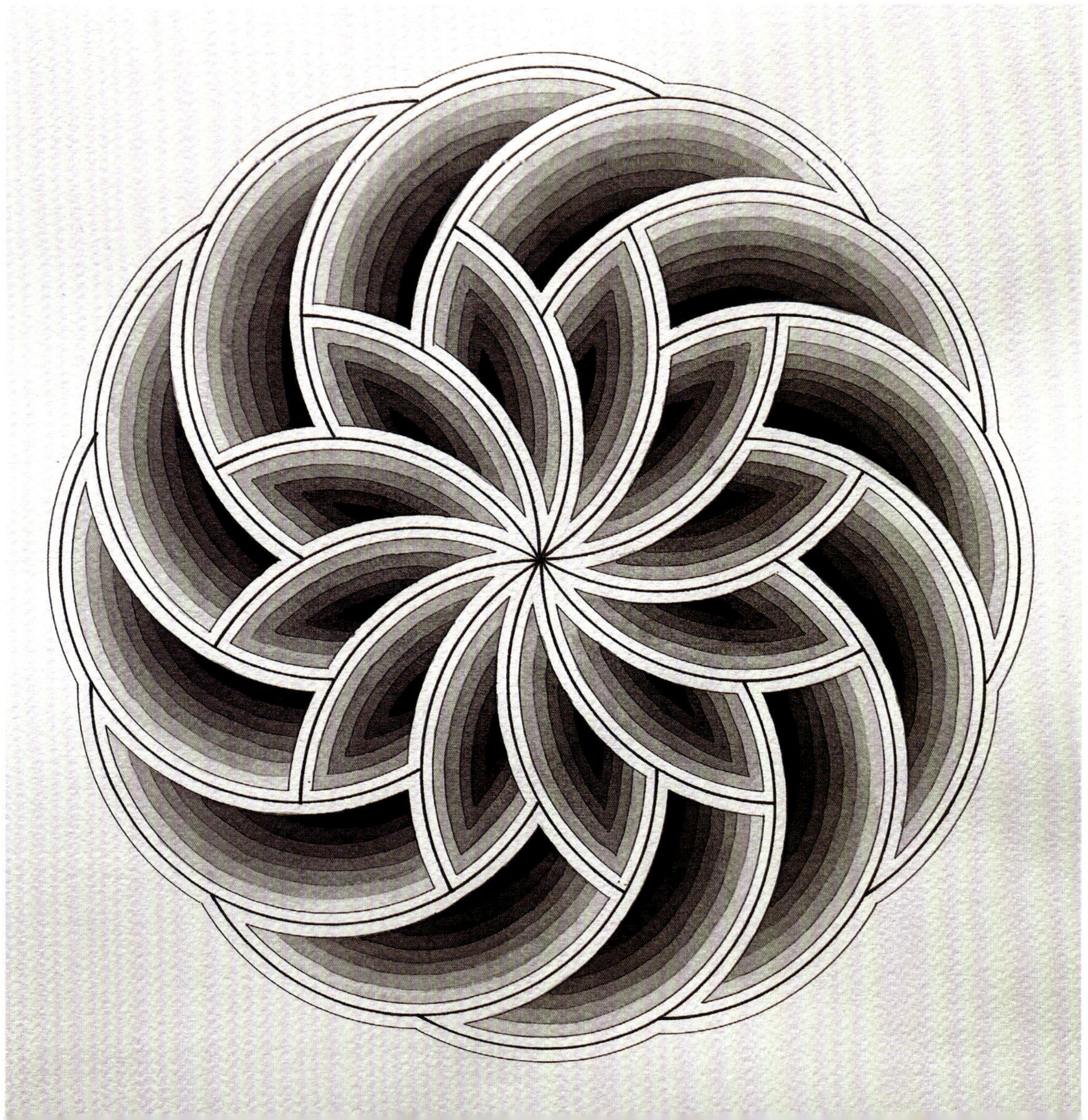

Imagination Mandalas

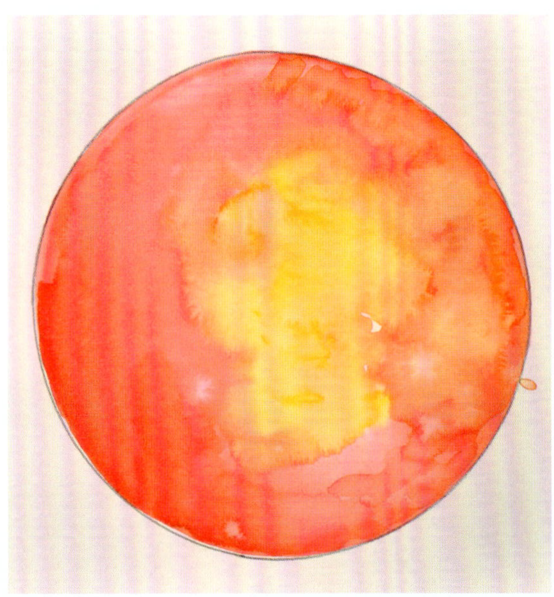

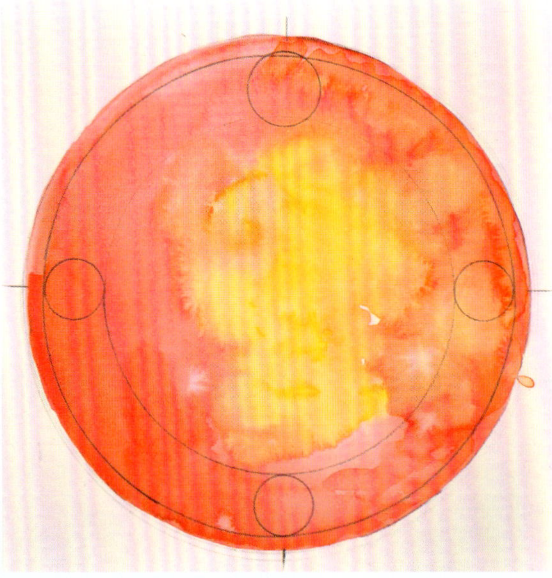

STEP ONE

Make a watercolor circle 7 inches in diameter (as in Chapter 8) as a basis for your mandala. For inspiration, consider some of your creative compost images or pick images based on the themes of this chapter. The central drawing can be natural, symbolic, realistic, or magical—anything that comes to mind is welcome. Here, my two-color wash is done is Alizarin Crimson and Winsor Yellow. I selected a fiery palette, planning a dragon theme in the center of my imaginative sketch.

STEP TWO

Use a variety of circular templates (plastic lids, dishes, coins, a compass) to make a band of concentric circles within the watercolor, leaving a 3- to 4-inch opening in the center.

STEP THREE

Divide the outermost band into a number of segments. Now, fill each space in the band with small images and simple geometric shapes. You can make each segment the same or unique to fill the band.

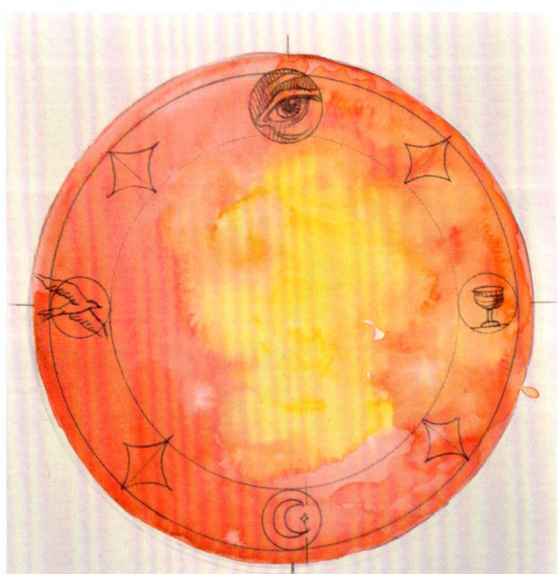

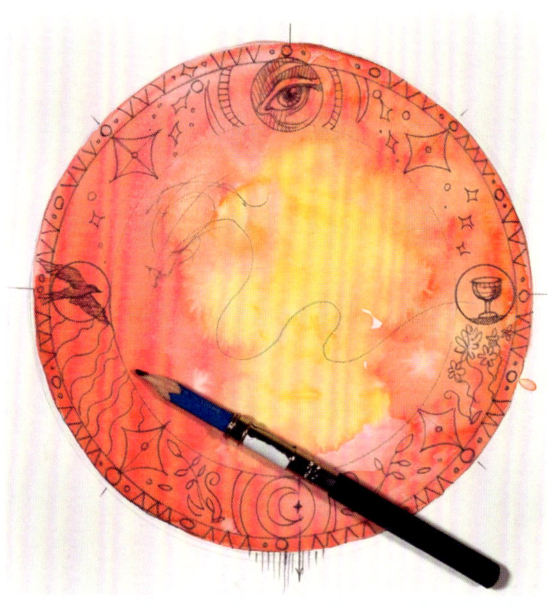

STEP FOUR

With the outer borders filled in, use a light pencil to make an invented drawing in the open center circle. Work as much as possible from memory and imagination, using reference only as a starting point. Lightly map out an image. Then, use stronger contours and values to define it. When the central image is done, revisit the borders and circles (retracing more darkly if needed) to balance the graphic qualities in the entire mandala. By breaking down the project into small parts, you learn a process you can adapt toward more ambitious work. Truly, everything you need here is within your imagination.

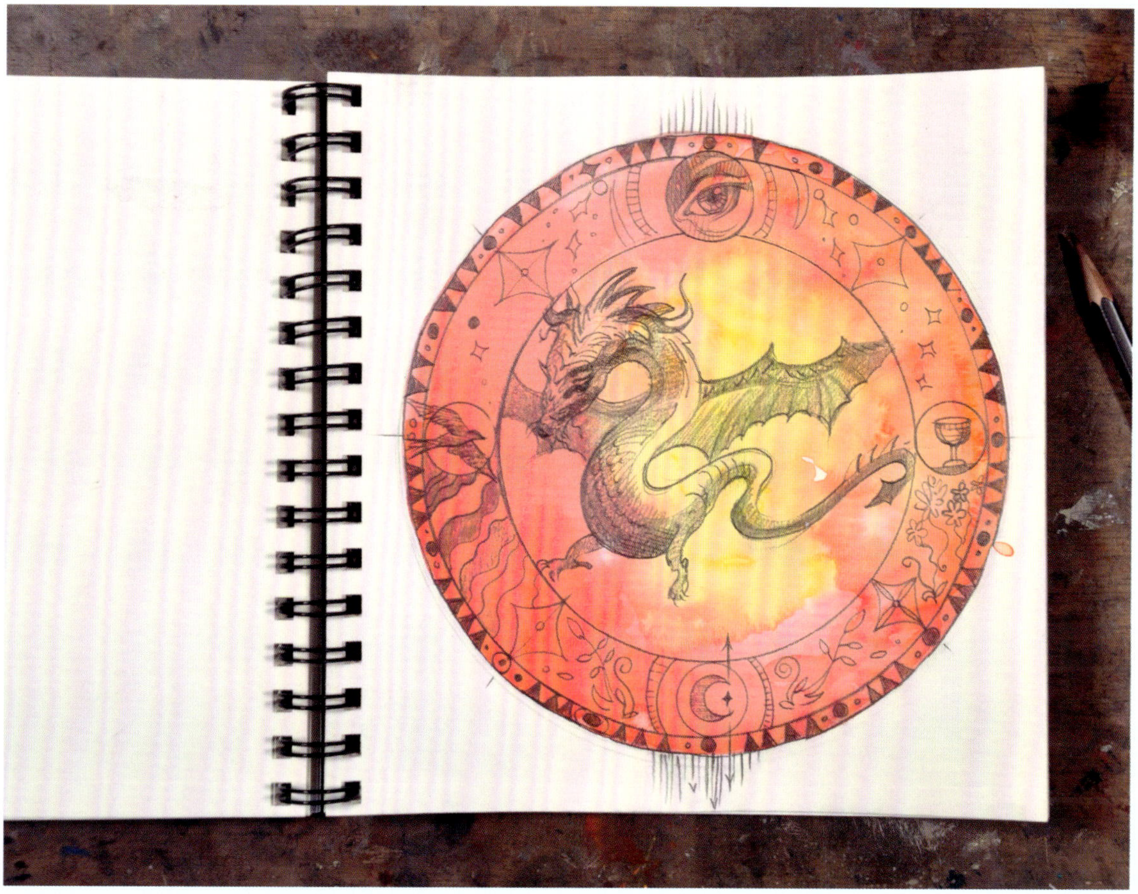

10

Developing Creative Ideas

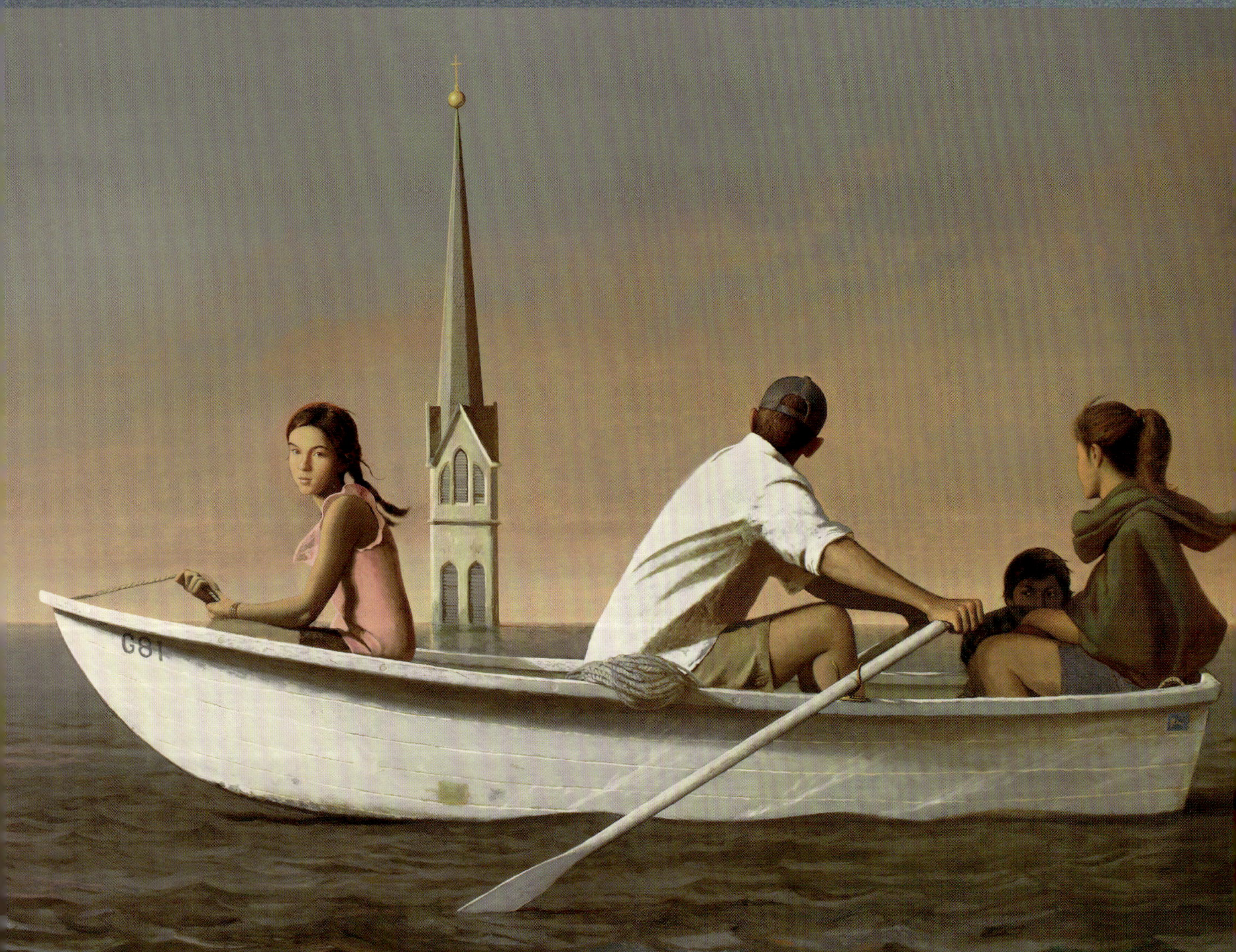

"I think one's art goes as far and as deep as one's love goes."

—ANDREW WYETH

How do artists go from fragments of ideas, the loosest of doodles, to a completed work? When you are trying to make your own work, what pathways will help you discern your voice and develop it into a realized piece and body of work? This part of the book will dig into strategies of the creative process—making sketches for your ideas, working from your imagination, and taking steps forward in producing more complex work. The themes of this chapter are not just for the beginner, but for all who hope to make creativity a significant part of their lives. Everyone starts at the beginning, and in the last couple of chapters, I hope to share some sustaining ideas for the long road.

A theme of this book is developing your personal vision through drawing. Often, young artists ask me, "Where do your creative ideas come from?" and "How did you find your own creative voice?" Within those questions lies a fundamental truth—creativity does not arrive fully formed like Athena from the head of Zeus. Instead, we develop through trial and experiment to arrive at a personal voice. Most new artists do not have an intrinsic and developed style and identity. More typically, this comes after decades of work. We tend to think that the artist appears, like Moses from Mount Sinai, full of visions and wisdom to impart. This is rarely true. Don't fret if you do not already have a vision of your creative output or purpose. All you need is a small burning ember motivating you to make art, and then don't quit.

For the majority of people, our creative voice is discovered while we accumulate piles of work. Over months and years, we gain understanding of what is pleasing and significant to ourselves. At first, it's easier to discern what others like through praise, a good grade, or "likes." Later, we start to see the difference between our own preferences and those of others. In time, we learn to trust our own choices, and thus our unique style emerges.

When you can see the creative process broken down into a series of small, manageable steps, it's much easier to visualize following this path yourself. Remember that grand figurative paintings are built one brushstroke at a time. Seeing the process makes it possible to imagine doing the same. In this chapter, I will share examples from artists who break down the process of creating large paintings through sketching. I will also discuss notans and thumbnails, two types of preparatory sketches that artists use to begin a composition.

Opposite: Bo Bartlett, *The Flood*, 2018, oil on linen, 82 x 100 inches (208 x 254 cm). Courtesy of the artist and Miles McEnery Gallery, New York.

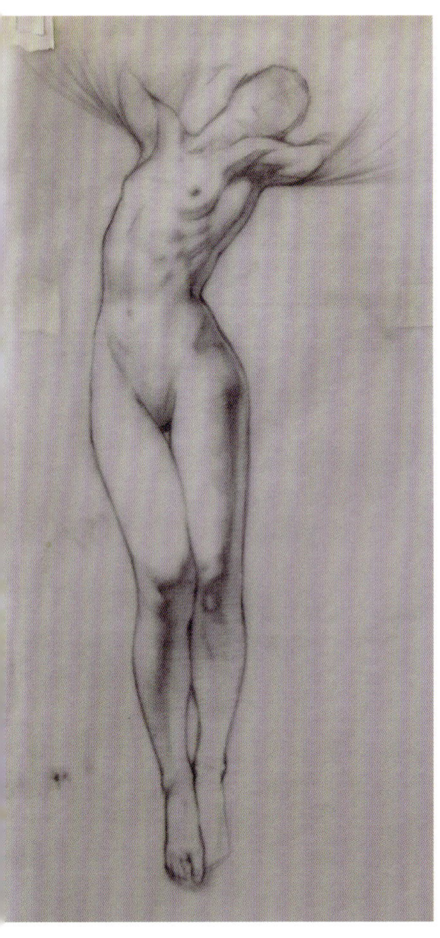

Above: Tenaya Sims, Drawing Study for *Semillas (1),* 2016, graphite on tracing paper, 14 x 11 inches (36 x 28 cm). Courtesy of the artist.

Opposite: Tenaya Sims, *Semillas,* 2016, oil and 23-karat gold leaf on linen, 110 x 80 inches (279 x 203 cm). Collection of Art Renewal Center.

WHAT IT TAKES TO MAKE A MASTERPIECE

Masterpiece is a scary word. I almost changed it so you wouldn't be intimidated and skip this section. But can we talk? Underneath all that anxiety, isn't that what the dream is all about? Making even *one* beautiful and worthwhile thing? And the feeling that you must at least *try*? So, let's allow space for big dreaming and work from the principle that if you shoot for the moon and miss, you land among the stars.

Great works of art don't just happen. They come to fruition in a particular place and time due to long preparation and planning, like a giant blossom on a hardy rose bush. A great master may knock off a song, a dance, a sketch in just a few minutes. It was the twenty years of living and practice beforehand that flowers in such a luminous quick burst.

To cultivate the conditions for serious work, you need:

CREATIVE COMPOST

By this system or another, you cultivate a renewable cycle of ideas. If you want to promote creative output, you must feed your artistic soul.

SLEEP/MEDITATION/QUIET

A time for quiet reflection, enough stillness to hear your own thoughts, and a (generally) uninterrupted chunk of time are essential. Rest, sleep, and the dream state are key to nurturing creative energy.

A COMMUNITY THAT INSPIRES AND UNDERSTANDS YOU

This can be just two or three people. You do not need crowds to appreciate the work you are pursuing. Because being alone too long on any road is discouraging and isolating, you need the company of folks who relate to your goals and obsessions, share feedback, and give encouragement. Ideally, your community also includes one or two people whose work you respect. A supportive mentor makes a world of difference. If you really want to meet a goal, tell a good friend. Sharing your goal aloud will make it more concrete and create a sense of accountability. Intentionally build a small tribe of like-minded people who encourage one another on their creative paths.

DISCIPLINE AND TRAINING

When you are new to art, try any and all things; freely experiment and dabble. Over time, you will discover your strengths, preferences, and tendencies. The longer you make art, the more focused you will become in your choices of mediums and techniques. Don't be tempted to mimic

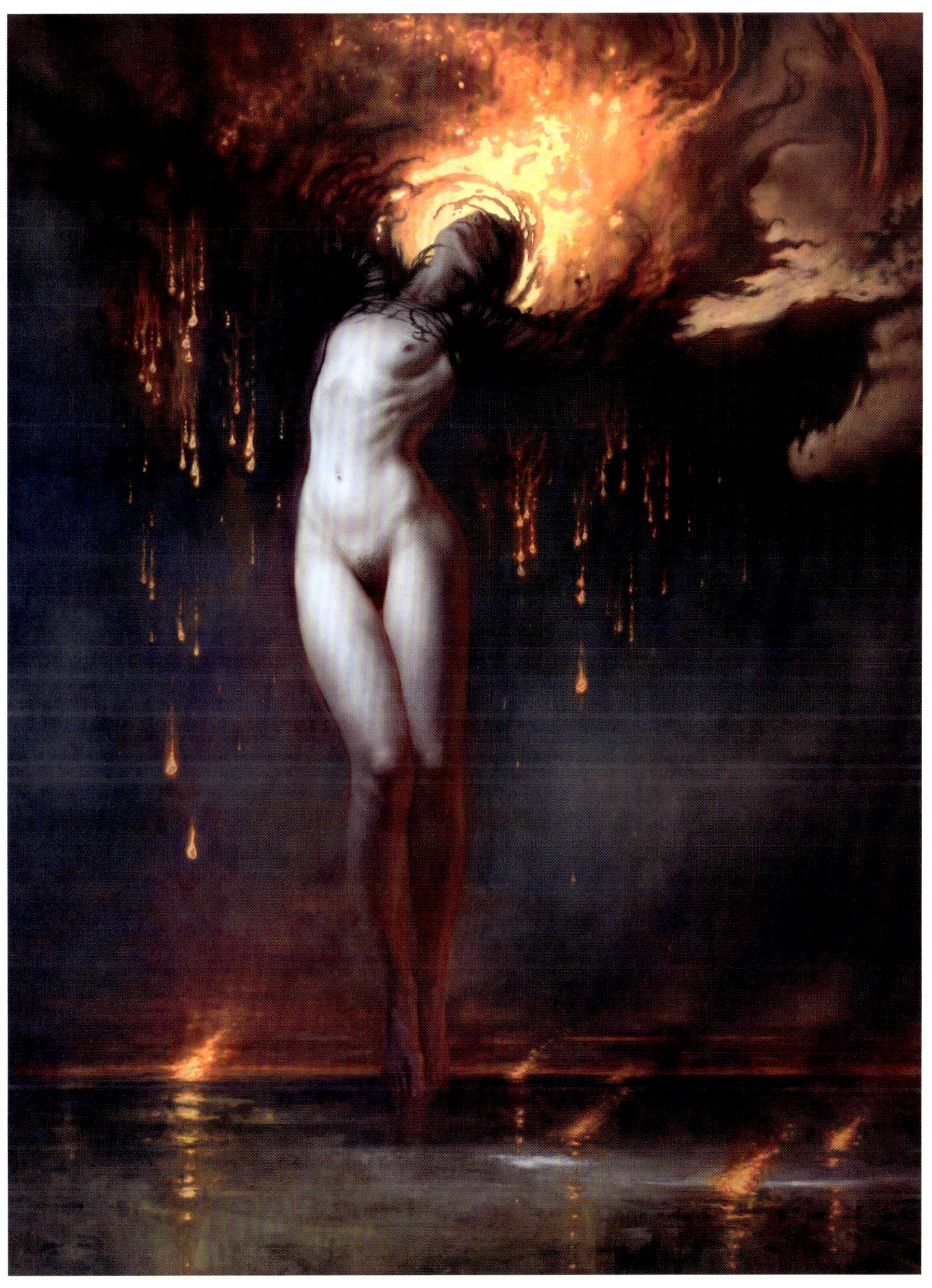

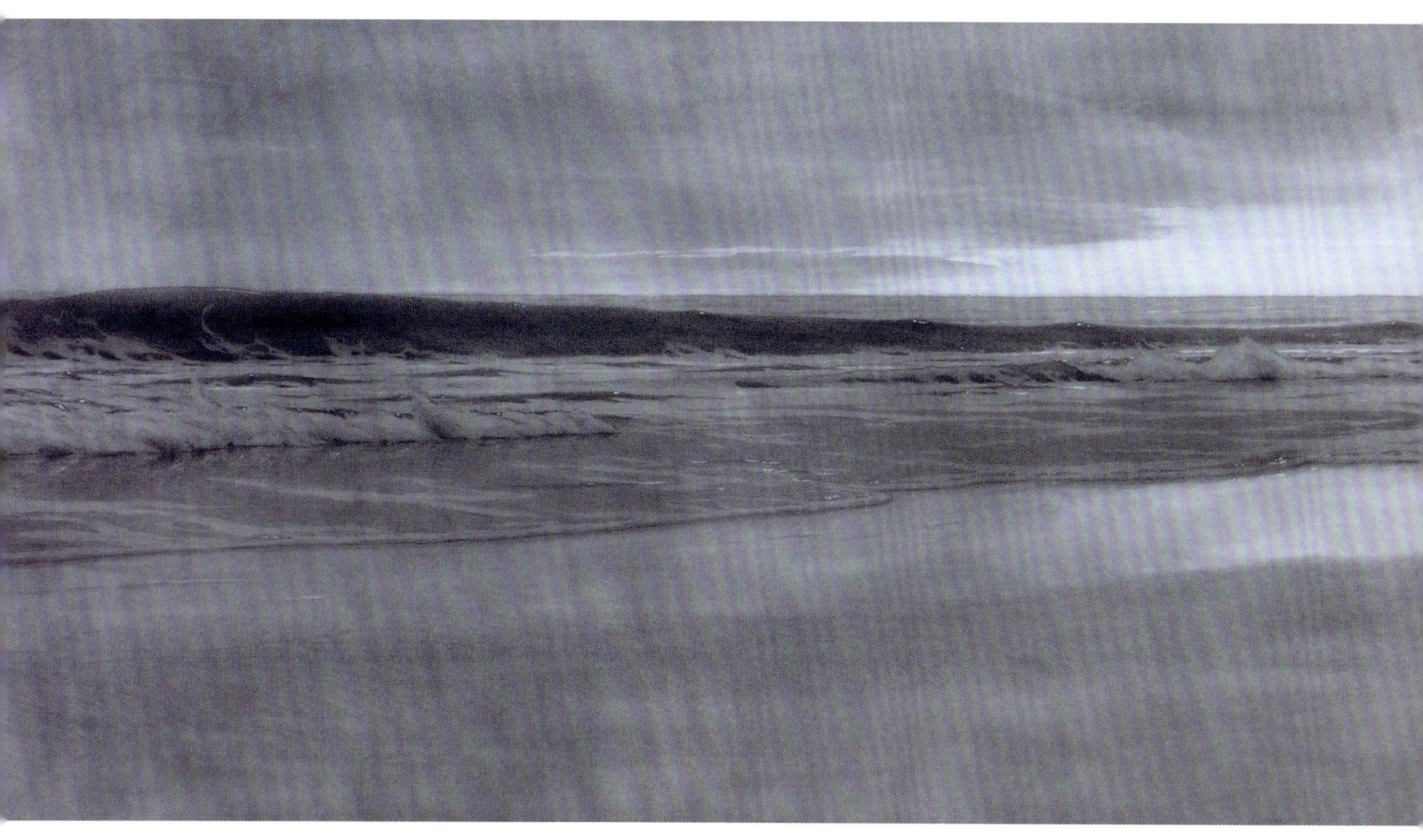

Edward Minoff, *Surf Drawing No. 3,*
2010, graphite, chalk, and gouache
on prepared paper, 9 x 22 inches
(23 x 56 cm). Courtesy of the artist.

popular styles, artists, subjects, and Instagram likes. The key to contentment
and success is remembering that you are the only person who can express
your thoughts, experiences, and emotions. Trust that in following a creative
path, this will become clear.

BELIEVE THAT YOU *CAN*

This may be the hardest one of all. You have to believe that you are worthy
of the time, the effort, and the solitary attention that your work requires
to complete. Absolutely no one will make the space or uninterrupted
time happen for you—you must claim it for yourself, defend it with some
fierceness, and love yourself enough to make it happen.

The above conditions are all internally related, but there is one outwardly
related element that is equally essential. What are you passionate about?
Yes, great, you love art, me too…but what else? What is an overriding force
that sustains your interest and effort? Art making is a process and passion,
but the subject of art is almost universally about something larger that
relates to our experience in society. When your art is just about art, you are

largely preaching to the choir. When you share your passions for larger human issues, you will communicate and connect more widely.

Landscape, for example, is not just about trees and water. The meaning contained within may be derived from love of place, humility before nature, the enchantment of color and light, environmentalism, or human impact. Botanical studies reflect scientific rigor and love for the beauty and mystery of nature. Still-life compositions can use symbols and carefully composed elements to create a poetic parable or a vision of a place and time. Unpack the layers of any subject and find the why and what-for of art.

Your *why* matters. In your own subjects and choices, find a connection to larger issues and tell a story of your point of view. For centuries, much art has centered around religious ideas—stories about human virtues, morality, and mortality. Narratives depict human experiences like love, hope, anguish, power, or jealousy—the dramas that recur in our personal lives.

Find the things that resonate with you. When you have passion for the subject and *meaning* of your efforts, you can sustain your creative path over years. Purpose gives struggle meaning. Heed your instincts and be guided by the love for the subject you are creating. If you lack a clear sense of direction or strong preference, lean into your curiosity. Any inkling of interest will suffice. Follow that path a bit to see where it leads. Just ask Alice: Rabbit holes can open new worlds.

WORLDBUILDING

If you have ever stayed up until 3:00 a.m. lost in a book, you understand the power of worldbuilding. J. K. Rowling's imagination has mesmerized millions through the elaborate magical world of Harry Potter. You can eat at the Leaky Cauldron and have a butterbeer. The origin of the word *fiction* comes from "to form." Whether in words, clay, pencil, or paint, the creation of fiction means inventing worlds to share with others.

Consider a great master like the Flemish artist Peter Paul Rubens, whose creations show us a world of a magical Rubensland: gods and monsters, wolf hunts, lords and ladies, all expressed in an artistically unified universe

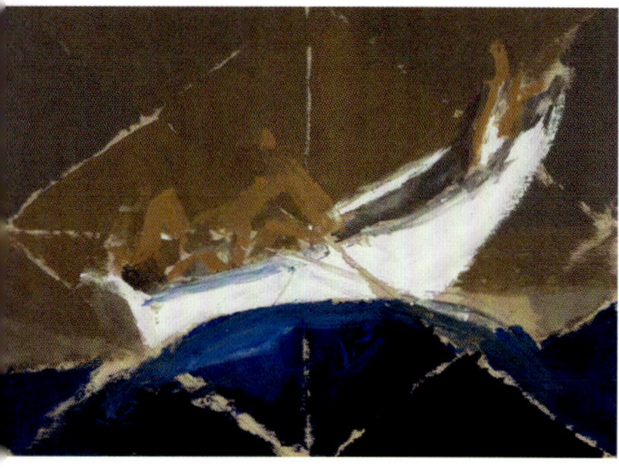
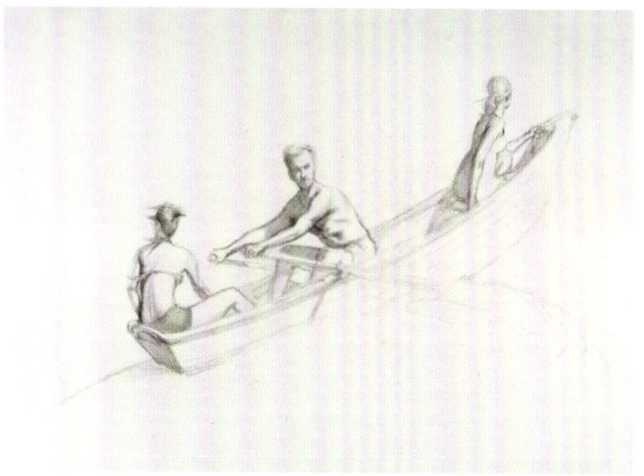
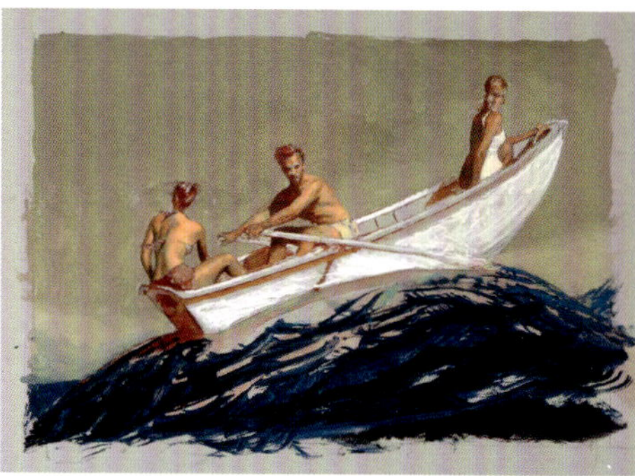
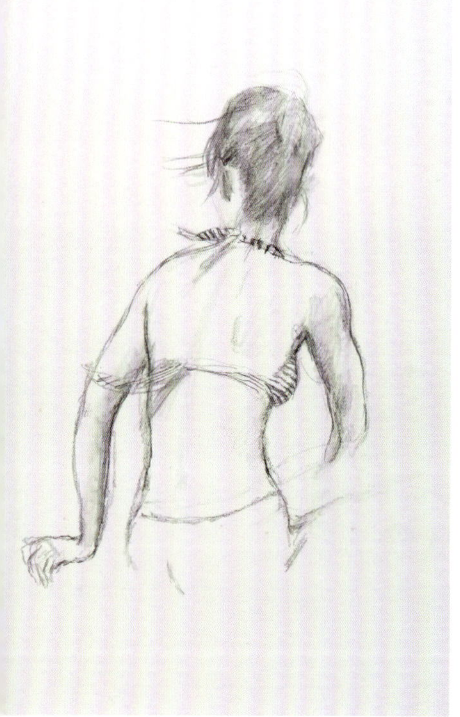
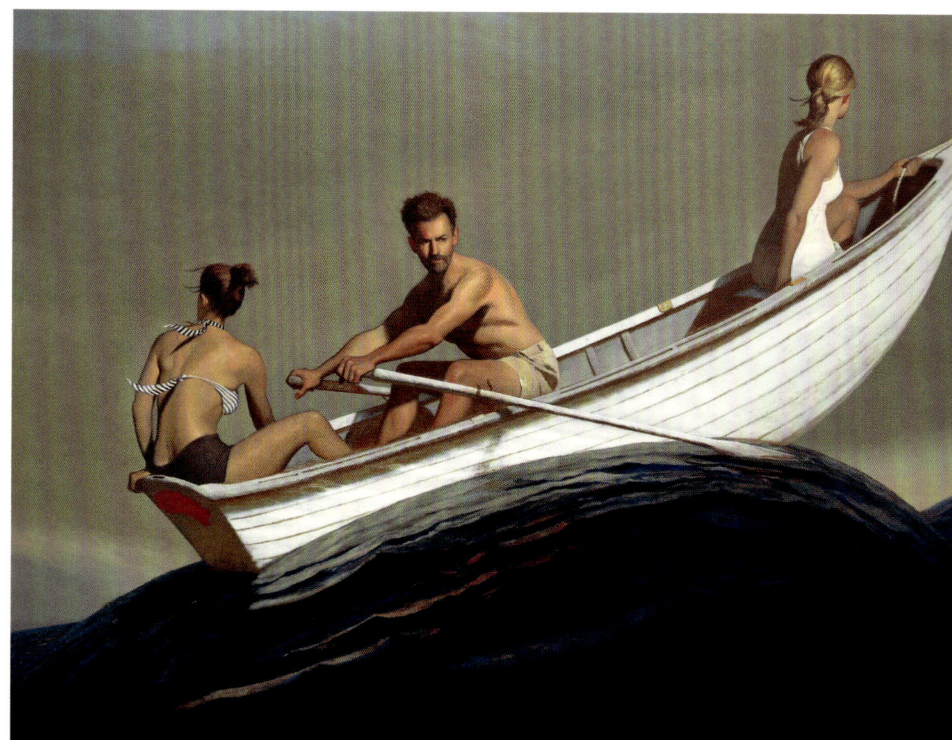

Bo Bartlett (top left, clockwise): *The Promised Land (Study of Quadrant and Color)*, 2015, oil on board, 9 x 12 in. (23 x 30 cm); *The Promised Land (Study of Swell)*, 2015, graphite on paper, 22½ x 30 in. (57 x 76 cm); *The Promised Land (Study)*, 2015, oil on board, 12 x 20 in. (30 x 51 cm); *The Promised Land,* 2015, oil on linen, 88 x 120 in. (224 x 305 cm); *The Promised Land (Study of Betsy)*, 2015, graphite on paper, 22 x 15 in. (56 x 38 cm). Courtesy of the artist / Miles McEnery Gallery, New York.

that looks like wonderful lusty fun to visit. A contemporary master like Bo Bartlett similarly imbues all his work with a signature air and light that parallels our realistic visual world but can be found only in his particular kingdom. These artists are using the language of realism to show us objects and places that we may identify, but the world in which they exist is not the same as real life.

Every fictional world has its own rules and limitations. In the realm of Harry Potter, an iPhone would make no sense, while flying skeleton horses are perfectly reasonable. In Rubens, the eagle may tear out your liver, but the Virgin Mary will shine down a beatific salve. What you must achieve in world building is the willing suspension of the viewer's disbelief. Get your audience to accept the fictional terms of your magical realm and you can do whatever you like within those boundaries. Imaginative artists paint their own worlds and invite us into their universe. I find myself wondering what the temperature is. Is it windy? What kind of home do these characters live in?

The artist Molly Judd evokes brooding mystery when she assembles a relatively simple collection of objects for her composition—a man with a nineteenth-century haircut and woolen coat, a beautiful shell, and a grassy seashore. Is he resting or fallen? His body seems insubstantial. What is the significance of the unusual conch shell? Judd's delicate control of line, value, and tone in the landscape makes the atmosphere feel calm but ominous. All these elements in her drawing make a particular universe unique to her creative world.

Tenaya Sims (p. 186) takes elements of representational drawing and departs into a fantastical realm of magic, spirit, and allegory. Here we are clearly in the world of fiction relative to our pedestrian view from town. Freely adding embellishments, Sims invites us to take in the scenery, unpack

Molly Judd, *Boy with Conch Shell*, 2018, charcoal on paper, 17 x 23 inches (42 x 59 cm). Courtesy of the artist.

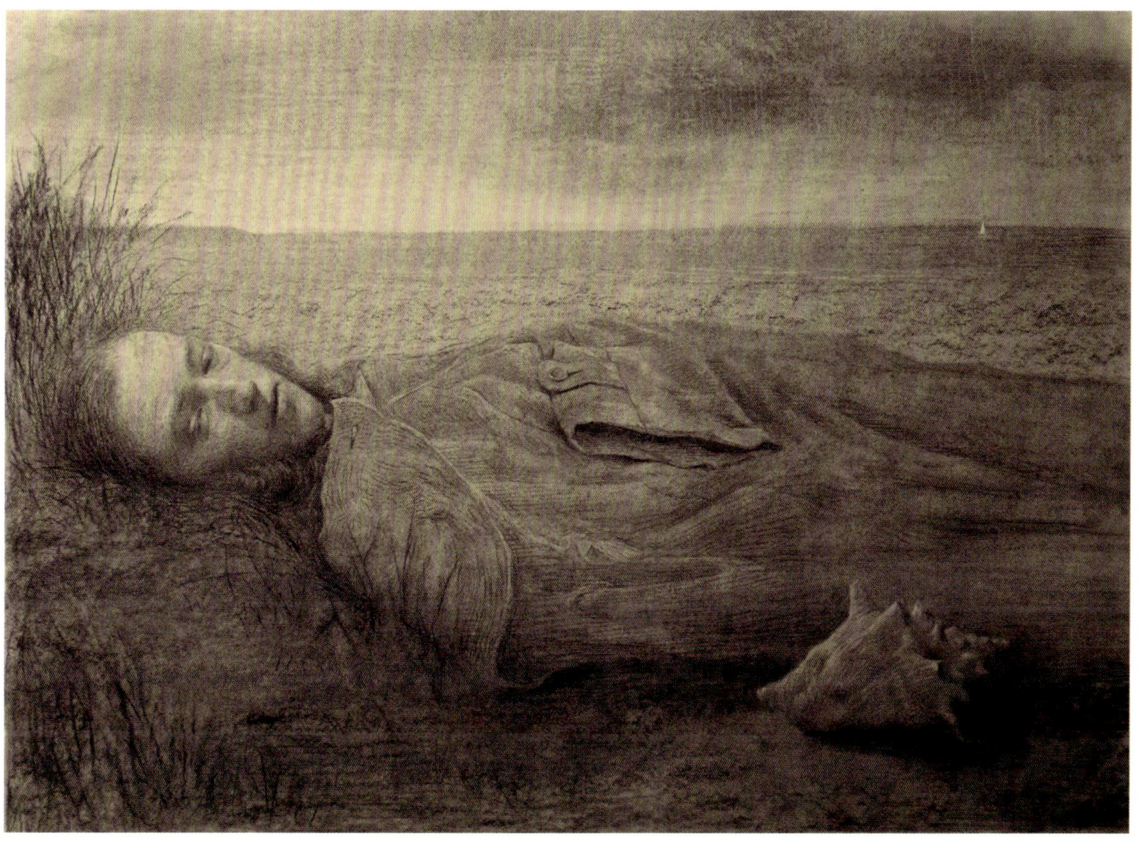

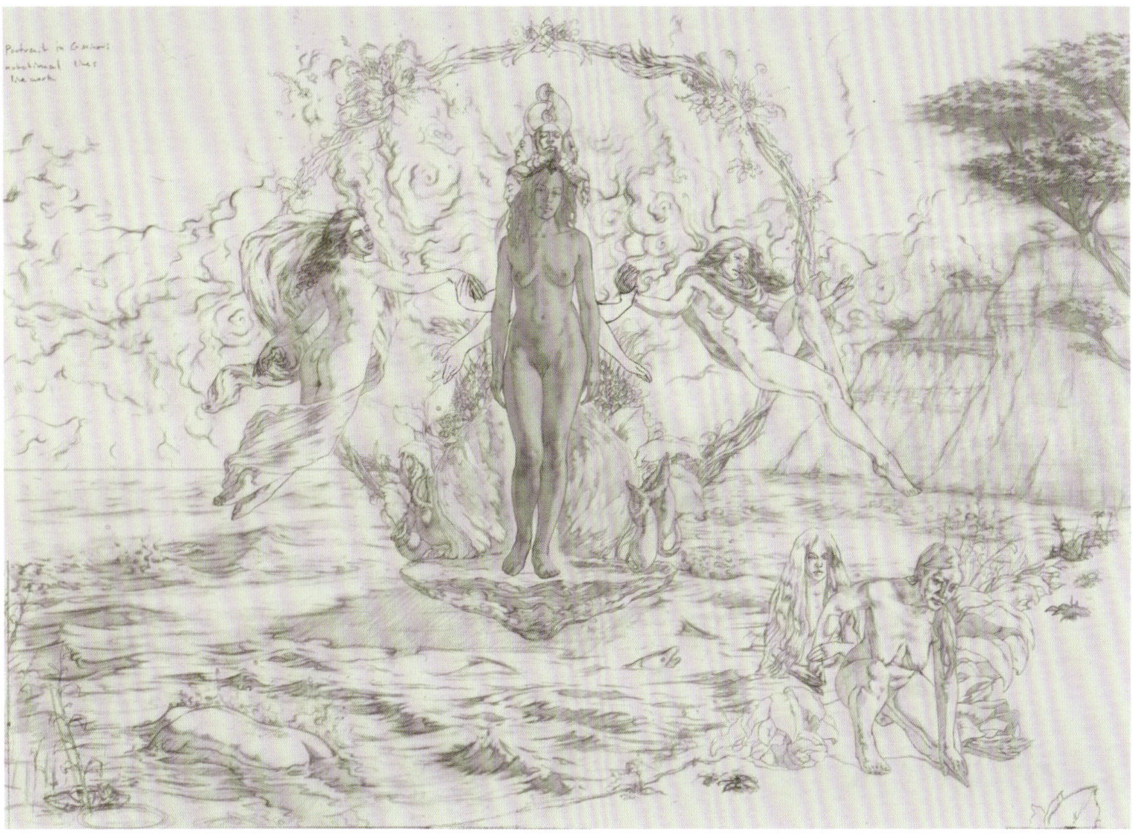

Above: Tenaya Sims, *Line Drawing Compilation for Birth of Venus,* 2014, graphite on paper, 19 x 27 inches (48 x 69 cm). Courtesy of the artist.

Opposite, top: Hyeseung Song, *Chapter 1: In the Cemetery,* 2018, oil on linen, 79 x 127 inches (201 x 323 cm). Courtesy of the artist.

Opposite, bottom: Hyeseung Song, *Watercolor Cut-Outs,* 2014, watercolor on Arches paper, 6 x 4 x 1 inches (15 x 10 x 3 cm). Courtesy of the artist.

the symbolism, and enjoy the aesthetic rhythms of his created world. Once you step away from documentary realism and into your own imaginative world, the terms of engagement and potential for expansion are endless.

STRATEGIES FOR DEVELOPING WORK

Passion is the word for the obsession the artist Hyeseung Song has with her subject, a sculpture from Père Lachaise Cemetery in Paris. Her emotional connection to this funerary monument sparked the inspiration for a cycle of large works in a connected narrative. To create the big canvas at the top of the opposite page, Song prepared many small pieces, including some plein air (outdoor) studies at the cemetery and concept sketches in the studio to distill her intended sense of mood. She researched each element—the statue, the cemetery tombstones, the tree, and the composition as a whole— before tackling the large canvas. By creating a paper cutout with watercolor (opposite, lower right), she was able to reposition her primary subject in her concept sketches to find her ideal placement. Using many quick and energetic sketches to quickly problem-solve helped her maintain her intensity with confidence on the large canvas.

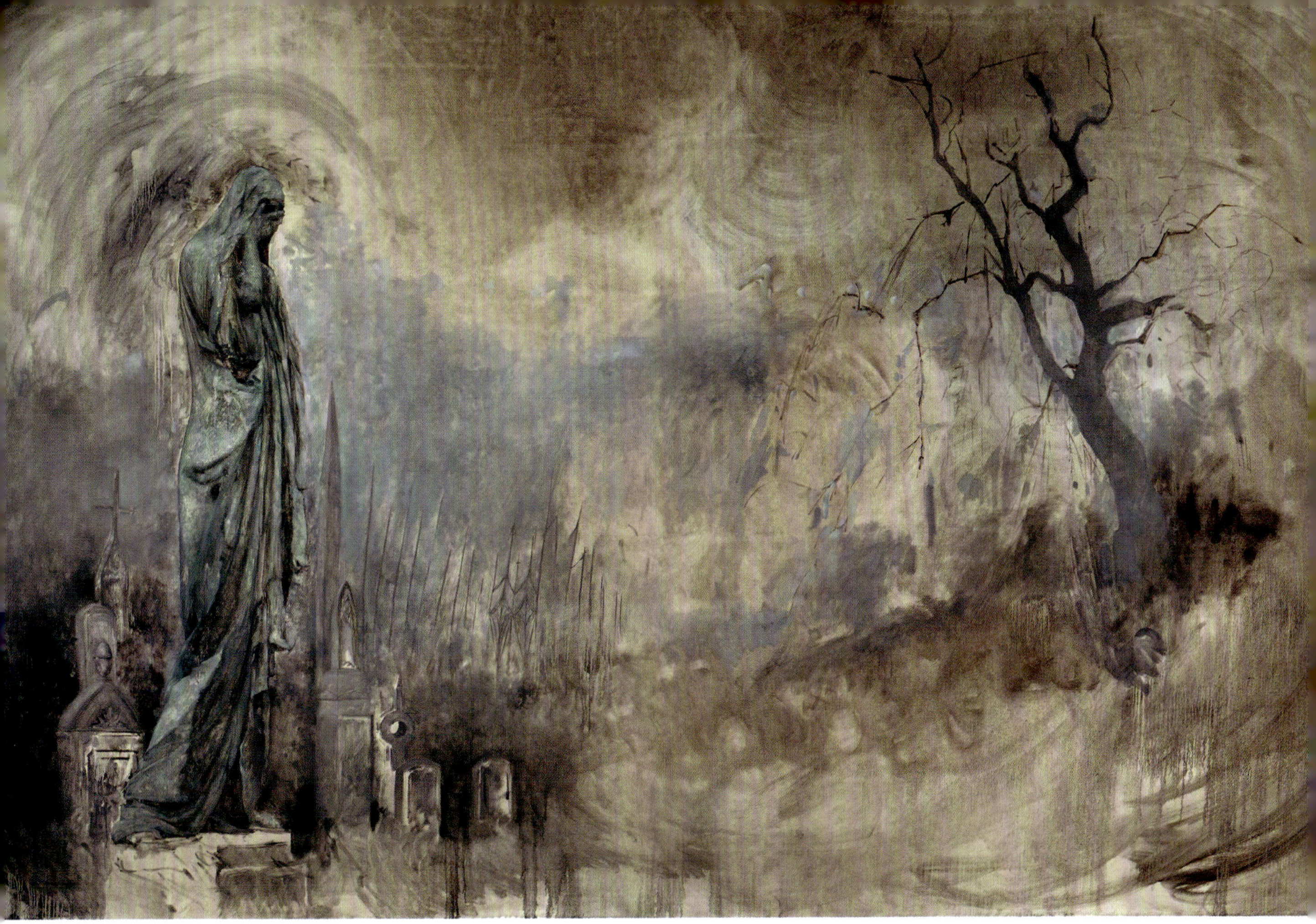

Artist James Gurney uses clay models, called "maquettes," to compose realistic paintings of long-lost dinosaurs with remarkable detail and naturalism. The clay model can be positioned and lit for realistic light and shadow details. For the work on the next page, he wanted to create the effect of a Spinosaurus submerged partially in water. He placed his clay dinosaur in a large pan with small rocks and sticks and added milky water to study how the shadows and reflections interacted. Using a 3-D model and making a lighting effect with natural objects, he was able to fuel his imagination.

"My work is not about paint. It is about paint in the service of something else."

—KEHINDE WILEY

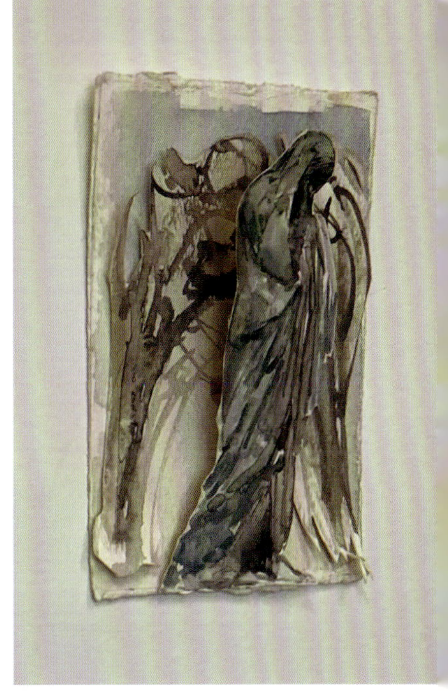

DIORAMAS AND MODELS

In the preceding chapter, we started looking at strategies for working from imagination. If you want more ways to build imaginative compositions, small models in paper are fun and spark endless ideas for building your own world.

The artist Anna Wakitsch executed this concept marvelously with a fantastic paper period room with careful architectural details and painted like a fine French interior. Can't go to Paris? Your viewer may never realize that your Parisian interior was made in miniature on your table in Springfield. Creating a small 3-D space and lighting it as if sunlight were pouring in through real windows gives a painter ample fuel to flesh out an image. Using models in this manner helps us build our spatial visual imagination and our ability to conceptualize pictorial space.

Below, left: James Gurney, *Spinosaurus* maquette, 2021, Sculpey over aluminum armature wire, length 8 inches (20 cm). © James Gurney, BDSP, 2021.

James Gurney, *Spinosaurus*, 2021, oil on board, 13 x 10 inches (33 x 25 cm). © James Gurney, BDSP, 2021.

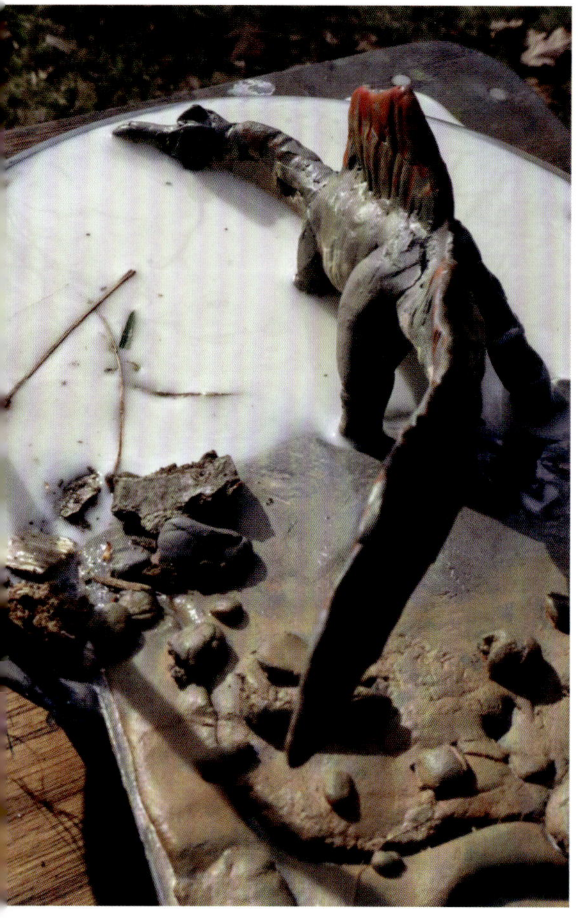

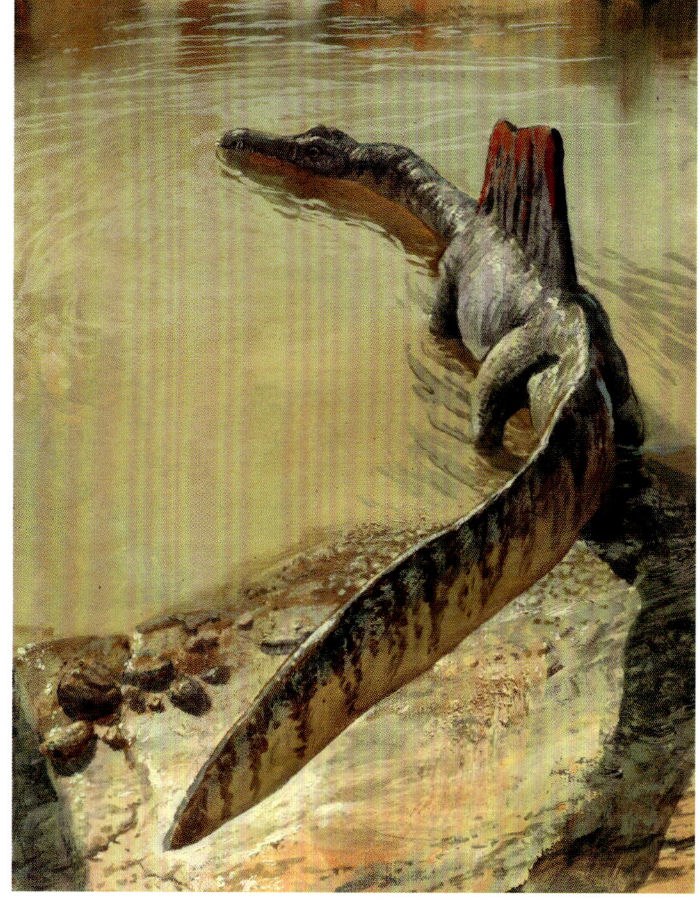

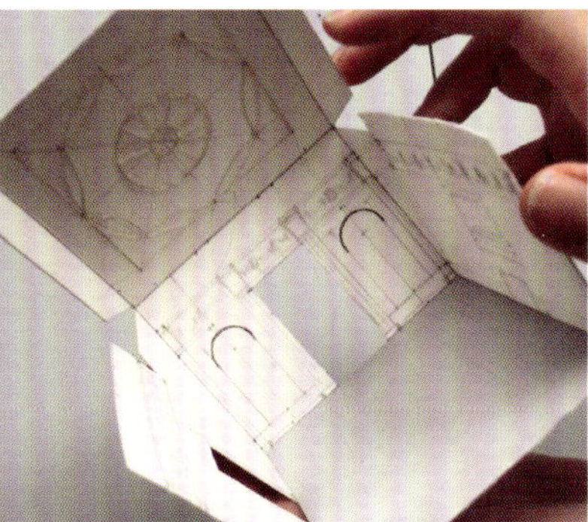

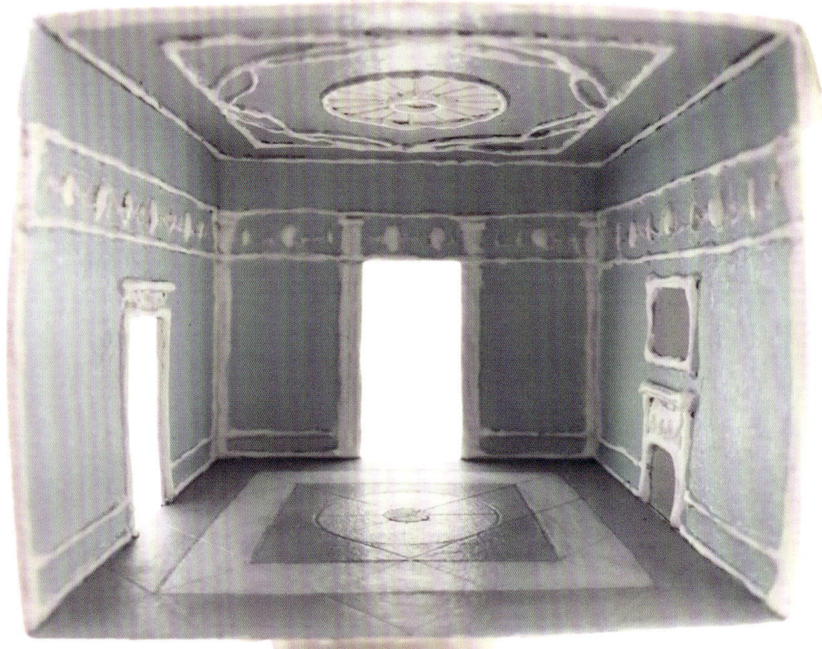

Anna Wakitsch creates complex paper maquettes that she can light as models to make realistic paintings of invented interiors. The circular painting at right below was made on a concave acrylic hemisphere; when viewed through an oculus, it creates a compelling illusion of 3-D space with a magical painterly atmosphere.

Above: Left: The paper model under construction; right, the model, painted and lit. Courtesy of the artist.

Right: Anna Wakitsch, *Withdrawing Room 1,* 2019, oil on acrylic hemisphere, 9 x 9 x 4½ inches (23 x 23 x 11 cm). Courtesy of the artist.

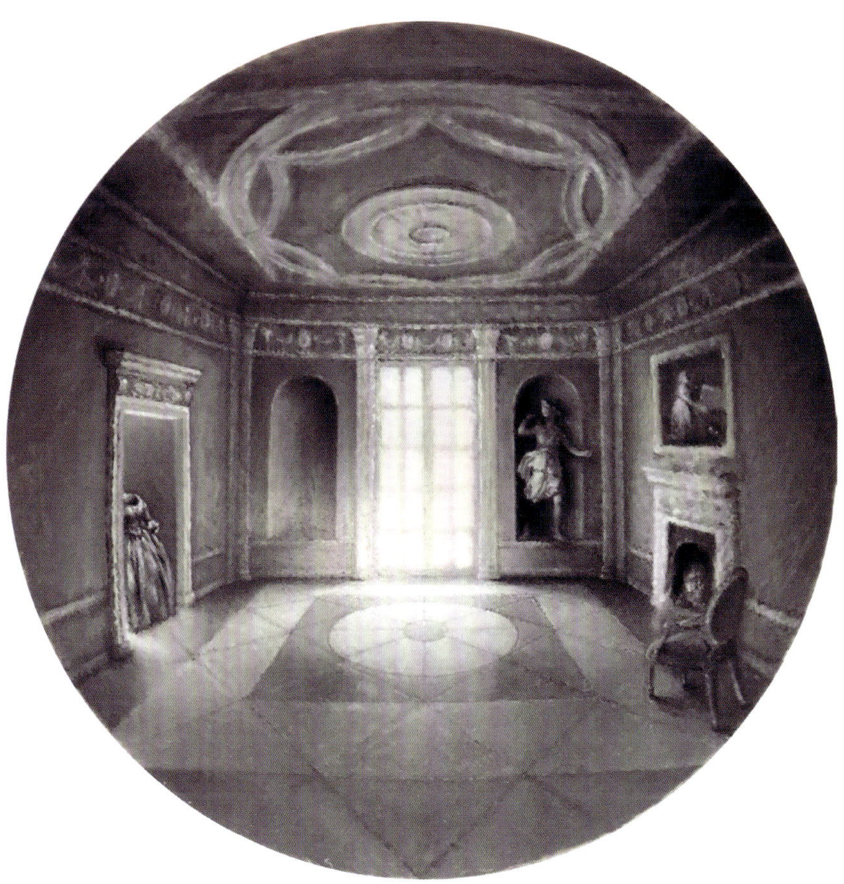

Make a Paper Playground

In this project, you will a simple paper model of a playground and then make a composition drawing of an imagined world. There's some structural drawing, using light and shadow. There's some perspective, building a few basic skills in the ground plane and picture plane. Then, creating the paper model itself gives you an opportunity to explore composition and placement within a picture. This will take a little more time, with two stages—first the model, then the drawing. I hope that this template of ideas gives you a bunch of adaptable concepts to embark on your own unique creations.

BUILDING THE MODEL

Materials for the paper playground:
· A couple of sheets of heavyweight paper or construction paper
· Plain white paper
· Scissors and glue stick
· Small photo or toy for a figure

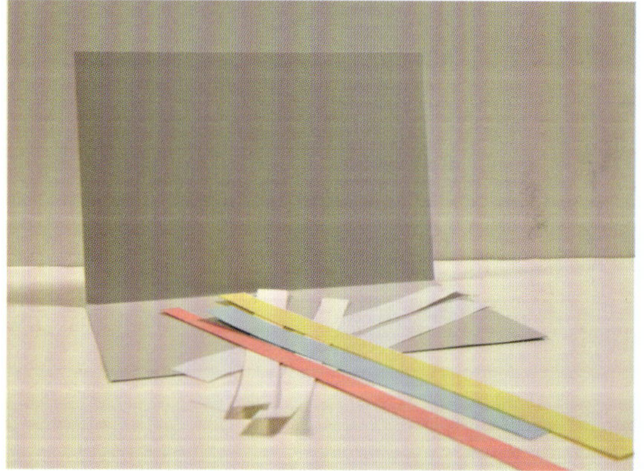

I used colored paper so you can see the components, but you can do this entirely on white paper. If you don't have heavy card stock, then plain copy paper will work, but at a smaller scale.

I folded a plain, light gray 8½ × 11-inch sheet of cardstock in half to make my "playground." When you do this with your sheet of paper, prop it up on a cardboard box if necessary.

I cut many strips of paper about ½- to 1- inch wide.

Next, I started folding and gluing my strips of paper. I didn't plan much; I just started with one element and added on from there. Play around with folding and curling the strips, and see what happens as you move them around. You are the director, placing elements on your paper stage.

Fold tabs and glue the ends of the paper in place to your paper base. Trim the strips as needed for big and small elements in your composition for a variety of shapes and sizes. Limit your objects to three to five. Trust me, it gets complicated fast.

To add a character to my story, I printed a small photo and glued it to a paper base (and folded a small tab to make it stand up). Using a small toy figure is good fun too. Got any monsters? Move your character around on your model to find various options for your composition.

Last—this is important—light your model with a single light source so you have clear light and

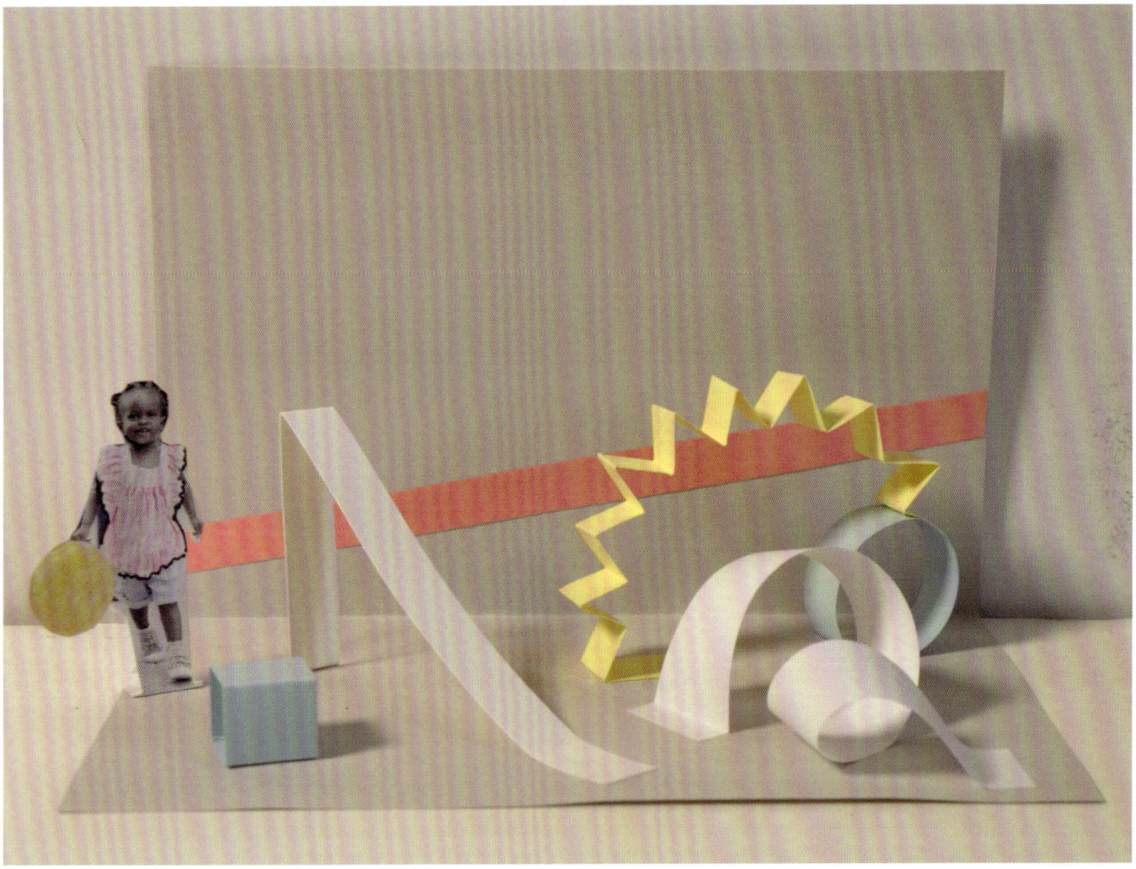

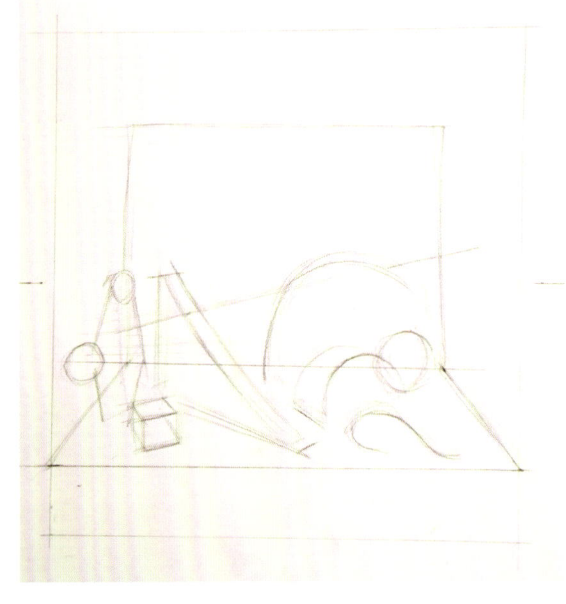

shadow shapes and cast shadows. This will make
it much easier to draw, and it will teach you
some basics about using light and shadow to move
through a composition.

DRAWING THE MODEL

The drawing portion of this project is nothing new
for readers thus far. Start with a block-in with
a light pencil (HB). This drawing is 8 × 9 inches.
Work between 5 × 7 inches and 8 × 10 inches.

Create a square or rectangular frame for a border.
The outer border becomes like the border around
a stage—the proscenium—that is like a picture
plane. All the parts of your pictorial world go within
that window.

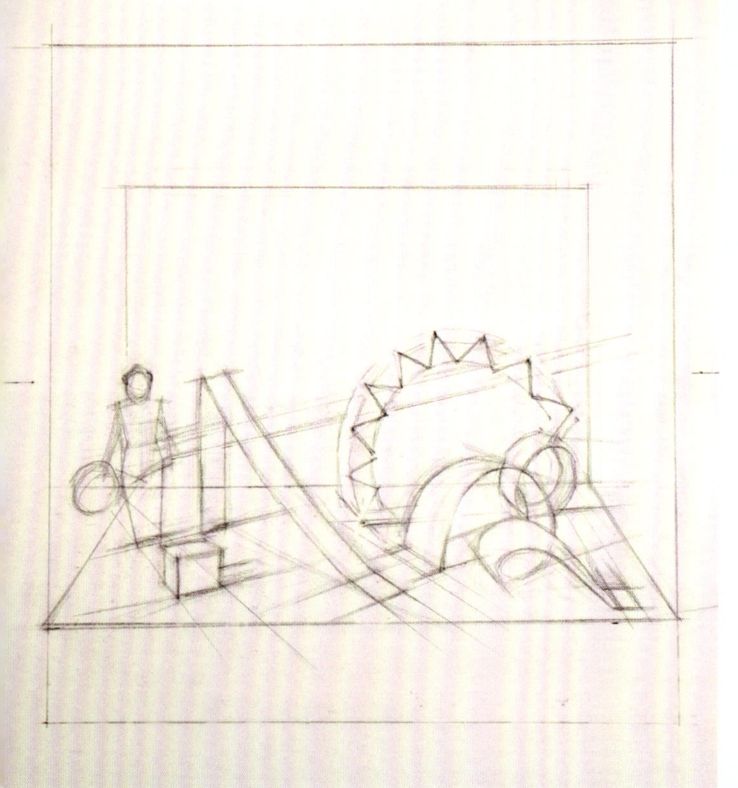

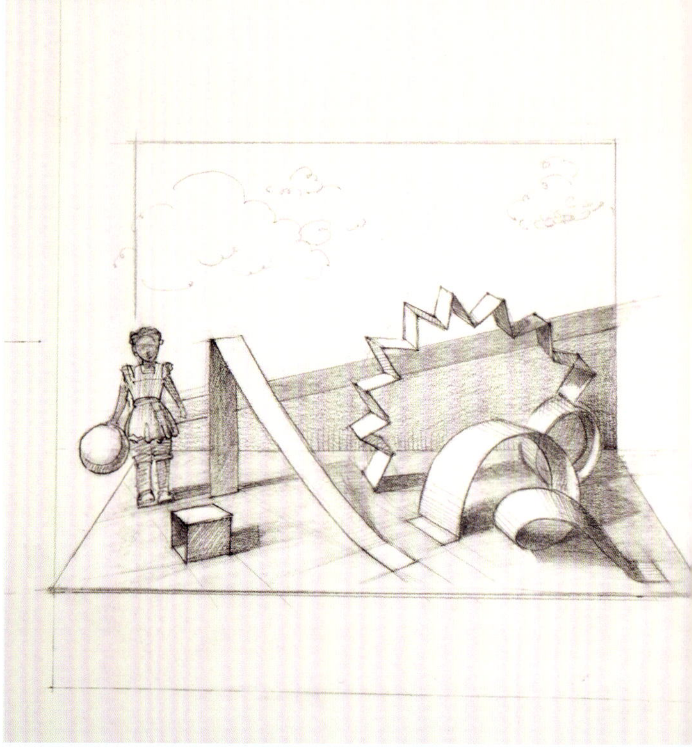

Start with the ground plane (the half of the paper on the table) and the backdrop (the upright half). This sets up your paper stage.

Use axis lines and block-in lines to sort out a general placement of the various elements. (Too complicated? It's OK to pull out one or two.) Use the basics of triangulation and measurement to check proportion.

Look at the ground plane carefully to help organize the placement of the playground objects—what comes in front? What's behind? How close are they to each other? I used longer axis lines to show the perspective and drew extra lines on the ground plane to check how they fit together. This is a helpful use of perspective.

When the block-in was sorted out, I switched to a darker (2B) pencil and added contours and shading. In particular, use the cast shadows on the ground plane and the form shadows to create dimension on your paper forms. I used my blending stump to even out some passages and lightly shade the ground plane. Erase and redraw to sharpen the details.

You do not need to make a finely detailed drawing (have fun if you want to!). Feel free to add more imaginative elements to yours. The intention of this project is to teach the basics of creating an imaginative preparatory sketch, and fine details in the drawing are not usually part of that process.

A bonus tip for this project—if you create your drawing on sturdy mixed-media paper, you can put a coat of clear acrylic matte medium on the drawing (let that dry completely) and make a painted sketch right on top in acrylics or oils. The drawing may smear a bit with the acrylic (use a fixative to ensure it doesn't), but it should hold up fine, and you can add color to explore your picture making further.

SMALL BETS

One of my favorite principles for developing work is *small bets*. This concept
states that through many small, quick sketches, we will navigate our way
efficiently to a successful idea and composition. Working in a small format
allows for quick development and multiple versions. Small bets encourage
exploration without the pressure of a big canvas or commitment if things go
south. I begin by drawing sketches, exploring line, shape, and composition.
For paintings, I will then make small sketches on paper to experiment with
color and value.

Small bets build our confidence in our voice and vision. When you
embrace this as a process over time, you can discern patterns and common
tendencies. This helps us identify our natural voice.

Ideas often emerge in fragments. You might have one or two clear
components but feel foggy about how it all works together. Fleshing out
the parts you "know" in little sketches helps you intuit your way toward a

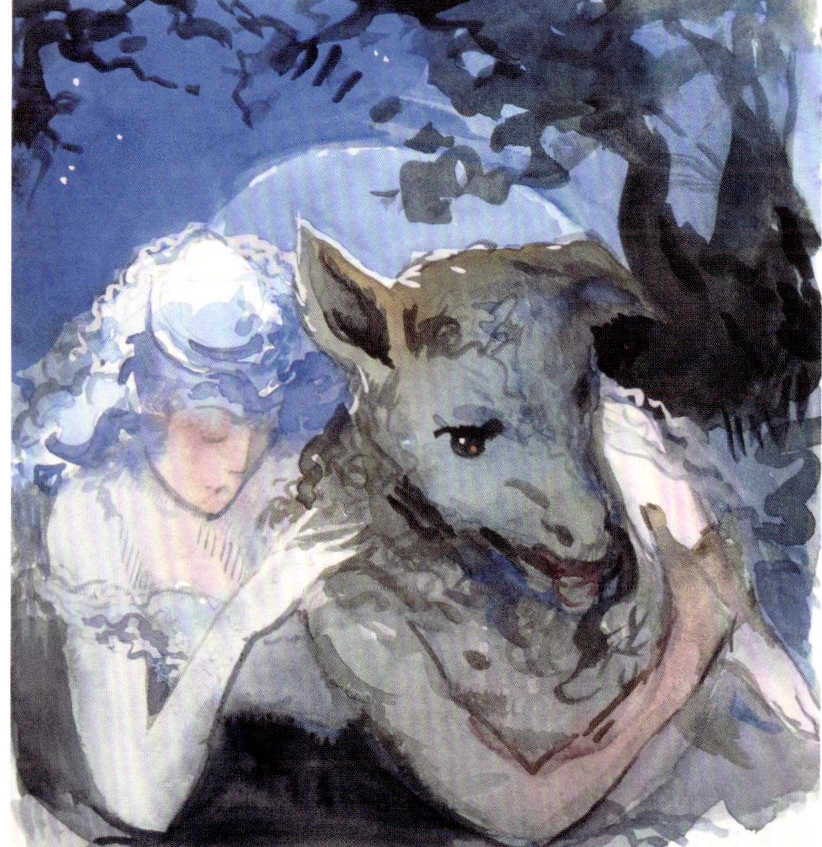

Patricia Watwood, *Titania and Bottom,* 2018, watercolor on paper, 7 x 6½ inches (18 x 17 cm). Courtesy of the artist.

To develop an idea for a painting, I did thumbnail drawings and a small watercolor sketch from imagination to explore the composition (below). Next, I did a drawing from a life model (opposite) to study the form and gesture of the figure.

Patricia Watwood, *Rachel, Moonlight Study*, 2017, 20 x 12½ inches (51 x 32 cm). Courtesy of the artist.

Below: Patricia Watwood, *Moonlight Thumbnail Studies*, 2017, pencil and watercolor on paper, each page 7 x 7 inches (18 x 18 cm). Courtesy of the artist.

solution. Sometimes the missing piece will arrive later to complete an idea.

Sketching allows for an editorial process. We often fall quite in love with our first ideas, becoming tunnel-visioned. This fervor can be heady, but you eventually learn that not all obsessions are healthy. I've learned to respect the distillation of ideas over time and to let my fervor cool a bit. I come back into the studio one clear morning and realize those proportions are really screwed up! Why didn't I see that? Time away allows you to see your own work with dispassion and clarity.

On the other hand, indecisiveness can be a stumbling block. If you have two options and have a hard time deciding, then it probably doesn't matter that much. Eeny, meeny, miny, moe and move on. It's important to notice the difference between stalling and editing.

A little time away can help you see freshly what work has the most potential. Falling out of love with your image a bit can be helpful. Was it important? Is this composition really the best version? I have little sketches that have sat around my studio for years, and some will eventually queue up to become finished pieces. After the sketches pile up for a while, priorities emerge. The images that lose their potency fade, and the sketches that continue to intrigue draw me back again and again until they manifest in their complete expression.

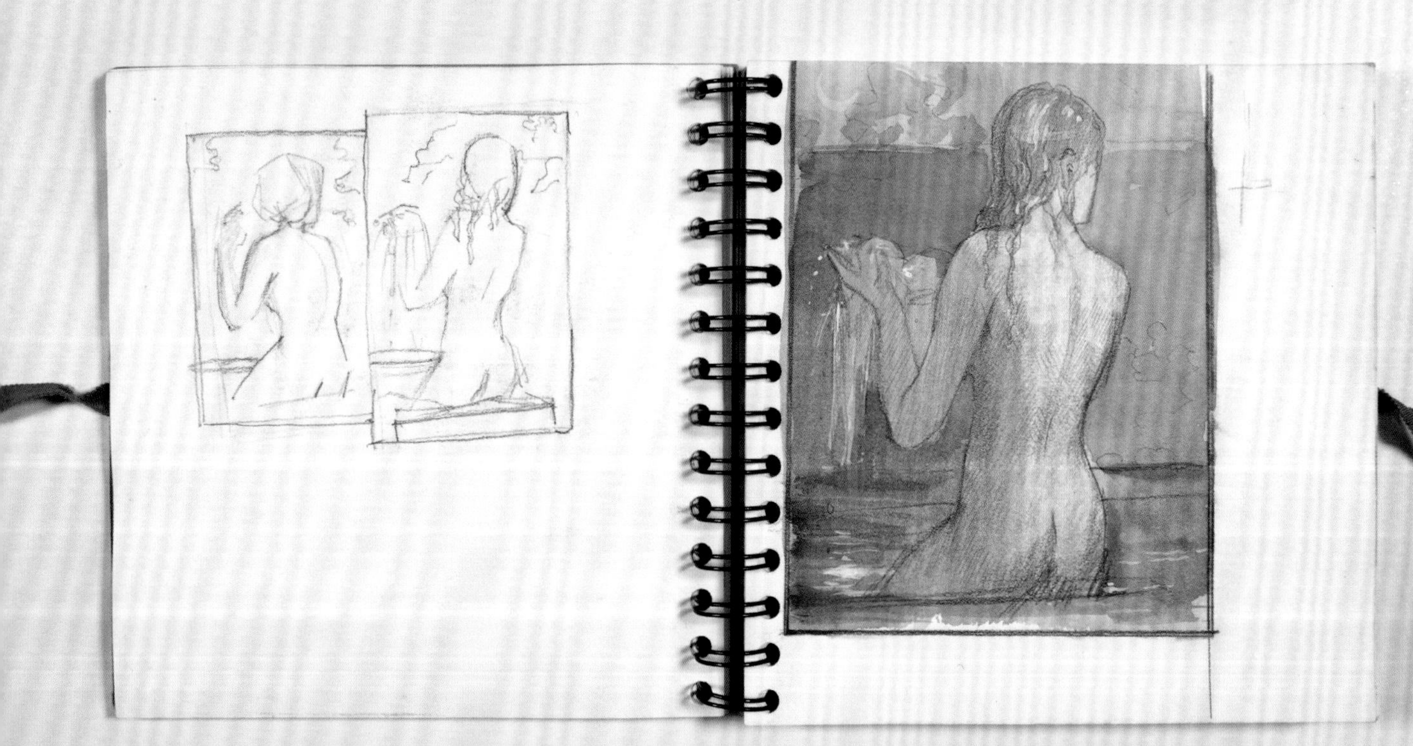

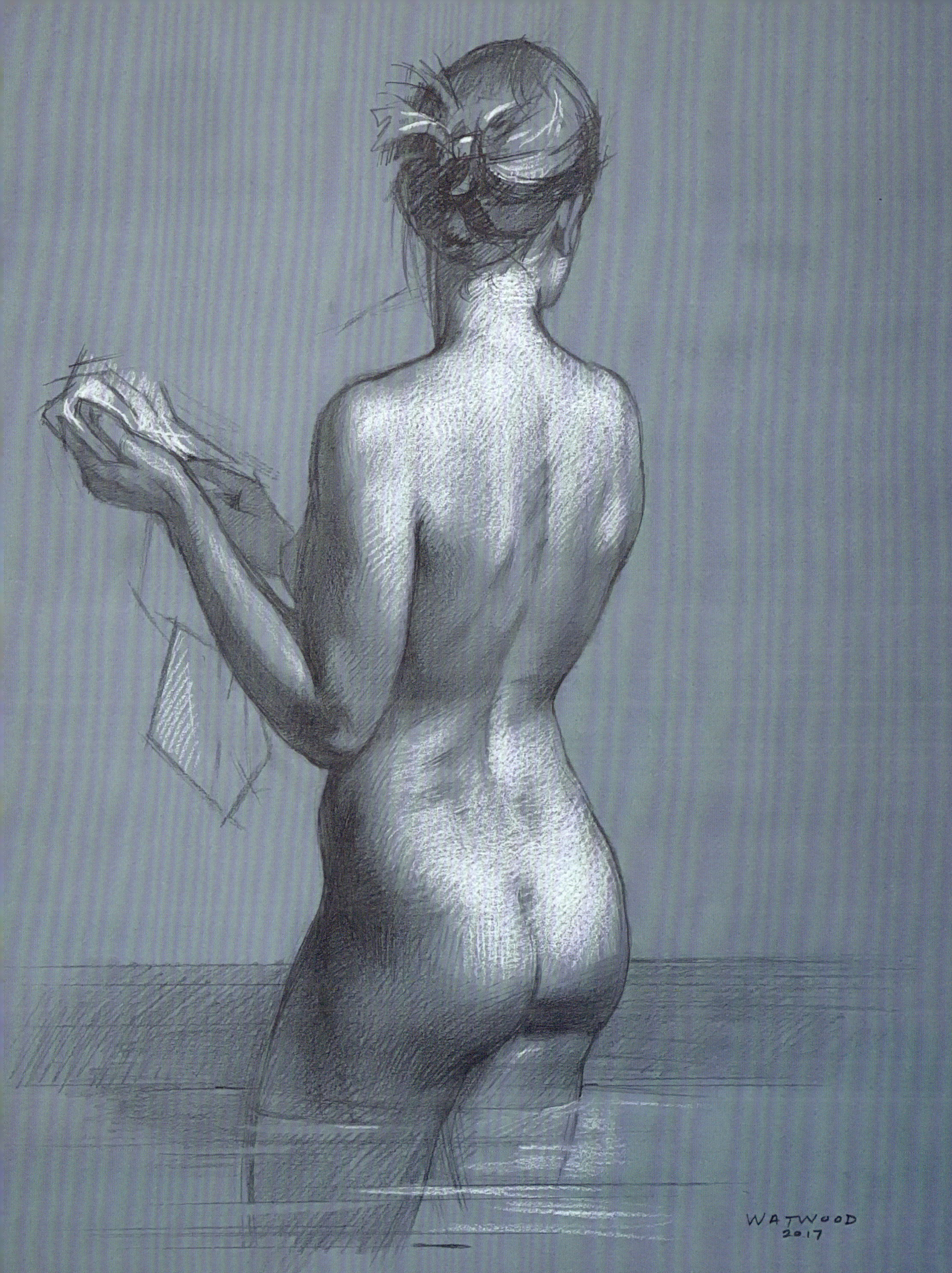

WATWOOD
2017

THUMBNAILS

A simple way to get started that's incredibly useful to all levels of artists is a thumbnail sketch. The key difference between a thumbnail and other preparatory works is the size. A *thumbnail* is a very small drawing or painting, created to plan the composition of a more finished work. Thumbnails are usually quite small, about the size of a credit card or postcard. Sometimes my idea for a painting feels like a butterfly in fog. Doodling out very small drawings, I try to catch a better look at the wispy image. It's trial and error, but the expression on the paper is essential to solidifying the thought.

Even the simplest of drawings is improved by thoughtful attention to composition and placement in relationship to the frame. *Placement* is the location and scale of a particular image on the page. *Composition* is the relationship among all parts of the picture to one another and the frame (often a rectangle). Thumbnails focus our attention on large elements before we get engrossed in details. Being small and quick, they allow us to experiment, try multiples, brainstorm, and discover what is most interesting and essential.

Artists use thumbnails as an *aide-mémoire*, gathering quick references when out and about to take home to the studio for development. You can add field notes to your sketchbook to record time of day, weather conditions, impressions of color, even your mood. Write what struck you about an

When exploring a new theme, I create multiple concept thumbnails in my sketchbook. Like those in my creative compost sourcebook, the images that persist in engaging my interest eventually develop into finished works. Below are multiple imaginative concept thumbnails in pencil and watercolor that I did in 2018 in an 8 x 8-inch sketchbook.

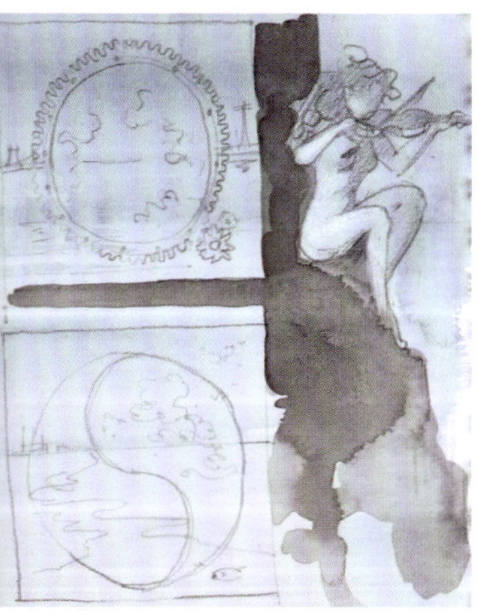
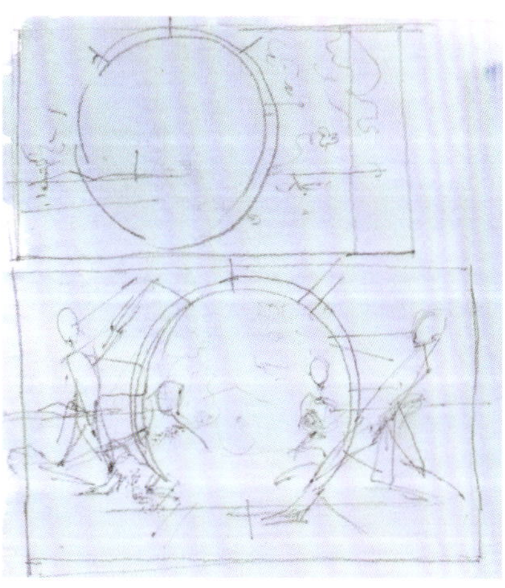
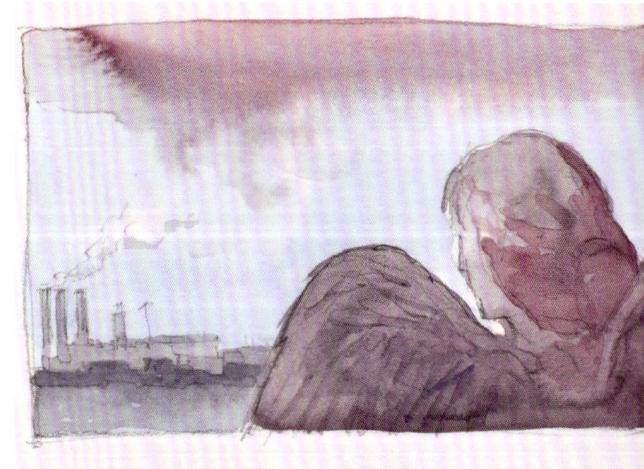

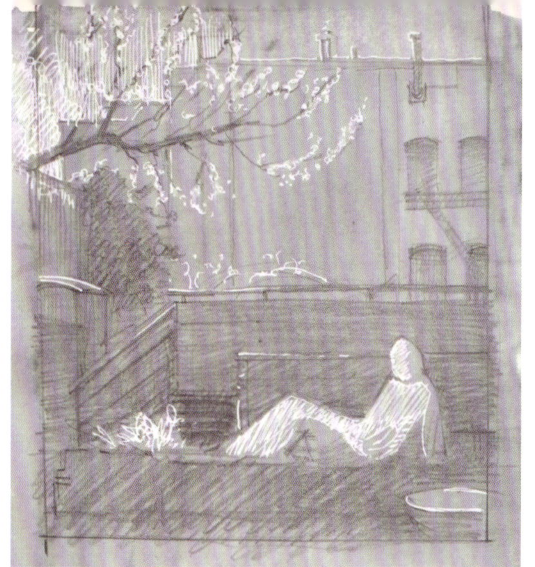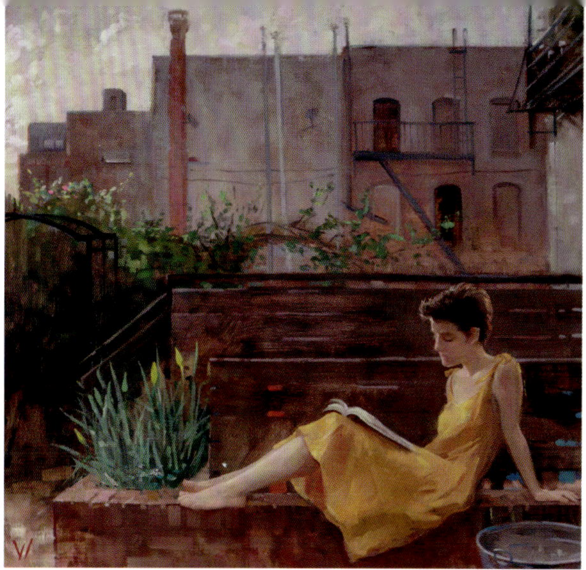

image, maybe "great expanse of vivid blue sky" or "blinding sunlight on the water." Jot down the angle of the light. These notes will help you recall both the visual image and the mood you experienced. You will be creating an archive of pictures you can return to for inspiration and learn more about your personal visual preferences. The artist Joseph Mallord William Turner (on p. 197) sketched thousands of thumbnails with notations to anchor scenes in his memory.

NOTAN

Arthur Wesley Dow's 1914 book *Composition* familiarized artists with the black-and-white *notan* as a particularly useful type of thumbnail. In recent years, notans are popular for cinematic storyboards and comic book

Before making the painting shown above, I needed a thumbnail sketch to decide what elements I wanted to include and how they would fit in my rectangle.

Above, left: Patricia Watwood, thumbnail sketch for *Quarantine*, 2020, watercolor, pencil, and white ink on paper, 6 x 4 inches (15 x 10 cm). Courtesy of the artist.

Above, right: Patricia Watwood, *Spring in Quarantine*, 2020, oil on linen, 19 x 20 inches (48 x 51 cm). Courtesy of the artist.

Gary Faigin, *Decomposition #2 (Study)*, 2002, charcoal on paper, 18 x 26 inches (46 x 66 cm). Courtesy of the artist.

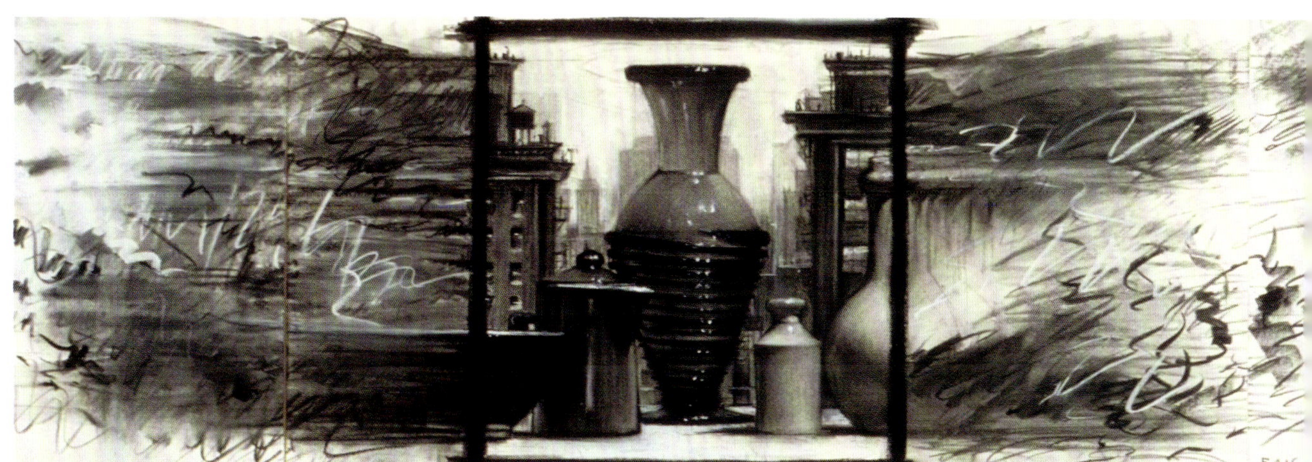

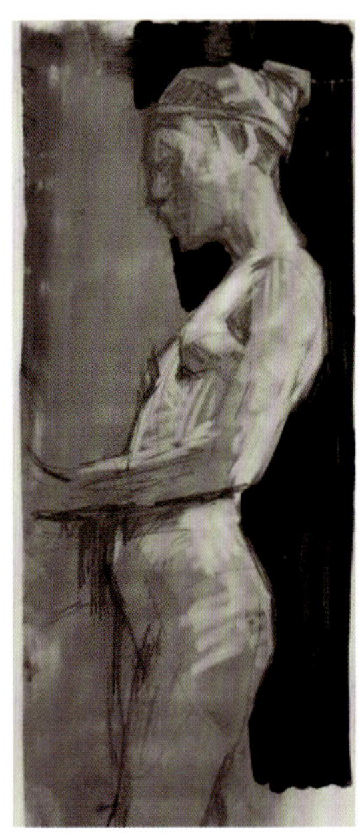

Brooks Frederick, *Daphne,* 2021, 6½ x 3 inches (17 x 8 cm). Courtesy of the artist.

Below: Casey Baugh, thumbnail sketches for *Nonchalant,* 2008, pencil on paper, 9 x 12 inches (23 x 31 cm), and *Nonchalant,* 2008, oil on linen, 20 x 16 inches (51 x 41 cm). Courtesy of the artist.

layouts. They are also extremely useful for artists in learning essentials of strong composition.

Notans come from a Japanese design principle, literally translating as "dark light." A notan composition is successful when it expresses an idea well and beautifully in two or three simple values. It may seem tricky to reduce all values and colors to only black and white. However, the understanding gained by such simplification is valuable and worth your attention in composing strong pictures. A notan should read clearly from a distance. When you adapt that clarity of impact to a fully developed work, your compositions will jump off the wall and get noticed.

The artist Casey Baugh began to explore ideas for his painting *Nonchalant* with fast and simple notans, trying out various placements of the figure in the frame. The successful result is built from a strong black-and-white thumbnail, its simple grouping of lights and darks giving the painting its unified and memorable shape.

Analyzing master works with notans is a powerful training tool for learning to organize a composition and strengthen the value structure in a work. Our mind processes visual images and values through grouping. The eye reads contrast first, so all the dark things will group together in a mush, as will all the light things. Only when we focus in on the small details do our eyes read specific variation. We want to learn to use this principle of grouping in our art to make better paintings. Notans show us how a few values and strong contrast create successful work.

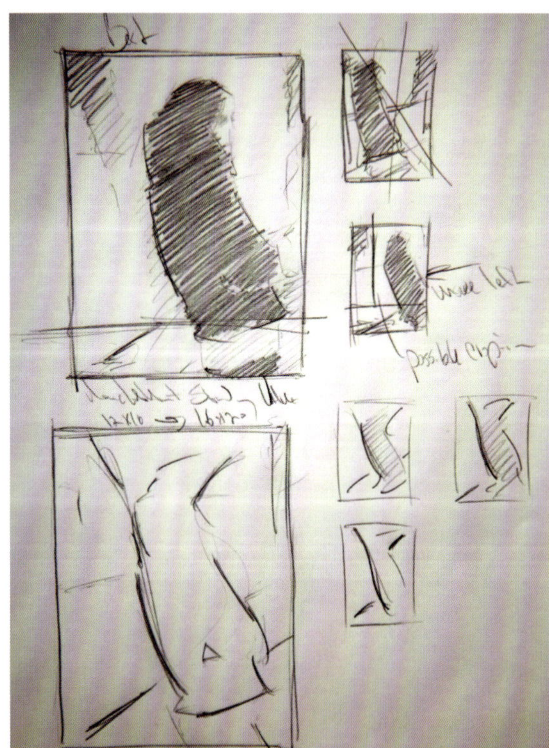

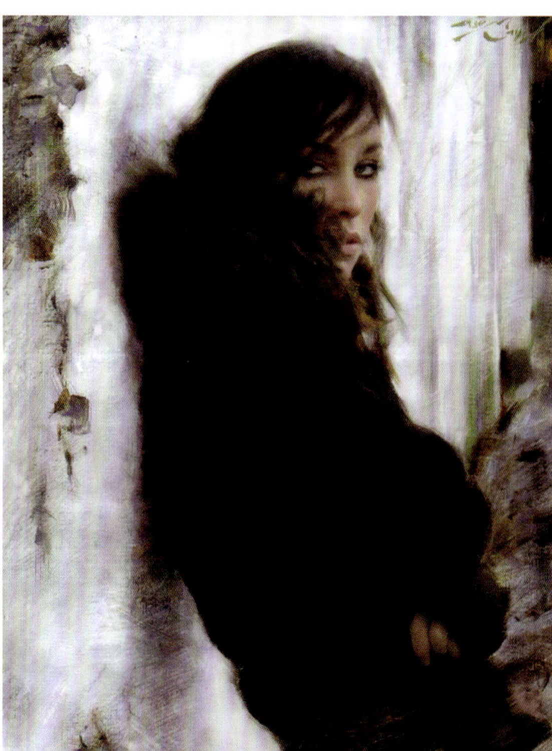

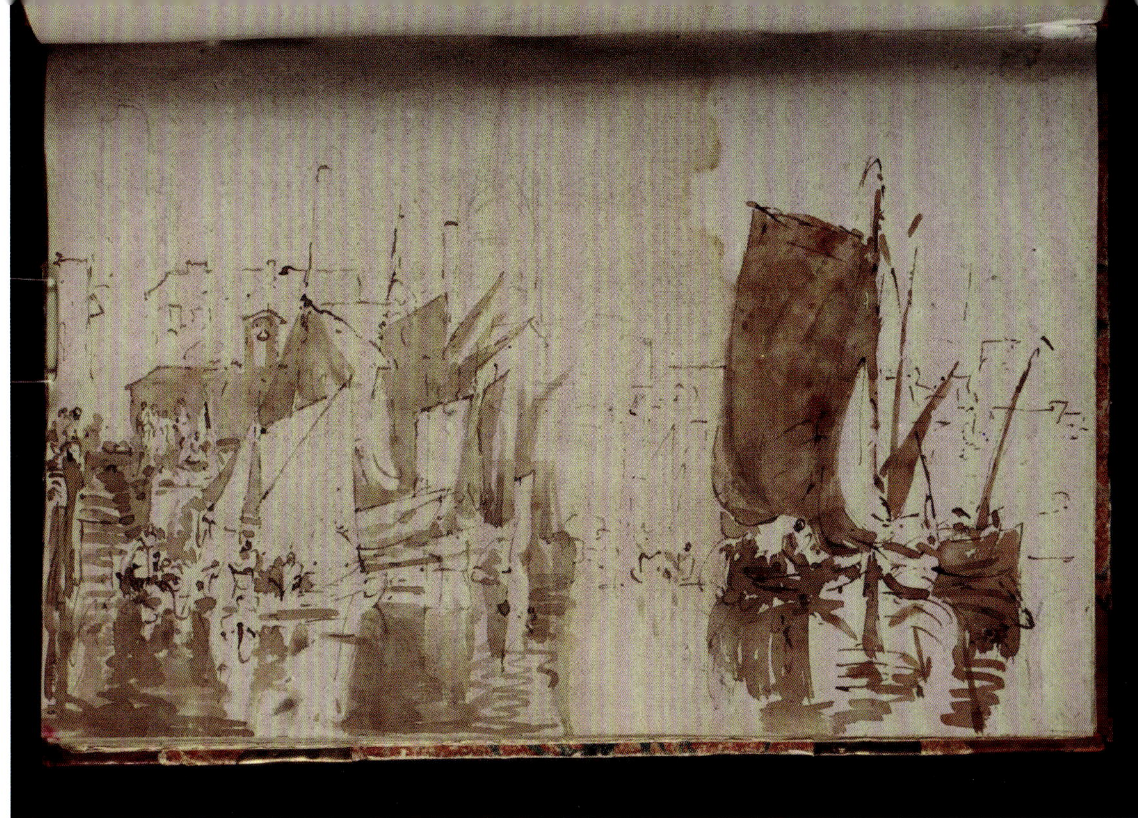

Above: Joseph Mallord William Turner (English,1775–1851), *London: St Dunstan-in-the-East and the Custom House from the Thames,* c. 1805–6, folio 14, recto, from Hesperides (1) Sketchbook, pen and ink and brown wash on paper, 6¾ x 10¼ inches (17.1 × 26.2 cm), Tate, London.

Below, left: Tanya Kramarenko, *Teapot,* 2022, colored paper collage, 8 x 10 inches (20 x 25 cm). Courtesy of the artist. Below, right: Tanya Kramarenko, *Mother and Child,* 2022, colored paper collage, 10 x 8 inches (25 x 20 cm). Courtesy of the artist.

Tanya Kramarenko simplified paintings into five values of gray paper to study contrast and composition.

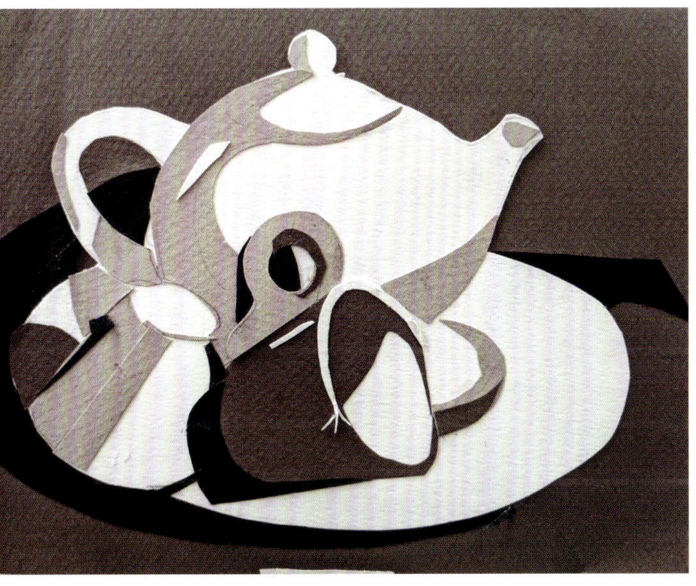

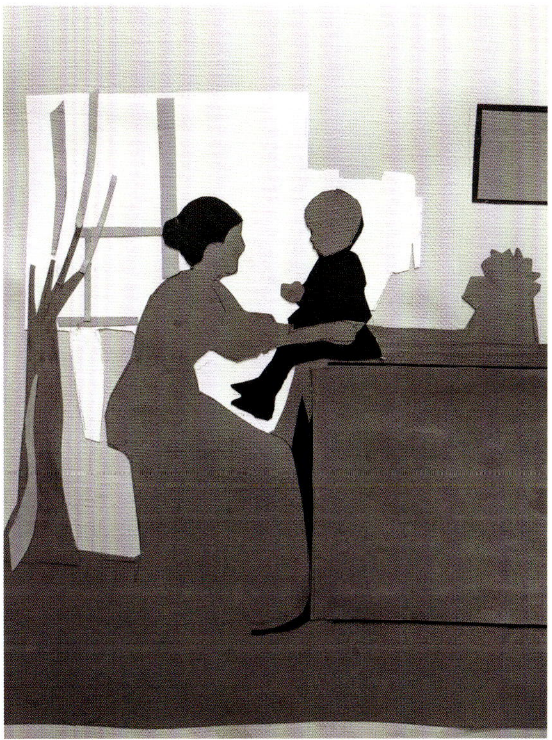

Notan Thumbnails

Let me show how I use a notan thumbnail to plan a composition. I explore options for where the primary subject should be anchored. Right in the middle? On the left or right? Artists often rely on regular divisions like thirds, quarters, and halfway points to plan a design. To work out the placement, I lightly subdivide my rectangle into one-half, one-third, or one-fourth divisions. Try a few options quickly to see what makes a pleasing design.

To start, draw a small rectangle. Try tracing a credit card—it's a perfect size. The relationship of the shapes inside to the edges is important, so start with a frame and revise the shape later if desired.

I encourage you to create your own from observation and references. With practice, aim to make a thumbnail in about five minutes. If you use these techniques to study great paintings, your memory and analysis of them will stick with you.

THREE NOTAN STUDIES

First working in pencil, I divided the rectangle in thirds with light lines to plan the composition. I chose to place a big tree in the right third, balanced with all the small trees on the left. I sketched in the primary shapes. For the notan, I used a Sharpie to color in the dark masses lined in the thin trees in the distance. The shadows on the ground were simplified into light and dark, with horizontal bands of black and white creating a ground plane.

Even if a tree might have been brown and green, I didn't consider the local color. I looked to see where shapes were in light *or* shadow, reducing the patterns to black and white. After I finished the marker, I erased any extraneous pencil marks.

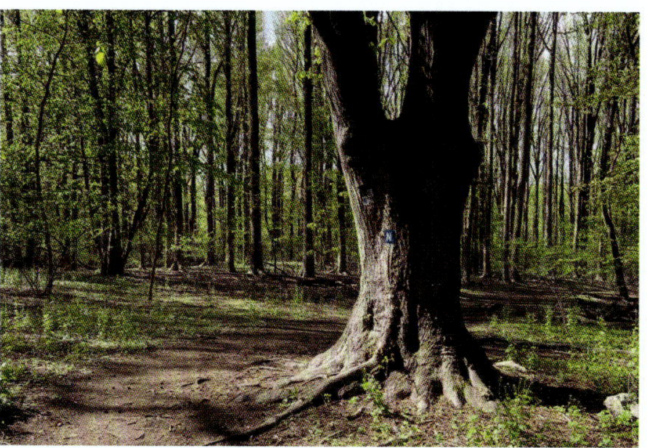

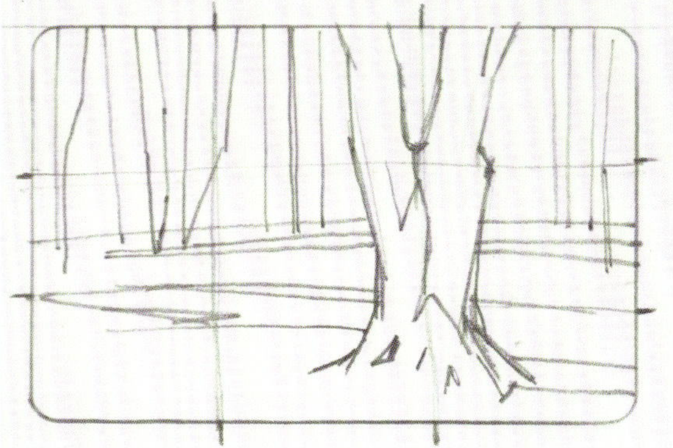

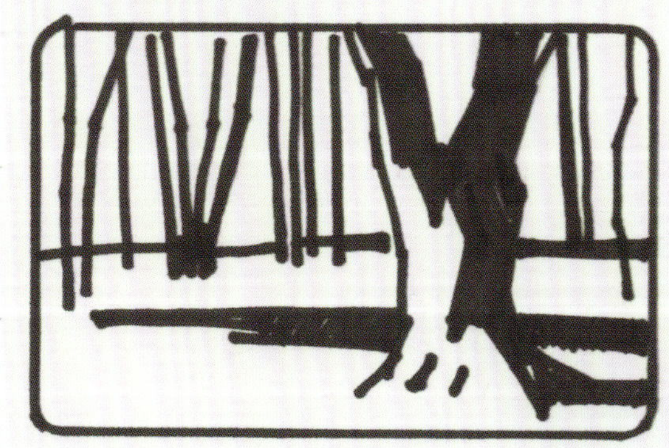

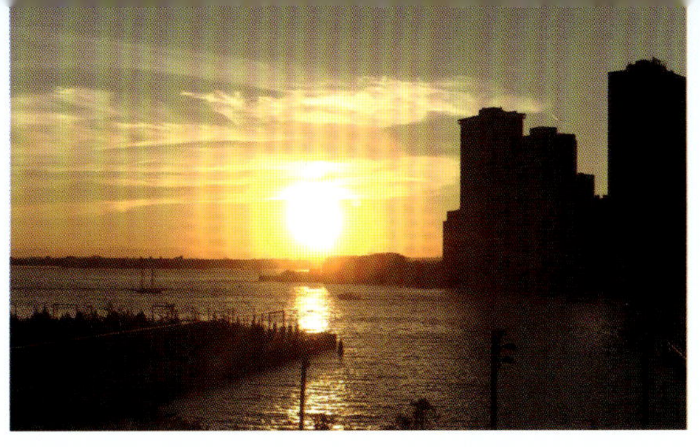

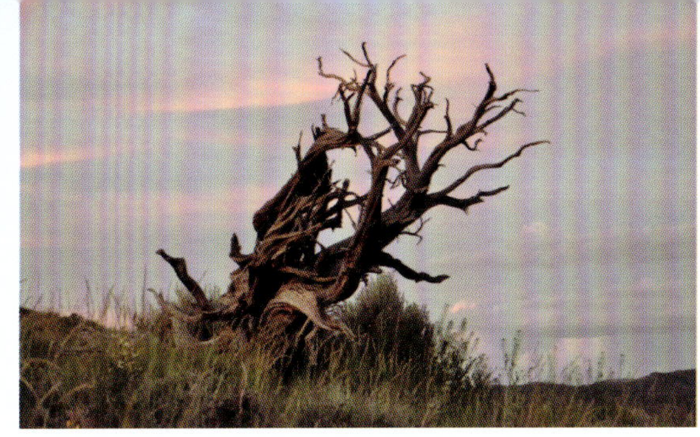

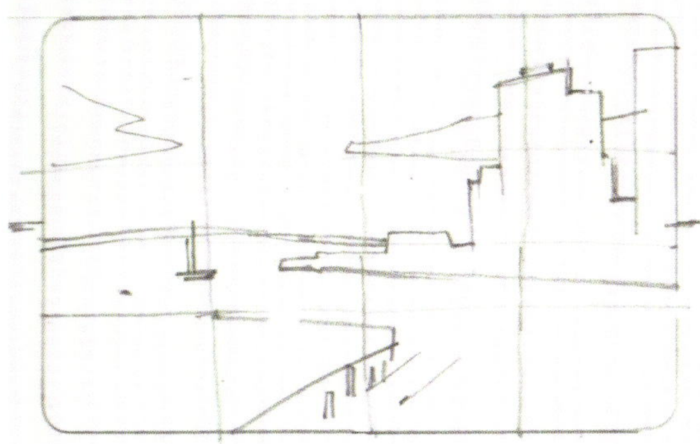

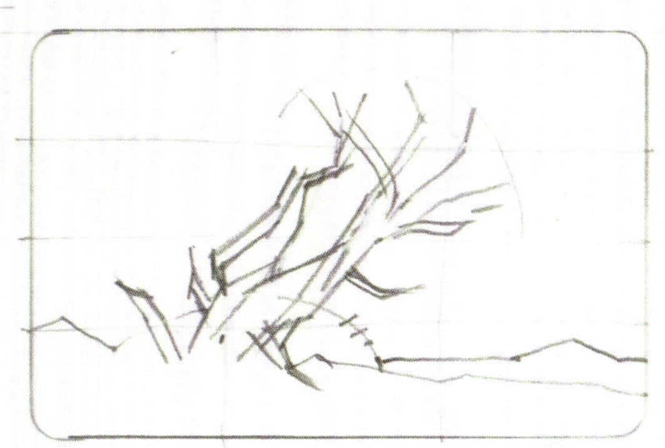

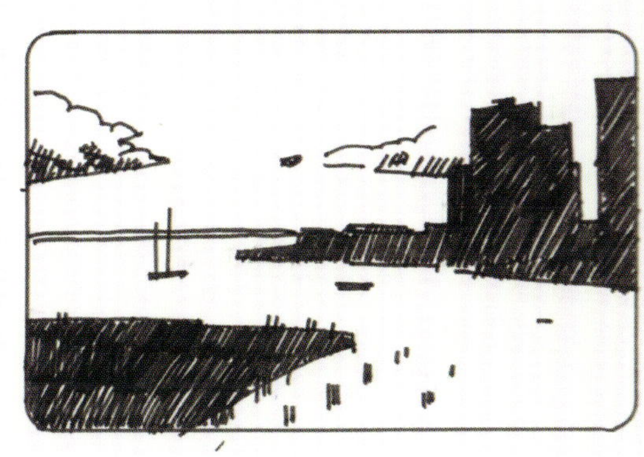

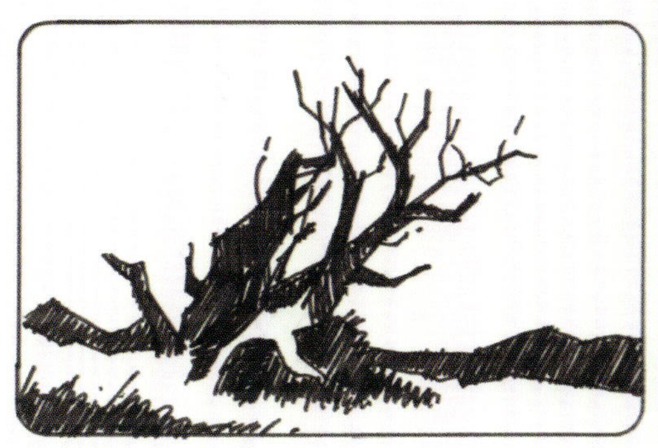

For this cityscape composition, I noticed that the horizon line in my reference fell right in the middle. So, I divided the frame vertically into quarters and horizontally with a centered horizon line and thirds for placing the pier and clouds. There is never one correct arrangement, but using the compositional divisions helped me organize my subject and created a harmonious placement. Experiment with different proportions and intervals and see how it changes the impact of the composition. Aim to have the simple black-and-white image tell the story and make dynamic shapes.

This notan of a juniper tree helped me plan out a satisfying placement of a single subject. Instead of plunking it right down in the center, I placed the mass of the base of the tree on the lower left third line, and the sweeping branches' counterweight over to the upper right third. The horizon line is low, along the bottom quarter of the composition, elevating and emphasizing the grandeur of the sculptural tree. Notice how the narrow bands of light and dark at the ground plane help define the layers of the landscape and distant mountains. A lot of information can be contained in the simple black-and-white shapes, and it helps you plan successful grouping in a composition.

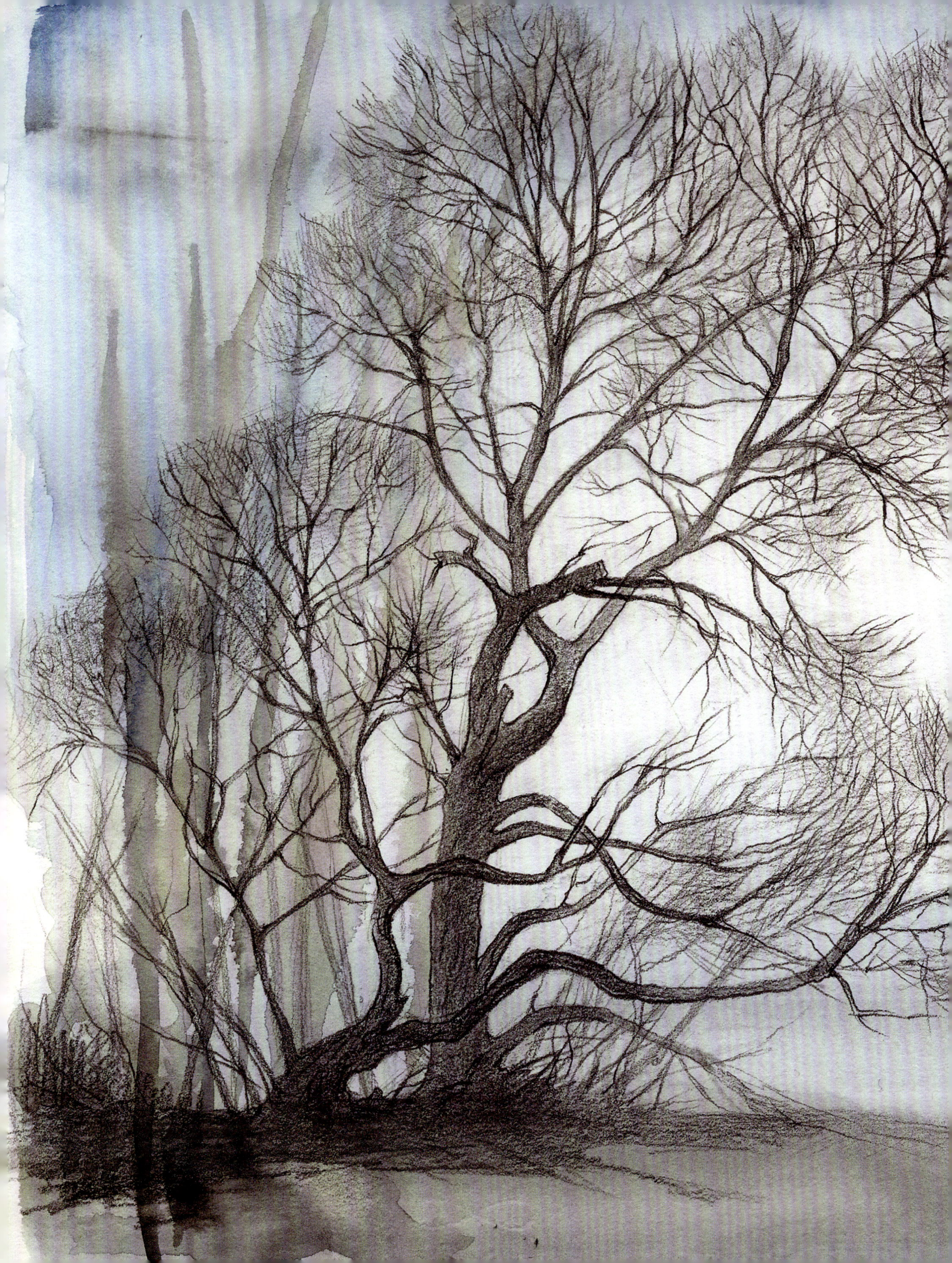

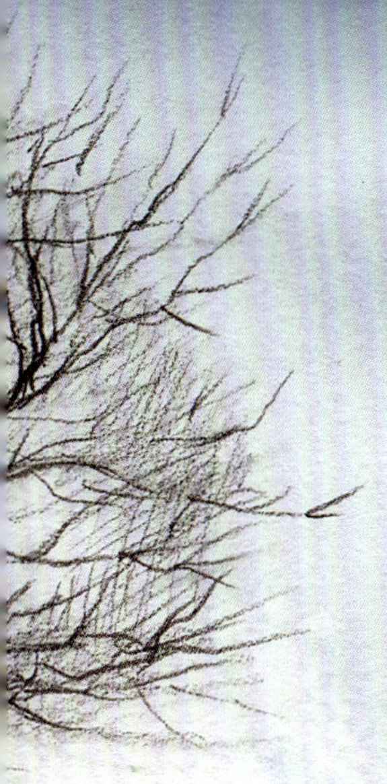

"This morning, like so many mornings,
we awoke feeling empty and frightened.
Don't retreat to the study to seek refuge in books.
Pick up an instrument
and let the beauty we love
become our composition.
There are innumerable ways to kneel and kiss the ground."

—RUMI, TRANSLATED BY MICHAEL R. BURCH

11

Lightworkers

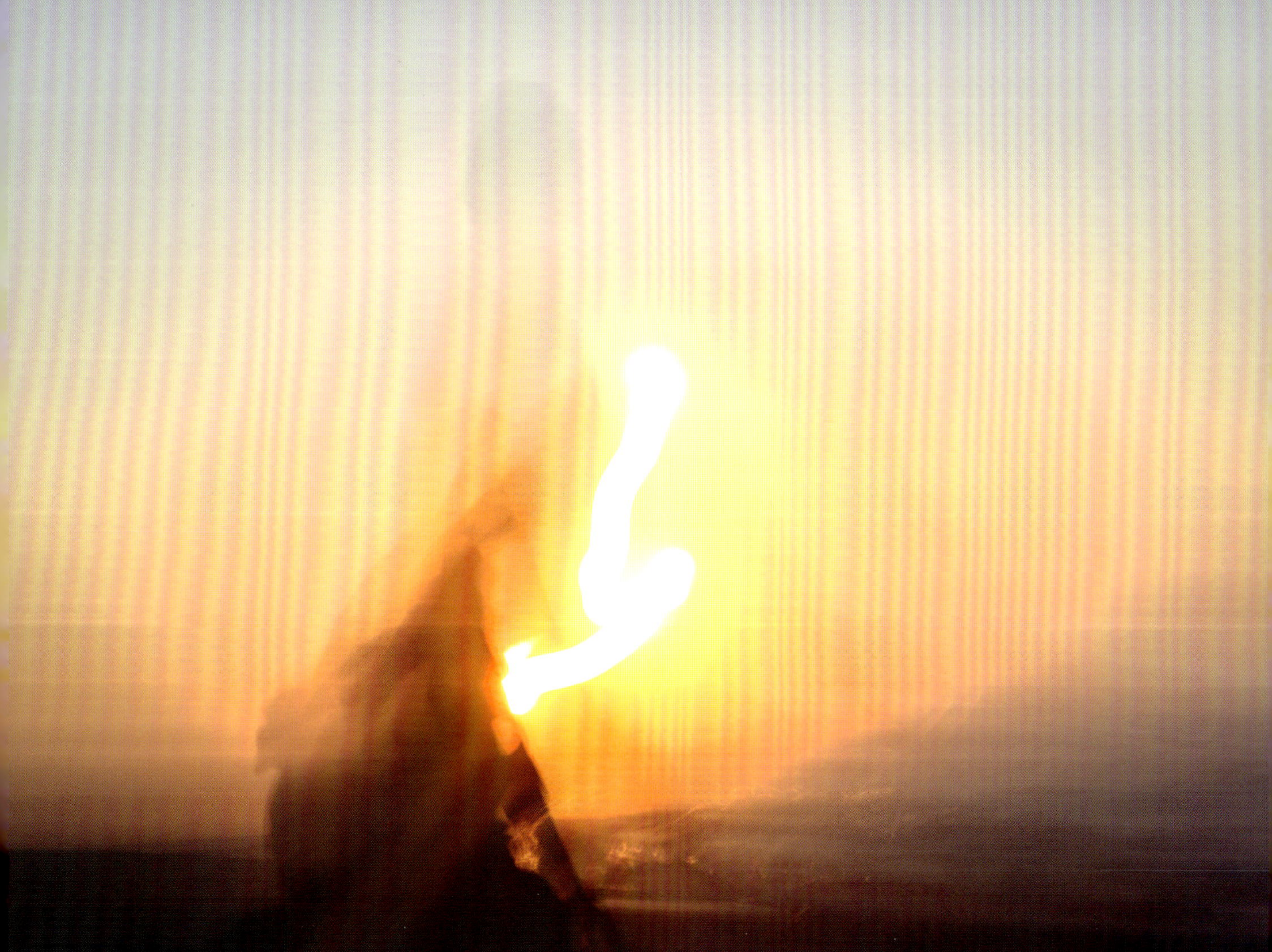

Any being who strives to leave the world just a little better than they found it is a lightworker. We have many parables. A child walks along the beach, where the sand is awash with starfish stranded on dry land. One at a time, she flings them as far as she can into the water. A man interrupts her and asks, "How are you possibly going to make a difference when there are thousands of stranded starfish?" "Well," she answers, "I made a difference to that one." Like Eleanor Roosevelt, she is a person who would rather light a candle than curse the darkness.

Whom do you know with a sunny disposition who just makes you smile? Over time, I have come to appreciate that these bright lights are not simply lucky and blind to the challenges of the world, but are guided by principle. They have made a choice, rising each new day to do their best to face it with a smile.

In creative work, there is the technical side, the process, the doing and making. While we are working, we experience the emotional side— the thoughts that rise and fall and the tide of feelings that come along. Interwoven and entirely interdependent, you never get one without the other. These two sides, the practice and the emotions, must both be treated in creative work as a sustainable and renewable cycle.

There will be sunny days and easy sailing. There will be fallow periods, winters, and discouragement, when both the practice and the mindfulness seem like a heavy empty bucket. Sometimes you have to push the cycle back up the hill—with effort, patience, intention, and hope. So, *my* hope for you is that the path of drawing will lead you to find ways to be a lightworker.

THE TOOLS OF THE LIGHTWORKER

There are two principles that I want to leave you with. One is self-love, and the other is gratitude. These are essential for any creative journey.

Your creative practice is a tool for managing that equilibrium and keeping the light burning.

For a creative path, we have looked at ways to fill and refill inspiration for visual ideas through practices like creative compost, sourcing from

Anna Wakitsch, *Power Outage,* 2013, graphite and white chalk on toned paper, 4 x 3 inches (10 x 8 cm). Courtesy of the artist.

Pages 202–203: Patricia Watwood, *Morning at Prospect Park,* graphite and watercolor on paper, 11 x 15 inches, (28 x 38 cm). Courtesy of the artist.

Opposite: Stefan Hagen, *Dawn, Long Island,* 2013, photograph. Courtesy of the artist.

Page 206: Thomas W Schaller, *Rooftops – Rome,* 2021, graphite on watercolor paper, 14 x 11 inches (36 x 28 cm). Courtesy of the artist.

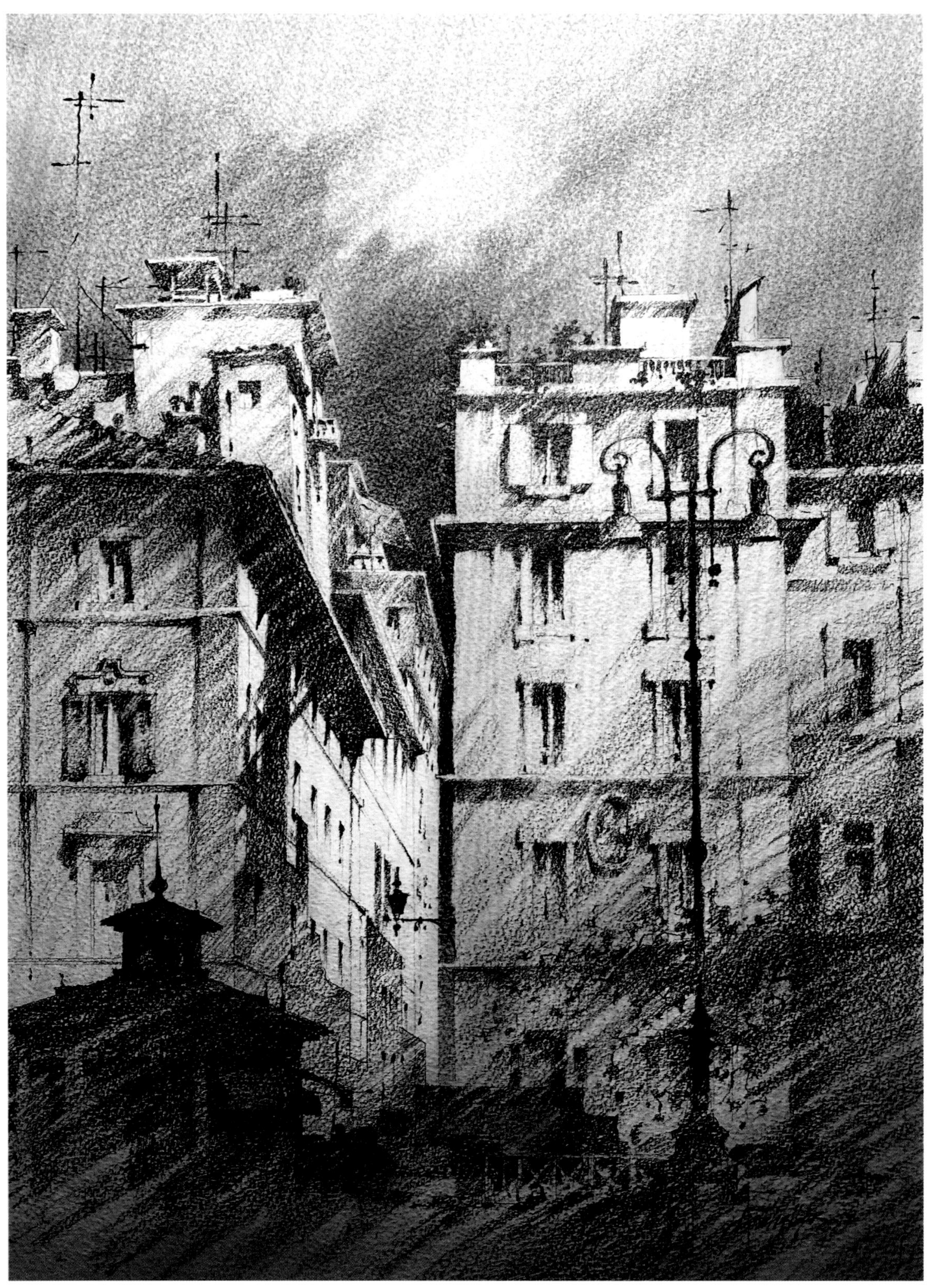

nature, and plumbing our imagination. On the side of mindfulness, we examined how, in happy emotional weather or sad, we can use a technical practice of pencil and sketchbook to anchor oneself. Over time, adhering to your creative practice will become like its own ritual of preparation. Pencil in hand, you will sail past the blank page and the demon of uncertainty without even noticing and travel off into the world of drawing. The very act of practice will restore equilibrium to the restive mind and settle you into a calm harbor of your personal creative work.

Below: I drew my eye in the center and added an array of wings. This is a personal emblem made to inspire faith in my own vision.

Patricia Watwood, *Seraphim*, 2017, digital composite; pencil and watercolor on paper, 11 x 15 inches (28 x 38 cm). Courtesy of the artist.

> *"Our deepest fear is not that we are inadequate. Our deepest fear is that we are powerful beyond measure. It is our light, not our darkness, that most frightens us…We are all meant to shine, as children do. As we're liberated from our own fear, our presence automatically liberates others."*
>
> —MARIANNE WILLIAMSON

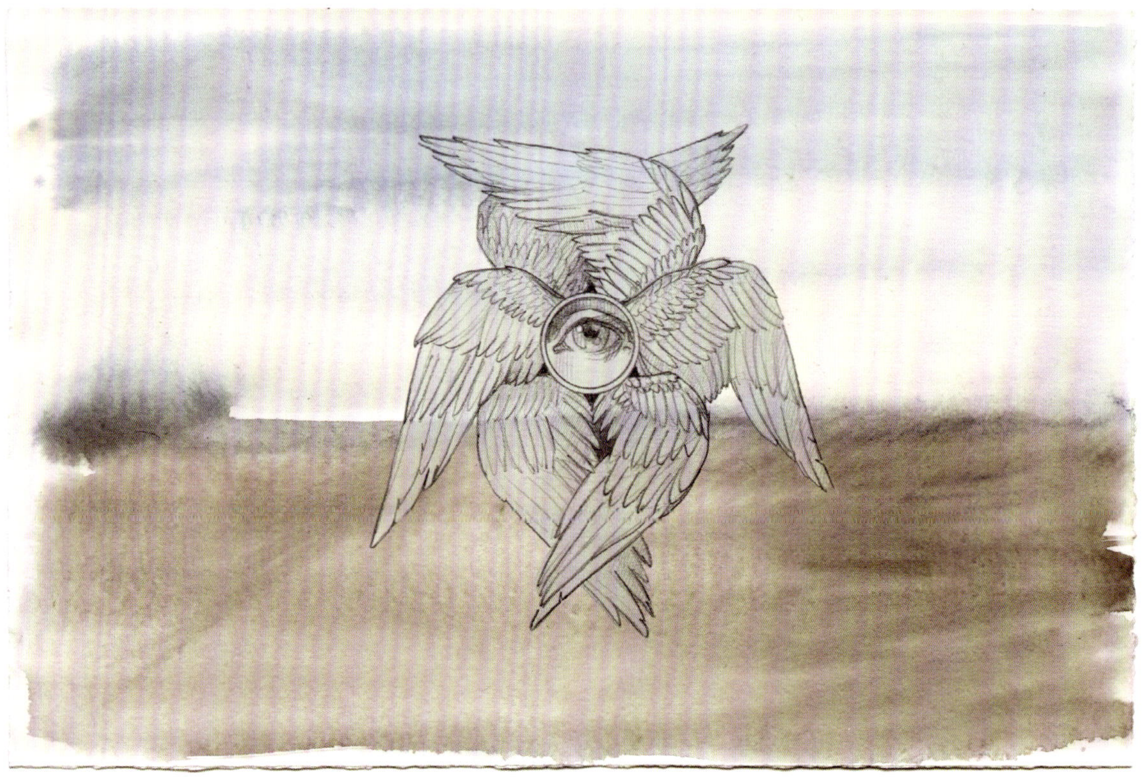

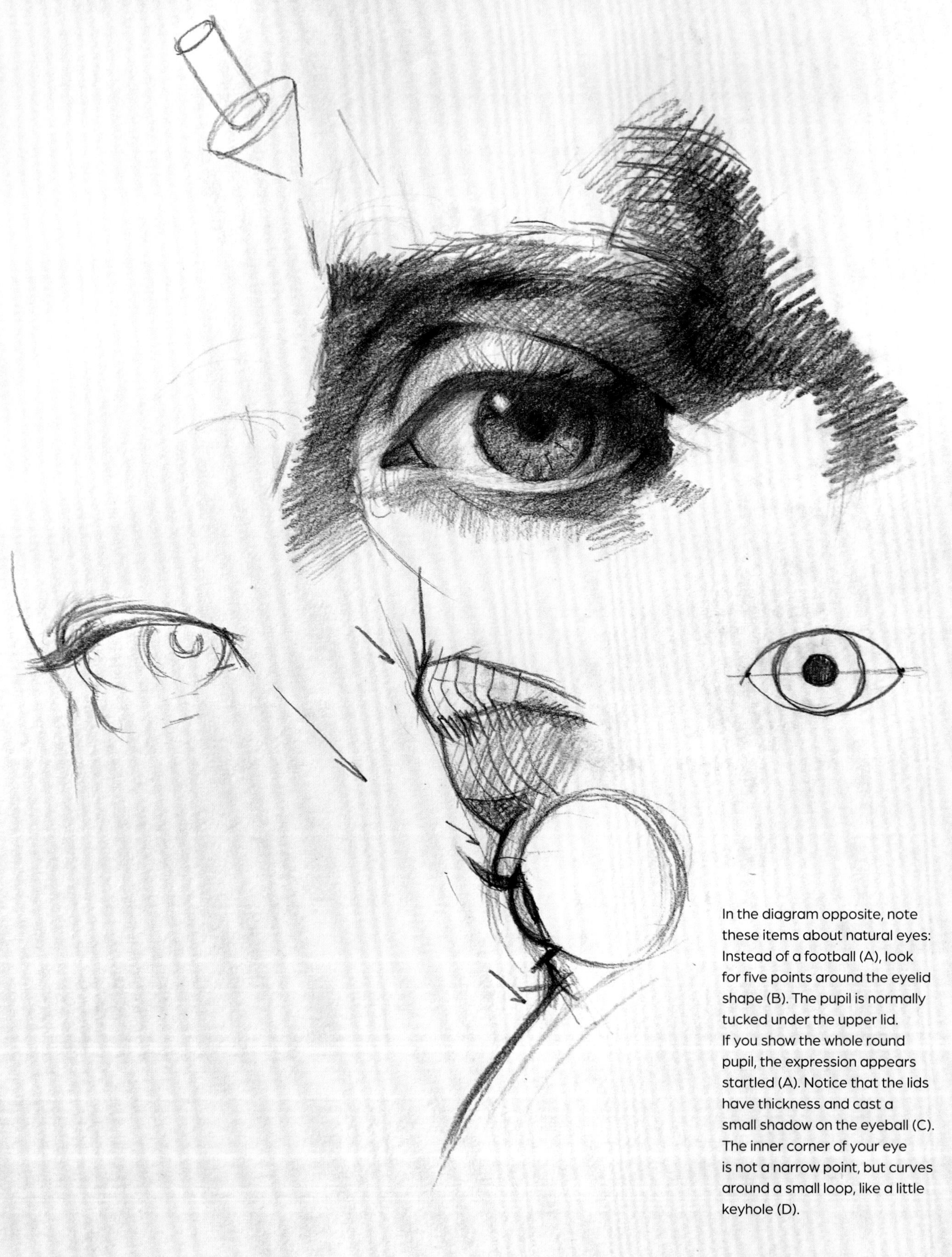

In the diagram opposite, note these items about natural eyes: Instead of a football (A), look for five points around the eyelid shape (B). The pupil is normally tucked under the upper lid. If you show the whole round pupil, the expression appears startled (A). Notice that the lids have thickness and cast a small shadow on the eyeball (C). The inner corner of your eye is not a narrow point, but curves around a small loop, like a little keyhole (D).

Draw Your Eye

This project gives some basics on drawing the eye—called "the window of the soul" and the gateway from the outer to our inner world. The view you take in from your door, the people you see, the beauty you discover—no other person can see the world from your point of view. Make a drawing of your own eye to honor and reflect on the uniqueness of your view of the world.

Before you start, let me share some tips on structure. Many novices will make a symbolic drawing of the eye that is football-shaped, with a full circle in the middle (A below). To draw a naturalistic eye, you must slow down and look carefully to notice the differences between a symbolic eye and the true organic structure.

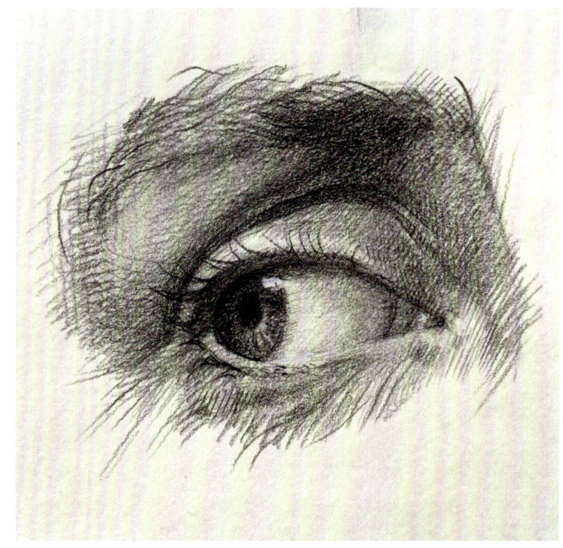

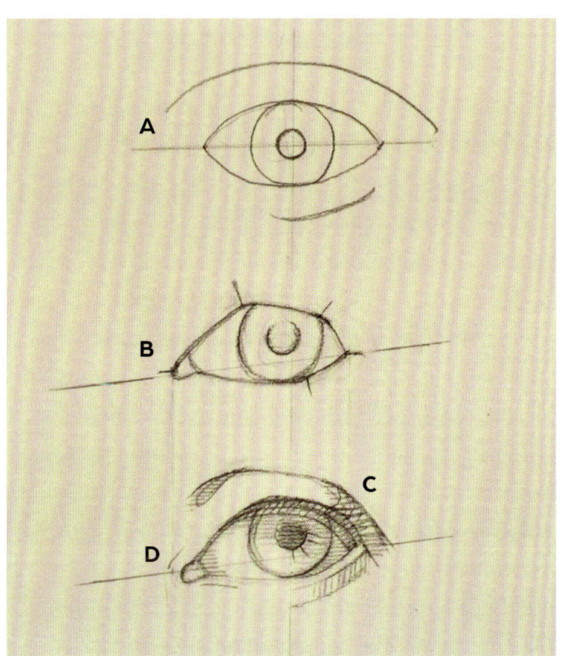

The pupil and the white of the eye are on a round ball, nested in the eye socket like an egg in a deep cup. The upper brow around the eye projects forward, over the eye, sheltering the ball under the bony brow. Notice that the top of the pupil is almost always covered a bit by the upper lid (B at left).

The lids are not thin and flat. The lids themselves have a thickness, and they stretch around the ball of the eye. When the pupil rotates in the socket, it pulls the lids to shape around the bulge of the cornea. The lids will cast little shadows on the eyeball (C at left).

For this drawing, work from a mirror, set up only a foot or two away from you, or take a photo and print it out. Make your drawing larger than life. Set up your placement to make the size of the eye at least 4 inches across. This will make it so much easier to manage the small details.

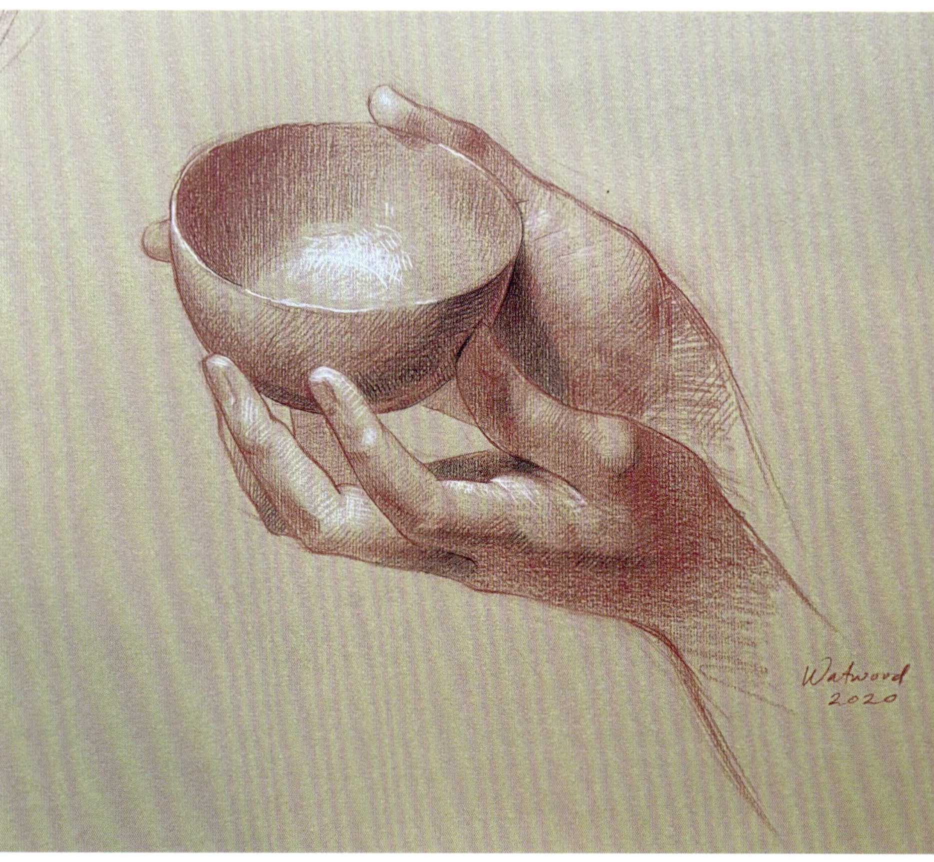

Patricia Watwood, *Two Hands and a Bowl,* 2020, sanguine colored pencil, Nero pencil, and white Prismacolor on tan paper, 12 x 16 inches (30 x 41 cm). Courtesy of the artist.

> *"Try to practice loving friendliness toward yourself."*
>
> —ELIZABETH GILBERT

PRACTICING SELF-LOVE

What does self-love make possible in your life? For the artist, self-love means time to work, prioritizing quiet and enough rest.

Many of us have been conditioned to think that claiming such time and space is selfish and that our role is to be helpful to others in some way other than making art. Words like *self-involved* and *narcissistic* crowd up next to the yearning to claim space for the creative self. How then can we reframe ideas of selfishness and self-involvement? These negative conditions exist when others are harmed by the way we might prioritize ourselves. But no one owes everyone else more than they give themselves. Some apparent selflessness is actually a form of self-annihilation, which then creates resentment, anger, and unhealthy boundaries. It can be a result of fear, a form of masochism, or even ego in disguise ("look how selfless I am, aren't I amazing?").

Love one another *as you love yourself.*

Self-love is healthy self-care. A healthy practice will also make it much easier to be decent and kind to others, even those you must come into

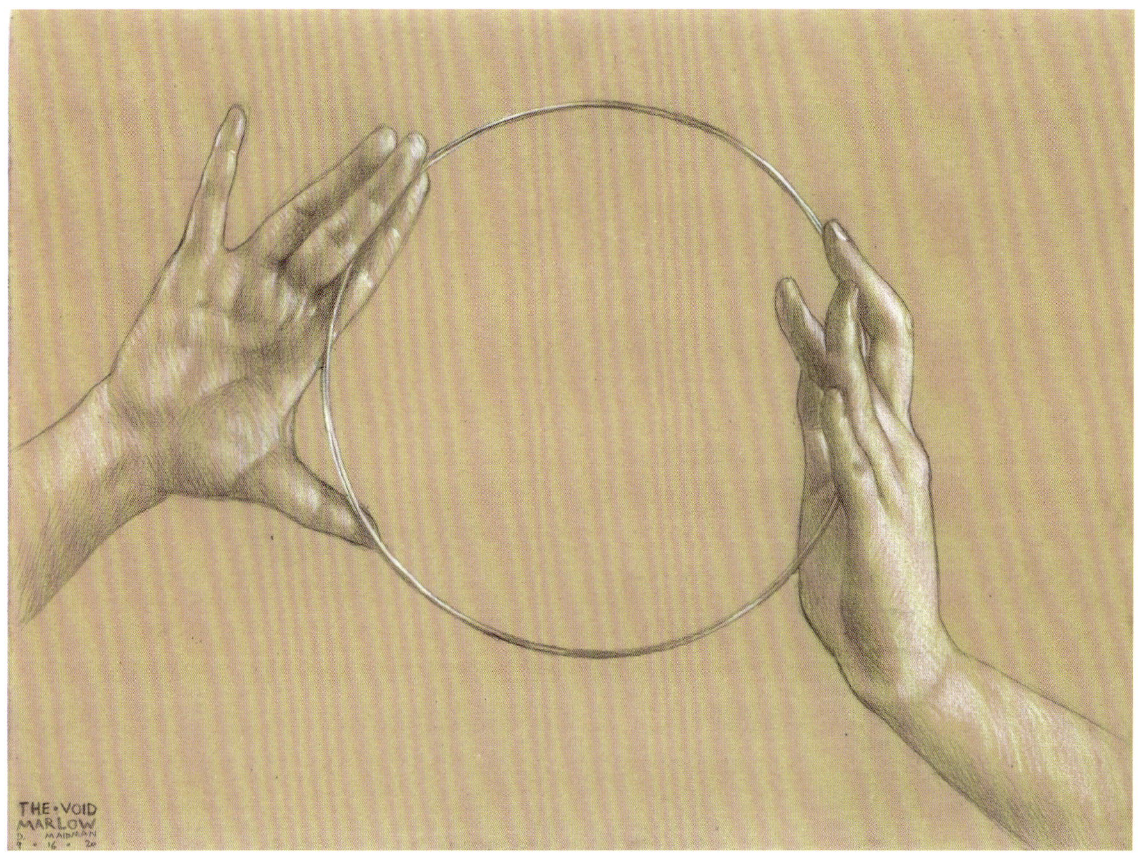

"You yourself, as much as anyone in the entire universe, deserve your love and affection."

—BUDDHA

conflict with. If you have a healthy self-regard, then others' barbs and taunts have less impact, and you are more able to see with compassion where that pain might be coming from in another person.

Self-love is self-compassion. Accept that imperfection, mistakes, are part of being human, as is forgiving ourselves over and over for our limitations and incompleteness. We accept that as part of the whole, and love the whole for its complexity.

Use a practice of positive self-talk while you do your creative work. When your monster pipes up—That's stupid! No one will like this! That's a terrible drawing!—intentionally counter that voice through a practice of positive self-encouragement. How would you speak to your best friend or

Daniel Maidman, *The Void*, 2020, graphite and white Prismacolor pencil on tan paper, 11 x 15 inches (28 x 38 cm). Courtesy of the artist.

your child? I bet most of us would never speak to them with the same tone of condemnation and hostility with which we speak to ourselves. Why don't you encourage yourself, just as you would a young child or your dear friend?

- You worked really hard on that!
- It's fantastic that you made time to draw!
- You were brave for trying that sketch!
- You got this!
- I'm proud of you!

Find a positive and true statement and encourage yourself. Speak it out loud or write it down for extra emphasis. However small your victory, use the power of your positive self-talk over and over to tamp down negativity to a manageable position. In time, your positive self-talk will become a habit and the negative voice will be rarer.

"When I was a boy and I would see scary things in the news, my mother would say to me, 'Look for the helpers. You will always find people who are helping.'"
—FRED ROGERS

HANDS OF GRATITUDE

Did you actually travel with me through this entire book? Thank you for sharing this journey with me.

The last tool for your creative journey is gratitude, the potent antidote to comparison. I learned that "jealousy is self-doubt in other people's clothing," and it helped me understand when I am noticing a feeling of jealousy toward another's success, it's usually because I want to work in that direction and my fear is telling me I can't.

To release a fear of lack, we must focus on abundance by recognizing the many blessings we already possess. Take a deep breath and pause a moment to ground yourself in the present moment. Now ask yourself: What makes me grateful, right now? Gratitude, even for a small blessing, is an indispensable element of creative work.

I believe that, as artists, we should always be grateful for our privilege when we have the freedom to spend even twenty minutes with our sketchbook. It is a privilege to have all the other basic needs met so that

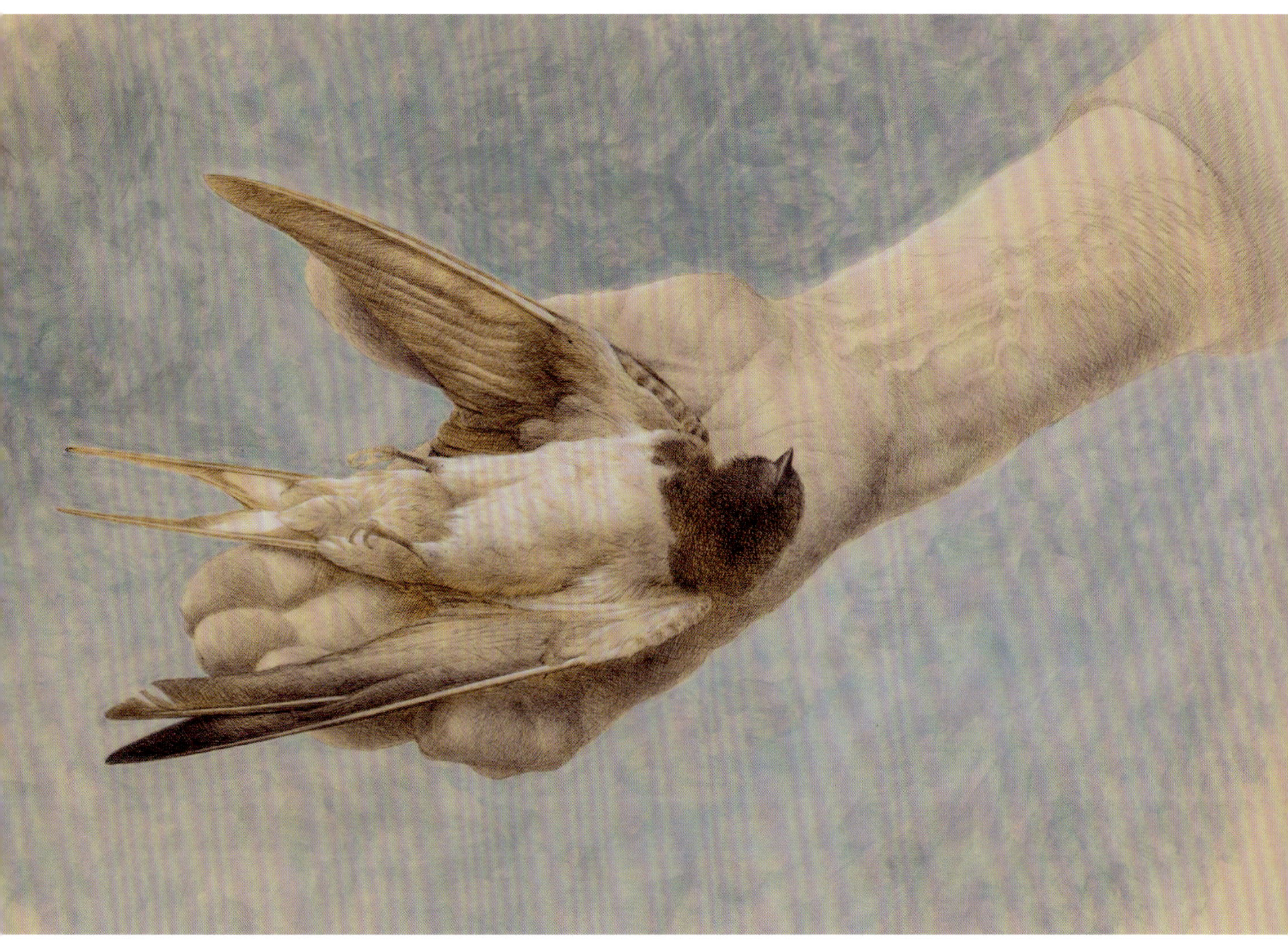

we can work on our art. Remember that even the time you have to make a terrible, screwed-up drawing is a privilege. Don't foist your struggles and insecurities on the world, which does not owe you anything. You don't have a "right" to be an artist. Resist the "poor me" and "if only I could." These sirens invite us to stay in frustration and jealousy, instead of our moving past them. Even with little financial abundance, we are blessed when we have the ability to invest our time in something we love.

I remember holding my grandmother's hand while sitting in a church pew on Sunday morning. Inattentive to the words from the lectern, I was mesmerized by the complex rippled surface of veins and tendons on the back of her hand. She did not fuss at me when I would delicately pull a bit of skin up and watch it—surprisingly slowly—rest back down on the surface.

This drawing is of a fallen sparrow in the hand of the artist's mother. Wade Schuman's mother has now passed on, but this drawing works a spell that turns loss and fragility into timeless beauty.

Wade Schuman, *Bird with Hand*, 2021, ballpoint pen on prepared paper with acrylic and white chalk, 32 x 40 inches (82 x 102 cm). Courtesy of Forum Gallery.

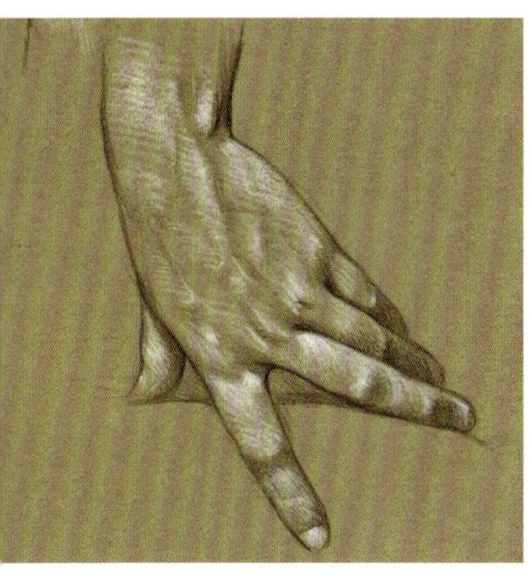

Above: Daniel Maidman, *Rachel's Hand*, 2015, graphite and white Prismacolor pencil on tan paper, 4 x 4 inches (10 x 10 cm). Courtesy of the artist.

Now, my own hands are crossed with raised blue veins, and the knuckles, grown larger, swirl with folds and creases. If I am lucky, they will become as wizened and knobby as my beloved grandmother's.

Place your hands on your lap and focus on them for a minute. How many things have your hands done for you—just today? Brushed your teeth? Poured your coffee? Fed you toast? Texted your friend? Artists are acutely aware of our dependence on and gratitude for our hands (and eyes!). How many of the projects in this book have your hands and eyes worked along with you in making?

Consider the complexity—there are twenty-six bones in your hand. (Did you know that? There are eight just in your wrist!) How many things can your hand do *without your even thinking about it*? Love the wrinkles, love the knobby bits. Your grandchild, wisely, will think they are wonderful and tell the story of the many things your hands have done.

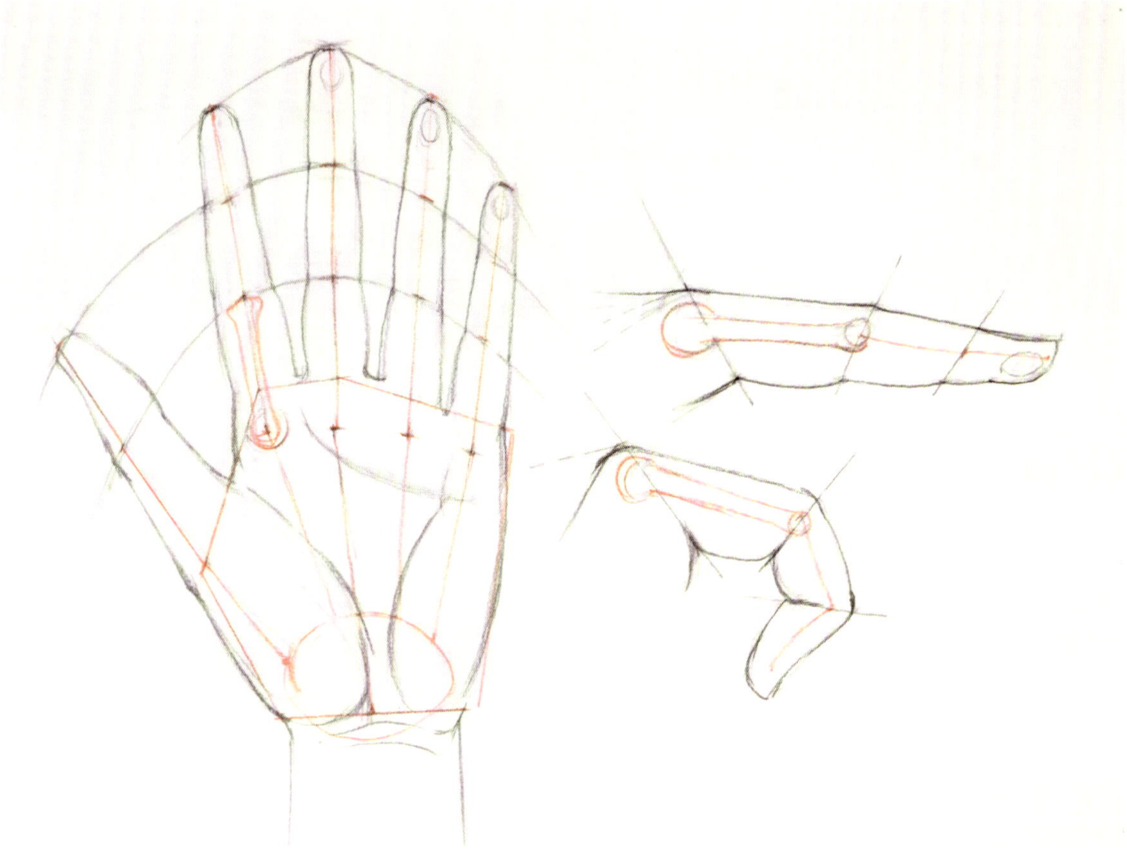

Knowing a bit more about what you are looking at will help your drawing. The palm and the middle finger are about the same length. The palm has

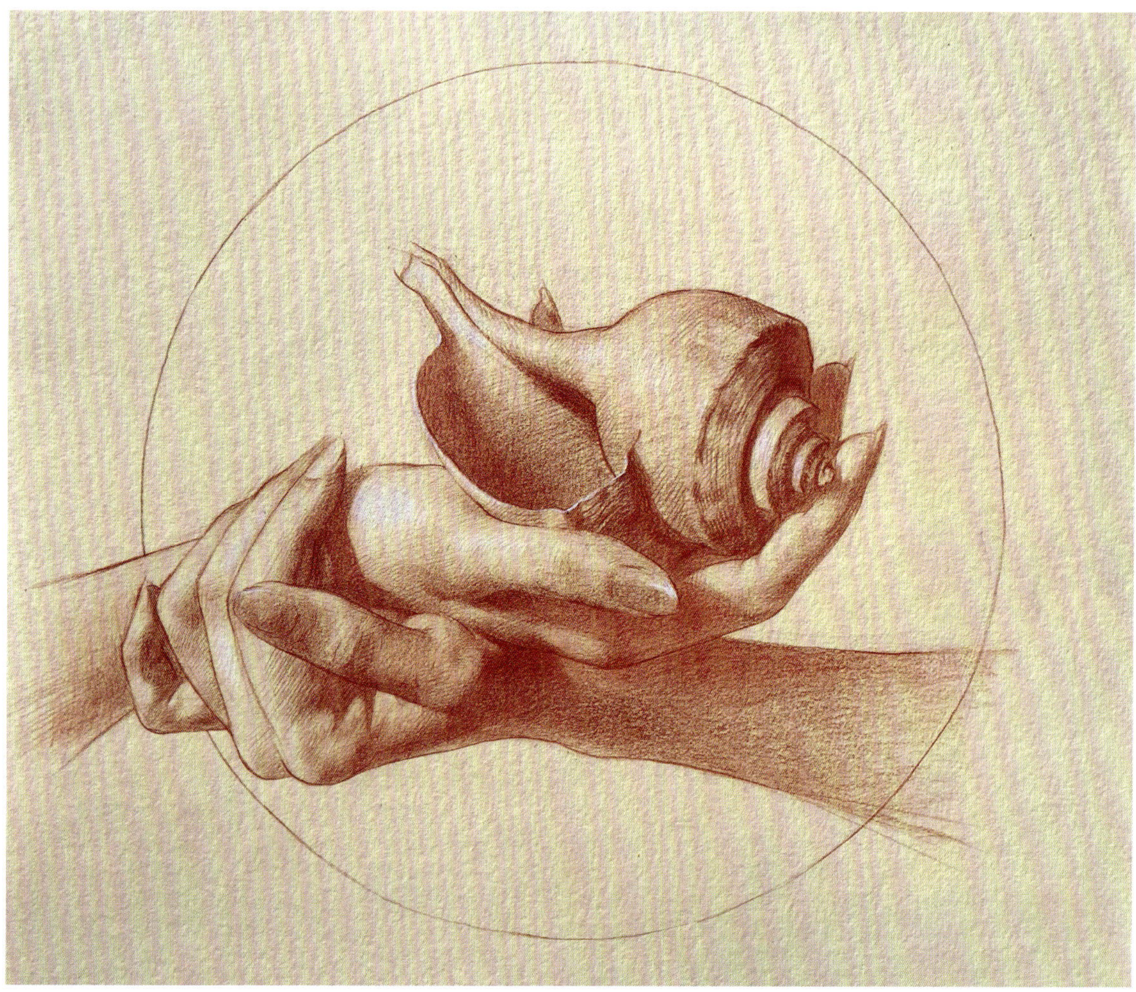

eight carpal bones in a cluster and five metacarpal bones. The two large muscles on the palm are the *thenar eminence* and *hypothenar eminence*. The classic creases in palm reading fold around these eminences and the fold at the base of the fingers. Look for a five-sided envelope shape around the palm.

The fingers begin in the palm and the knuckles on the back of your palm show the base of those bones. The fingers look a bit shorter on the palm side and longer on the back side. Each finger has three bones and each segment gets smaller and tapers going out to the tip. The thumb is unique; it has only two bone segments, and the tip of the thumb bends back as well as forward. The diagram on the opposite page shows the relative lengths of the fingers and how the bone segments follow a proportional pattern. While the nails seem to attract a lot of attention, in drawing they are considered a minor form and should be handled quite delicately.

Patricia Watwood, *Two Hands and a Shell,* 2021, sanguine colored pencil, Prismacolor, and watercolor on tan paper, 14 x 14 inches (36 x 36 cm). Courtesy of the artist.

Draw Your Hand

For this drawing, I took a photo of my hand, with a good single directional light, and made a print. You can work from observation of your hand, but I find it more difficult to hold my hand in a pose while working. This was done on a loose, single-color wash—yellow for joy.

STEP ONE

Make an envelope of the outer points of the hand and fingers, and check the measurements of width to length.

STEP TWO

Find the center of the palm (on your own hand, find the spot where a few drops of water will settle). This will be right below the very bottom of your middle finger. Note that on your drawing. Draw a center line from the middle of the wrist to that center circle and then out the middle finger. Now, create central axis lines for the other fingers. Note the gentle flow of the gesture of each finger.

STEP THREE

Develop the block-in of the contours. First, break down the center lines of the fingers into three segments for the knuckles and digits. Each bone segment gets a little smaller as it radiates out.

Notice two key details: The fingers taper toward the tips, so make the sides narrow down. Second, look for the small spaces *between* the fingers at the palm, rather than crowding them all together at the knuckles.

STEP FOUR

Refine the contours and add cross-hatching and tone to shape the forms. Pay more attention to the large shapes, and simplify or omit small details. Your hand is beautiful and unique, as is every other part of yourself.

"Your work is to discover your work, and then with all your heart, give yourself to it."
—SIDDHARTHA GAUTAMA BUDDHA

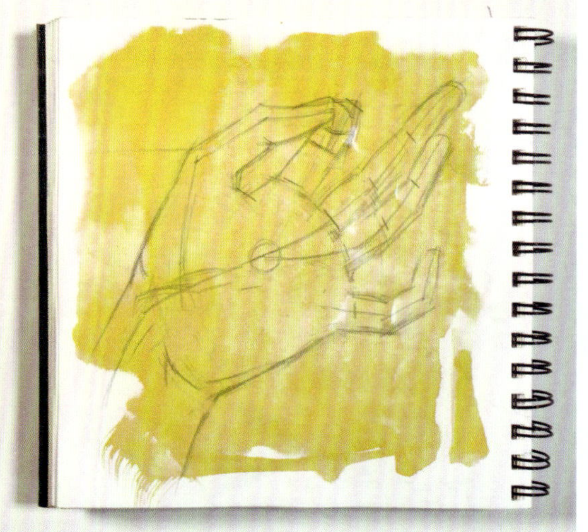

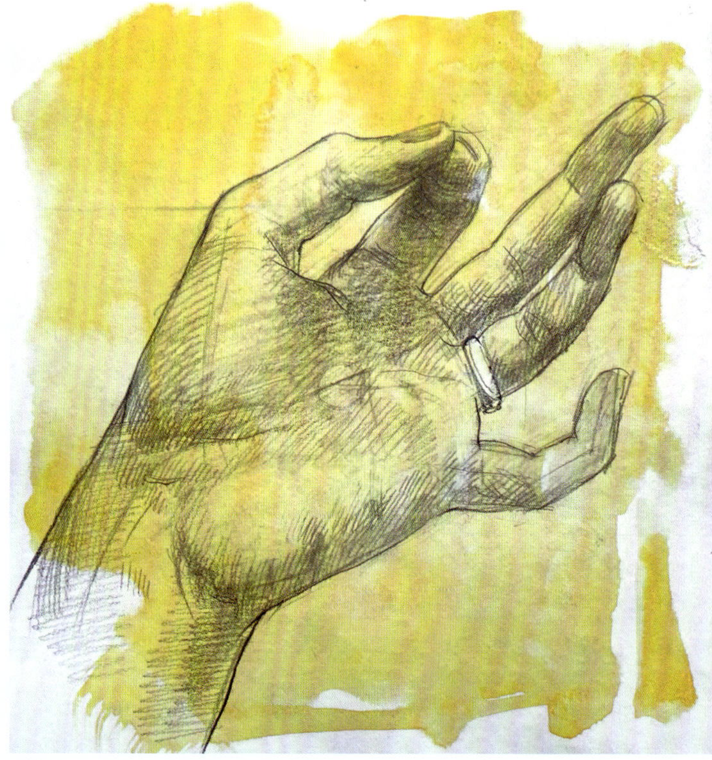

THE PATH ONWARD

In my opening, I dedicated this book to the lightworkers, and it is my hope that now, you will be one, too. Now that you have picked up a pencil and heeded a small voice guiding you to make some art, I hope that this book becomes a source you return to for encouragement when you need a reminder of just how big the world can be if you travel the path of drawing. If you are able to set an intention, stay engaged, and maneuver past a few monsters, the journey can take you a lifetime and bring you many beautiful vistas.

On my path, I've discovered that creative work is not just the thing that calls me from afar, but the structure that pushes me forward. Sometimes I feel energetic and I make art. Sometimes I need energy and I make art. If hope is the living water at the bottom of the well, your drawing practice is the pump that brings it to the surface. Do not wait for inspiration. Do not wait for free time. Do not wait for enough money or release from other responsibilities. Tend the pump that feeds your soul, quiets your mind, and helps you hear the muses speak.

Don't quit. That's the secret. Absolutely everyone who begins and does not quit will discover personal growth and enjoyment. Whether you are led to a rewarding hobby or an art profession, by making time and space for drawing, you will be changed for the better by the journey.

Go in peace and traveling mercies.

"May today there be peace within…
May you not forget the infinite possibilities that are born of faith…
and allow your soul the freedom to sing, dance, praise and love.
It is there for each and every one of us."

—TERESA OF ÁVILA

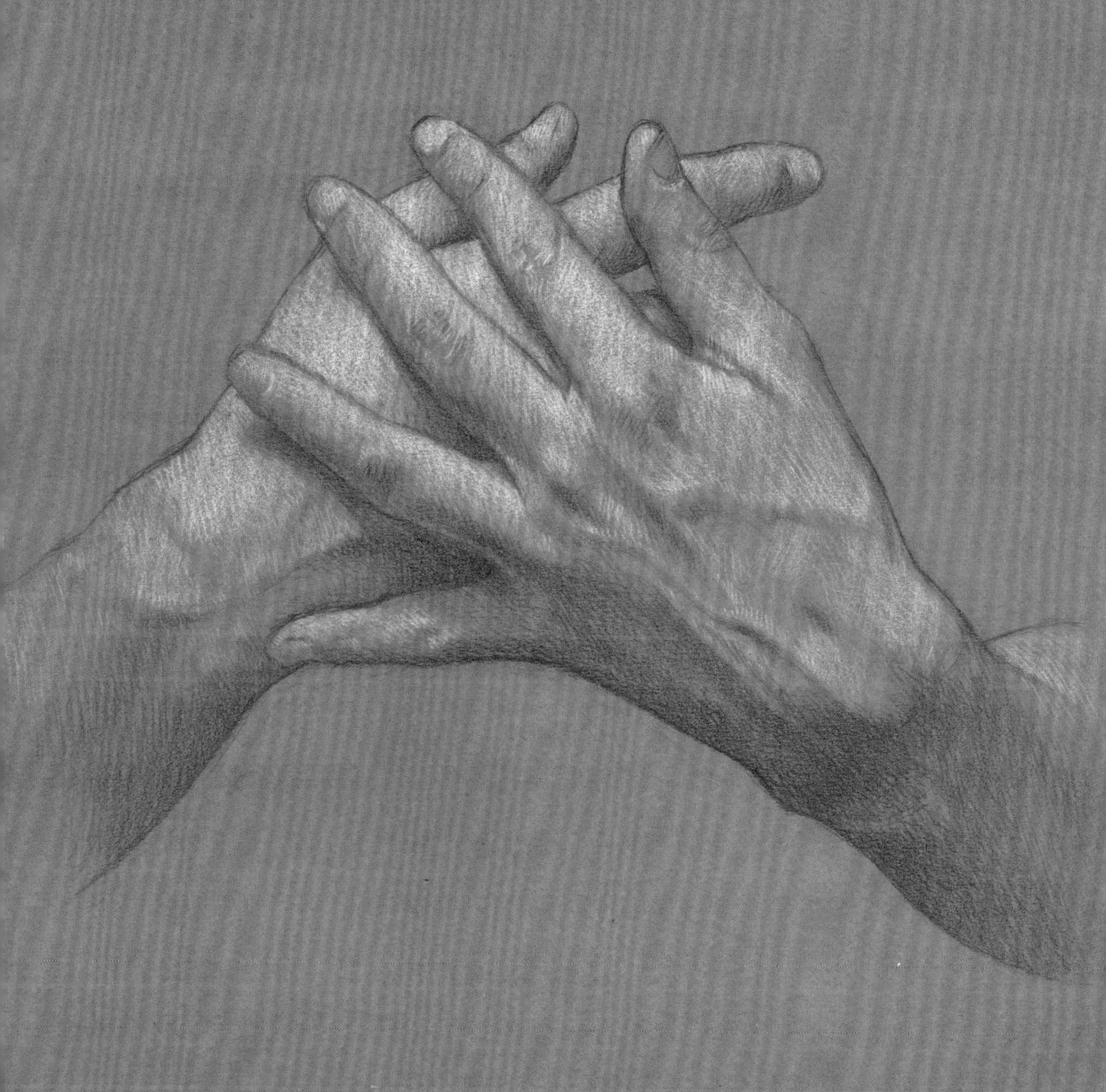
D. MAIDMAN
4 · 3 · 2015

Glossary

Accent shadow: The darkest part of the shadow, where there is no ambient or reflected light. (*Chapter 7*)

Block-in: The preliminary stage of a drawing in which the basic composition is mapped out. Also called "blocking in." (*Chapter 5*)

Block-in lines: Light lines that guide the composition of a drawing. (*Chapter 5*)

Cast shadow: The shadow created by an object when it blocks the light from the primary light source. (*Chapter 7*)

Central axis lines: Lines marking the center and length of an elongated or symmetrical form. (*Chapter 5*)

Composition: The arrangement of the shapes in pictorial space in relationship to one another and the frame (usually a rectangle). (*Chapter 5*)

Contour: The line that defines the edge or shape of an object. (*Chapter 6*)

Creative compost: Personal source material gathered for inspiration, reflection, and resources; anything that feeds your artistic soul and imagination. (*Chapter 4*)

Cross-contour lines: Lines that suggest the surface of a form by mimicking the contours of the depicted object. Cross-contour lines can go in multiple directions across a three-dimensional surface, like a web. (*Chapter 6*)

Cross-hatching: A layer (or layers) of parallel lines angled against the original hatching marks. (*Chapter 2*)

Dark light: The area of the light mass where it gets darker as it approaches the terminator. (*Chapter 7*)

Envelope: An irregular shape with three to six sides that plots the major components of a complex composition or shape. (*Chapter 5*)

Form: The three-dimensional shape of something, as opposed to the space around it. (*Chapter 7*)

Form shadow: The part of the object not illuminated by the primary light source; the part of the form in shadow. (*Chapter 7*)

Hatching: Parallel lines used for shading, modeling form, or describing texture. (*Chapter 2*)

Highlight: The lightest spot on a form. The location of the highlight will depend on your point of view. (*Chapter 7*)

Light mass: The part of the subject that is illuminated by the light source. (*Chapter 7*)

Light shape: Any part of the form in the light, as distinct from the shadow shape. (*Chapter 7*)

Limited palette: Using a selection of only a few colors or pigments in a painting for the purpose of efficiency, harmony, or experimentation. (*Chapter 8*)

Mixed media: Use of multiple materials in a single work, e.g., graphite and watercolor. (*Chapter 8*)

Modeling or rendering form: The aspects of drawing and painting, such as shading, that convey a subject's three-dimensionality. (*Chapter 7*)

Mood board: An assembly of resources for inspiration and visualization. (*Chapter 4*)

Plane: The spatial orientation of a given surface of a three-dimensional object, particularly as relative to the artist's observation point, and the direction of the light source. (*Chapter 5*)

Reflected light: Part of the form shadow where ambient light brightens the value of the shadow as it curves away from the terminator. (*Chapter 7*)

Shadow shape: A general term for the shadows, including both the form shadow and cast shadow. (*Chapter 7*)

Sketch: A quick drawing, first attempt, or preparatory lines, as opposed to a more refined work. (*Chapter 6*)

Terminator: The boundary between the light and shadow on a form; i.e., the form shadow edge.

This is the point on the form where the light (from a single light source) no longer touches the object and falls past it. (*Chapter 7*)

Third contour: Another term for the *terminator,* which shows the dimensionality of a form. The third contour shows the edge from the point of view of the light, where the light no longer touches the object and falls past it. (*Chapter 7*)

Tone: Shading that is even and smoothly blended, as opposed to hatched, for example. (*Chapter 7*)

Triangulation: Comparing three points on an object to improve accuracy of a drawing. (*Chapter 5*)

Value: The lightness or darkness of anything we observe. (*Chapter 7*)

Value step scale: A chart of evenly spaced tones from lightest to darkest in a given medium. (*Chapter 7*)

Vision board: A collection of images and words gathered in poster format to remind you of your goals and dreams. (*Chapter 4*)

Visual literacy: The capacity to identify and comprehend our visual observations. (*Chapter 3*)

Selected Bibliography

These selected books have guided my development in drawing and creativity and will lead the reader to further understanding. *The Path of Drawing* does not delve into figurative art as a subject. However, I was primarily trained in life drawing and figurative art, so I also include volumes here that have been essential references and works I recommend to my students. Last, I include a short list of favorite works of poetry.

Drawing and Figure Drawing:

Ackerman, Gerald M. *Charles Bargue with the Collaboration of Jean-Léon Gérôme: Drawing Course*. Paris: ACR Edition, 2003.

Aristides, Juliette. *Lessons in Classical Drawing*. New York: Watson-Guptill, 2011.

—*Classical Drawing Atelier*. New York: Watson-Guptill, 2006.

Faigin, Gary. *The Artist's Complete Guide to Facial Expression*. New York: Watson-Guptill, 1990.

Jacobs, Ted Seth. *Drawing with an Open Mind*. New York: Watson-Guptill, 1991.

Lawlor, Robert. *Sacred Geometry: Philosophy & Practice*. London: Thames & Hudson, 1982.

Osti, Roberto. *Dynamic Human Anatomy*. New York: Monacelli Studio, 2021.

Peck, Stephen Rogers. *The Atlas of Human Anatomy for the Artist*. Oxford: Oxford University Press, 1951.

Ruskin, John *The Elements of Drawing*. New York: National Library Association, 1859. gutenberg.org /files/30325/30325-h/30325-h.htm.

Ryder, Anthony. *The Artist's Complete Guide to Figure Drawing: A Contemporary Perspective on the Classical Tradition*. New York: Watson-Guptill, 2000.

Zeller, Robert. *The Figurative Artist's Handbook*. New York: Monacelli Studio, 2016.

Composition:

Arnheim, Rudolf. *Art and Visual Perception: A Psychology of the Creative Eye*. Oakland: University of California Press, 1974.

Dow, Arthur Wesley. *Composition*. Garden City, New York: Doubleday, Page, and Co., 1914. gutenberg.org /files/45410/45410-pdf.pdf.

Creativity and Creative Living:

Barry, Lynda. *Making Comics*. Montreal: Drawn & Quarterly, 2019.

Bayles, David, and Ted Orland. *Art & Fear*. Santa Cruz, California: The Image Continuum, 1993.

Brown, Brené. *Daring Greatly*. New York: Avery, 2012.

Cameron, Julia. *The Artist's Way: A Spiritual Path to Higher Creativity*. New York: Jeremy P. Tarcher/Putnam, 1992.

Gilbert, Elizabeth. *Big Magic: Creative Living Beyond Fear*. New York: Riverhead Books, 2015.

Henri, Robert. *The Art Spirit*. Boulder, Colorado: Westview Press, 1984. (*originally published in 1923*)

Johnstone, Chris, and Joanna Macy. *Active Hope: How to Face the Mess We're in without Going Crazy*. Novato, California: New World Library, 2012.

Oliver, Mary. *Blue Pastures*. New York: Harcourt, 1995.

Tharp, Twyla. *The Creative Habit: Learn It and Use It for Life*. New York: Simon & Schuster, 2006.

Poetry:

Mitchell, Stephen, ed. *The Enlightened Heart*. New York: Harper Perennial, 1989.

Oliver, Mary. *A Thousand Mornings: Poems*. New York: Penguin Books, 2012.

Rilke, Rainer Maria. *Rilke's Book of Hours: Love Poems to God*. Translated by Anita Barrows and Joanna Macy. New York: Riverhead Books, 1996.

Notes

1. Maia Duerr, The Center for Contemplative Mind in Society, "The Tree of Contemplative Practices," accessed May 18, 2022, contemplativemind.org/practices/tree.

2. Emma Brockes, "When Alexandria Ocasio-Cortez met Greta Thunberg: 'Hope is contagious,'" *The Guardian*, June 29, 2019, theguardian.com /environment/2019/jun/29/alexandria-ocasio-cortez-met-greta-thunberg-hope-contagious-climate.

3. Brené Brown, Speaking.com Leadership Speaker, December 29, 2013, youtube.com/watch?v=KuWK WjVXcwo&list=PLrunGv2JGx52ej-e9R8OyfJMcRVGNBBXt&index=3.

4. Twyla Tharp, *The Creative Habit: Learn It and Use It for Life* (New York: Simon & Schuster, 2006), 15.

5. Lynda Barry, "Documenting All the Small Things That Are Easily Lost," *New York Times*, Sunday, May 3, 2020, nytimes.com /2020/05/01/arts/lynda-barry-diary-project.html.

6. Robert Lawlor, *Sacred Geometry: Philosophy & Practice* (London: Thames & Hudson, 1982), 14.

7. Richard Henry, email to author, July 30, 2020.

8. Ted Seth Jacobs, *Drawing with an Open Mind* (New York: Watson-Guptill, 1991), 39.

9. Ibid. 46.

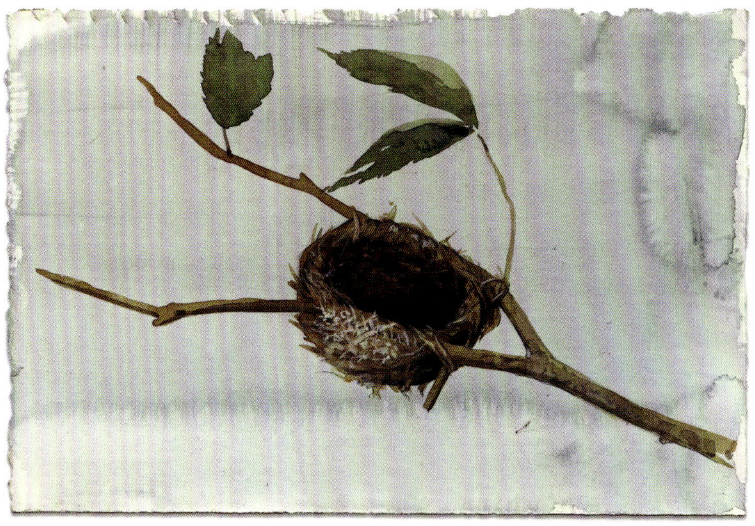

10. Alexis Hilliard, email to author, November 7, 2021.

11. David Bayles and Ted Orland, *Art & Fear* (Santa Cruz , California: The Image Continuum, 1993), 36.

12. Anthony Ryder, *The Artist's Complete Guide to Figure Drawing: A Contemporary Perspective on the Classical Tradition* (New York: Watson-Guptill, 2000), 29.

13. Julia Cameron, *The Artist's Way: A Spiritual Path to Higher Creativity* (New York: Jeremy P. Tarcher/Putnam, 1992), 153.

14. Ibid.

15. Ibid, 11.

16. Elizabeth Gilbert, *Big Magic: Creative Living Beyond Fear* (New York: Riverhead Books, 2015), 19.

17. Brené Brown, Speaking.com Leadership Speaker, December 29, 2013, youtube.com/watch?v=KuWK WjVXcwo&list=PLrunGv2JGx52ej-e9R8OyfJMcRVGNBBXt&index=3.

18. Gilbert, *Big Magic: Creative Living beyond Fear*, 26.

16. Chris Johnstone and Joanna Macy, *Active Hope: How to Face the Mess We're in without Going Crazy* (Novato, California: New World Library, 2012), 75.

Thumbnail Index
of Artist Illustrations

All images and illustrations in the book are by author
Patricia Watwood, unless credited otherwise.

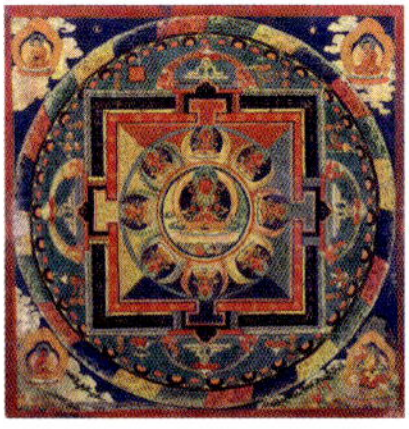

**19th-Century
Tibetan School**

174

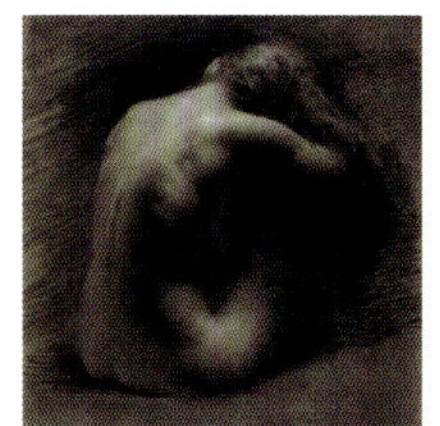

Aristides, Juliette

9, 10

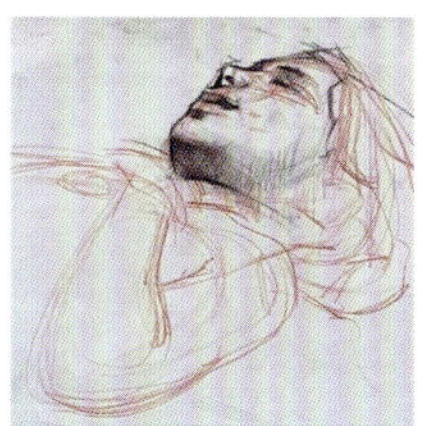

Banholzer, Craig

152

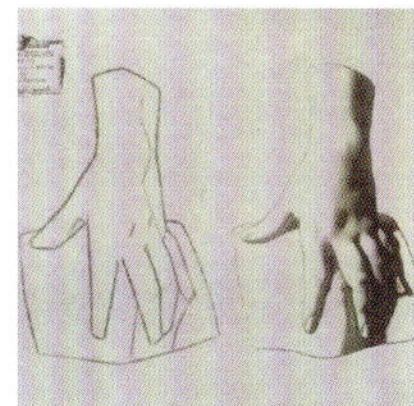

Bargue, Charles

94

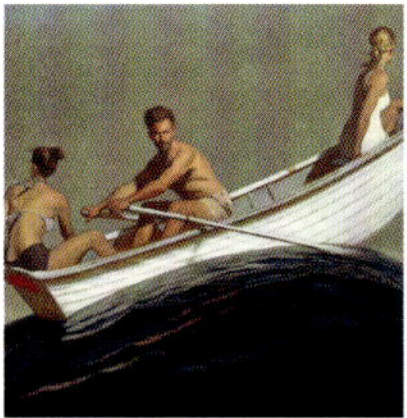

Bartlett, Bo

178, 184

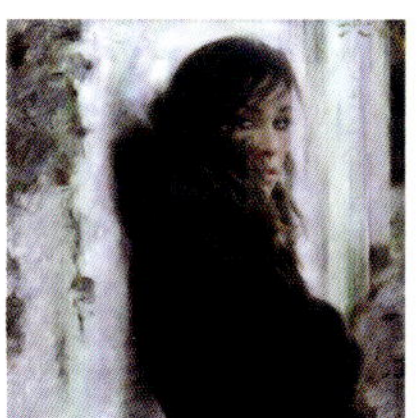

Baugh, Casey

198

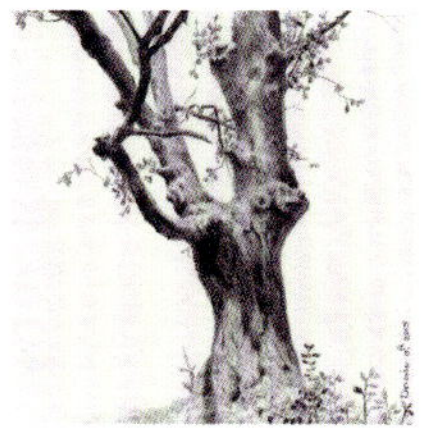

Brodsky, Dina

32, 33, 50, 112

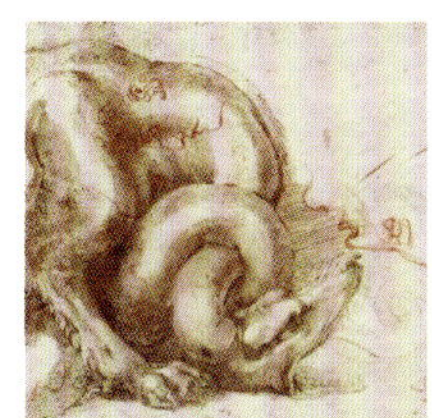

**Buonarroti,
Michelangelo**

89, 160

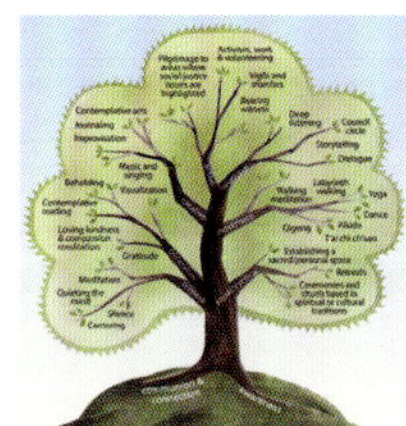

**The Center for
Contemplative
Mind in Society**

13

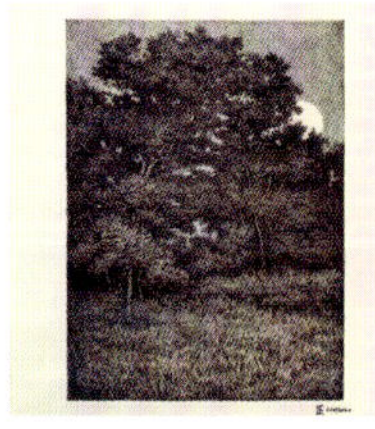

Colan, Luis

12, 26

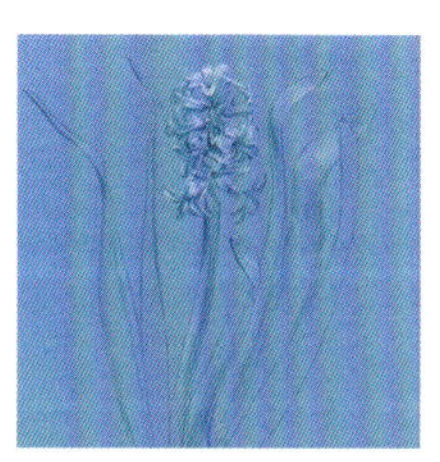

Conklin, Andrew S.

115

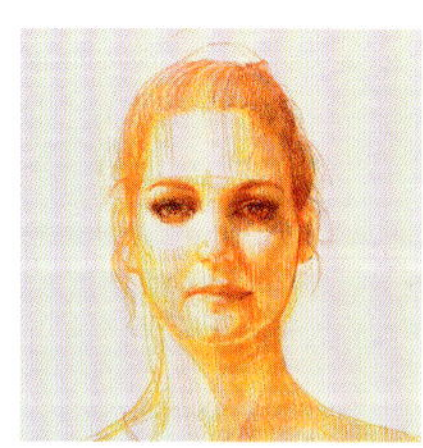

Cook, Janet A.

151, 153

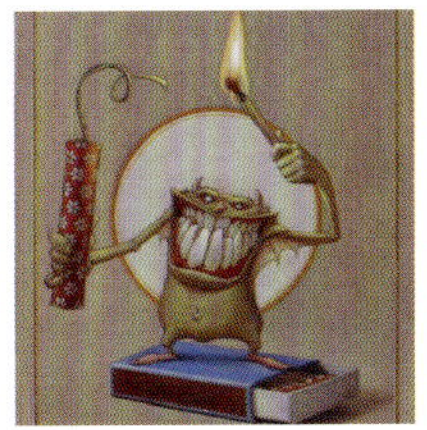

Curanaj, Tony

43, 165, 172, 173

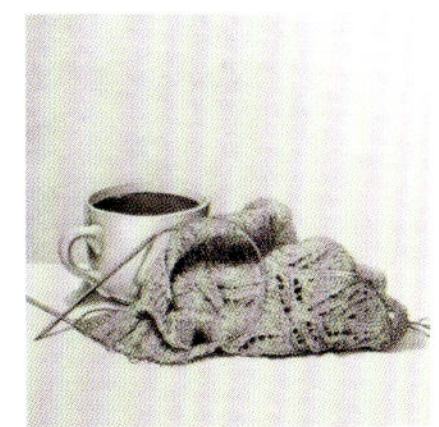

Davidson, Margaret

83

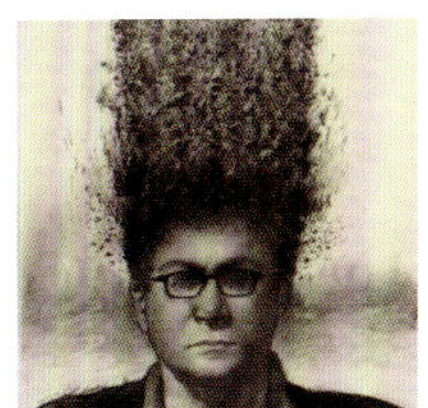

Faigin, Gary

56, 125, 197

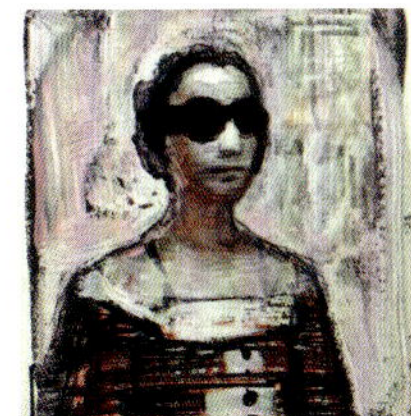

Frederick, Brooks

149, 152, 198

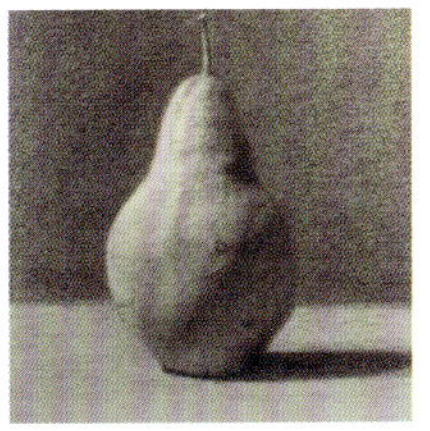

Gilbert, Sonya

122

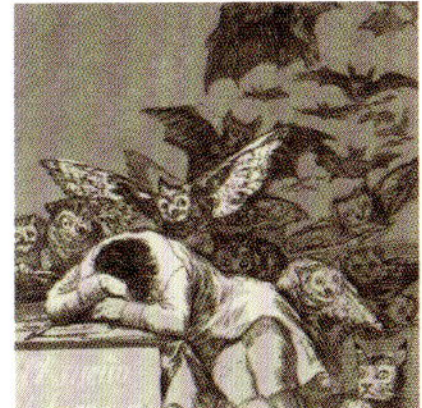

de Goya y Lucientes, Francisco José

162

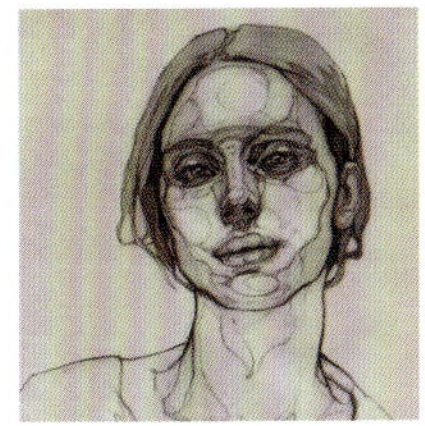

Grochulska, Agnes

2, 14, 103, 105, 106

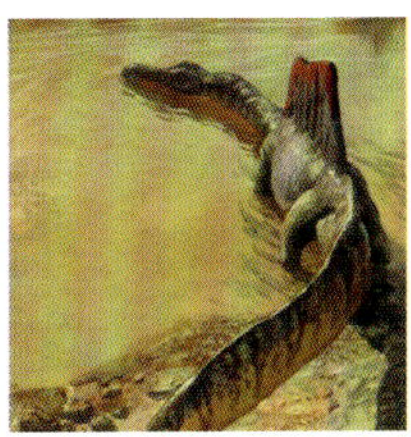

Gurney, James

188

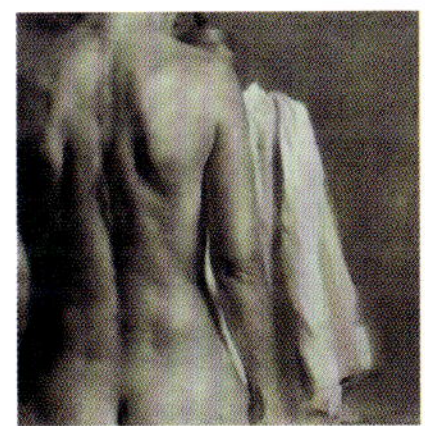

Gurpide, Amaya

68

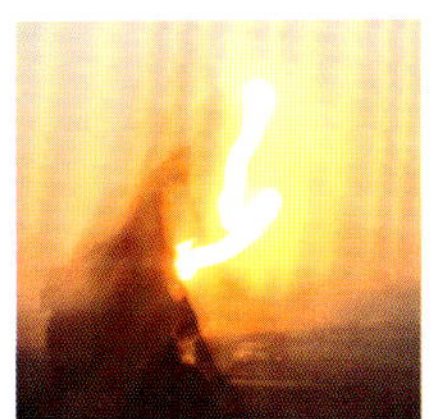

Hagen, Stefan

204

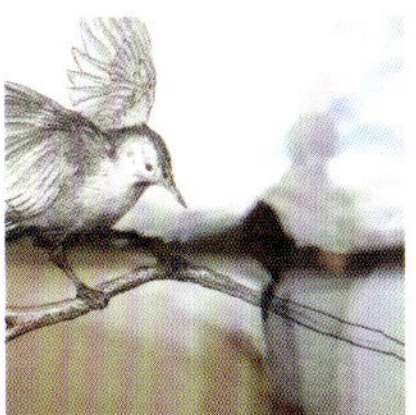

Hagen, Stefan and Patricia Watwood

55

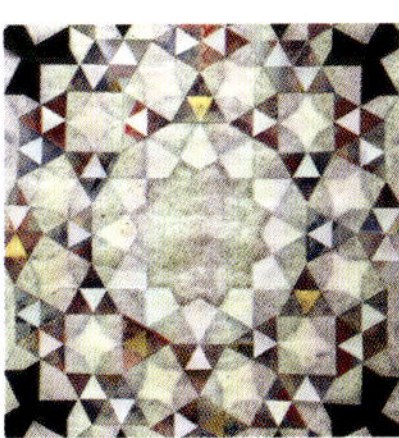

Henry, Richard

34, 42

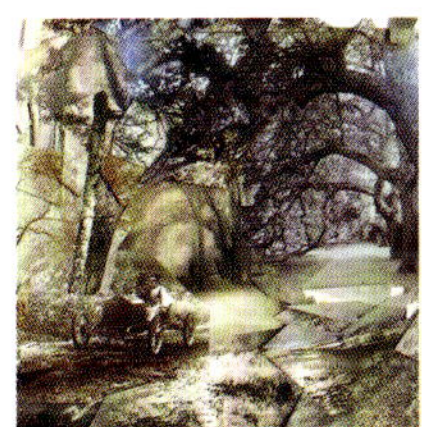

Hilliard, Alexis

69

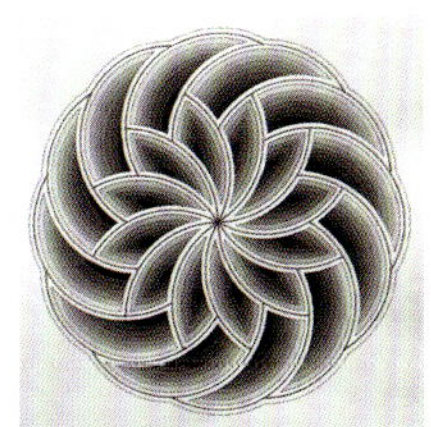

Iqbal, Aziza

174, 175

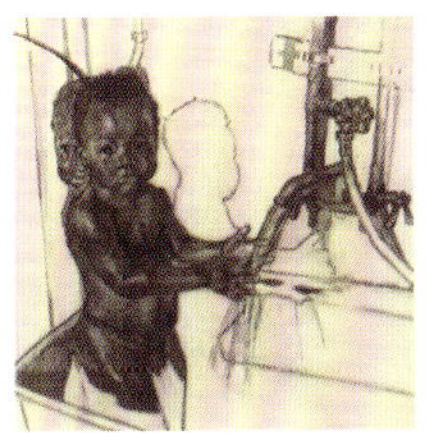

Johnson II, Steven Anthony

82, 84, 102

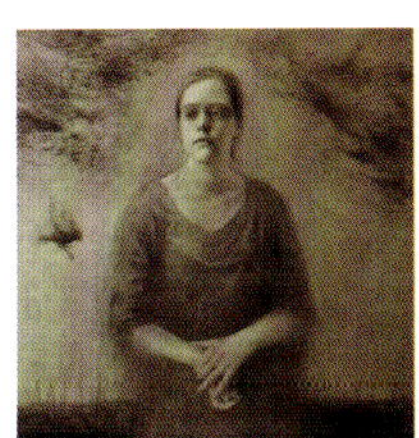

Judd, Molly

59, 185

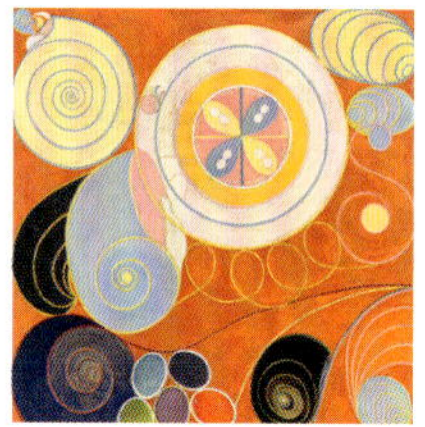

af Klint, Hilma

36, 46

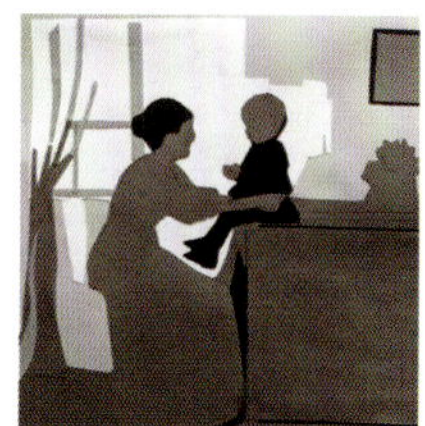

Kramarenko, Tanya

199

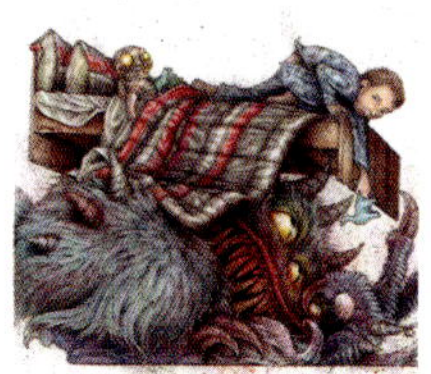

Lamph, Tyler

164

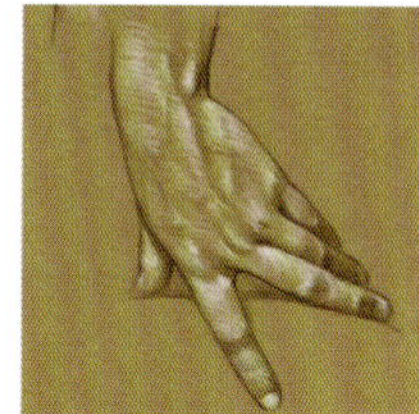

Maidman, Daniel

37, 211, 214, 219

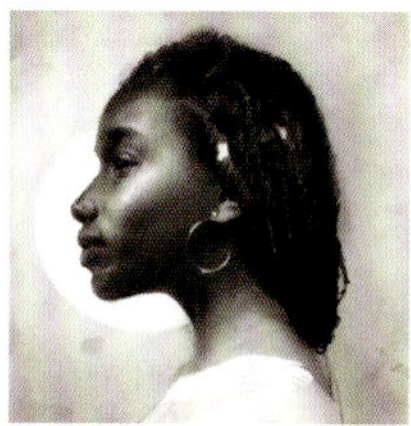

Meadors, Michael

129, 153

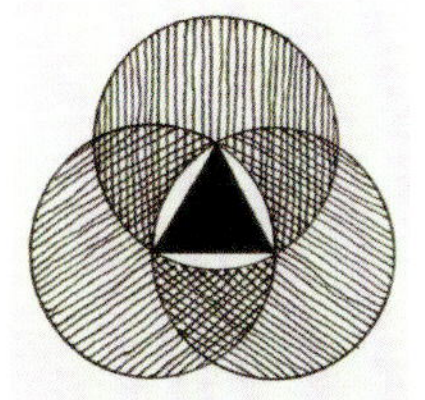

Milne, Marie

40

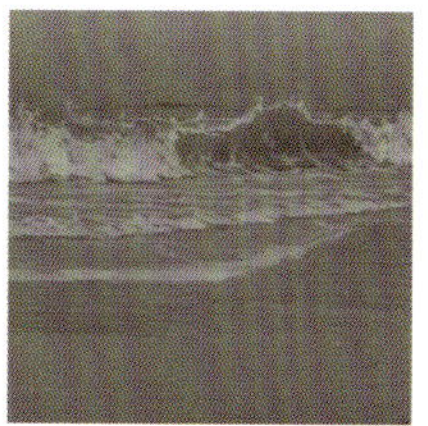

Minoff, Edward

57, 182

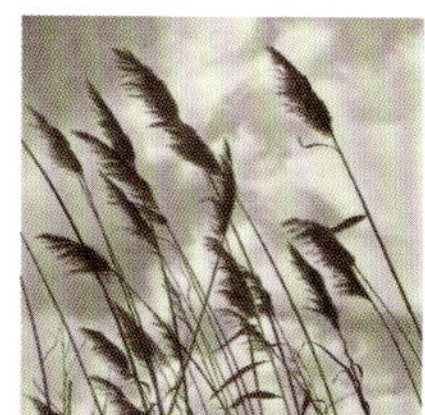

Reilly, Mary

5, 51

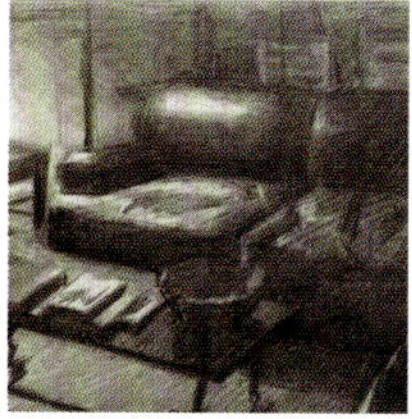

Rochat, Edmond

122

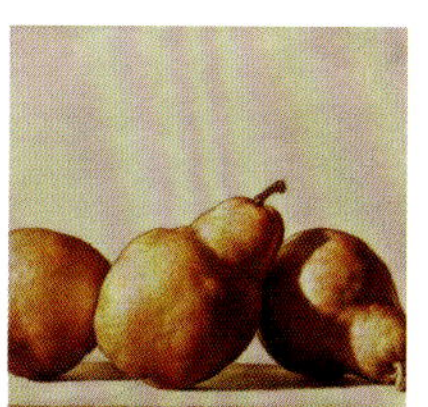

Ryder, Anthony

120

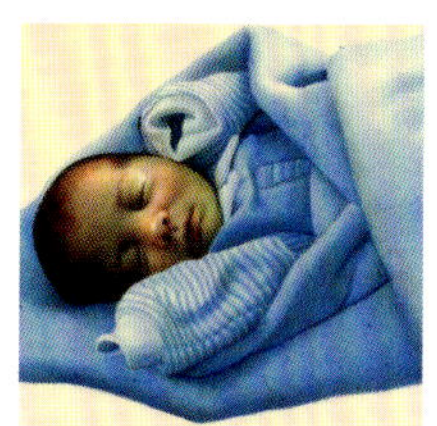

Sanchez, Nicholas

150

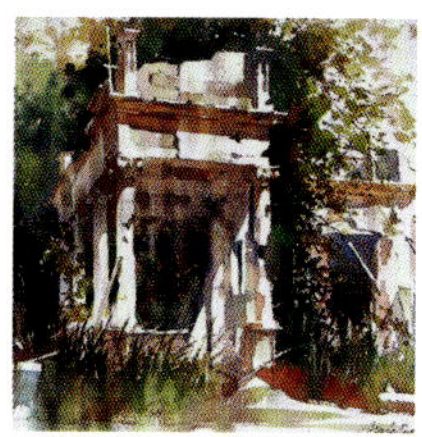

Schaller, Thomas W.

145, 147, 206

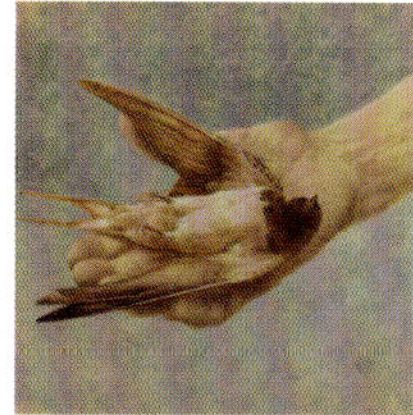

Schuman, Wade

93, 213

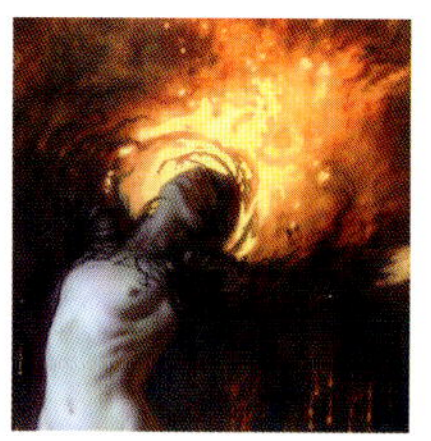

Sims, Tenaya

139, 180, 181, 186

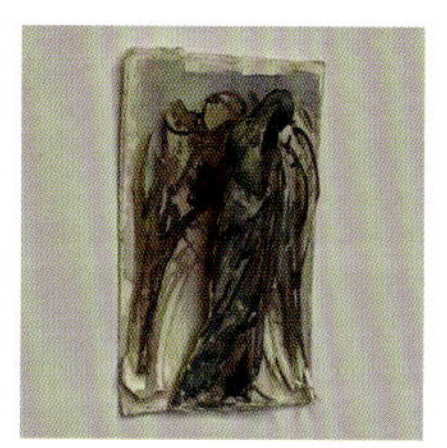

Song, Hyeseung

187

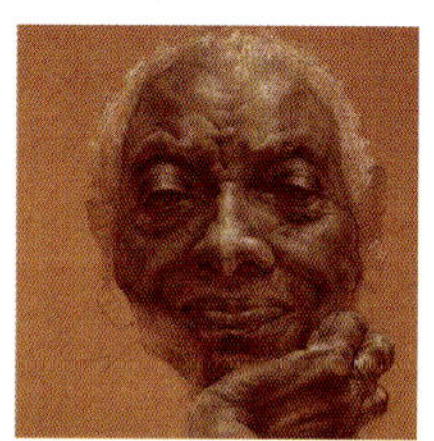

Steele, Alexey

19, 79

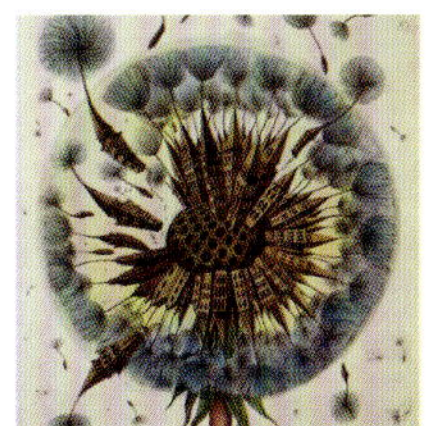

Terauds, Marina
29, 61, 62, 114

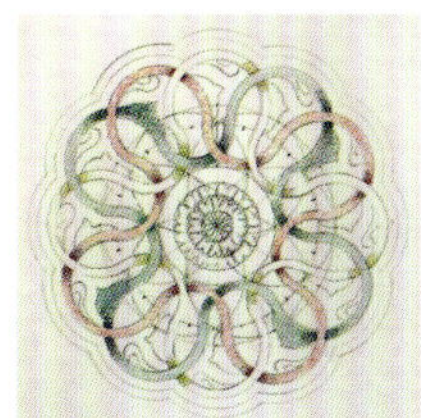

Theis, Mandy
41

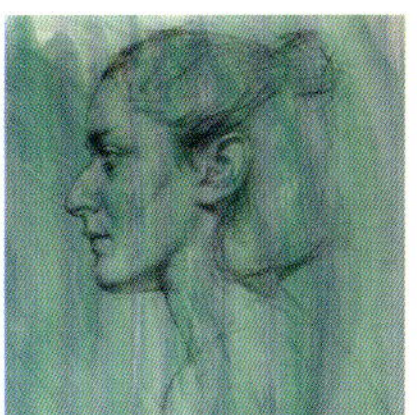

Tully, Nichole Michelle
95, 150

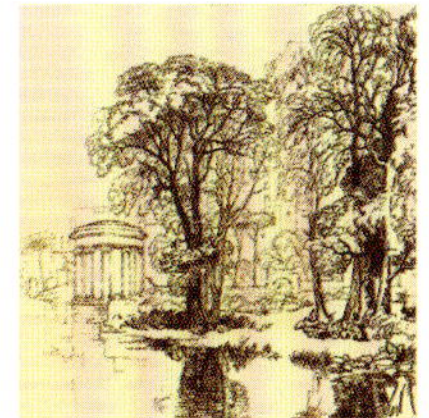

**Turner, Joseph
Mallord William**
113, 199

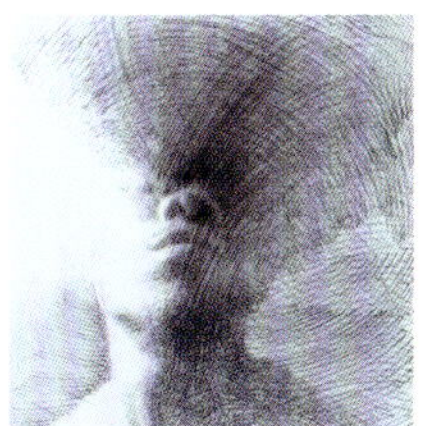

Uzor, Austin
107, 151

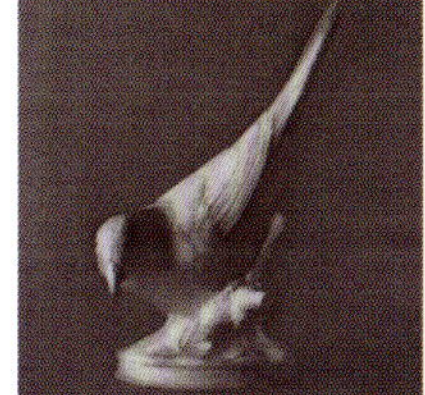

Valeri, Sadie J.
136

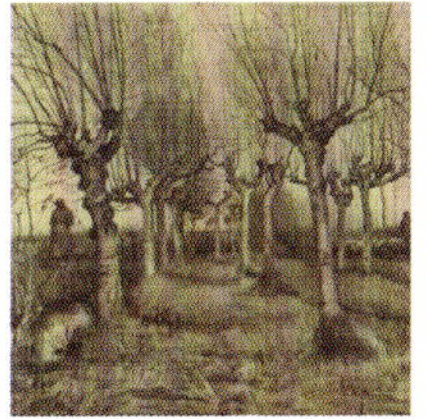

Van Gogh, Vincent
167

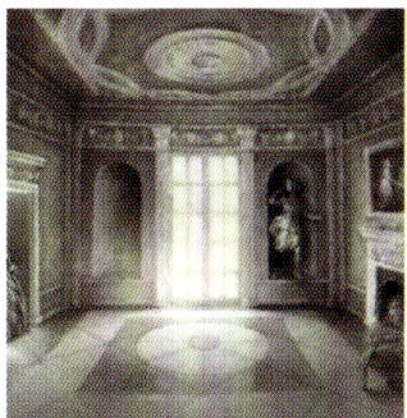

Wakitsch, Anna
189, 205

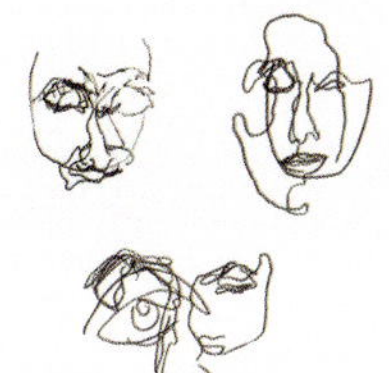

Watwood, Beaux
106

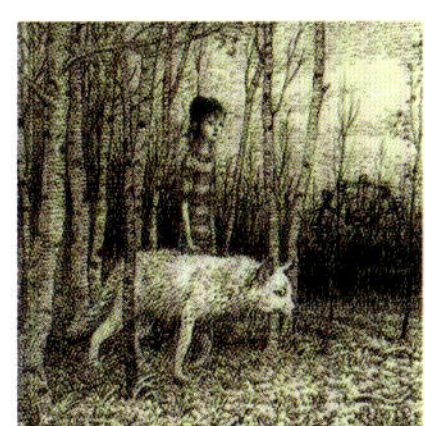

Wiesenfeld, Aron
76, 104, 108

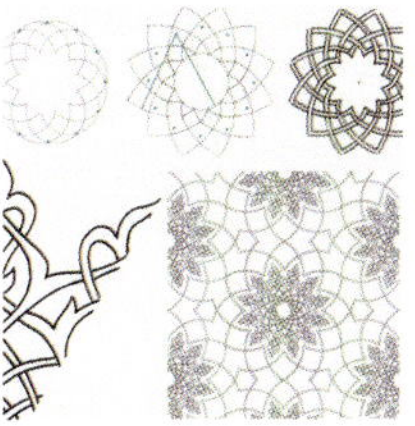

Williamson, Adam
42

About the Author

Patricia Watwood is a visual artist known for her realist drawings, oil paintings, and portraits.

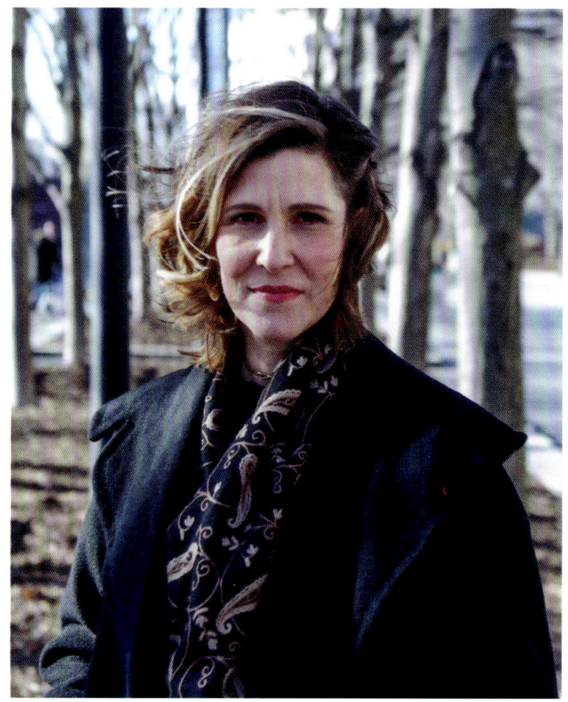

A leading figure in the contemporary figurative art movement, she has exhibited at the Beijing World Art Museum, the European Museum of Modern Art, and the Butler Institute of American Art, and her work is held in public and private collections around the world. Her commissioned portraits hang in institutions such as St. Louis City Hall, Washington University, the Harvard Kennedy School of Government, and the Harvard Art Museums.

Watwood earned her MFA with honors from the New York Academy of Art, and was a founding member of the Water Street Atelier. She is a signature member of the Portrait Society of America, and has been named a Living Master by the Art Renewal Center. She is the current First Vice President of the Salmagundi Club of NYC. Watwood has produced classes with Streamline Art Video and the streaming platforms, Craftsy.com and Terracotta.org.

She has served as a professor of drawing at New York Academy of Art and has written for and been featured in *American Artist* and *Fine Art Connoisseur*, among other publications.

Index

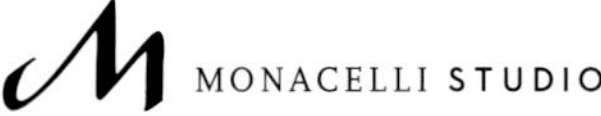

Monacelli
A Phaidon Company
111 Broadway
New York, New York 10006
www.monacellipress.com

Front cover/back cover: Patricia Watwood, *The Path of Drawing,* 2022,
sanguine colored pencil, Nero pencil, white gouache and watercolor on
paper, 12 x 19¼ inches (30 x 49 cm). Courtesy of the artist.

Endpapers by Patricia Watwood, 2017.

Title page: Agnes Grochulska, *Liquid Line 1,* 2020, graphite on canvas,
30 x 30 inches (76 x 76 cm). Courtesy of the artist.

Page 5: Mary Reilly, *Shoreline, Staten Island,* 2011, graphite pencil on
paper, 23½ x 18 inches (60 x 46 cm). Collection of Eskenazi Museum of
Art at Indiana University. Courtesy of the artist.